Expert Delphi

Robust and fast cross-platform application development

Marco Cantù

Paweł Głowacki

Expert Delphi

Group Product Manager: Kunal Sawant
Publishing Product Manager: Akash Sharma
Book Project Manager: Manisha Singh
Senior Editor: Esha Banerjee
Technical Editor: Rajdeep Chakraborty
Copy Editor: Safis Editing
Indexer: Tejal Daruwale Soni
Production Designer: Ponraj Dhandapani
DevRel Marketing Coordinator: Shrinidhi Manoharan

First published: June 2017

Second edition: February 2024

Production reference: 1090224

Published by Packt Publishing Ltd.

Grosvenor House
11 St Paul's Square
Birmingham
B3 1RB, UK

ISBN 978-1-80512-110-7

www.packtpub.com

When I joined Embarcadero, Paweł greeted me saying "It is great that you are now on board, and we are both working for the same company and making Delphi better!"

Working on a new edition of his work has been great. Therefore, this book is dedicated to the late Paweł Głowacki, a friend and one of the most passionate Delphi evangelists, and to the fond memories of the time spent together.

– Marco Cantù

Foreword

In mid-December 2017, the sad news of Paweł Głowacki's passing broke in the Delphi developer community. I had the pleasure of working closely alongside Paweł for over 6 years until mid-2017, covering 10 major Delphi product launches with him.

Behind each product launch, there were new demos to create, events to attend, and new webinars to organize and attend to help share details about the new features available to Delphi developers. Between all these activities, Paweł's enthusiasm for programming shined brightly, a light that shone so brightly that it was dearly missed when it left us all too soon. The outpouring of love from around the world showed how well he, and his content, was loved and the magnitude of his global stardom within the Delphi community.

I remember the time when I started working at Embarcadero and Paweł was in the UK office ahead of an event. I met him in the lead-up to the launch of XE2; I noticed that he had a really thick book about shader languages that he was reading intensely... He joked about how it was really interesting, but, how it could also double up as a pillow! (He'd had an early flight in). But this summed up his approach. He always wanted to bring great content, founded in a deep technical understanding of developers, and delivered it with a smile and in a fun way.

This is something that Expert Delphi brings to you. Many of the chapters lean heavily on Paweł's years of making content understandable yet fun to learn. *Chapter 2* starts off with one of his favorite Developer Direct webinar sessions that we ran for multiple series called *Mind Your Language*.

This second edition has been lovingly revised by Marco Cantù, to bring its content up to date with the latest developments in Delphi. With Paweł's voice still shining through, you will learn how easy it is with Delphi to develop across the stack. Expert Delphi covers everything from front-end application development for mobile and desktop to 3D development, to embedding database access and building and using backend multi-tier architectures touching on both SOAP and REST with RAD Server.

As David I commented in the original edition's foreword, "In Expert Delphi, Paweł encapsulates the knowledge gained through years as a world-class Delphi engineer, an entertaining presenter, a community leader, and a passionate advocate. With his words, step-by-step instructions, screenshots, source code snippets, examples, and links to additional sources of information, you will learn how to continuously enhance your skills and apps."

And, as Paweł and I used to say at the end of our developer sessions… Thanks for joining us today and Happy Coding everyone!

Stephen Ball

Presales Director, Embarcadero
@DelphiABall

Contributors

About the authors

Marco Cantù is an experienced Delphi expert, who started working with the product since its introduction in 1995. He is currently working as a Product Manager for RAD Studio at Embarcadero Technologies, an Idera company. Prior to that, Marco was a Delphi trainer and consultant for Wintech Italia. Over the years, Marco has written 20 books on Delphi, from the classic *Mastering Delphi* series to the *recent Object Pascal Handbook*. Marco has been a speaker at many Delphi and programming conferences worldwide, including over 10 Borland US Conferences, the Software Development Conference, Borland European conferences, EKON (Germany), DCon (UK), Conference to the Max (Holland), DelphiTage, the Italian Delphi Day, and a few editions of Delphi Developer Days. Marco is based in Italy.

Paweł Głowacki was Embarcadero's European Technical Lead for Developer Tools. Previously, Paweł spent over 7 years working as a senior consultant and trainer for Delphi within Borland Education Services and CodeGear. Apart from working with Embarcadero customers across the region, he represented Embarcadero internationally as a conference and seminar speaker. Paweł passed away in mid-December 2017, but he is alive in the hearts of the Delphi developers community, worldwide.

Marco Cantù (left), Paweł Głowacki (right)

About the reviewer

Mauricio Marcelo Paiva de Abreu has been passionate about technology since he was 9 years old. His first computer was Sharp's MSX HotBit, in which he started programming with Basic. He has closely followed the development of many programming languages and PCs, including CP500, Prológica – Solution16, and several others since then.

Mauricio's first contact with Delphi was in version 5.0. A self-taught person in Delphi, he developed projects for intern companies in Access and Delphi. He managed these contracts and worked on Delphi 7 videoconferencing room rental projects with SQL Server as the database. At present, he has a software development company that creates new ideas for the Brazilian market, which uses Delphi for 99% of its ERP development.

He is knowledgeable in several versions of Delphi, including 2010, XEs, Berlin, Tokyo, Alexandria, and Athens.

Table of Contents

Part 2: Going Mobile

9

Desktop Apps and Mobile Bridges 235

Part 3: From Data to Services

10

Embedding Databases 265

11

Integrating with Web Services 299

15

Preface

The world of mobile app development is becoming more and more complex. Technology is continuously evolving. Every day, new versions of mobile operating systems are released in the market. Mobile devices are getting new capabilities. User expectations are constantly growing, and it is harder and harder to meet them.

The only way to meet and exceed all challenges in the contemporary world of mobile development is to become a developer superhero. Superheroes have super tools. In this book, we are going to embark on the journey of mastering Delphi development to build mobile apps. We will learn how to develop amazing productivity powers and rapidly build stunning cross-platform mobile apps from one codebase.

We will start by getting comfortable in using Delphi's Integrated Development Environment. Next, we will review the key constructs in the Object Pascal language and everyday programmer tasks so you can easily understand and write solid and maintainable source code. Over the course of this book, the fun levels will only increase. We will start our adventure with mobile development with Delphi by building small projects that will make you feel like a real Delphi developer. Having mastered simple things, we will be ready to do more serious stuff. We will go deep into understanding the concept of FireMonkey styles, which is the cornerstone of building stunning cross-platform user interfaces that will make a difference in the end-user experience of your apps. The rest of the journey is all about gaining practical knowledge of using more complex Delphi frameworks. We will get down to the metal and harness the full power of mobile hardware and operating systems. We will be working with sensors, building data-driven user interfaces, embedding mobile databases, integrating with REST web services and the Cloud, and defining scalable, multiuser backends.

But why Delphi? There are two main platforms for mobile apps that are dominating the mobile market: Android and iOS. It is a common requirement to develop an app for both platforms. This typically means using different tools, frameworks, and programming languages. If you want to build a mobile app for iOS, you would typically use the Xcode development environment from Apple and use Swift as the programming language. Android development requires different tools. For Android, you would typically use a tool like Android Studio from Google and the Java programming language. These are two different worlds that speak different languages. If you want to build your app for both, this typically means having two different sets of skills and in practice two different teams of developers. Mobile app development gets more and more fragmented. One can be an iOS developer, and somebody can specialize in Android.

This is where the advantage of a tool like Delphi becomes significant: You can write a single application, and the same source code written with a single programming language and using a single set of user interface controls will work on both iOS and Android. Not only does it work but it also works great, leveraging the platform features and adapting to the different UI requirements.

Not only that, Delphi also offers you the ability to build the backend for your mobile apps, offering REST-based access to your own services from your mobile app.

With Delphi, you can become a mobile developer superhero and develop unmatched productivity powers to build complete mobile apps using just one tool, one framework, and one programming language to create mobile apps for both iOS and Android and desktop applications for Mac and Windows. At the same time, you can also build scalable REST API backends that will power your mobile apps on all platforms.

Who this book is for

This book is intended for software developers who know the foundations of programming and can write code in at least one programming language, as it will not teach you the foundations of programming. In other words, if you have never written any line of code in your life, this book is not for you.

This book is meant for developers who might not have used Delphi or for developers who have used Delphi in the past but only for Windows VCL applications, not FireMonkey mobile ones. There is little for Windows and desktop development here, as the focus is on building mobile iOS and Android apps.

This book is packed with practical code examples and best practices for you to become an excellent mobile developer! It is focused on learning by doing – more than just offering many theoretical discussions, it will guide you step by step in rebuilding projects. That is why no expertise in Delphi is required: In most cases, the steps do not assume you have a pre-existing knowledge of the tool or the programming language.

Given the information built on what was presented in previous chapters, though, if you are new to Delphi mobile development, we encourage you to go through the book in sequence: Jumping right away to the final chapters would be a very steep learning curve.

What this book covers

Chapter 1, Fasten Your Seat Belts, introduces you to the Delphi IDE and guides you on the first step for building an app for various platforms.

Chapter 2, Mind Your Language, offers an introduction to Delphi's Object Pascal language, covering some of its foundations and some of the most recent extensions to the language.

Chapter 3, Packing Up Your Toolbox, delves into some of the core runtime library features, focusing on managing files in different formats, including JSON and XML.

Chapter 4, Using the Parallel Programming Library, focuses on multi-threading, parallel programming, and threads synchronization.

Chapter 5, Playing with FireMonkey, introduces the FireMoney UI library, covering its foundations while guiding you in the development of an actual app.

Chapter 6, FireMonkey in 3D, goes over the development of 3D apps in FireMonkey, showing multiple different techniques.

Chapter 7, Building User Interfaces with Style, delves into the styles architecture, which is the core architectural element of FireMonkey.

Chapter 8, Working with Mobile Operating System, focuses the attention on the device sensors, cameras, and integrated web browsers.

Chapter 9, Desktop Apps and Mobile Bridges, touches on desktop development with UI controls more interesting for desktop than mobile, and how desktop and mobile apps can work together via a technology called tethering.

Chapter 10, Embedding Databases, introduces database development, the FireDAC data access library, and live bindings.

Chapter 11, Integrating with Web Services, how to call external web services via HTTP, REST clients, SOAP clients, or Cloud access libraries.

Chapter 12, Building Mobile Back-ends, starts looking into the development of server libraries you can use as the backend of your mobile apps, covering WebBroker and DataSnap.

Chapter 13, Easy REST API Publishing with RAD Server, is fully focused on the RAd Server technology available in the high-end versions of Delphi.

Chapter 14, App Deployment, covers the deployment of apps to the mobile stores, Apple's App Store and Google's Play Store.

Chapter 15, The Road Ahead, is a short conclusion suggesting things you can do after you've finished reading the book.

To get the most out of this book

This book will teach you the development of apps with Delphi and FireMonkey and does it through practical demos and step-by-step guides. For this reason, you need to have a copy of Delphi at hand and possibly a mobile device you can deploy your applications to. For macOS and iOS development, you need an Apple Mac, while for Android a Windows machine with Delphi and the integrated Android SDK is sufficient. Some specific additional requirements are listed below.

Software/hardware covered in the book	Operating system requirements
Embarcadero Delphi IDE	The IDE runs on Windows or on a Windows VM hosted in a different operating system. You need a license of Delphi, although most of the content and demos will work using the Community Edition, which is available for free (with some limitations)
Android development	Requires only an Android phone or tablet, possibly with a recent version of the operating system
iOS development	Requires a Mac and a (paid) Apple developer account to deploy to your device and an actual iPhone or iPad.
DataSnap and RAD Server Frameworks	Available only in the high-end, paid versions of Delphi
App Store Deployment	Require paid developer accounts on Apple or Google online stores

If you are using the digital version of this book, we advise you to type the code yourself or access the code from the book's GitHub repository (a link is available in the next section). Doing so will help you avoid any potential errors related to the copying and pasting of code.

Download the example code files

You can download the example code files for this book from GitHub at `https://github.com/PacktPublishing/Expert-Delphi_Second-edition`. If there's an update to the code, it will be updated in the GitHub repository.

We also have other code bundles from our rich catalog of books and videos available at `https://github.com/PacktPublishing/`. Check them out!

Conventions used

There are a number of text conventions used throughout this book.

`Code in text`: Indicates code words in text, database table names, folder names, filenames, file extensions, pathnames, dummy URLs, user input, and Twitter handles. Here is an example: "This will add a form inherited from `TForm3D`."

A block of code is set as follows:

```
const
  DEFAULT_OPACITY = 1;
  POS_X = 150;
  POS_Y = 150;
  SUN_RADIUS = 50;
  RAY_COUNT = 12;
  RAY_LENGTH = 100;
```

When we wish to draw your attention to a particular part of a code block, the relevant lines or items are set in bold:

```
procedure TForm1.PaintBox1Paint(Sender: TObject;
  Canvas: TCanvas);
begin
  Canvas.BeginScene;
  try
    // access "Canvas" methods and properties here
  finally
    Canvas.EndScene;
  end;
end;
```

Any command-line input or output is written as follows:

```
procedure TMViewForm.FormCreate(Sender: TObject);
begin
    MultiView1.Mode := TMultiViewMode.PlatformBehaviour;
    ComboMode.ItemIndex := 0;
end;
```

Bold: Indicates a new term, an important word, or words that you see onscreen. For instance, words in menus or dialog boxes appear in **bold**. Here is an example: "Now select the grid, right-click on it, or see the commands at the bottom of the Object Inspector and open its **Items Editor**."

> **Tips or important notes**
> Appear like this.

Get in touch

Feedback from our readers is always welcome.

General feedback: If you have questions about any aspect of this book, email us at customercare@ packtpub.com and mention the book title in the subject of your message.

Errata: Although we have taken every care to ensure the accuracy of our content, mistakes do happen. If you have found a mistake in this book, we would be grateful if you would report this to us. Please visit www.packtpub.com/support/errata and fill in the form.

Piracy: If you come across any illegal copies of our works in any form on the internet, we would be grateful if you would provide us with the location address or website name. Please contact us at copyright@packt.com with a link to the material.

If you are interested in becoming an author: If there is a topic that you have expertise in and you are interested in either writing or contributing to a book, please visit authors.packtpub.com.

Share Your Thoughts

Once you've read *Expert Delphi*, we'd love to hear your thoughts! Scan the QR code below to go straight to the Amazon review page for this book and share your feedback.

https://packt.link/r/1-805-12110-3

Your review is important to us and the tech community and will help us make sure we're delivering excellent quality content.

Download a free PDF copy of this book

Thanks for purchasing this book!

Do you like to read on the go but are unable to carry your print books everywhere?

Is your eBook purchase not compatible with the device of your choice?

Don't worry, now with every Packt book you get a DRM-free PDF version of that book at no cost.

Read anywhere, any place, on any device. Search, copy, and paste code from your favorite technical books directly into your application.

The perks don't stop there, you can get exclusive access to discounts, newsletters, and great free content in your inbox daily

Follow these simple steps to get the benefits:

1. Scan the QR code or visit the link below

https://packt.link/free-ebook/9781805121107

2. Submit your proof of purchase
3. That's it! We'll send your free PDF and other benefits to your email directly

Part 1:
Building Blocks

You've just installed Delphi and have its main window in front of you, how do you start building the next successful mobile app? We will get to it but before we get deeper into the main topic of this book, it's important to focus on some of the foundations and building blocks of Delphi development.

In particular, we are going to take you on a tour of the IDE, explore Delphi's Object Pascal programming language, and look into some core elements of the **RunTime Library** (**RTL**) focusing on ways to manage files using different formats and on multi-threading.

We'll do this by building a small and focused example. Something that will help you get started on the main goal of the book to help you become an expert Delphi mobile developer.

This part has the following chapters:

- *Chapter 1, Fasten Your Seat Belts*
- *Chapter 2, Mind Your Language*
- *Chapter 3, Packing Up Your Toolbox*
- *Chapter 4, Using the Parallel Programming Library*

1

Fasten Your Seat Belts

The key benefit of Delphi in mobile development is that you can design your app once and you can natively compile it for both Android and iOS from the same source code. This chapter is exactly about this capability. We are going to install Delphi, create a simple one-button "Hello World" app, and then run the same app on an Android phone and an iOS device.

The **integrated development environment** (**IDE**) is where the programmer spends most of their time. Learning best practices of using the IDE will pay off in the future and will increase your developer productivity. Before building apps, you need to feel comfortable working in the Delphi IDE.

The objective of this chapter is to help you install the Delphi IDE, learn basic IDE functionality, and prepare it for mobile development.

In this chapter, we will cover the following topics:

- Delphi installation
- Riding the IDE
- Deploying to mobile devices

Delphi installation

Delphi is a Windows program, so you need to have a computer with a proper version of Windows installed and enough free space on your hard drive. You may want to install Delphi on a physical computer or a Windows virtual machine image using one of the available virtualization solutions, such as VMWare. In this case, you can also use a Mac computer with a Windows virtual machine. Installing it on a virtual machine has some advantages in cross-platform development. To create iOS apps, you will need to have access to a Mac computer anyway. This could be another computer available on the local network or the same physical machine configured with a virtual machine to run the IDE. Whether you choose to install Delphi on a physical or virtual Windows machine, the installation process is the same.

Delphi is implemented as a native Windows 32-bit executable, but it is recommended to install it on 64-bit versions of Windows 11, or a recent 64-bit version of Windows 10.

Delphi versions

Delphi comes in different versions, so before downloading the installer, we need to decide which version to choose. There are four Delphi versions: **Community Edition (CE)**, Professional, Enterprise, and Architect:

- **CE** is a free version of Delphi with very few technical limitations compared to the Professional edition, but a license valid only for hobbyists, startups, and other scenarios in which the developer or company revenues do not exceed 5,000 US dollars a year. Refer to the product's **End User License Agreement** (**EULA**, available online) for more details on the CE license limitation and to make sure you are using it legally. The version of the CE edition generally lags several months behind the paid product versions, but it offers a great way to get started with Delphi, and it's free.

- The next version is **Professional**. It contains all the features required for mobile development as it can target Windows, macOS, Android, and iOS. The Professional edition is a viable choice if you plan to build Delphi applications with no need for advanced database access, multitier support, and some of the other advanced features available in the *Enterprise edition*.

- The third version is **Enterprise**. This is the full version of Delphi and contains everything that is in **Professional**, plus support for building Linux server applications, access to all databases, DataSnap and RAD Server multitier solutions, and some more additional features. This is the version of Delphi that we are going to use in this book, although most of the examples and features we'll cover are also available in the Professional edition.

- The highest Delphi version is **Architect**. This is a product bundle that contains Delphi "Enterprise" and separately installed tools from Embarcadero sister companies, such as Aqua Data Studio from Idera and Ext JS from Sencha. We are not going to cover any of those additional tools in this book.

Delphi is available as a standalone product, but it can also be used as part of RAD Studio. RAD Studio contains Delphi and C++Builder. Delphi and C++Builder are two different **IDE personalities** of **RAD Studio**; both can be installed from the same RAD Studio installer into one deeply integrated environment. Both products, Delphi and C++Builder, share the same component libraries but differ in the programming language being used. Delphi uses Object Pascal, while C++Builder uses standard C++. As this book's title implies, here, we are focusing on Delphi.

In this book, we are going to use **Delphi 12.0 Enterprise edition**. Delphi is produced by Embarcadero, and you can find more information about different Delphi versions and features on the Embarcadero Delphi home page: `http://www.embarcadero.com/products/delphi`.

You can get Delphi directly through the Embarcadero website, including a 30-day trial and the CE version of Delphi (at the time of writing, this is version 11.3). After purchasing Delphi, you will receive an automatically generated email with the download link to the Delphi installer and the serial number needed during the installation.

Running the Delphi installer

The Delphi installer is available in two different formats. You can either choose to install Delphi using the so-called **Online Installer**, or you can use the **Offline Installer**, based on an ISO image you can download upfront. The first option is the default one and makes it for faster installation; it is also the only option available for the CE version. The Online Installer (also called Minimal Installer) is a small application that downloads and installs only some minimal parts of Delphi. After this "minimal Delphi" is ready, you can choose to install the support for different platforms and features. Even if you install from the ISO image, the process is the same as the minimal installation, followed by the platform selection. This is useful when internet access is slow, unreliable, or for some security reasons, the Windows machine that you want to install Delphi on does not have internet access.

In this section, we are going to use the standard Online Installer, using the download link provided by the website (for trial or CE versions) or in the confirmation email. You will need to have administration rights on Windows to be able to install Delphi. On one of the first installer screens, you will be prompted to enter the serial number that you have received from Embarcadero, and you will need to enter your **Embarcadero Developer Network** (**EDN**) username and password. If you do not have an EDN account, you can quickly create one from within the installer or on the website (`my.embarcadero.com`). It is free and it makes the connection between the serial number that you have received and you as the user of the software.

After the initial installation, as shown in *Figure 1.1*, you can choose which platforms and additional features you want to install. You can always add or remove platforms and features from the **Tools | Manage Platforms** menu item of the Delphi IDE after the installation is complete:

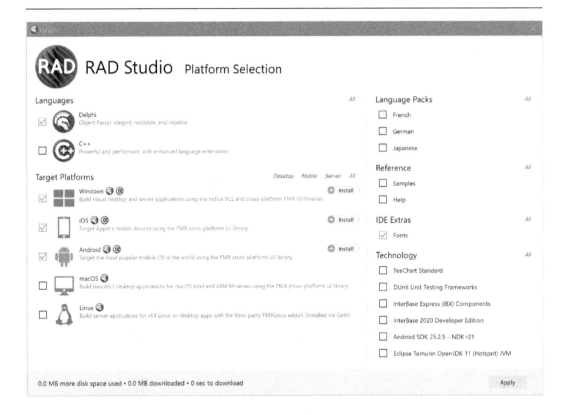

Figure 1.1: Platform Selection in Delphi 12

The list that's displayed depends on your license, which might include both Delphi and C++ languages (as in the preceding screenshot) or only Delphi. I recommend going for the full installation, selecting all platforms and all additional features, except for languages other than English. At the end of the installation, you will see the message that the installation is complete, and you can start working.

If you run into problems during the installation, you can review Delphi Installation Notes on Embarcadero DocWiki at `https://docwiki.embarcadero.com/RADStudio/en/Installation_Notes`.

Delphi will be installed. Run it – the first thing you will see is the **Welcome Page** area, as shown in *Figure 1.2*:

Figure 1.2: The Delphi Welcome Page area

From the **Welcome Page** area, you can create new applications (in the **Create New** section) open recent projects (in the **Open Recent** section), access new or promoted add-on packages in GetIt, and check recent YouTube videos by Embarcadero (in the **Learn** section). The projects that you frequently work with can be marked as **Favorite** projects and will show at the top of the **Open Recent** list. Now, let's look at extending Delphi with new components.

Installing custom components

The Delphi IDE has an open architecture and provides many ways to extend its functionality through additional packages. You can see the list of currently installed packages by clicking the **Installed Packages...** option available from the **Component** menu. The most typical Delphi building block is a *component*. Technically, this is about taking object-oriented programming principles and moving them one step further. With components, you can manipulate regular programming language object instances at design time before the project is built for a given platform. Packages may also contain custom property editors and the Open Tools API extension to the IDE itself, which may add custom functionality to the IDE, such as additional menus and windows.

Out of the box, with the default Delphi installation, you will get a few hundred components already preinstalled. Depending on your Delphi version and selected features, this list may differ. As shown in *Figure 1.3*, you can click on the **Install Packages** option in the **Component** menu to verify which components are installed:

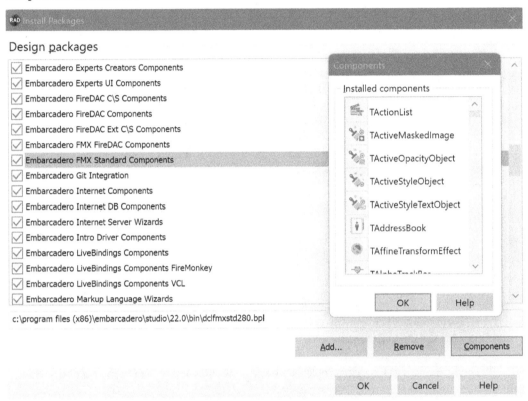

Figure 1.3: The Install Packages window shows the components in a package

Many additional free and commercial component packages are not installed by default. They can be installed with the integrated **GetIt Package Manager**. It is available either from the **Welcome Page** area or from the **Tools** menu. See *Figure 1.4*.

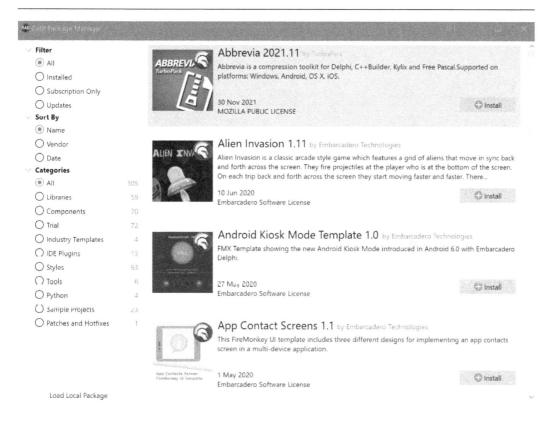

Figure 1.4: The Delphi GetIt Package Manager dialog box

If you want to install any of the available component packages, just click on the **Install** button to the right of the package. The installation process is very straightforward. After accepting the license, the components are downloaded from the internet, possibly compiled, and installed into the IDE. Notice that some special add-on components and premium styles are available only to customers with an active update subscription and, for this reason, they cannot be installed with the CE version.

How do you customize other areas of the Delphi IDE? You can use the **Options** dialog.

IDE options

You can manage all aspects of how the Delphi IDE works from the **Options** dialog, which is available from the **Tools** menu. Here, you can customize various aspects of how Delphi operates as a whole. See *Figure 1.5*.

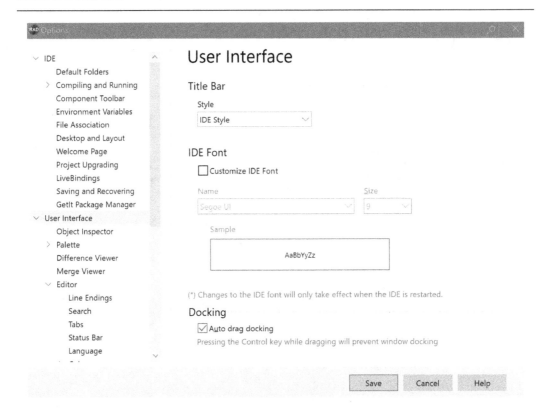

Figure 1.5: One of the many pages of the Delphi IDE Options dialog box

You cannot understand the assorted options of this dialog box until you have a better understanding of the different capabilities the Delphi IDE offers, which is what I am going to focus on in the next section.

Riding the IDE

In a nutshell, Delphi is a program for making other programs. The program responsible for generating executable files from the source code is a compiler. It is typically implemented as a command-line application, but it can also be invoked directly from the IDE. When executing the compiler as a command-line application, you can pass to it command-line parameters. As depicted in *Figure 1.6*, compilers take different command-line parameters, including the location of source code files necessary to generate the resulting binary file:

Figure 1.6: A simplified compiler architecture

It is possible to write your programs using a text editor such as Notepad and then execute the compiler from the command line, but it is not the most efficient way of creating applications. Most programmers use IDEs to work on apps. The idea of an IDE originates from Delphi's ancestor – Borland Turbo Pascal, in the 1980s – and it comes from the integration of three previously separate programs: Code Editor, Compiler, and Debugger.

Delphi compilers and toolchains

The Delphi IDE contains different compilers for generating apps for different platforms. The IDE manages all the necessary source code files for building an app. It also takes care of passing correct parameters to the right compilers and manages their output. In the IDE, it is possible to build, deploy, and run an app directly on the mobile device connected with a USB cable by just pressing the **Run** button. It is also possible to generate an application executable without running it by using the `Compile` or `Build` commands. Sometimes, it is very handy to be able to step into an application as it is executed in the host operating system. This process is called **debugging**. In the Delphi IDE, you can run your program "with" or "without" debugging.

Nine Delphi compilers come installed with **Delphi 12.0**, as indicated in *Table 1.1*. All compilers are available in all product editions, except for the Linux compiler, which is only in the Enterprise and Architect versions:

Delphi Compiler	Target Platform
Dcccaarm	32-bit Android
dccaarm64	64-bit Android
dcciosarm64	64-bit iOS
dcc32	32-bit Windows
dcc64	64-bit Windows
dccosx64	64-bit macOS (Intel)
dccosxarm64	64-bit macOS (ARM)
dcciossimarm64	iOS simulator for macOS ARM
dcclinux64	64-bit Linux (Intel)

Table 1.1 – The Delphi compilers for the different target platforms

These compilers are typically installed into the `bin` folder of the product installation folder (by default, this is under `C:\Program Files (x86)\Embarcadero\Studio\`). The `bin` folder of Delphi is added to the Windows path by the installer, so you can try and execute them directly from the command line. As shown in *Figure 1.7*, executed with no parameters, the Delphi compilers will just display their version numbers and the available command-line switches:

```
Command Prompt        ×    +  ∨                              —    □    ×

C:\>dccaarm
Embarcadero Delphi for Android compiler version 35.0
Copyright (c) 1983,2022 Embarcadero Technologies, Inc.

Syntax: dccaarm [options] filename [options]

  -A<unit>=<alias> = Set unit alias
  -B = Build all units
  -CC = Console target
  -CG = GUI target
  -D<syms> = Define conditionals
  -E<path> = executable/library output directory
  -G = Output map file
  -GD = Output map file and .drc file
  -H = Output hint messages
  -I<paths> = Include directories
  -JH = Generate .hpp file
  -LN<path> = package .dcp and .a output directory
  -LU<package> = Use package
  -M = Make modified units
```

Figure 1.7: The Delphi Android compiler invoked from the command prompt

In the IDE, we don't need to invoke command-line compilers directly. The IDE does this for us when we choose to either run, build, or compile our project. It will also take care of outputting the resulting binary files into a separate folder for each supported platform and build configuration. When we build, deploy, and run our apps, we can see the commands being executed in the message log pane, including the parameters passed to them and their output.

The "Hello World" app

Starting with a new programming language or framework typically involves creating a program that displays the classic `Hello World` message; we will follow this convention. Our app will have just one button. When you press this button, the message `Delphi Hello World!` will be displayed. Later in this chapter, we are going to put this app on an iPhone and an Android device.

To start, click on the **Multi-Device Application – Delphi** option in the **File | New** menu (see *Figure 1.8*) or the welcome page:

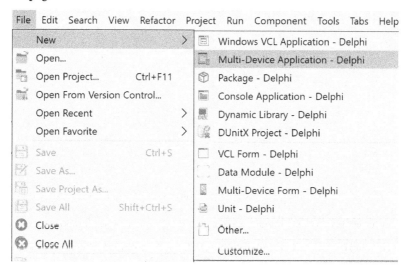

Figure 1.8: The Multi-Device Application – Delphi menu option

This will display a wizard with different multi-device project templates, as shown in *Figure 1.9*.

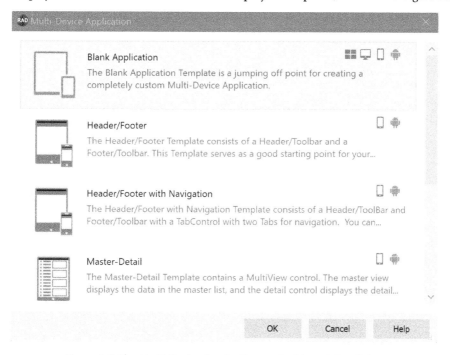

Figure 1.9: The Multi-Device Application project templates dialog

Double-click on the **Blank Application** project template. This will create a new project and open its main form in the IDE. See *Figure 1.10*.

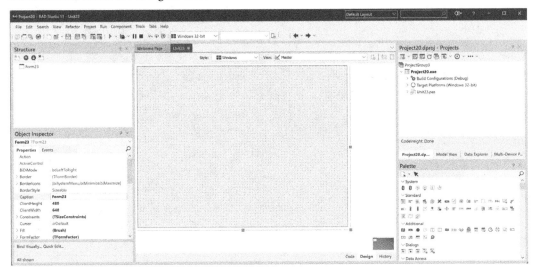

Figure 1.10: A new, blank multi-device application in the IDE

The first thing you must do after creating a new project is to save it all. The Delphi project is made up of multiple files that are managed by the IDE. The IDE will also create subfolders in the project directory for managing different artifacts, such as compiled executable files, editor history, and recovery files, so it is always a good idea to save a new project into a new empty directory.

Click on the **Save All** button in the Delphi toolbar just below the main menu (see *Figure 1.11*) to save all the files in the project. Remember that Delphi does not automatically save the files in the editor, so you need to do that from time to time. As an alternative, you can configure the IDE so that it saves the source code files when you start the debugger. In any case, the IDE does save temporary files in a separate location so that in case of a crash, it can recover unsaved files:

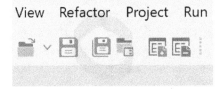

Figure 1.11: The "Save All" speed button

First, we will be asked to save the main form for our application. Enter uFormHelloWorld in the file save dialog and click **Save**. Next, a second file save dialog will be displayed. Here, we need to give our project a name. Enter DelphiHelloWorld and click **Save**.

Delphi organizes all the necessary files to build an app into a "project." The Delphi IDE contains several windows that help us work on our projects. There are different project types. It is possible to create a project group inside the IDE, keeping several projects at hand, but at any given moment, there could be only one project active. You can see the name of the active Delphi project in the title bar at the top-left corner of the Delphi window. Its name is also displayed in bold font in the **Project Manager** area.

Let's add a button to the form. The fastest way to work in the IDE is to use **IDE Insight**. There are hundreds of different options, components, and windows in the IDE. If you know what you are looking for, you can just press *F6* or press *Ctrl + .* keys at the same time. The **IDE Insight** combo box, in the IDE title bar, will receive focus. You can also just click on the **IDE Insight** combo box itself. We want to add a button to the form. Just start typing what you are looking for and notice how, with every keystroke, the list of available items in the **IDE Insight** combo box changes. Type *b*, *u*, and *t*; and after three keystrokes, the **TButton** component will be the first element of the list. See *Figure 1.12*.

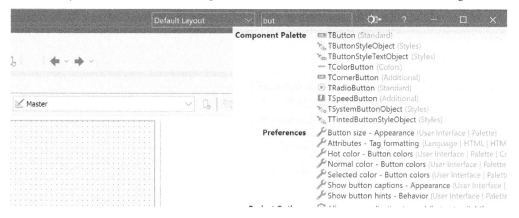

Figure 1.12: Incremental filtering in the IDE Insight combo box

Just press *Enter* and a button will be added to the form. IDE Insight is probably the single most useful productivity feature of the IDE. It only takes five or six keystrokes to add the component to the form. Alternatively, we could locate the **TButton** component in the **Tool Palette** window (by navigating over the available components categories or typing in the local search box, as shown in *Figure 1.13*) and double-click it to add it to the form:

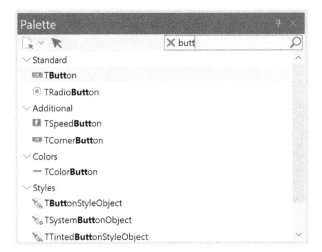

Figure 1.13: Searching for the Button component in the Tool Palette window

We now have a button in the middle of an empty form. Let's start working on how our app will look – that is, in the form designer. Later, we will focus on what our app is going to do – that is, coding in the editor window. Click on the button and move it more toward the window's top-left corner. In the bottom left part of the IDE, there is an **Object Inspector** pane. Here, we can modify the properties and events of a component. In this case, we want to change the text that's displayed on the button. Make sure that `TButton1` is selected in the **Object Inspector** pane and find its `Text` property. As I've done in *Figure 1.14*, replace the default caption, `Button1`, with the text `Hello World`:

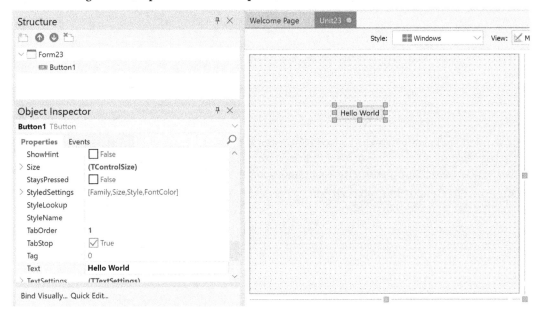

Figure 1.14: Changing the button's text in the Object Inspector pane

Now, find the `Name` property of the button control and change it to `BtnHelloWorld`. Notice that the component's new name is immediately reflected in the **Structure** view above the **Object Inspector** pane. The change, however, also affects the application code skeleton we've generated so far. Now, select the form. You can click somewhere on the form in the Form Designer to select it or just click on the form's node in the **Structure** view above **Object Inspector**. That is how the IDE works. Different windows are synchronized with each other, so selecting a component changes the current component selection in other views. Find the `Name` property of the main form and change the default, `Form1`, to `FormHelloWorld`. Now, find the `Caption` property of the form and change it to `Delphi Hello World`. Save everything.

It is always a good practice to give components and their properties meaningful names. There are different naming conventions. One of the most popular ones is to use an abbreviation of the component type at the beginning of its name so that, from the name, we can immediately figure out the type of the specific component. You also want to keep names short. If names are too long, you need to type more. Long names in the source code also tend to be less readable. It is up to you to decide what naming convention to use, but once you have decided, it is important to stick to it for consistency.

Now that we have built the user interface, we need to define what will happen when the user of our app clicks on the button. For this, we need to attach an event handler to the `OnClick` event of the `BtnHelloWorld` button. We can select the button, switch to the **Events** tab in the **Object Inspector** pane, locate the `OnClick` event, and double-click in the space next to it to generate an empty event handler. However, there is a faster way: just double-click on the button on the form. Either way, the IDE will switch from the Form Designer to the Code Editor and the cursor will be placed just at the beginning of an empty line between "begin" and "end," where we need to enter some code in the Object Pascal language. This code will be executed by our app in response to the click event – that is when the user clicks on the button. It could be misleading that this event is called `OnClick` as you can only use a mouse on desktop computers. Don't worry – if we compile our app to mobile targets, this event will be triggered in response to tapping on the button on the mobile device's screen.

In the code of our event handler, we will invoke the built-in `ShowMessage` function and pass to it `Delphi Hello World` as the string that we want to display in the message. The editor should look like what's shown in *Figure 1.15*:

```
procedure TFormHelloWorld.BtnHelloWorldClick(Sender: TObject);
begin
  ShowMessage ('Delphi Hello World');
end;
```

Figure 1.15: The button's OnClick event handler code

Click on **Save All** again. Now, let's run the application directly. Press *F9* or click on the green run arrow icon under the main menu to build and run the project. You can see the application running in *Figure 1.16*:

Figure 1.16: The Delphi "Hello World" multi-device app running on Windows

We are on Windows so, by default, we will compile our multi-device app as a Windows 32-bit executable. This is extremely useful when developing mobile apps with Delphi. During development, it is quicker to run our multi-device app on Windows to see that it does not contain any mistakes. If it compiles fine on Windows and runs with no problem, then there is a big chance that it will also compile OK with mobile compilers and run on a device. Building and deploying it to a mobile device typically takes longer.

Every Delphi form is made of two source code files. When we entered `uFormHelloWorld` as the name of the main form of our app, the IDE created two files: `uFormHelloWorld.pas` and `uFormHelloWorld.fmx`.

You can switch between these files by clicking on a specific button of the toolbar with a "Toggle Form/ Unit (F12)" hint, press *F12*, or use the **Code** and **Design** tabs at the bottom of the editor or form designer. The first file is what we can see in the **Code** tab: it's the source code of the form and the file in which we added the event handler code. You can see this code in *Figure 1.17*:

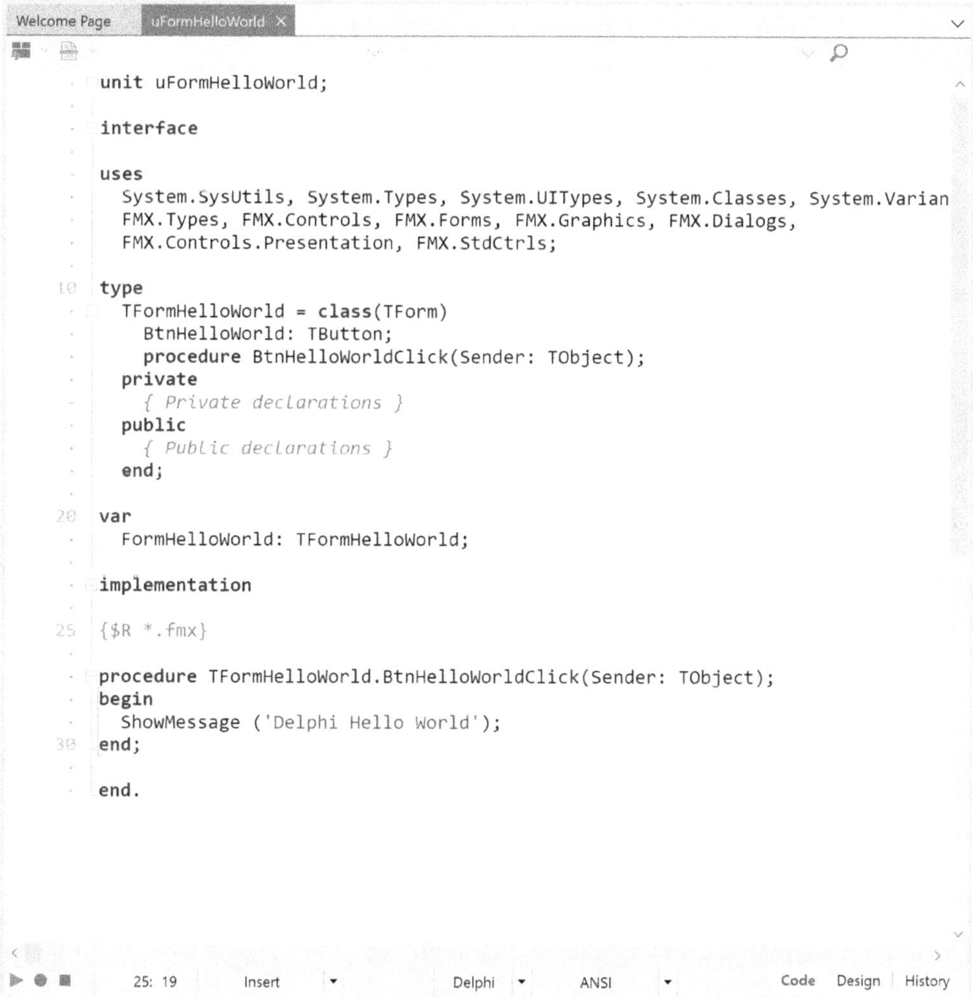

Figure 1.17: The Code Editor with the unit of the "Hello World" app

The content of the fmx file is managed by the Form Designer and we generally do not edit it directly. Every time we change something in the **Object Inspector** pane or the **Form Designer**, these changes are stored in the fmx file. The **Form Designer** gives us a "*what you see is what you get*" user experience so that we can see what our app will look like even before we run it.

You can preview the text representation of the form file by right-clicking somewhere on the form and selecting the **View As Text** option from the context menu, as shown in *Figure 1.18*.

```
1  object FormHelloWorld: TFormHelloWorld
       Left = 0
       Top = 0
       Caption = 'Delphi Hello World'
       ClientHeight = 376
       ClientWidth = 431
       FormFactor.Width = 320
       FormFactor.Height = 480
       FormFactor.Devices = [Desktop]
10     DesignerMasterStyle = 0
       object BtnHelloWorld: TButton
         Position.X = 160.000000000000000000
         Position.Y = 80.000000000000000000
         TabOrder = 1
         Text = 'Hello World'
         OnClick = BtnHelloWorldClick
       end
   end
```

Figure 1.18: The Delphi Form Designer, after calling View as Text

To return to the form view, just right-click in the editor again and select **View As Form** from the context menu.

The most important window in the IDE is **Project Manager** (see *Figure 1.19*). It provides a graphical interface to work with all the files that make up our projects and lets us switch between different compilers and build configurations. You can build your applications in either **Debug** or **Release** mode. **Debug** mode is used during an app's development. The resulting binary file will contain additional binary information that can be used by a debugger. When our app is ready to be built for distribution to an app store, then we can switch to **Release** mode. This will generate an app in a form that is suitable for distribution, removing useless debug information and optimizing the generated code:

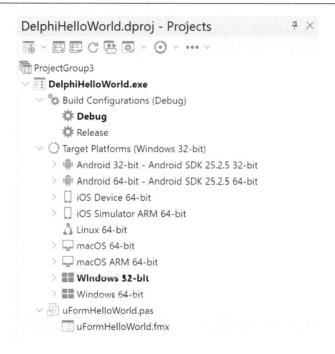

Figure 1.19: The Delphi Project Manager

Let's have a look at the different files that make up a Delphi project. If you want to quickly find the folder where the current project is located, you can right-click on one of the project files in the **Project Manager** area and use the **Show in Explorer** command.

You should now see all files and folders that make up our DelphiHelloWorld project, as shown in *Figure 1.20*:

Name	Date modified	Type	Size
_history	6/10/2023 12:26 PM	File folder	
Win32	6/10/2023 12:18 PM	File folder	
DelphiHelloWorld.dpr	6/10/2023 12:15 PM	Delphi Project File	1 KB
DelphiHelloWorld.dproj	6/10/2023 12:15 PM	Delphi Project File	83 KB
DelphiHelloWorld.dproj.local	6/10/2023 12:15 PM	LOCAL File	1 KB
DelphiHelloWorld.identcache	6/10/2023 12:22 PM	IDENTCACHE File	1 KB
DelphiHelloWorld.res	6/10/2023 12:18 PM	RES File	110 KB
uFormHelloWorld.fmx	6/10/2023 12:15 PM	FireMonkey Form	1 KB
uFormHelloWorld.pas	6/10/2023 12:15 PM	Delphi Source File	1 KB

Figure 1.20: The files that make up a Delphi project in Windows Resource Explorer

Among others, you will see two files named uFormHelloWorld and two project files with the same name as our project, DelphiHelloWorld, but with different extensions. The first one has an extension of dpr, which stands for "Delphi Project" and contains the main program file of our application. We can preview this file inside the IDE (see *Figure 1.21*) by going to the **Project** | **View Source** menu:

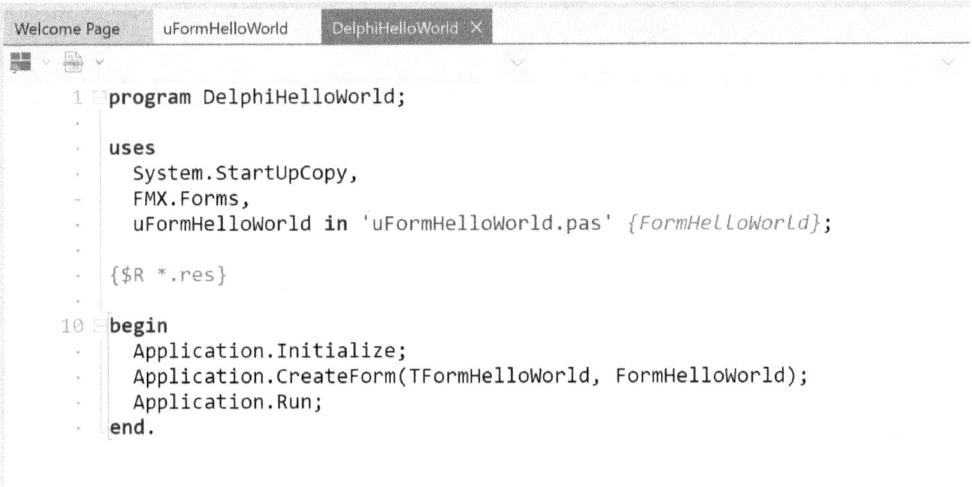

```pascal
program DelphiHelloWorld;

uses
  System.StartUpCopy,
  FMX.Forms,
  uFormHelloWorld in 'uFormHelloWorld.pas' {FormHelloWorld};

{$R *.res}

begin
  Application.Initialize;
  Application.CreateForm(TFormHelloWorld, FormHelloWorld);
  Application.Run;
end.
```

Figure 1.21: The Delphi project source code

This is the application's main program file, which is managed by the IDE, and most of the time, we do not need to change anything there. The second project file has a dproj extension. If we open it in an external editor (in *Figure 1.22*, below UltraEdit, but Notepad will also be fine), we will see that it contains XML code with build instructions for the MSBuild engine that is used by Delphi to manage all files and resources that are needed to build our project for different targets and configurations:

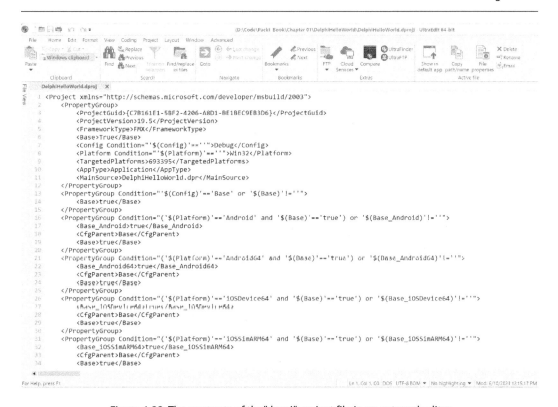

Figure 1.22: The contents of the "dproj" project file in an external editor

There is also a `win32` subfolder here. It contains a subfolder called `debug` and two files: `DelphiHelloWorld.exe` and `uFormHelloWorld.dcu`. The first file is a regular Windows 32-bit executable program that we have just built. We could copy this file to another computer to run it, although it doesn't do much, as it only displays a message. The second file is the product of compiling a single Object Pascal file and it is only useful for the IDE during the build process. You can safely delete the `win32` folder and its contents. The next time you run the application, these folders and files will be recreated. That is the difference between "building" and "compiling" the project. The first time, both commands do the same thing. They generate all binary files in the output folder. `dcu` files are generated first and the `exe` file is generated next. If we select **Build** every time, all binary files are recreated. If we select **Compile**, only the units (Object Pascal files and matching `dcu` files) that have changes recreated. This speeds up compiling a large project.

Deploying to mobile devices

Our `DelphiHelloWorld` project is now ready for deployment to mobile devices. We have already built and run it on Windows. Now, we are going to deploy it to an Android device, and then to iOS.

There is a one-time preparation phase for mobile development that you need to go through after Delphi is installed. We want to get to the point in which you can see your devices as targets inside the **Project Manager** area.

For Android, all the steps to configure your system to detect your device are described at `https://docwiki.embarcadero.com/RADStudio/en/Configuring_Your_System_to_Detect_Your_Android_Device`.

Deploying to Android

Deploying apps from Delphi to Android devices is simpler than deploying to iOS. You only need to have an Android device and a USB cable to connect your device to a Windows machine where you have Delphi installed.

The first step is to enable USB debugging on the device. This option can be set in **Developer options** on your device. However, this option is not easy to find because you need to enable development support on the device itself first. Follow these steps to do so:

1. On your Android device, go to **Settings | About phone**. Tap on **Build number** seven times to become a developer! This makes the developer options available.

2. Under **Settings | System | Developer options** (or **Settings | Developer options** on older versions of Android), check the **USB Debugging** option.

3. Connect your Android device with a USB cable to a computer where your PC is running. The first time you connect your Android device, you may see a message displayed on the device to `Allow USB debugging` from the computer identified by a string of hexadecimal numbers that represent the computer's RSA key fingerprint. Check the **Always allow from this computer** option and click on OK. More information on enabling USB debugging on Android devices is available at `https://docwiki.embarcadero.com/RADStudio/en/Enabling_USB_Debugging_on_an_Android_Device`.

4. The next step is to install the USB driver for your Android device on the machine where Delphi is installed. This feature is not part of Delphi but of the Android SDK. You can install the SDK by enabling it in the **Additional Features** area available in the Delphi installer and **Platform Manager**, or manually after downloading it from Google. The Delphi installer configures the Android SDK, but the USB driver installation is a manual step. Depending on your device, the steps may be different. You can find detailed information on how to install the USB driver for your Android device at `https://docwiki.embarcadero.com/RADStudio/en/Installing_the_USB_Driver_for_Your_Android_Device`.

Now, let's go back to the Delphi IDE. For each platform we want to target outside of Windows, we need to configure a specific **SDK Manager**. Open the **Tools | Options** dialog box and select the **Deployment | SDK Manager** section in the tree on the left. Now, click on the **Add** button to add a new SDK, as shown in *Figure 1.23*. Select the **Android 32-bit** platform:

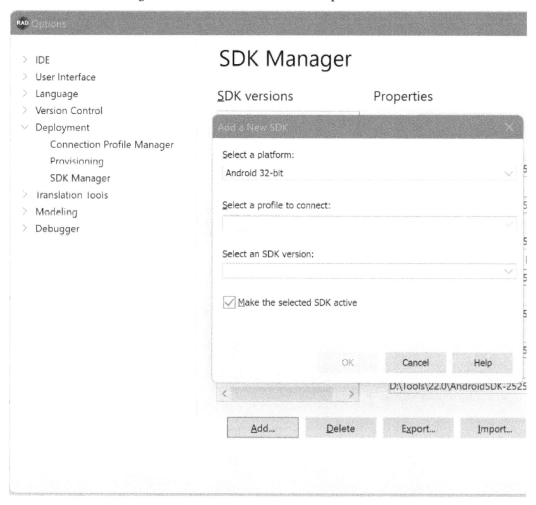

Figure 1.23: Adding a new SDK in the Delphi IDE SDK Manager

In this case, we don't need to configure a remote connection (that's for Apple OSs and Linux). In the last combo box, we must select the Android SDK installation folder, in the GetIt Catalog Repository (or the location of your manual installation of the Android SDK).

You might want to repeat the same steps to install an SDK for the Android 64-bit platform (the steps are identical).

At this point, you can get back to the `DelphiHelloWorld` project, reopening it in the Delphi IDE if it's not still open. In the **Project Manager** area, expand **Target Platforms** and double-click on the **Android 32-bit** node or the **Android 64-bit** node to select one of the two available Android targets. It should display the name in bold font, indicating that this is now the current project compilation and execution target.

Expand the **Target** node under the Android platform; if you have an Android device connected via USB, with the proper developer configuration and permissions, you'll see the device's name listed. See *Figure 1.24*.

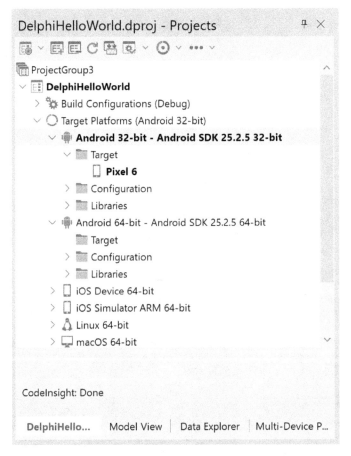

Figure 1.24: Selecting a target device in the Delphi Project Manager area

Now, when you click on the green run arrow, the IDE will build our *DelphiHelloWorld app* using the Delphi Android compiler, create an APK package, deploy the app, install it on the device, and run it – all in just one click. You can see the app running in *Figure 1.25*:

Figure 1.25: The Delphi "Hello World" app running on Android

Deploying to iOS

Deploying apps from Delphi to an iOS device is significantly more complex than the Android counterpart. Here is a quick checklist of what you need:

- An Apple Mac computer running macOS. It can also be an Intel or ARM version, but the ARM version is needed if you want to run your apps in the iOS simulator.

- The Apple Xcode (free) development environment installed on your Mac. There is no separate SDK for iOS; the development tools are only available as part of the Apple developer IDE. The reason is that during the process of deploying to an iOS device, an app needs to be digitally signed with the special command-line tool that comes with Apple Xcode installation.

- A paid Apple iOS Developer Program account.

- A physical iOS (or iPadOS) device. To be able to deploy apps to the iOS device, it needs to be provisioned first. The process of provisioning an iOS device, joining the Apple iOS Developer Program, and installing various certificates is the same as in the case of any app developed with Xcode. You can follow the documentation provided by Apple to learn about this process.

In addition to these requirements, which depend on Apple procedures and are the same regardless of the development tool of your choice, one extra step is required by Delphi. You need to install a special **Platform Assistant Server (PAServer)** program on the Mac where you have Xcode installed. The PAServer installable package is installed in the "PAServer" subdirectory of the Delphi installation folder. Just copy it over to your Mac and execute it.

PAServer is implemented as a command-line app. After it is launched on Mac, it will display a command-line interface where you will be prompted to enter your Mac password. Your Mac will also display a dialog, asking if it is OK to give PAServer debugging permissions. Accept it.

You can think about PAServer as an agent that performs operations on behalf of the Delphi IDE that runs on a remote Windows machine. For Delphi to be able to connect, you need to know the IP address of the machine where PAServer is running. You can find out the IP address by issuing the i command from PAServer's command prompt. The list of all available command-line parameters to PAServer is displayed when you enter ? in the command prompt. See *Figure 1.26*.

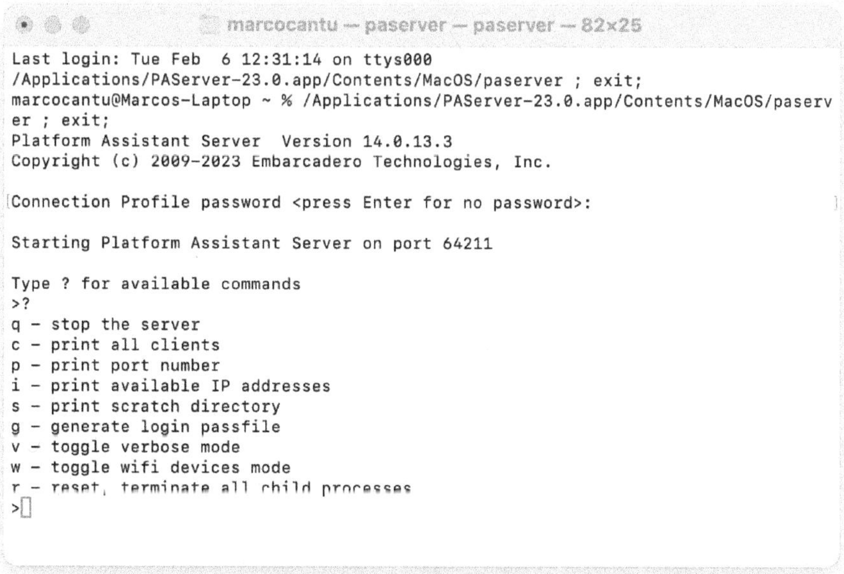

```
Last login: Tue Feb  6 12:31:14 on ttys000
/Applications/PAServer-23.0.app/Contents/MacOS/paserver ; exit;
marcocantu@Marcos-Laptop ~ % /Applications/PAServer-23.0.app/Contents/MacOS/paserv
er ; exit;
Platform Assistant Server   Version 14.0.13.3
Copyright (c) 2009-2023 Embarcadero Technologies, Inc.

Connection Profile password <press Enter for no password>:

Starting Platform Assistant Server on port 64211

Type ? for available commands
>?
q - stop the server
c - print all clients
p - print port number
i - print available IP addresses
s - print scratch directory
g - generate login passfile
v - toggle verbose mode
w - toggle wifi devices mode
r - reset, terminate all child processes
>
```

Figure 1.26: The PAServer tool running on Mac

Now, you need to configure Delphi so that it can find the iOS device you want to deploy to. The goal is to find your device listed in the **Project Manager** area. In general, you could have multiple different Macs visible to your Delphi installation. For every Mac you want to deploy to, you need to define a connection profile.

Like what we have done for Android, we need to configure the SDK for iOS. Again, open the **Tools | Options** dialog box and select **Deployment | SDK Manager**. This time, you have to select the **iOS Device 64-bit** platform. At this point, you have to pick an existing or define a new profile to connect. A profile is a configuration that points to the IP address of the Mac where PAServer is running.

When you select **Add New** in the **Connection Profile** combo, the **Create a Connection Profile** wizard will be displayed (see *Figure 1.27*). Enter a profile name. Click **Next**. On the next tab of the wizard dialog, we need to enter the address and port of the remote machine. Keep the default port of **64211** and enter your Mac password in the last field:

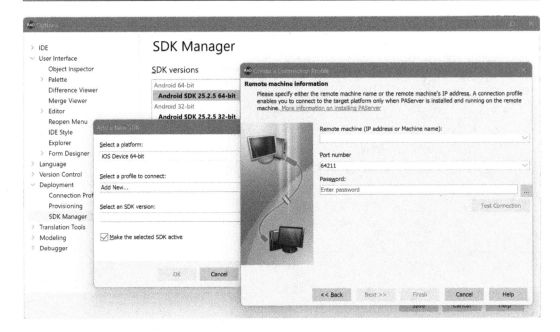

Figure 1.27: The Create a Connection Profile dialog, which is used to configure an iOS SDK in Delphi

Now, click on the **Test Connection** button to verify that the IDE can communicate with the remote PAServer. If everything went well, you should see a message stating that the connection to your Mac succeeded. Click on **Finish**, then proceed with the following steps in the SDK Manager configuration (see *Figure 1.28*):

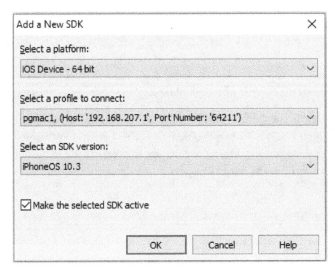

Figure 1.28: The Add a New SDK dialog

Once the cache has refreshed, the IDE should automatically update the iOS 64-bit **Target** node and you should see your device listed there. In *Figure 1.29* you can see the project with the configuration of the iOS Simulator target.

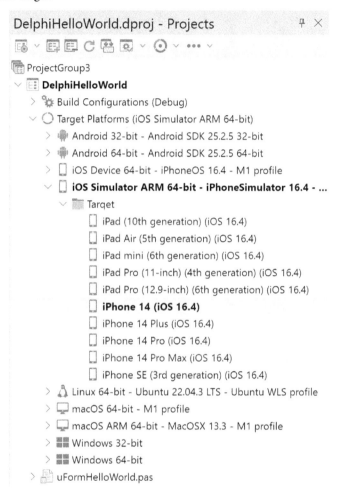

Figure 1.29: The Project Manager area with an iOS simulator configuration listed as a target

Now, click on the **Run** button. This will locally build the iOS `ipa` executable file and send it to the Mac machine where PAServer is running. PAServer will invoke the command-line tool from Xcode installation to digitally sign the executable, after which it will be deployed and run on the physical iOS device, all in one operation.

Figure 1.30 shows what our *Delphi Hello World app* looks like on an iOS simulator.

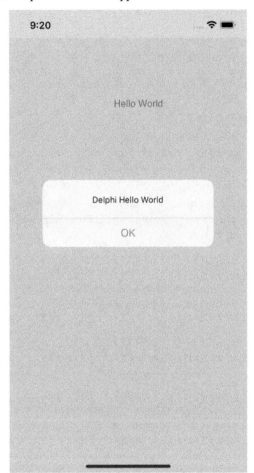

Figure 1.30: The Delphi "Hello World" app running on iOS Simulator

More information about deploying apps to iOS devices from Delphi can be found online at `https://docwiki.embarcadero.com/RADStudio/en/IOS_Mobile_Application_Development`.

Summary

In this chapter, we installed Delphi and configured it for mobile development, configuring the SDKs for Android and iOS. We also learned about some of the basic functionalities of the IDE.

Now, we are going to change gears and focus on the Object Pascal programming language. This is the programming that's used by Delphi – the language itself is also known as the Delphi programming language.

2

Mind Your Language

The **Object Pascal** language used in Delphi is constantly evolving. With every new version of Delphi, there are new features added to the language. Even though there are different Delphi compilers for each of the platforms, the language is the same. Minor differences depend on whether the target platform is 32-bit or 64-bit, and some other platform nuances. But in almost all cases, the same source code compiles and works across all platforms. This wasn't the case in the early days of Delphi mobile compilers, which implemented **Automatic Reference Counting (ARC)** and other features not found in the desktop counterpart.

Fluency in using the Object Pascal language (also known as the **Delphi language**) is a key skill for every Delphi developer. It's easy to underestimate how a good knowledge of the language can make you a better (and faster) developer.

This chapter will cover the following:

- Do you speak Object Pascal?
- The Object Pascal language phrasebook

The objective of this chapter is to gain fluency in using the Object Pascal language. This chapter is not a definitive reference to every single feature of the programming language of Delphi, as that would easily take an entire book. The goal is to cover most of the everyday constructs, to be able to understand the **FireMonkey library source code,** and to write solid and maintainable code.

Do you speak Object Pascal?

The Pascal language was designed to teach good programming practices, and its modern counterpart, the Object Pascal language, in use today, still holds true to some of the core tenets in terms of readability and clarity. The Object Pascal language in today's Delphi is a high-level, modern, strongly typed compiled language that supports structured and object-oriented programming.

To solve a problem using a computer, you need to define a finite set of actions that operate on certain data – or in other words, to define an algorithm. An algorithm expressed in a programming language is a computer program and its actions are described as programming language instructions.

One or more actions that are performed on certain data can be encapsulated in Object Pascal language as a routine or a class. In most programming languages, routines are called functions. In Object Pascal, if a function does not return a value, it is called a procedure. Classes are the cornerstones of object-oriented programming, which is the most important approach to building apps in Object Pascal. Classes group data and operations performed on this data together, providing encapsulation and reusability.

In the previous chapter, we learned about compilers. The job of a compiler is to process one or more files that contain the text of programs that we write in a programming language and generate a binary file that can be loaded by an operating system and executed. In this chapter, we are going to focus on the contents of files that contain the source code of our programs. Source code files are regular text files that can be opened in an arbitrary text editor. The default extension of a file that contains Object Pascal source code is `pas`. When you install Delphi, it will register itself with Windows as the default program for opening different file types related to Delphi programming, including `pas`, `dpr`, `dpk`, and `dproj`.

The source code file needs to contain proper content according to the rules of the programming language. If you try to compile a file that is not properly structured or contains programming language errors, the compiler will stop the compilation and report an error message describing the location and the nature of the error. Sometimes the error message might not be obvious, but we would typically get the name of the source file and the line number where the error is located.

Program structure

Each Object Pascal program begins with a `program` declaration, which specifies the name of the program. It is followed by a `uses` clause to refer to other source code files in the program, and then a block of declarations and statements. Object Pascal programs are typically divided into modules of source code called **units**. The optional `uses` clause contains the list of units used by the program. These units in turn may use other units specified in their own `uses` clauses.

Every Object Pascal program uses the built-in `System` unit. This unit contains predefined constants, types, functions, and procedures, for example, basic functions to write and read from the command line or work with files. If you explicitly place `System` in the `uses` clause, you will get an error message that this unit is already used, and it is not permitted to use a unit multiple times in one unit. Apart from the `System` unit, Delphi comes with many units that are not used automatically. They must be included in the `uses` clause. For example, the `System.SysUtils` unit is typically used in every Delphi project because it provides some basic functionality such as the declaration of an exception class that is needed for structured exception handling. Unit names may contain dots, as in the case of `System.SysUtils`. Only the last part is the actual unit name, and all preceding identifiers constitute a namespace, which is used to logically group units. In some cases, it is possible to skip the namespace part, and the compiler will still be able to compile the unit. The order of the units listed in the uses clause is important and determines the order in which they are referenced and initialized.

The first time you compile an app, the compiler produces a compiled unit file (with the .dcu extension) for each unit in the project. These files are then linked to create an executable file. In the **Project** menu or the **Project Manager** context menu, there are options to either compile or build the current project. When you compile your project, individual units are not recompiled unless they have been changed since the previous compilation or their compiled units cannot be found. If you choose **Build**, all compiled units are regenerated. In fact, the compiler just needs the compiled unit to generate the executable, so it might not have access to the source code of a unit at all. With pre-compiled units, you can build even noticeably big projects very quickly.

Console application

The simplest possible type of program that can be written in Delphi is a console application. It does not contain a graphical user interface. Console programs can be executed from the command prompt and can optionally take command-line parameters. A console application may output some text back to the command line, perform some calculations, process files, or communicate with remote services running somewhere on the internet.

Let us create a simple Delphi console app. It will be an interactive program that will take our name from the command line and display a greeting.

To get started, from the **File** menu, select **New and Console Application - Delphi**. The IDE has generated a console application for us that currently does nothing.

The next thing we always do after creating a new project is to save it. Click on **Save All** in the **File** menu, click on the **Save All** icon in the toolbar, or just press the *Ctrl + Shift + S* keys on the keyboard.

Always save a new project into an empty folder. Enter Greeter as the name of the new project and click on **OK**. Note that the IDE changed the identifier in the first line of code and the name of the file where the program is stored. Once you save the project, it will look as shown in *Figure 2.1*.

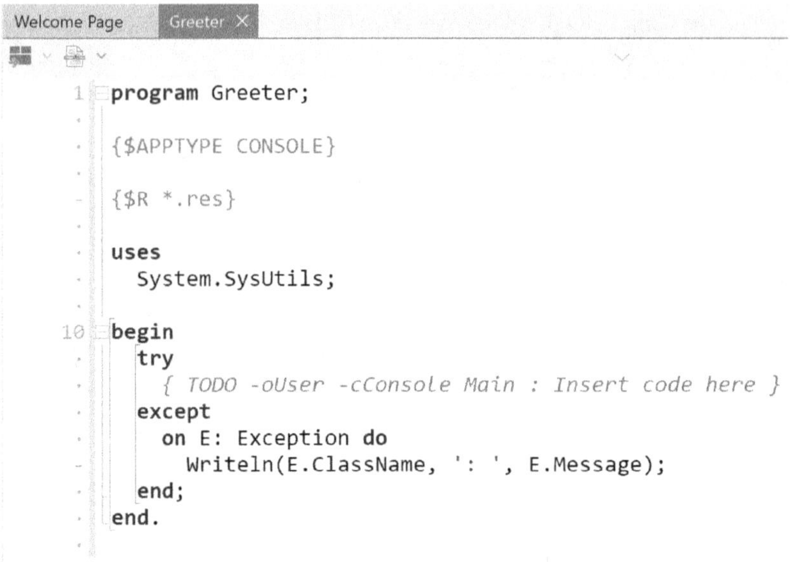

Figure 2.1: The default code of a Delphi console application

All Delphi executable program source code needs to start with the Object Pascal `program` keyword followed by the name of the program. The program's name, the identifier in the code, should match the physical filename or the compiler will fail to process the file.

If you now browse the folder where we saved the project, you will find there two files named `Greeter`, but with different extensions. One is the `Greeter.dpr` file, which contains the source code of the program that we see in the code editor. By convention, the main file of the Delphi app, the one that starts with the `program` keyword, does not have a `pas` extension but a `dpr` extension, which stands for *Delphi project*.

The second file is `Greeter.dproj` and contains MS Build XML code that the IDE uses to store different settings that belong to the project and are used for compilation. We already looked at one `dproj` file in the previous chapter.

Let us replace the contents of our program with the following code:

```
program Greeter;

var
  S: string;

begin
  Write('Enter your name: ');
  Readln(S);
```

```
    Writeln('Welcome ' + S + '!');
    Readln;
end.
```

Save and run the application. It should display the `Enter your name:` message and then display the welcome message. On my machine, it looks as shown in *Figure 2.2*:

Figure 2.2: The output of the Greeter console application

Procedures for reading and writing to the console come from the built-in `System` unit. So, in our simple demo program, there is no need for a `uses` clause at all. The last empty `Readln` statement is there in the program, so it is possible to actually see the output from the previous `Writeln` statement before the program closes. `Write` is used to output text to the console and `Read` is used to read the input from the console into a string variable. The `Writeln` and `Readln` variations of these methods additionally advance to the next line in the console.

Before the `begin` keyword, there is a declaration of a variable. Since Object Pascal is a strongly typed language, you need to declare a variable and its type before you can use it. In our example, `S` is declared as `string`, so it can hold an arbitrary string of Unicode characters. Traditionally, in the Pascal language, individual characters of a string can be accessed with a 1-based index, using the square bracket notation, such as `S[2]`.

The code editor helps us to visually work with our code. In the screenshot from the code editor in *Figure 2.1*, on the left side, in the gutter, there is a green line. It is completely green because I have just saved the code. If I were to start typing, the color of the gutter next to the modified row would change to yellow to indicate that there are some unsaved changes. Every time you save a file, its local copy is stored in a hidden `__history` folder. At the bottom of the code editor, there is a **History** tab. In the **History** view, you can browse through changes, compare file versions, and restore a file to a previous revision.

Blue dots in the gutter indicate all executable lines of source code. This is where you could place a breakpoint if you would like to debug this program and stop when that line is reached. The instructions that make up the Object Pascal program start with the `begin` keyword and end with the `end` keyword followed by a dot (`.`) character. Everything that goes between these keywords contains statements. Each statement is separated with a semicolon (`;`) character. It would still be a valid program if we were to remove the semicolon after the last `Readln` instruction because the semicolon's role is to be a separator and not a terminator (as is the case in many other programming languages, including the many derived by the C-language syntax and using curly braces).

Indentation of source code and text formatting does not have a meaning for the compiler, unlike in Python, but it is a good practice to use indentation and empty spaces for better readability. That is why the `begin` and `end` keywords start from the beginning of the line and all other statements are indented two spaces. To increase the indentation of a block of code in the code editor, you can select the lines keeping the *Shift* key pressed and use the *Ctrl + Shift + I* key combination. For the decrease indentation, or unindent, use *Ctrl + Shift + U*.

You can put arbitrary text in your source code in the form of comments that are ignored by a compiler. Comments are multi-line or single-line. Multi-line comments are enclosed with curly braces (`{  }`) or the old-style parentheses and star character combination (`(*  *)`). The two types of multi-line comments can be nested within each other.

There are some other instructions that look like multi-line comments but start with a dollar sign. They are displayed in a distinct color in the code editor because they are compiler directives. In the default source code generated for a console application, there are two optional compiler directives. The first tells the compiler that this program is a console app and the second one, with the R switch, instructs the compiler to embed in the resulting executable any binary resources (for example, an icon) that might be found in the resource file that has the same name as our project, but with the `res` extension.

Still, the most common type of comments is one-line comments. They start with two slashes (`//`) and continue up to the end of the line. One-line comments are also handy for commenting out a block of code. The Delphi editor offers the *Ctrl + /* key combination for this purpose. If a comment starts with three slashes, it is treated as a special XML documentation comment that can be used for displaying documentation hints in the code editor and documentation generation. It is good practice to properly document your code with comments, so it is easier to read and maintain it.

Building a forms application

It is time to start building our first fully functional mobile app: *The Game of Memory*. In this chapter, we are only going to create the main architecture. Our app is going to be quite simple. There will be two forms:

- A main form with a grid of squares that will serve as the game board
- A second form that will contain game settings

This simple architecture will help us understand the structure of typical Delphi **Forms** applications.

Close the Greeter program if it is still open. Create a new application with **Multi-Device Application - Delphi**. Select the **Blank Application** template and click on **Save All**. Save the file that contains the main form of the application as uFormMain and the project as GameOfMemory. Change the Name property of the application form to FormMain. Add another form to the project.

In the **File | New** menu, select **Multi-Device Form - Delphi**. In the dialog to select the form type, keep the default **HD** selection. The other option is **3D**. We will get to building 3D user interfaces later in the book. The HD stands for high definition and is just a fancier way of specifying that we want just a regular 2D form. Save the file as uFormSettings and change the Name property of the new form to FormSettings. You should end up with a project structure similar to the one depicted in *Figure 2.3*.

Figure 2.3: The structure of the project in the Project Manager

Exploring the project file

Our project contains two forms now. Where is the program file of our app? Click on the **View Source** option in the **Project** menu or the context menu in the **Project Manager**. Now you should see the following code. This is the main program of our GameOfMemory app:

```
program GameOfMemory;

uses
  System.StartUpCopy,
  FMX.Forms,
  uFormMain in 'uFormMain.pas' {FormMain},
  uFormSettings in 'uFormSettings.pas' {FormSettings};

{$R *.res}

begin
  Application.Initialize;
  Application.CreateForm(TFormMain, FormMain);
  Application.CreateForm(TFormSettings, FormSettings);
  Application.Run;
end.
```

The main program file in our project is managed automatically by the IDE and, in most cases, there is no need to edit it manually. This is a very typical Delphi project file.

The first line contains the program heading, which must match the filename. The following lines contain `uses` clauses, referring to library units and the units included in the project. Next, there is a `$R` compiler directive linking the project's resource file to the program.

The logic of a program is defined between the reserved `begin` and `end` words. The project file ends, like all source code files, with a period.

In this program, statements are method calls to the global `Application` object of the project. The block can also contain declarations of constants, types, variables, procedures, and functions, although in general, the main project source file is kept simple, and all the application code is in secondary units, such as the form units.

The Delphi code editor has a built-in hyper-navigation functionality to quickly jump to other units. For example, we may want to see where the `Application` global object variable reference is declared. If we move the mouse cursor over the word `Application` somewhere in the code, we will see a hint that tells us in which unit a given symbol is defined. See *Figure 2.4*.

```
12      Application.Initialize;
        Application.CreateForm(TFormMain, FormMain);
        var FMX.Forms.Application: TApplication - FMX.Forms.pas (1396)
   en
```

Figure 2.4: Moving the mouse over a symbol shows a tooltip

If you press the *Ctrl* key at the same time, the symbol turns into an underlined hyperlink that you can click to quickly jump to the unit where a given symbol is declared. Alternatively, you can right-click on the symbol in the editor and select the **Find Declaration** option.

The blue arrows in the IDE toolbar (see *Figure 2.5*) let you move back and forth through the history of your navigation in the code editor.

Figure 2.5: The arrows of the code navigation toolbar

Currently, at the startup of our program, both application forms are created. In fact, we do not need to create the `Settings` form when the application starts. It is possible that the end user will just play the game and close the application without going into **Settings**. Another important consideration in mobile apps is the application startup time. It is ideal to keep it to a minimum. The call to create the `Settings` form, depending on the processor speed of your mobile device, may delay the moment when the end user sees the screen of the app by a couple of milliseconds. We can just manually delete the following line of code in the code editor:

```
Application.CreateForm(TFormSettings, FormSettings);
```

There is, however, a more elegant way of doing so. In the **Project** menu, click on **Options** at the bottom of the menu. In the **Project Options** dialog, select the **Forms** node and move **FormSettings** from the list of auto-created forms to the list of available forms, as displayed in *Figure 2.6*:

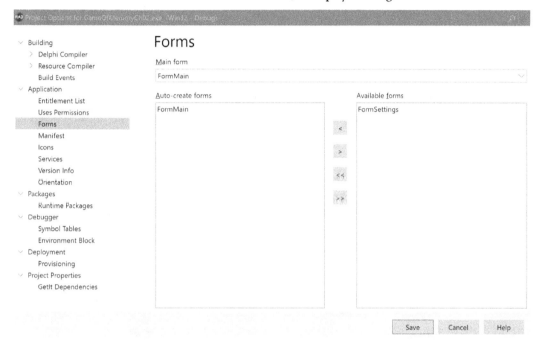

Figure 2.6: The Forms page of the Project Options dialog box

Notice that by making this change in the **Forms** configuration page, the line of the source code responsible for creating the Settings form disappears from the project source code.

The form units

Now we are going to implement basic navigation between the forms, and at the same time have a closer look at the structure of the Object Pascal unit.

The main form of the application is displayed at the application startup. Its lifetime is the same as the application. Let us add a toolbar to the main form of the app and a speed button in the top-right corner that will display the Settings form. In the Settings form, we will also add a speed button at the left side of the toolbar with the *left arrow* image for going back to the application's main form.

Adding a toolbar

Make sure that the FormMain unit is open in the Form Designer. If you are in the code editor, you can switch to the Form Designer by clicking on the **Design** tab at the bottom of the screen. Press the *Ctrl* and . keys at the same time to move the input focus to the IDE Insight box and just start typing TToolbar, which we want to add to the form. After the first three letters, the toolbar should be at the top of the list. Just double-click on it to add it to the main form, as in *Figure 2.7*:

Figure 2.7: Finding a component in IDE Insight

It will automatically align to the top of the form. In the same way, using IDE Insight, add the TSpeedButton component to the toolbar. Change its Align property to Right so it always stays at the top-right corner of the screen regardless of its size or orientation. Change the Name property of the speed button to SpdbtnSettings. Now we need to give it a nice icon. We can do so by changing its StyleLookup property.

By default, when we create a new multi-device form, it uses the default Windows style. What we really want is to see how the form will look on the mobile target, iOS or Android. Change the selection from **Windows** to **iOS** in the combo box above the Form Designer, visible in *Figure 2.8*.

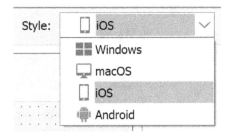

Figure 2.8: The selection of a platform in the Form Designer

Now, if we open the `StyleLookup` property of the speed button in the Object Inspector, we should be able to select from one of the built-in iOS styles for a given control. Select the `drawertoolbutton` style from the list, as you can see in *Figure 2.9*.

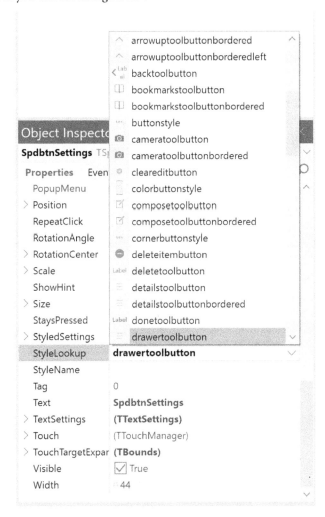

Figure 2.9: Picking a style for the button

If we switch to **Android**, the look and feel of the form will change, including the styling of the toolbar and icons available for styling the speed button.

Save the form. Now go to the `Settings` form. Change **Style** in the combo box above the form to **iOS**. Following the same steps as previously, add a toolbar and a speed button. Change the `Name` property of the speed button to `SpdbtnBack`, its `StyleLookup` property to `arrowlefttoolbutton`, and the `Align` property to `Left`.

Using form units

Now we will implement the functionality to navigate between these forms. In the main form, when we click on the **Settings** button, we want to call the Show method of the Settings form. However, **FormMain** does not know about the **FormSettings** form. We need to add **FormSettings** to the uses clause of **FormMain**. We could do it manually, but the IDE can again help us with it. Make sure that the uFormMain file is open in the code editor and click on the **Use Unit** option in the **File** menu.

In the **Use Unit** dialog, select the **FormSettings** form and keep the default selection to add this unit to the uses clause of the implementation section of the uFormMain unit. This dialog lists all other units in the current project not yet used by the currently selected unit. See *Figure 2.10*.

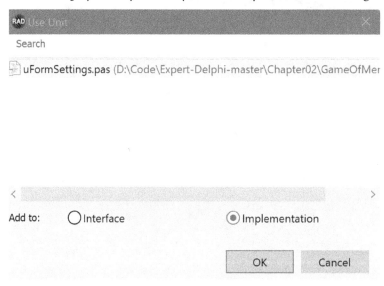

Figure 2.10: The Use Unit dialog box

The next step is to do the same thing in the **FormSettings** form. Add uFormMain to the implementation section of the **FormSettings** uses clause. Double-click on the **Back** speed button and enter a line of code to show the main form of our application:

```
procedure TFormSettings.SpdbtnBackClick(Sender: TObject);
begin
  FormMain.Show;
end;
```

The forms application – units structure

The source code file for a form is a simple Object Pascal unit. Every unit file begins with a unit heading, which is followed by the two main sections, called the interface section and implementation section. In addition, there could be two optional sections, called the initialization section and the finalization section. The interface section of the unit starts with the reserved `interface` word and continues until the implementation section. The interface section indicates what the unit makes available to other units in the program. It declares constants, types, variables, procedures, and functions visible to other units. The interface section, instead, does not contain any executable code. The declaration of a procedure or function includes only its heading. The block of the procedure or function follows in the implementation section. The interface declaration for a class includes declarations of all its members, including the ones that are private to the class and not accessible to the code outside of the declaring unit. The interface section may include its own `uses` section, which must appear immediately after the `interface` keyword.

The implementation section of a unit starts with the `implementation` keyword and continues until the beginning of the initialization section or, if there is no initialization section, until the end of the unit. The unit has a special termination, marked with the *end* keyword followed by a period. The implementation section contains declarations of constants, types, variables, procedures, and functions, which are visible only to the declaring unit. This introduces better organization to the program structure, through encapsulation and the separation of concerns. The implementation section of the unit contains the actual code defined in either standalone functions and procedures or in methods of classes. Only those functions and procedures that additionally have their headings declared in the interface section of the unit are visible to the code residing in other units. The implementation section of the unit may have its own `uses` clause section that follows immediately after the `implementation` reserved word.

A given Object Pascal unit may contain a reference to other units only once, in either its implementation or interface section. If you are unsure where to put a unit reference, put it in the implementation part of the unit. Sometimes you have to put a unit reference in the interface section of the unit. For example, our uFormSettings unit declares the `TFormSettings` class, which is inherited from the `TForm` class defined in the `FMX.Forms` unit, so this unit must be listed in the interface section of the unit.

If unit A depends on unit B and unit B depends on unit A, then they are mutually dependent. This is the case between the two units in our `GameOfMemory` project. If the two units are mutually dependent, at least one of them should list the other unit in its implementation `uses` clause and not its interface `uses` clause.

The initialization section is optional. It starts from the `initialization` keyword and continues until the beginning of the finalization section, or if there is no finalization section, until the end of the unit. The initialization section contains statements executed at the program startup. That is why the order in which units are listed in `uses` clauses is important, because it determines the order in which initialization statements are executed.

The finalization section is also an optional section, as you can have an initialization without a finalization. However, it can only appear in units that have an initialization section. In other words, you cannot have a finalization section without an initialization section.

The finalization section starts from the reserved `finalization` word and continues until the end of the unit. The finalization section contains statements that are executed when the program terminates, in the opposite order from the `initialization` section.

The TFormSettings class

The `uFormSettings` unit contains a declaration of the `TFormSettings` type. Type declarations follow the reserved `type` word. After the declaration of the form's type, there is a variable declaration, `FormSettings`, of the `TFormSettings` type. Variable declarations start with the `var` keyword. When you define a variable, you must also state its type. As mentioned before, the Object Pascal language is strongly typed. The more complex your programs begin, the more you will appreciate the fact that it is not the job of a compiler to guess the type, but it is you – the programmer – who decides about types. The Delphi compiler works in a top-down fashion and typically just reads in sequence all dependent units in your project. That also means that the `TFormSettings` type needs to be declared before it can be used to declare the type of the variable. Because the `FormSettings` variable is defined in the interface section of the unit, it can be used outside of the unit, for example, in the main program file.

Inheritance is a very important concept in object-oriented programming. Our `Settings` form has everything that a standard multi-device form has. You can inspect the declaration of the `TForm` class in the `FMX.Forms` unit. A class declaration defines the name of the class and the class it inherits from in the brackets after the `class` keyword. The class declaration is divided according to visibility. Different class members can also be *private*, where they are visible to the defining class only. It is also possible to have members defined as *protected*. This means that a given member – variable field, constant, or method – is also visible to descendant classes. The two other important visibility specifiers are *public* and *published*. The first means that class members are visible to all other units in the project. Any `published` member has public visibility, but published class members are also accessible at design time in the IDE.

The three lines right after the class declaration of the form contain two field declarations, for the toolbar and the Speed button. There is also a method, or more specifically an event handler, for the `OnClick` event of the button. These declarations do not have an explicit visibility specifier and they are treated as published. This part of the form class is managed by the IDE. Every time you add a component to the form, or create an event handler, the corresponding declaration is added automatically. Also, the interface `uses` a clause that is updated by the IDE every time a different component is added to the form in the Form Designer. The form's class declaration also has placeholders for optional private and public declarations that programmers may want to add.

The implementation section of the unit starts with the $R compiler directive, which instructs the compiler to link to the unit the form file that is managed by the IDE and contains component properties that are set by the Form Designer and Object Inspector. What follows is the implementation of the TFormSettings.SpdbtnBackClick (Sender: TObject) event handler. Its name is made of two parts separated by a period. The first part is the name of the class, and the second part is the name of the method. In parentheses, there is the Sender parameter, which is passed to the method, and in this case, is a reference to the SpdbtnBack control of the form. The Show method in the body of the event handler has been inherited from the TForm class and as such is available in the descendant TFormMain class reference defined in the other form.

Handling the button OnClick event

One last thing is to implement the functionality to show the Settings form in the OnClick event of the main form. Remember that we have removed TFormSettings from the list of auto-created forms. This means that we are now responsible for creating an instance of this class before we can manipulate it in code.

Enter the following code in the OnClick event handler of the SpdbtnSettings speed button:

```
uses
  uFormSettings;

procedure TFormMain.SpdbtnSettingsClick(Sender: TObject);
begin
  if FormSettings = nil then
    FormSettings := TFormSettings.Create(Application);

  FormSettings.Show;
end;
```

With this code, we are displaying the form, creating it in case it doesn't exist.

The lifetime of a secondary form

The global FormSettings variable stores the reference to an instance of the TFormSettings class. We only need to create the Settings form once in the code. This is a common lazy creation pattern, where an object is created just before it is used for the first time in code. If the end user never clicks on the **Settings** button, this object is never created. Here, we are entering a whole new world of different expressions and instructions of the Object Pascal language. What happens here is that if the FormSettings variable is nil, we assign to it the reference to the newly constructed instance of the TFormSettings type. Create is a special **constructor** method that may perform the initialization of an object, but most importantly, it allocates memory for the object. There are also **destructor** methods that are responsible for freeing the object's memory. The TForm class, which is an ancestor of TFormSettings, is in turn inherited from the TComponent class. This is where the `Create(AOwner: TComponent)` constructor is defined. Here, we specify that the global `Application` object is the owner of the newly created form, and it will be responsible for calling the form's destructor at the application's termination.

This is another feature of Object Pascal. Not only do you need to define types of variables, but you are also responsible for managing memory. Once you get some memory through a call to a constructor, you should also think about when it is released. In the case of this secondary form, it's OK to release it when the program terminates.

The Object Pascal language phrasebook

This book is aimed at Delphi programmers with some previous Delphi experience. The Object Pascal language of Delphi keeps evolving and knowing it well is of primary importance to every, even experienced, programmer. Not all the concepts that you can find in many Object Pascal tutorials are discussed here, but the idea is to have a solid understanding of some of the fundamental language concepts, with a focus on newer constructs.

Tokens

Tokens are the smallest meaningful pieces of text that a compiler understands. The tokenization is the very first thing that the compiler does when starting to process a source code file. There are different types of tokens, including identifiers, numbers, string constants, and special symbols. An Object Pascal program is made up of *tokens* and *separators*. A separator is either a blank space or a comment. There must be at least one separator between tokens.

In an Object Pascal source code, you can use any Unicode characters for identifiers, but it makes a lot of sense to stick to just ASCII characters and consistently use just English language in your code. Different elements of the Object Pascal language are in English, and it makes it easier to work with other programmers who might have other languages as their mother tongue.

The Delphi code editor displays different elements of the Delphi source code using distinct colors. Some words are displayed in bold and some others in italics. The color scheme of the Code Editor can be customized in the IDE options, but here we will stick with the defaults.

The Object Pascal language defines a set of *reserved words* that the compiler knows about and cannot be used as identifiers in our code. Keywords are displayed in bold, so they are easy to spot. Keywords have special meaning to the compiler. For example, if you try to save your program as `program`, you will get an error message that `program` is a reserved word and cannot be used as an identifier. If for some reason you truly want to use a keyword as an identifier in your code, you can escape it by prepending an identifier with & character. This is not recommended, though, as it could confuse some of the Delphi plugins and tools.

Identifiers are used for constants, types, variables, procedures, functions, units, programs, and fields in records. An identifier must begin with a letter or an underscore character and cannot contain spaces. Letters, digits, and underscore characters are allowed after the first character. Identifiers and reserved words are not case sensitive, which is a distinguishing feature of Object Pascal compared to many other programming languages. In case of potential ambiguity and for clarity, you can qualify an identifier with its unit name in front of it.

Constants

A constant is an identifier that refers to a value you cannot change. Normal decimal notation is used for numbers that are integers or real constants. A hexadecimal integer constant uses a dollar sign as a prefix. It is also possible to use engineering notation where an exponent follows the E or e character:

```
const
  One = 1;
  OneReal = 1.0;
```

A character string is a sequence of zero or more characters, written in one line in the program and enclosed with single quotes. A character string with nothing between the single quotes is called a *null* string. Two sequential single quotes in a character string denote a single quote character in the string itself.

For example, a string constant would print out as just `Paweł's computer`:

```
const
  Name = 'Marco';
  Computer = 'Paweł''s computer';
```

Object Pascal allows the use of constant expressions. The compiler evaluates them at compile time and not when executing the program.

Object Pascal makes it possible to embed control characters in character strings. The # character followed by an unsigned integer in the range 0 to 255 means a character of the corresponding ASCII value. A useful example of this capability is embedding a new line character in a string constant, so it displays in multiple lines, like in the following code snippet:

```
const
  EL = #13;

procedure TForm1.ButtonMultilineClick(Sender: TObject);
begin
  ShowMessage('Welcome!' + EL + 'Good morning!');
end;
```

Embedding the new ASCII character number 13, or new line control character, displays the message in two lines. For readability, the actual new line character is defined as a constant. In this specific case, the line break value is already available in a library constant called `SLineBreak`.

Types

Writing applications in Object Pascal starts with defining custom types. Only the simplest programs can get away with just using built-in types. Once you define your types, you start writing code and implementing algorithms that operate on your types and data structures. The more carefully your types are designed, the cleaner and more readable your code will be.

Object Pascal comes with many different built-in types that you use to define your own custom types. With experience, it will become more obvious how to model your problem domain. If you write an app to manage grades in a school, you will want to model the abstraction of a school grade. Should it be constant, an enumerated type, a record, or a class?

Every country and education level has different grading schemes. As an example, let us consider the grading system that was used in my primary school in Poland. There were only four grades: very good (5), good (4), sufficient (3) and insufficient (2). At first, as shown in the following example, we could be tempted to use numbers as grades in our code:

```
var
   Grade: Integer;
```

That is not an optimal design. What if our application by mistake assigned a value to a `Grade` variable that was negative or too big?

In this case, it would be better to define a school grade as an enumerated type. This will make our code less error prone and much more readable. There are two ways you can define an enumerated type. Traditionally, we would define `TSchoolGrade` enumeration as follows:

```
type
   TSchoolGrade = (sgVeryGood, sgGood, sgSufficient,
     sgInsufficient);
```

Somewhere in our code, we have a variable of the `TSchoolGrade` type that can only hold one of the four grades defined by this type. Now our code looks better. The `sg` prefix helps us to remember that, for example, the `sgGood` identifier is in fact one of the possible school grade values. The other possibility is to use enumerated values in the fully qualified form. With the SCOPEDENUMS ON compiler directive, we can enforce using the fully qualified form of an enumeration:

```
{$SCOPEDENUMS ON}
type
  TSchoolGrade = (VeryGood, Good,
    Sufficient, Insufficient);
```

```
procedure DoWork;
var
  SG: TSchoolGrade;
begin
  SG := VeryGood; // error, needs scope
  SG := TSchoolGrade.VeryGood; // correct syntax
```

Now we do not really need the SG prefix anymore. It is up to you which form of defining enumerated types to use. The first one is more compact. The second one may be more readable and less error prone in case of conflicting enumerated values.

Inline variables declaration

Starting with recent versions of Delphi, it's possible to declare a variable within a code block by adding the var keyword in front of it:

```
var X := 20.0;
var I: Integer := Trunc(X);
```

While this can be seen as a nice alternative syntax, there is a bit more to it. First, you can use it to set the result of a complex expression as the initial value. Second, inline variable declaration can rely on type inference, so you can omit the type of the variable when the compiler has enough information to determine it:

```
var I := Trunc(X);
```

Third, and most important, an inline var declaration introduces a new visibility rule and lifetime logic for variables, as the scope of these variables is limited to the code block they are declared in. In the case of a variable declared in a nested block, the visibility is the block itself, not the entire method or function. As an example, the variable of a for loop can be defined inline with its type inferred from the context, and therefore it cannot be used after the for loop itself:

```
for var J := 1 to 10 do
begin

end; // J goes out of scope
```

In this book, I'm going to use inline variables where I think they make sense. I will also try to avoid overusing them – which is a risk one may incur in trying to leverage a new feature of the language at all costs.

Sets and arrays

After defining a type, we are going to use it in our code, either as a standalone variable or as a collection. The most basic collection type is a set. It is a very powerful type and one not available in other programming languages. We could, for example, define the set of qualifying school grades. Elements of a set are enclosed in square brackets:

```
type
  TSchoolGrade = (sgVeryGood, sgGood, sgSufficient,
    sgInsufficient);
  TSchoolGrades = set of TSchoolGrade;
const
  Qualifying_Grades: TSchoolGrades =
    [sgVeryGood, sgGood, sgSufficient];

function IsQualifyingGrade(SG: TSchoolGrade): boolean;
begin
  Result := SG in Qualifying_Grades;
end;
```

Using the `in` operator, we can check whether a given value belongs to a set. It is also possible to use other operators to combine sets, calculate their intersections, and, in general, implement other set theory operations.

Another built-in type for dealing with collections of values is an array. Arrays can have either a fixed or a varying size. If it is fixed, then we need to define up front how many elements an array can hold. It is also possible to use dynamic arrays. In this case, we can change the size of an array in code using the `SetLength` procedure and check its current size with the `Length` function. Once we are done with using a dynamic array, we should pass it to the `Finalize` procedure, so the memory it occupies can be properly freed.

One interesting usage scenario for fixed arrays is defining a record constant array. Such an array needs to have a fixed size, because it is embedded in the program at compilation time. This way, you can avoid writing code for initializing an array and adding elements to it.

Let's consider chess. Chess pieces do not change and sometimes it makes sense to assign a relative value to them. So, a simple chess program can make decisions based on the concept of exchanging pieces. Why not hardcode this information? The following code example uses fixed values for the chess pieces:

```
type
  TChessPiece = record
    Name: string;
    Value: Double;
  end;
```

```
const
  Chess_pieces_count = 6;

  Chess_pieces: array[0..Chess_pieces_count-1]
    of TChessPiece =
    (
      (Name : 'Pawn'; Value : 1),
      (Name : 'Knight'; Value : 3),
      (Name : 'Bishop'; Value : 3),
      (Name : 'Rook'; Value : 5),
      (Name : 'Queen'; Value : 9),
      (Name : 'King'; Value : 0)
    );
```

Obviously, this is only an example, and chess piece valuations can be different depending on the phase in the game and expert opinions.

Instead of using an array of a fixed size, it is more common to use dynamic arrays. We can initialize them as if they were a fixed size and perform set operations on them:

```
var
  Fruits: array of string;
begin
  Fruits := ['Apple', 'Pear'];
  Fruits := Fruits + ['Banana', 'Orange'];
```

Dynamic arrays also allow the use of the Insert and Delete procedures for adding and removing a specified number of elements from a given position in an array.

Helpers

Manipulating types in code can be even more readable when we define type **helpers**. Helpers extend a type vertically. You can define them in simple types, enumerations, records, or even dynamic arrays. Delphi already comes with helpers defined for many built-in types, so they are easier to use in code. One good example is the quite common task of converting an integer into a string, so it can be displayed:

```
begin
  var I := 10;
  var S := IntToStr(i); // old style
  S := I.ToString;  // more readable modern style
  S := 10.ToString; // that would work too
```

Just right-click on the `ToString` method in this code and jump to the declaration. In the `System.SysUtils` unit, you will see helpers defined for many built-in types, providing some additional useful methods, for example, minimum and maximum values for a given built-in numerical type.

It is easy to define your own helper classes. We already have the `TSchoolGrade` custom enumerated type. It would be useful to provide methods to convert a school grade value into a string or a number. With a helper, it can be done elegantly. Let's start with the enumeration and a set based on it:

```
type
  TSchoolGrade = (sgVeryGood, sgGood,
    sgSufficient, sgInsufficient);
  TSchoolGrades = set of TSchoolGrade;
```

Next, we define a constant with qualifying grades:

```
const
  Qualifying_grades: TSchoolGrades =
    [sgVeryGood, sgGood, sgSufficient];
```

To make it easier to work with these values, we can now define a helper for the enumeration:

```
type
  TSchoolGradeHelper = record helper for TSchoolGrade
  public
    function ToString: string;
    function ToInteger: Integer;
    function IsQualifying: Boolean;
  end;
```

Finally, we need to implement the methods of the helper:

```
function TSchoolGradeHelper.IsQualifying: Boolean;
begin
  Result := self in Qualifying_grades;
end;

function TSchoolGradeHelper.ToInteger: Integer;
begin
  case self of
    sgVeryGood: Result := 5;
```

```
      sgGood: Result := 4;
      sgSufficient: Result := 3;
      sgInsufficient: Result := 2;
    end;
  end;


  function TSchoolGradeHelper.ToString: string;
  begin
    case self of
      sgVeryGood: Result := 'Very Good';
      sgGood: Result := 'Good';
      sgSufficient: Result := 'Sufficient';
      sgInsufficient: Result := 'Insufficient';
    end;
  end;
```

We use the `self` pseudo-variable in the implementation of a helper method to refer to the current value of the type we operate on.

Also, the function to check whether a given grade is qualifying has been refactored as a helper method. It is more readable and improves the code structure.

Generics

One of the most powerful concepts in the Object Pascal language is a **generic type**. Using this feature, we can write our code in a more generic way, so the same algorithm can operate on not just one data type but many. Generics are data structures or methods that can be parameterized by type. The code is not fully specified, leaving the implementation details to the code that is using generics, creating a specific instance of the generic. There could be generic types, where the whole type definition is parameterized by an unspecified type, or we can just define generic methods that operate on a type that is not fully specified.

As an example, let's consider a `fillable` class. Many languages have a concept of **nullable** values, but we will be different and use `fillable`. It seems more natural. One of the useful examples of using *nullables*, or *fillables*, is mapping between data stored in a relational database and entities in our code. A field in a database record may contain a value, such as a string or integer, or it might be `null`. To properly represent data coming from a database in our code, we need an extra logical flag that would say if a value of a given type contains a valid value or is `null`. If we could represent this data using an object, we would have the possibility to have a nil reference, but it is more efficient to work with plain, simple built-in types whose lifetime does not need to be directly managed. Without generics, we would need to implement a `fillable` class for every field type duplicating the same logic for clearing the flag, returning information if the value is filled, or adding two `fillables` together:

```
type
  TFillable<T> = record
    Value: T;
    IsFilled: Boolean;
  end;

  TFillableString = TFillable<string>;
  TFillableInteger = TFillable<Integer>;
  // ...
```

If our implementation cannot deal with an arbitrary type, we can specify a constraint on the type parameter using a colon notation. We can, for example, say that the generic TFmxProcessor type can be parameterized by any type, but it needs to be a class derived from TFMXObject and it needs to have a public constructor:

```
type
  TFmxProcessor<T: TFMXObject, constructor> = class
    // ...
  end;

  TRecordReporter = class
    procedure DoReport<T: record>(X: T);
  end;
```

Another example where generics are useful is a custom sorting algorithm. There are many implementations, such as bubble sort or quick sort. It does not matter whether we are sorting characters, integers, or real numbers – the algorithm's logic is the same. With generics, you do not need to implement the sorting algorithm for each possible type it can operate on. You just need to have a way to compare two values, so they can be ordered properly.

Delphi comes with a System.Generics.Collections unit that defines many useful generic collection types, such as enumerations, lists, and dictionaries, that we can use in our code.

Consider the following TPerson class:

```
unit uPerson;

interface

type
  TPerson = class
    FirstName, LastName: string;
    constructor Create(AFirstName, ALastName: string);
    function Fullname: string;
  end;
```

```
implementation

{ TPerson }

constructor TPerson.Create(AFirstName, ALastName: string);
begin
  FirstName := AFirstName;
  LastName := ALastName;
end;

function TPerson.Fullname: string;
begin
  Result := FirstName + ' ' + LastName;
end;

end
```

Before the introduction of generics, you could manage a list of objects with the TList class. Let's compare the differences in managing lists with and without generics.

Here is some code that would iterate through an object list of the TPerson instance and log their full names using TList:

```
procedure DoPersonsTList;
var
  Persons: TList; P: TPerson;
begin
  Persons := TList.Create;
  try
    // not safe, can add any pointer
    Persons.Add(TPerson.Create('Kirk', 'Hammett'));
    Persons.Add(TPerson.Create('James', 'Hetfield'));
    Persons.Add(TPerson.Create('Lars', 'Ulrich'));
    Persons.Add(TPerson.Create('Robert', 'Trujillo'));

    for var I := 0 to Persons.Count-1 do
    begin
      P := Persons.Items[I];
      Log(p.Fullname);
    end;
  finally
    Persons.Free;
  end;
end;
```

The TList class is defined in the System.Classes unit and can be used to manage a list of pointers of an arbitrary type. To access the Fullname method of the TPerson class, we need to perform a typecast through assigning a reference to a variable of a proper type. If the object is not a TPerson, or a descendant class instance, we would get an error at runtime:

```
procedure DoPersonsGenerics;
var
  Persons: TObjectList<TPerson>; P: TPerson;
begin
  Persons := TObjectList<TPerson>.Create;
  try
    // safe, can only add TPerson or descendant
    Persons.Add(TPerson.Create('Kirk', 'Hammett'));
    Persons.Add(TPerson.Create('James', 'Hetfield'));
    Persons.Add(TPerson.Create('Lars', 'Ulrich'));
    Persons.Add(TPerson.Create('Robert', 'Trujillo'));

    for P in Persons  do
      Log(P.Fullname); // no typecast needed

  finally
    Persons.Free;
  end;
end;
```

Using a generic list is much cleaner. The compiler at compile time knows that it is dealing with a list of TPerson objects and will not compile code that tries to add incompatible references. We can use a more readable for..in..do loop and there is no need for a typecast. Using generics in general improves the quality of your code.

Anonymous code

Anonymous code is all about treating code as data. You can assign an implementation of a function or procedure to a variable; you pass functions as parameters to other functions and receive them as results. This is an enormously powerful feature of the modern Object Pascal language. With anonymous code, the source code of your app can be more compact and maintainable.

A declaration of an anonymous method type has a syntax like this:

```
type
  TStringProc = reference to procedure (S: string);
```

We are saying that TStringProc is a procedure that takes a string parameter. Now, we can define variables of this TStringProc type, assign to them an implementation, pass them as parameters to functions, or simply just call them:

```
procedure CallMe(const Proc: TStringProc; Msg: string);
begin
  Proc(Msg);
end;


procedure DoStringProc;
var
  Proc: TStringProc;
begin
  Proc := procedure(X: string)
  begin
    Log('Declared proc got: ' + X);
  end;

  CallMe(Proc, 'Hello');

  CallMe(
      procedure(V: string)
      begin
        Log('Inline code got: ' + V);
      end,
      'World');
end;
```

Here, we have a CallMe procedure, which takes as a parameter a chunk of code compatible with TStringProc and a string variable. There is also a Proc local variable of the TstringProc type. In the first lines of the DoStringProc routine, we are assigning an implementation to the Proc variable. Notice that there is no identifier after the procedure keyword. Parameter declaration follows immediately. That is why it is called an anonymous method. It does not need a name, because it is never referenced by name. In the first call to CallMe, we are passing the Proc variable as a parameter. The second call to CallMe is even more compact. We are defining the implementation of an anonymous procedure in place.

A more useful example of using anonymous code could be generic list sorting. We can define the `TPersonList` class and implement a `SortByFullName` method. Let's look at the interface of the unit first:

```
interface

uses
  System.Generics.Collections, // TObjectList<T>
  uPerson;  // TPerson

type
  TPersonList = class(TObjectList<TPerson>)
    procedure SortByFullName;
  end;
```

The only method in the implementation section is in the following code snippet:

```
uses
  System.Generics.Defaults, // IComparer, TComparison
  System.SysUtils; // CompareStr

procedure TPersonList.SortByFullName;
var
  Comparer : IComparer<TPerson>;
  Comparison : TComparison<TPerson>;
begin
  Comparison := function(const P1, P2: TPerson): integer
  begin
    Result := CompareStr(P1.FullName, P2.FullName);
  end;
  Comparer := TComparer<TPerson>.Construct(Comparison);
  inherited Sort(Comparer);
end;
```

The generic object list class defines a `Sort` method that can be overridden in descendent classes. As its parameter, it expects a generic `comparer` class that is just responsible for comparing any two elements of the underlying class and returns an integer value that needs to be negative if the first element is less than the second, 0 if they are the same, or a positive value if the first element is greater than the second. Here, we construct the `TComparer` class, which is responsible for comparing the two `TPerson` objects. Luckily, in the `System.SysUtils` unit, there is a very handy `CompareStr` function, which we can use directly. Our comparer is referenced by its implementing interface and that is why we do not need to free it afterward. It will be freed automatically by the interface reference-counting mechanism.

Operator overloading

Your code can be made more readable with operator overloading. You cannot add new operators that don't exist in the language, but you can overload the meaning of any of the existing operators in the language (including match, logical, and comparison operators). You can also implement implicit conversion operators that make it possible to assign different data types to a given type and define what would happen during the assignment. You can also define comparison operators to define the result of the = or < > built-in operator.

Operator overloading leads to more compact, more readable code. For example, Delphi comes with a `System.Math.Vectors` unit with different useful types, such as `TVector3D`, with useful overloaded operations. Here is an example of how to use `TVector3D`:

```
uses
  System.Math.Vectors;

procedure DoSomeVectorMath;
var
  A, B, C: TVector3D;
begin
  A := TVector3D.Create(1,2,4);
  B := TVector3D.Create(2,3,1);
  C := A + B;
  // ...
```

Another good example is the `TAlphaColorF` record type defined in the `System.UITypes` unit, which defines different operations on colors using real numbers.

Operator overloading cannot be used with class types, only with records.

Runtime type information

RTTI (or **runtime type information**) provides what other programming languages call **reflection** to the Object Pascal language. Reflection is the ability of a programming language to explore and interact with the data types, methods, properties, and other elements of the program itself. Reflection enables different types of meta-programming scenarios. You can, for example, write code that will be able to operate on objects that it does not know about, as it is accessing them by name.

The RTTI generated by the Delphi compiler provides abstractions for all the types and access to this data through the `System.Rtti` unit. If you want to programmatically inspect a type and what members it contains, you can use an instance of the `TRttiContext` type. This record has a `GetType` method, which returns an instance of the `TRttiType` class, which in turn has methods that let you *inspect* a given type and iterate through all its members.

You can see as follows a sample code snippet, which gets the metadata for the TButton class, reads the list of its methods, scans them in a for loop, and outputs the names of the public methods:

```
procedure TFormDemo.BtnRTTIClick(Sender: TObject);
var
  Ctx : TRttiContext;
  T : TRttiType;
  M : TRttiMethod;
begin
  T := Ctx.GetType(TButton);
  for M in T.GetMethods do
    if M.Visibility = TMemberVisibility.mvPublic then
      Log(Format('Type = %s; Method = %s',
        [T.Name, M.Name]));
end;
```

The result is a very long list of methods, starting with the following:

```
Type = TButton; Method = Create
Type = TButton; Method = Destroy
Type = TButton; Method = SetNewScene
Type = TButton; Method = Create
Type = TButton; Method = Destroy
Type = TButton; Method = AfterConstruction
Type = TButton; Method = ToString
Type = TButton; Method = Change
Type = TButton; Method = Create
Type = TButton; Method = Destroy
Type = TButton; Method = HasPresentationProxy
...and so on
```

Custom attributes

Custom attributes let you add custom information to a class itself or to its individual members. Many libraries that come with Delphi use custom attributes. They are useful when we want to mark certain types, or type members, that need to be treated in a special way. For example, in the DUnitX unit testing framework that comes with Delphi, we use a Test custom attribute to mark a method as testable and optionally provide parameters to be used by the unit test runner. Another example is the REST API resources that are published from a RAD Server module. With custom attributes, we can tell the framework what the name of the REST resource should be to access a certain method.

A custom attribute is just a regular class that is inherited from the TCustomAttribute type defined in the built-in system unit.

Let's consider a definition of a custom documentation attribute. A programmer could use such an attribute to associate a given class member in code with a custom URL with more information about it:

```
unit uDocAttribute;

interface

type
  DocAttribute = class(TCustomAttribute)
  private
    FURL: string;
  public
    constructor Create(URL: string);
    property URL: string read FURL write FURL;
  end;

implementation

{ DocAttribute }

constructor DocAttribute.Create(URL: string);
begin
  FURL := URL;
end;
```

To apply an attribute, it needs to be placed just before the element it applies to in square brackets. Optionally it can take parameters that just come as a list in brackets. This will implicitly call the custom attribute constructor:

```
uses
  uDocAttribute;
type
  [Doc('http://mydocs/MySuperClass')]
  // skipping "...Attribute"
  TMySuperClass = class
  public
    [DocAttribute(
      'http://mydocs/MySuperClass/DoSomething')]
    procedure DoSomething;
  end;
```

By convention, custom attribute class names end with the word `Attribute`. The Delphi compiler allows you to skip the optional `Attribute` part of the `attribute` class name when referring to that class.

That's nice, but how do I know that there are attributes applied to classes that my code operates on? This can be discovered by using the same RTTI access mechanism covered in the previous section.

In our documentation attribute example, we can use RTTI to retrieve documentation URLs for the type itself and its methods:

```
uses
  RTTI, uDocAttribute, uMySuperClass;

procedure TFormDemo.btnDocAttributeClick(Sender: TObject);
var
  Ctx : TRttiContext;
  T : TRttiType;
  M : TRttiMethod;
  A : TCustomAttribute;
begin
  Ctx := TRttiContext.Create;
  T := Ctx.GetType(TMySuperClass);
  for A in T.GetAttributes do
    if A is DocAttribute then
      Log(Format('Type = %s; Attribute = %s, URL = %s',
        [TMySuperClass.ClassName, A.ClassName,
        DocAttribute(A).URL]));

  for M in T.GetMethods do
    for A in M.GetAttributes do
      if A is DocAttribute then
        Log(Format(
          'Type=%s; Method=%s; Attribute=%s, URL=%s',
          [TMySuperClass.ClassName, M.Name, A.ClassName,
          DocAttribute(A).URL]));
end;
```

The RTTI context object owns all intermediate objects that represent different class members, such as `TRttiMethod` or `TRttiAttribute`, and it frees them all on destruction. This cleanup happens automatically because the RTTI context is a managed record that goes out of scope at the end of the method using it.

Summary

In this chapter, we have covered different basic as well as more advanced elements of the Object Pascal language used in Delphi. There are many tutorials and language primers that cover all elements of the language in detail. A good and deep knowledge of the language is important to be able to master Delphi, but this chapter should have helped you cover some of the basics and touched upon some of the features used later in the book.

In the first part of the chapter, we reviewed the structure of a typical Delphi application from the memory game app that we will build in the next few chapters. The second part of the chapter covered select elements of the Object Pascal language, such as type helpers, generics, and anonymous code, that are needed to better understand the code that comes with the Delphi installation and you need to use very frequently, such as generic lists of objects.

In the next chapter, we are going to build on our language knowledge and review the functionality of some key classes for doing common things every programmer needs to know how to do, such as working with files and streams.

3

Packing Up Your Toolbox

There are many simple everyday programming skills that every Delphi developer needs to have. Pack your everyday programmer toolbox with everything you will need for simple things such as file input/output and more complex ones such as working with JSON and XML. These techniques are all part of the Delphi **Runtime Library** (**RTL**), a very large collection of core functions and classes that don't involve the user interface and generally work on all target platforms.

This chapter will cover the following topics:

- Working with files and streams
- Working with JSON
- Working with XML

The objective of this chapter is to become fluent in using Delphi programming through useful techniques such as working with files, streams, JSON, and XML.

Technical requirements

All the code in this chapter can be found in the following link: `https://github.com/PacktPublishing/Expert-Delphi_Second-edition`

Working with files and streams

Almost every app needs to persist data. Imagine that you have just downloaded an app and worked with it for a while. The next time you open it, you would like to see that it has remembered what you have done so far. An app can store its data in the cloud, in an embedded database, or in a file. This last option is the easiest to use, and so it's the one we want to start from.

A local file can store information in different formats. It could be a binary file, which is just an array of bytes that is left to an app to make sense of, or it could be a text file. Your app can store information in plain text or it can use file formats such as JSON or XML to make it easier to process structured information, even if saved as text.

Imagine that you would like to write a small mobile app to keep track of your favorite locations on the internet. To keep it simple, it could be just a list of favorite items made up of two strings: a URL and a caption. Let's go for it!

To start, we should create another multi-device application in Delphi. We will skip the ready-to-use templates and select the blank application template. Once we have the skeleton app, we can save the main form as `uFormFavMain` and then save the whole project as `FavoritesDemo`. Once this is done, we add a new unit to the project and save it with the name `uFavorite`. Let's define a simple `TFavorite` class for individual favorite items. It will contain only two public string fields, URL and `Caption`. For convenience, let's add a constructor that will take the initial values for both fields. We could have used public fields, given the simplicity, but it is better to use properties mapped to private fields, as this offers better encapsulation and a more sound approach:

```
type
  TFavorite = class
  private
    FCaption: string;
    FURL: string;
    procedure SetCaption(const Value: string);
    procedure SetURL(const Value: string);
  public
    property URL: string read FURL write SetURL;
    property Caption: string read FCaption write SetCaption;
    constructor Create(AURL, ACaption: string); overload;
  end;
```

The implementation of these three methods is very simple, so it's not listed in the book. You can refer to the companion code repository. There is also the `TFavorites` class definition: a generic object list of `TFavorite` objects. Adding this definition makes it easier to use it in code. Even if not required, it's recommended to define a proper generic type rather than just using the same in multiple locations in code:

```
uses
  System.Generics.Collections;

type
  TFavorites = class(TObjectList<TFavorite>);
```

We will be first storing favorites in a text file, using a convention that every two consecutive strings in the file represent one favorite entry: the first line for URL and the second line for `Caption`. Later in the chapter, we will use specialized file formats such as JSON and XML to give our file a better structure.

The main form of our demo app will contain a private field, accessible through a public property, with a list of sample favorite items, which we are going to access from other forms in the application to avoid duplicating code. External code will not be able to destroy this instance because the reference is read-only.

We need to create an `OnCreate` event for the main form, where we are going to construct the `Favorites` list and add some sample favorite entries, and then define an `OnDestroy` event handler, in which we are going to destroy the list.

To avoid long identifiers, in many places of the demo app, we just use `Favs` as a handy abbreviation. This is the interface of the main form class:

```
type
  TFormFavMain = class(TForm)
    procedure FormCreate(Sender: TObject);
    procedure FormDestroy(Sender: TObject);
  private
    FFavs: TFavorites;
    procedure AddSampleItems(AFavs: TFavorites)
  public
    property Favs: TFavorites read FFavs;
  end;
```

In the implementation of the `FormCreate` and `FormDestroy` event handlers, the application creates and destroys the list of favorites and fills it by calling the `AddSampleItems` private procedure:

```
procedure TFormFavMain.FormCreate(Sender: TObject);
begin
  FFavs := TFavorites.Create;
  AddSampleItems (FFavs);
end;

procedure TFormFavMain.AddSampleItems (
  AFavs: TFavorites);
begin
  AFavs.Add(TFavorite.Create(
    'www.embarcadero.com/products/delphi',
    'Delphi Home Page'));
  AFavs.Add(TFavorite.Create(
    'docwiki.embarcadero.com/RADStudio/en',
    'RAD Studio online documentation'));
end;

procedure TFormFavMain.FormDestroy(Sender: TObject);
begin
  FFavs.Free;
end;
```

There are many different ways of creating files in code. For example, we could use the Pascal classic built-in functions such as `AssignFile`, `Rewrite`, `Reset`, and `CloseFile`. Another option is to use functionality from specialized classes, such as `TMemo` or `TIniFile`, which provide methods such as `SaveToFile` and `LoadFromFile` that could be used directly. There is also a `TFile` class in the `System.IOUtils` unit, which can be used to write and read different types of data such as strings or just raw arrays of bytes.

Probably the easiest way to work with files is to use the `TStreamWriter` and `TStreamReader` classes from the `System.Classes` unit. They provide an elegant programming model for doing file operations.

The main form of our demo app will work as a menu to display other forms, where we will be trying different approaches to working with text files. Let's add a new multi-device form to our project. Save it in the `uFormFavTextFiles` unit and rename the form `FormFavTextFiles`. That is another useful convention to follow: the name of the unit that stores a form starts with u followed by the name of the form.

> **Note**
>
> The use of the initial u for unit names is the approach Paweł used in the first edition of this book. While I'm not a particular fan of this technique, it is used a lot and I wanted to preserve the original coding and writing style, where it makes sense. For this reason, I'm keeping this convention in this book's code.

First, we are going to add some navigation code for moving from the main form to the additional form and back. After that, we add the new form to the `uses` statement in the implementation part of the main form. Then, we add a button to the form with a call to show the form, as in the following code:

```
uses
  uFormFavTextFiles;


procedure TFormFavMain.BtnTextFilesClick(Sender: TObject);
begin
  FormFavTextFiles.Show;
end;
```

In the other form, we add exactly the same logic to display back the main form.

Now, we can focus on implementing the functionality to write the favorites from the list in memory in our main form into the text file and read it back. Add two buttons to the form and align them to the top. In this way, they will always look good at different screen resolutions on mobile devices. Also, add a `TMemo` component, rename it `MemoLog`, and align it to the client area. Optionally, change all four margins of the memo from 0 to 4, for example, so that there is a little margin around the memo, which looks better on a mobile screen. The first button will be used to write favorites to a text file and the second to read this information back and display it in the memo, so we know that things work OK.

The form at design time, if we select the **Android** preview style, should look like the one in *Figure 3.1*:

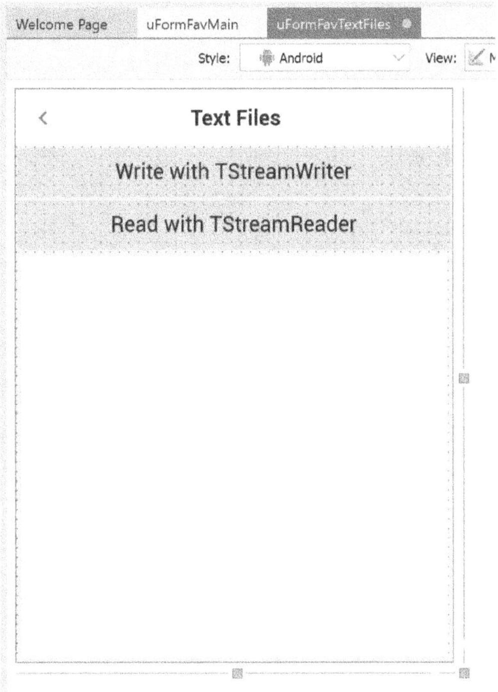

Figure 3.1: FormFavTextFiles at design time in Delphi

First, we are going to define a separate `GetFilename` function that will centralize accessing the name of the file, so that functions for both writing and reading are accessing the same file, without duplicating code.

On mobile operating systems, unlike traditional desktop ones, an app can only create and read files from its own `Documents` folder. In the `System.IOUtils` unit that ships with Delphi, the `TPath` class offers a number of class methods to work with paths. The location of the `Documents` folder can be obtained with the `TPath.GetDocumentsPath` call. In order to construct the full path to our file, we also need to use a delimiter between the path and the actual filename. A delimiter, however, depends on the target filesystem, as it can be either a slash or backslash. It is good practice not to hardcode it, but to rely on the Delphi RTL instead. You can directly access the delimiter, as well as use specific methods to create a path, as we'll do in the following code block. If our text file is called `favs.txt`, then the actual code to get the full filename of the favorites text file could look like this:

```
uses
    uFormFavMain, uFavorite, System.IOUtils;
function TFormFavTextFiles.GetFilename: string;
begin
```

```
    Result := TPath.Combine(TPath.GetDocumentsPath, 'favs.txt');
  end;
```

Double-click on the first button on the form and enter the following code to save the favorites information into the plain text file:

```
procedure TFormFavTextFiles.BtnWriteClick(Sender: TObject);
var
  SW: TStreamWriter;
  Fav: TFavorite;
  Favs: TFavorites;
begin
  Favs := FormFavMain.Favs;
  SW := TStreamWriter.Create(GetFilename, False, TEncoding.UTF8);
  try
    for Fav in Favs do
    begin
      SW.WriteLine(Fav.URL);
      SW.WriteLine(Fav.Caption);
    end;
  finally
    SW.Free;
  end;
end;
```

In this example, we are using the Favorites list from the main form. To simplify the code, in the first line, we put this property reference into the local Favs variable, which is easier to use in code. The rest of the implementation is quite trivial. We are constructing an instance of the TStreamWriter class and, in the for loop, writing the URL and Caption properties of each TFavorite item in the list.

Now, let's read this information back. In the OnClick event of the second button, write the following code:

```
procedure TFormFavTextFiles.BtnReadClick(Sender: TObject);
var
  SR: TStreamReader;
begin
  SR := TStreamReader.Create(GetFilename, TEncoding.UTF8);
  try
    while not SR.EndOfStream do
      MemoLog.Lines.Add(SR.ReadLine);
  finally
    SR.Free;
  end;
end;
```

Now, run the app. Navigate to the **Text Files** screen and click on the **Write with TStreamWriter** button first and then on the **Read with TStreamReader** button. You should see the list of favorites in the memo, as in *Figure 3.2*:

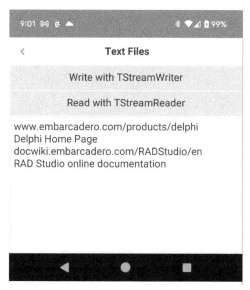

Figure 3.2: The FormFavTextFiles running on Android

The problem with this approach is that there is no structure in the data. By convention, we know that every two lines of text contain one favorite entry. The first is the URL and the second is the caption.

Working with JSON

A better format for storing favorite entries is JSON. This is currently the most popular data interchange format. Its strength is its simplicity. The JSON specification is an interesting read and can be found at `http://json.org`. With a very simple type system, JSON is able to represent complex data structures. One of the key design objectives of JSON is to keep it simple. Most programming languages can process JSON, and Object Pascal is not an exception.

There are two main ways to work with JSON in Delphi. The first approach is to build an in-memory representation of the JSON tree using objects from the `System.JSON` unit. The second approach is based on streaming and provides sequential access to JSON data. In reality, both ways have their advantages and disadvantages. Let's look at both.

JSON is a very popular format for sharing information and all kinds of datasets. Imagine you have just locally downloaded a piece of JSON. Now what?

Here is the favorites information expressed as JSON:

```
{
  "Favorites": [
    {
      "URL": "www.embarcadero.com/products/delphi",
      "Caption": "Delphi Home Page"
    },
    {
      "URL": "docwiki.embarcadero.com/RADStudio/en",
      "Caption": "RAD Studio online documentation"
    }
  ]
}
```

Notice that, unlike the first file created as plain text, the favorites data in JSON is more structured. Here, we have an object with just one property called Favorites and its value is an array made of two objects. Each object contained in the array has two string properties, URL and Caption. For a programmer, a typical objective might be to convert JSON data into programming language constructs that can be manipulated in code, or to output JSON text from a program.

Let's add another form to the demo app and call it FormFavJSON. We can add all the functionality to navigate to this form and back to the main form exactly as we did for the FormFavTextFile form.

Writing JSON

First, let's look at different ways of generating JSON. We will save this information to a file and, later, we will read this information back into a local favorites list.

Again, we are going to start by implementing a GetFilename function, but this time, to write and read from the favs.json file:

```
function TFormFavJSON.GetFilename: string;
begin
  Result := TPath.Combine(TPath.GetDocumentsPath, 'favs.json');
end;
```

We will also need a simple function to write a string with JSON text to a file. With the `TStreamWriter` class, as we saw earlier, it is quite simple to implement this:

```
procedure TFormFavJSON.WriteJsonTextToFile(txt: string);
var
  sw: TStreamWriter;
begin
  sw := TStreamWriter.Create(GetFilename, False, TEncoding.UTF8);
  try
    sw.WriteLine(txt);
  finally
    sw.Free;
  end;
end;
```

The first approach for generating JSON is based on building an in-memory graph of JSON data and then converting it to string in one operation. For this, we will define the `FavListToJsonTextWithDOM` method, which will return JSON text generated from our global `TFavorites` list in the main form of the demo app:

```
uses
  System.IOUtils, uFormFavMain, System.JSON.Writers,
  System.JSON.Types, System.JSON.Builders,
  System.Generics.Collections;


function TFormFavJSON.FavListToJsonTextWithDOM: string;
var
  Fav: TFavorite; Favs: TFavorites;
  ObjFavs, ObjF: TJSONObject; ArrFavs: TJSONArray;
begin
  Favs := FormFavMain.Favs;

  ObjFavs := TJSONObject.Create;
  try
    ArrFavs := TJSONArray.Create;

    for Fav in Favs do
    begin
      ObjF := TJSONObject.Create;
      ObjF.AddPair('URL', TJSONString.Create(Fav.URL));
      ObjF.AddPair('Caption',
        TJSONString.Create(Fav.Caption));
      ArrFavs.Add(ObjF);
    end;
```

```
  ObjFavs.AddPair('Favorites', ArrFavs);

  Result := ObjFavs.ToString;
finally
  ObjFavs.Free;
end;
end;
```

In this approach, we need to define local variables for all JSON objects to build a graph in memory and then output it with the `ToString` method of the root `ObjFavs` instance. Note that we only need to free the root object. All other objects are owned by the root object; if we try to free them in code, we will get an error.

Note that, with this approach, it is not very easy to visualize the exact JSON that this function will generate.

Let's add a button to the form, align it to the top, and change its `Caption` property to `Write with JSON DOM`. Double-click on the button and enter the following code in its `OnClick` event to implement the actual functionality of writing JSON to the file:

```
procedure TFormFavJSON.btnWriteDOMClick(Sender: TObject);
var
  S: string;
begin
  S := FavListToJsonTextWithDOM;
  WriteJsonTextToFile(S);
end;
```

The second approach for generating JSON involves using the `TJsonTextWriter` class. Let's define the `FavListToJsonTextWithWriter` method in the form class that is returning a string. In the first part of the code of this method, we initialize the JSON structures and create the array:

```
uses
  System.JSON.Writers, System.JSON.Types;


function TFormFavJSON.FavListToJsonTextWithWriter: string;
var
  Fav: TFavorite;
  Favs: TFavorites;
  StringWriter: TStringWriter;
  Writer: TJsonTextWriter;
begin
  Favs := FormFavMain.Favs;

  StringWriter := TStringWriter.Create();
  Writer := TJsonTextWriter.Create(StringWriter);
```

```
  try
    Writer.Formatting := TJsonFormatting.Indented;
    Writer.WriteStartObject;
    Writer.WritePropertyName('Favorites');
    Writer.WriteStartArray;
```

In the central portion of the code of the method, we create two JSON name-value pairs for each object:

```
    for Fav in Favs do
    begin
      Writer.WriteStartObject;
      Writer.WritePropertyName('URL');
      Writer.WriteValue(Fav.URL);
      Writer.WritePropertyName('Caption');
      Writer.WriteValue(Fav.Caption);
      Writer.WriteEndObject;
    end;
```

At the end, we close the JSON structure, copy the resulting string, and destroy the temporary data structures:

```
    Writer.WriteEndArray;
    Writer.WriteEndObject;

    Result := StringWriter.ToString;

  finally
    Writer.Free;
    StringWriter.Free;
  end;
end;
```

The constructor of the TJsonTextWriter class expects as its argument an instance of TTextWriter, which will be responsible for the actual process of outputting the resulting JSON text. Notice that the TTextWriter class has virtual abstract methods that just define the interface to the text-writing functionality. The class itself cannot be used as is. You need to use one of the text writer subclasses such as TStringWriter. This is a very elegant approach and makes it easy to use other types of writers without changing the logic for JSON writing.

Before calling different "write*" methods, we set the Formatting property of the writer to TJsonFormatting.Indented, so the resulting JSON will be nicely formatted. Note that, in the DOM approach, we just got JSON in one, non-formatted string. The code to write JSON with text writer is much more verbose and does not allocate any temporary objects. Now, the code is much more readable. Just by glancing at it, we can figure out what the resulting JSON is going to look like.

The third approach for generating JSON is based on using fluent builders. The idea is to make the code even more verbose, resembling the resulting JSON more closely. Again, we first need to set up the proper classes, then create and initialize them:

```
uses
  System.JSON.Builders;

function TFormFavJSON.FavListToJsonTextWithBuilder: string;
var
  StringWriter: TStringWriter;
  Writer: TJsonTextWriter;
  Builder: TJSONObjectBuilder;
begin
  StringWriter := TStringWriter.Create();
  Writer := TJsonTextWriter.Create(StringWriter);
  Builder := TJSONObjectBuilder.Create(Writer);
  try
    Writer.Formatting := TJsonFormatting.Indented;
```

As in the previous example, we still need `TStringWriter` and `TJsonTextWriter` instances, but on top of those, we need to instantiate `TJsonObjectBuilder`, which accepts `TJsonTextWriter` as an argument to its constructor.

The core of the algorithm is the use of the JSON `Builder` for creating the data structure, and concatenating the calls to the various methods (a technique known as the fluent interface method):

```
    Builder
    .BeginObject
      .BeginArray('Favorites')
        .BeginObject
          .Add('URL',
            'www.embarcadero.com/products/delphi')
          .Add('Caption', 'Delphi Home Page')
        .EndObject
        .BeginObject
          .Add('URL',
            'docwiki.embarcadero.com/RADStudio/en')
          .Add('Caption',
            'RAD Studio online documentation')
        .EndObject
      .EndArray
    .EndObject;
```

Now, we can extract the resulting string and clean up the various objects used in the method:

```
    Result := StringWriter.ToString;

  finally
    Builder.Free;
    Writer.Free;
    StringWriter.Free;
  end;
end;
```

Just from the structure of this source code, we can visualize what kind of JSON we are going to generate. The problem is that we cannot really use fluent builders for outputting data coming from an external data structure, such as our TFavorites list, because it is just one long chain of method calls on the builder class instance.

In the demo application, we can read the JSON as text and display it, to see what has been generated, as in *Figure 3.3*:

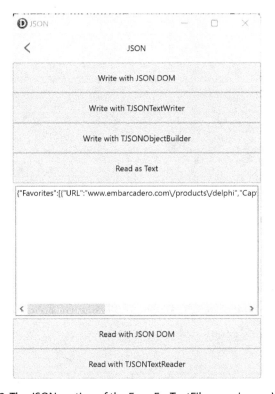

Figure 3.3: The JSON section of the FormFavTextFiles running on Windows

This is the code we can use to write the favorites data to a file in JSON format. Next we need to be able to read it back from the file.

Reading JSON

JSON specification does not provide any way for expressing the "schema" or metadata describing the structure of JSON information. Consequently, when we write code that processes JSON, we are hoping to find certain data structures. There are two ways of reading JSON: one is based on its in-memory representation and the second is based on streaming.

The key to parsing JSON using DOM is the `ParseJSONValue` class method belonging to the `TJSONObject` type. This is an overloaded method defined in the `System.JSON` unit and it takes JSON text in the form of a string, stream, or array of bytes, parses it, and returns a `TJSONValue` reference, which points to the root of a graph of the JSON objects in memory. If the JSON text passed to this method is malformed, then this method does not raise an exception but just returns a `nil` reference.

In this code, we need a number of intermediate objects representing the various elements of the JSON data structure, as you can see in the `var` declarations and the initial portion of the method shown here:

```
uses
  System.JSON.Readers, System.JSON.Types;


procedure TFormFavJSON.BtnReadDOMClick(Sender: TObject);
var
  Favs: TFavorites;
  ValRoot: TJSONValue;
  ObjRoot: TJSONObject;
  ValFavs: TJSONValue;
  ArrFavs: TJSONArray;
  I: integer;
begin
  Favs := TFavorites.Create;
  try
    ValRoot := TJSONObject.ParseJSONValue(ReadJsonTextFromFile);
```

From now on, the code continues reading data structures and checking that they are not `nil`, which will happen if the JSON doesn't have the expected structure:

```
if ValRoot <> nil then
begin
  if ValRoot is TJSONObject then
  begin
    ObjRoot := TJSONObject(ValRoot);
    if ObjRoot.Count > 0 then
```

```
      begin
        Valfavs := ObjRoot.Values['Favorites'];
        if ValFavs <> nil then
        begin
          if ValFavs is TJSONArray then
          begin
            ArrFavs := TJSONArray(ValFavs);
            for I := 0 to ArrFavs.Count-1 do
            begin
              if ArrFavs.Items[I] is TJSONObject then
                ProcessFavObj(Favs,
                  TJSONObject(ArrFavs.Items[I]));
            end;
          end;
        end;
      end;
    end;
  end;

  DisplayFavsCount(Favs);
finally
  Favs.Free;
end;
end;
```

In the preceding method, the code for reading individual entries of the favorite objects list is demanded by a separate method, ProcessFavObj. This method is responsible for processing a single TJSONObject representing just one TFavorite item:

```
procedure TFormFavJSON.ProcessFavObj(
  Favs: TFavorites; FavObj: TJSONObject);
var
  Fav: TFavorite; Val: TJSONValue;
begin
  Fav := TFavorite.Create;

  Val := FavObj.Values['URL'];
  if Val <> nil then
    if Val is TJSONString then
      Fav.URL := TJSONString(Val).Value;

  Val := FavObj.Values['Caption'];
  if Val <> nil then
    if Val is TJSONString then
```

```
      Fav.Caption := TJSONString(Val).Value;

  Favs.Add(Fav);
end;
```

There is also a `DisplayFavsCount` method, which is called at the end of the processing to verify that we actually successfully parsed JSON. There should be two `TFavorite` items in the resulting list:

```
procedure TFormFavJSON.DisplayFavsCount(Favs: TFavorites);
begin
  if Favs <> nil then
    ShowMessage('Favorites count: ' + Favs.Count.ToString)
  else
    ShowMessage('Favorites reference is nil');
end;
```

As you can see, processing JSON in this way is very tedious. Even for a simple JSON, such as in our demo sample, the resulting code is quite complex and involves a lot of checking for `nil` and typecasting to expected types of JSON values. There is also an overhead of having to create a lot of in-memory objects that represent JSON.

A much better way is to use a streaming model and process JSON text sequentially with the `TJsonTextReader` class:

```
procedure TFormFavJSON.BtnReadReaderClick(Sender: TObject);
var
  Jtr: TJsonTextReader;
  Sr: TStringReader;
  Favs: TFavorites;
begin
  Favs := TFavorites.Create;
  try
    Sr := TStringReader.Create(ReadJsonTextFromFile);
    try
      Jtr := TJsonTextReader.Create(Sr);
      try
        while Jtr.Read do
        begin
          if Jtr.TokenType = TJsonToken.StartObject then
            ProcessFavRead(Favs, Jtr);
        end;
      finally
        Jtr.Free;
      end;
    finally
```

```
      Sr.Free;
    end;

    DisplayFavsCount(Favs);
  finally
    Favs.Free;
  end;
end;
```

By using this approach, we no longer need to create temporary objects. We just move through the stream of JSON tokens. Notice that we do not need to encapsulate the structure of the whole JSON in this code. It could be part of a bigger structure. We just iterate through tokens and, if we encounter the `BeginObject` token, we can start a separate process in the specialized procedure that only cares about objects that represent one favorite.

Again, the reading of individual objects takes place in a separate method:

```
procedure TFormFavJSON.ProcessFavRead(
  Favs: TFavorites; Jtr: TJsonTextReader);
var
  Fav: TFavorite;
begin
  Fav := TFavorite.Create;

  while Jtr.Read do
  begin
    if Jtr.TokenType = TJsonToken.PropertyName then
    begin
      if Jtr.Value.ToString = 'URL' then
      begin
        Jtr.Read;
        fav.URL := Jtr.Value.AsString;
      end
      else if Jtr.Value.ToString = 'Caption' then
      begin
        Jtr.Read;
        Fav.Caption := Jtr.Value.AsString;
      end
    end
    else if Jtr.TokenType = TJsonToken.EndObject then
    begin
      Favs.Add(Fav);
      exit;
    end;
```

```
    end;
  end;
```

Using JSON readers instead of DOM is faster and requires less memory and processing power.

Using the JSON wizard in Delphi 12

There is a new, additional approach to processing JSON, which was introduced for the first time in Delphi 12. It is based on the idea of directly mapping the JSON data structure to Delphi objects. The IDE offers a new wizard that can generate the mapping code automatically, starting with a JSON data structure and creating the target objects and mapping code.

This new JSON Data Binding Wizard offers a large number of alternative options, which we have no room to explore in depth here. If you create a new application, you can start the wizard from the **New Items** dialog box and select the **Web** section. The wizard first asks you to enter a JSON file or JSON text. In this case, I've used the JSON file produced in the previous demos. As you can see in *Figure 3.4*, there is a main decision to make in terms of mapping – I've decided to go with the **REST. Json** mapping library and kept the other options as default.

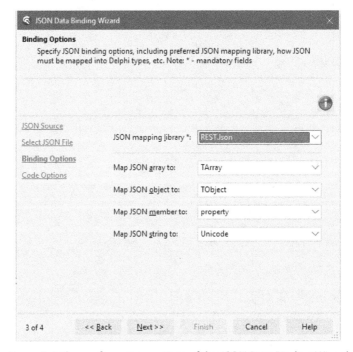

Figure 3.4: The configuration options of the JSON Data Binding Wizard

If you accept the default values on the final page of the wizard, it will end up generating the skeleton classes in *Figure 3.5*, decorated with attributes used by the serialization code, which is part of the RTL.

```
type
  [JsonSerialize(jmAllPubProps)]
  TFavorite = class(TPersistent)
  private
    FURL: string;
    FCaption: string;
  public
    property URL: string read FURL write FURL;
    property Caption: string read FCaption write FCaption;
  end;

  [JsonSerialize(jmAllPubProps)]
  TData = class(TPersistent)
  private
    FFavorites: TArray<TFavorite>;
  public
    destructor Destroy; override;
    property Favorites: TArray<TFavorite> read FFavorites write FFavorites;
  end;
```

Figure 3.5: The classes generated by the JSON Data Binding Wizard

Mapping JSON to objects is very powerful, reduces a lot of the code you need to write to read and process JSON, and offers a higher level of abstraction. This is the new, recommended approach.

Working with XML

Before JSON dominated the world, XML was the most popular format for data interchange. With the addition of many new specifications, XML became very complex to process in code, and very cumbersome for a number of use cases. However, at a practical level, XML is still used in many circumstances and it's important to understand how to process XML in case you need to.

XML processing in Delphi is based on building an in-memory representation of the XML file using XML parsers from different vendors. The key component for working with XML is TXMLDocument. XML parsing is considerably more difficult than it is with JSON. TXMLDocument has a pluggable XML parser architecture, and Delphi comes with a number of XML parser implementations from different vendors. There are different vendor implementations available depending on the target platform, as you can see in *Figure 3.6* for Windows.

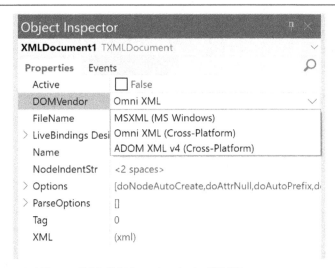

Figure 3.6: The available DOM vendors in the TXMLDocument component

Let's have a look at how to implement writing and reading XML information from a file. In the **New Items** dialog, there is a **Web Documents** category, in which you can find a wizard to create a new XML file. We can add an XML file directly to our `FavoritesDemo` project. Click on the **XML File** icon and save the file as `favs.xml`.

Our favorites sample data expressed in XML could look like this:

```
<?xml version="1.0" encoding="UTF-8"?>
<Favorites>
  <Favorite>
    <URL>www.embarcadero.com/products/delphi</URL>
    <Caption>Delphi Home Page</Caption>
  </Favorite>
  <Favorite>
    <URL>docwiki.embarcadero.com/RADStudio/en</URL>
    <Caption>RAD Studio online documentation</Caption>
  </Favorite>
</Favorites>
```

The XML standard has two different formats for describing metadata. The first one is **DTD**, which is short for **Document Type Definition**. It is very old and hardly used. The second one is called **XML Schema** and is used more often. With XML Schema, we can validate the structure of an XML file and it can be also used to automatically generate code for processing XML files. Delphi provides **XML Data Binding Wizard**, which can be found in the **New Items** dialog in the **XML** category of new **Delphi Projects**.

With this wizard, we can generate an Object Pascal unit for processing XML files of a known structure. Let's double-click on the wizard icon. In the first screen of the wizard, we need to specify either an XML or Schema file as the source. In the second screen, visible in *Figure 3.7*, we can preview the simple and complex types detected in the source file.

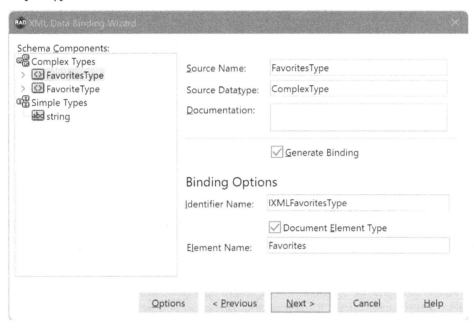

Figure 3.7: The second page of XML Data Binding Wizard

In the last screen, we can preview the source code that is about to be generated by the wizard. The actual XML Schema with all modifications done in the wizard, which will be used by the wizard to drive the code generation, can be optionally saved into an xdb file.

After clicking on the **Finish** button, the wizard will generate a Favs.pas file that is automatically added to the current project. This binding file contains interface and type definitions that correspond to all complex types detected in the source data. In our case, there are the IXMLFavoritesType and IXMLFavoriteType interfaces and their corresponding type declarations. The first interface is derived from the IXMLNodeCollection class because it could contain multiple favorite items, and the second interface inherits from just IXMLNode because it represents just an object.

Working with XML in code is all about traversing a graph of objects in memory that represents individual pieces of data. It is similar to the JSON DOM support we saw earlier. We could just use the TXMLNodeCollections and TXMLNode classes to write similar code as in the case of JSON, where we deal with objects from the System.JSON unit.XML Data Binding Wizard adds type information to XML nodes so there are properties that map to elements from the XML or XML Schema files. This helps to simplify the code we need to write.

At the end of the interface section of the unit generated by the wizard, there are three global functions that can be used to work with XML:

```
function GetFavorites(Doc: IXMLDocument):
  IXMLFavoritesType;
function LoadFavorites(const FileName: string):
  IXMLFavoritesType;
function NewFavorites: IXMLFavoritesType;
```

The first can be used to obtain the IXMLFavoritesType interface from existing data loaded into a TXMLDocument. The second one can be used for reading information from a file, and the last one can be used to create a new XML file.

Let's add another form to our FavoritesDemo project for writing and reading XML. We are going to call it FormFavXML. The first thing is to add the navigation to and from the main application form in the way described earlier in the chapter. We will also need the already-known method for getting the full filename of the favs.xml file that we are going to write and read.

The next step is not obvious. We want to make sure that our app will use the correct XML parser implementation that would work on mobile platforms. For this, we need to make sure that somewhere in the uses clause of our project, there are correct units added so the XML parser implementation gets compiled into our app. The easiest way to do so is to drop on the form a TXMLDocument component, select the desired value in the DOMVendor property, and save the form. Correct units will be added automatically to the form interface uses clause. If we select **Omni XML** as the DOM vendor, the following units will be added:

```
uses
  // ...
  Xml.xmldom, Xml.XMLIntf, Xml.XMLDoc, Xml.omnixmldom;
```

The first three are related to TXMLDocument components, and the last one is the actual DOM vendor implementation.

Now, let's add a button to the form, align it to the top, and change its Text property to **Write XML**. Double-click on it, and in the OnClick event handler, enter the following code:

```
procedure TFormFavXML.BtnWriteClick(Sender: TObject);
var
  Favs: TFavorites;
  Fav: TFavorite;
  FavsXML: IXMLFavoritesType;
  FavXML: IXMLFavoriteType;
  AXMLDoc: IXMLDocument;
begin
  Favs := FormFavMain.Favs;
```

```
  FavsXML := NewFavorites;
  for Fav in Favs do
  begin
    FavXML := FavsXML.Add;
    FavXML.URL := Fav.URL;
    FavXML.Caption := Fav.Caption;
  end;

  AXMLDoc := NewXMLDocument;
  AXMLDoc.DocumentElement := FavsXML;
  AXMLDoc.SaveToFile(GetFilename);
end;
```

Reading the XML is even more straightforward:

```
procedure TFormFavXML.BtnReadClick(Sender: TObject);
var
  Favs: TFavorites;
  Fav: TFavorite;
  FavsXML: IXMLFavoritesType;
  I: integer;
begin
  Favs := TFavorites.Create;
  try
    FavsXML := LoadFavorites(GetFilename);
    for I := 0 to FavsXML.Count-1 do
    begin
      Fav := TFavorite.Create;
      Fav.URL := FavsXML[I].URL;
      Fav.Caption := FavsXML[I].Caption;
      Favs.Add(Fav);
    end;

    DisplayFavsCount(Favs);

  finally
    Favs.Free;
  end;
end;
```

The call to `LoadFavorites` takes the filename and returns the reference to the `IXMLFavoritesType` interface, which we can use to iterate through the favorites data and populate a local favorites list. Similarly to the JSON example, after we have done the processing, we are calling the `DisplayFavsCount` method. This displays the number of items read and helps us in verifying that we have the correct number of favorite items in the list.

Summary

In this chapter, we have learned some useful everyday skills that Delphi developers can benefit from.

In the first part, we looked into working with text files. Later, we moved on to taking advantage of popular structured file formats such as JSON and XML. We have looked into working with both file formats by building their in-memory representation. In the case of JSON, we have also looked into reading and writing data using dedicated readers and writers. While the focus of the chapter was on reading and writing files of different formats, we took advantage of this topic to explore many practical Delphi techniques and compared different approaches to accomplish the same task.

In the next chapter, we'll focus on another core building block of the Delphi RTL – namely, the support for threads, tasks, and parallel programming. This is a complex topic but one you cannot ignore.

4

Using the Parallel Programming Library

Any modern CPU has a multi-core architecture. This means multiple applications can run in parallel at the same time in the foreground or the background. That's not specifically interesting for developers. What's relevant, though, is that a multi-core CPU allows single applications to use more than one core at the same time, spawning additional threads of execution and running them in parallel.

While this feature offers a lot of power to CPU-bound applications (applications that need to perform a lot of calculations or CPU operations), it is one of the most difficult to use as a developer. This is because multithreaded applications need to be written with a lot of care since different threads might access the same resources at the same time. Hence, threads need to synchronize any shared resource access, which is far from a simple operation in many cases.

This chapter will cover the following parts:

- Using threads
- Access synchronization
- The Parallel Programming Library

Writing multithreaded code is commonly perceived as one of the most difficult things in programming. This chapter cannot be an exhaustive guide to the topic, but it aims to offer a good, solid introduction, focused on what Delphi provides in this area.

Technical requirements

All the code in this chapter can be found in the following link: `https://github.com/PacktPublishing/Expert-Delphi_Second-edition`

Using threads

When an operating system starts an app, it creates a process for it and starts a thread of execution, often called the **main thread**. As I mentioned before, in each process, there could be one or more threads running, which is more relevant at a time when all processors that power computers and mobile devices have multiple cores. This means that there could be multiple threads executing in parallel on each core. A typical app executes in one thread, which runs on just one processor core. All other cores do nothing.

There are, however, multiple reasons for using threads. The most important is not the extra performance, but keeping an app responsive while it is doing some heavy calculations or waiting for external information (for example, using an HTTP request). Another scenario is using multiple threads for faster calculations, which is more enticing but, as mentioned, also the most complex one.

Since the early versions of Delphi, there is a `TThread` class in the **Runtime Library** (**RTL**), which represents the concept of the operating system thread. There is also a simple wizard that can help get you started with threading. Once you have created a new application in Delphi, you can use the **New Items** dialog box (from the **File | New | Other** menu), select **Individual Files**, and then **Thread Object**, as shown in *Figure 4.1*:

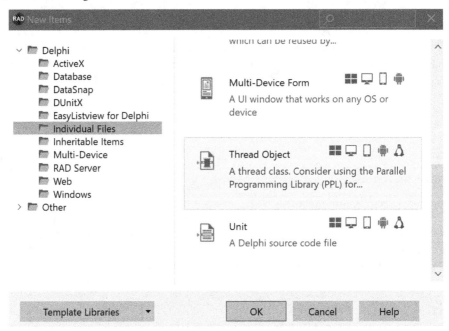

Figure 4.1: Selecting the Thread Object wizard in the New Items dialog box

The wizard in itself is very simple, as you can see in *Figure 4.2*. It offers the ability to indicate the thread class name and optionally set a thread name – a feature exclusively used when debugging.

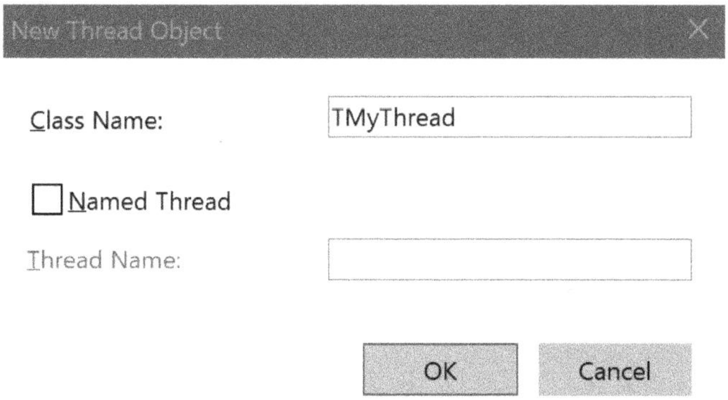

Figure 4.2: The simple Thread Object wizard

While the parameters are simple, this wizard is handy as it helps you lay down the structure of a thread class. At the operating system level, a thread is a function that is executed in parallel. In Delphi terms, the thread code is written in the Execute function of a class that is derived from TThread, and this wizard's role is to create such a method in a proper class, helping you get started. This is the generated class declaration:

```
type
  TMyThread = class(TThread)
  private
    { Private declarations }
  protected
    procedure Execute; override;
  end;
```

The generated body of the Execute method is just a placeholder:

```
procedure TMyThread.Execute;
begin
  { Place thread code here }
end;
```

How do you create such a thread? In the main form, or somewhere else in your application, you can write code as shown here:

```
var AThread := TMyThread.Create;
AThread.FreeOnTerminate := True;
AThread.Start;
```

In this case, I'm calling a custom `Create` constructor of the `TMyThread` class, but in general, you can also create a `TThread` directly. The base class constructor has a parameter, `CreateSuspended`, indicating whether the thread should immediately start or not. The reason is that you might need to pass it some parameters before the execution starts. The other value I'm setting here is `FreeOnTerminate`, which determines whether the thread object should remain in memory or be immediately deleted. You might need to keep it around to read some of its results.

In this case, I don't need extra initialization code, so starting the thread manually is useless. However, I added it to help explain how things work.

What are we going to do in this simple application? To keep things simple, I'm going to do some fairly useless numeric processing, generating a hundred million numbers in an in-memory list and picking the minimum and maximum one:

```
procedure TMyThread.FillList;
begin
  Randomize;
  CS.Acquire;
  try
    for var I := 1 to 100_000_000 do
      FIntList.Add(Random (MaxInt));
  finally
    CS.Release;
  end;
end;
```

I am skipping some of the details of the code, as the complete source is available in the GitHub repository. Here is the initial part of the `Execute` method:

```
procedure TMyThread.Execute;
var
  LMin, LMax: Integer;
begin
  FillList;

  LMin := 100_000_000;
  for var I := 0 to FIntList.Count - 1 do
  begin
    if FIntList [I] < LMin   then
      LMin := FIntList [I];
  end;
```

Now, the thread has one of its results available, LMin, but how is it going to display it on the main form? In general terms, a secondary thread should never access the UI because, at the operating system level, there is a main thread or UI thread that has exclusive access to the user interface objects and controls. In other words, our thread cannot touch the main form controls. However, it can ask the main thread to execute some code on behalf of the threads by means of the special thread function, Synchronize. This function receives an anonymous method as a parameter, which will be executed in the main thread, blocking any other code of the main thread at the same time. The thread, in turn, is going to stop and wait for this Synchronize function to be executed before continuing. Here is the code in my example:

```
Synchronize(
  procedure
  begin
    FormThread.ShowMin(LMin);
  end);
```

The ShowMin function here is a simple method to update the Text of one of the labels of the user interface:

```
procedure TFormThread.ShowMin(AMin: Integer);
begin
  Label1.Text := 'Min: ' + AMin.ToString;
end;
```

I added it to better separate the UI design from the code in the thread. In *Figure 4.3*, you can see the resulting application running on Windows:

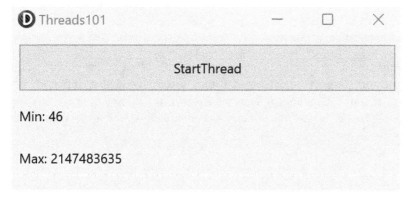

Figure 4.3: The Threads101 project running on Windows

This is the basis of threading in Delphi. It doesn't seem so complicated at first, but there is more you really need to understand to be able to use threads effectively.

Access synchronization

When synchronizing access, as we saw in the previous demo, one of the main issues with multithreaded applications is the need to avoid multiple threads accessing the same variable or the same resource at the same time. If one thread is making a change to a data structure while another thread is reading from it, the result will be totally unpredictable. *Synchronized access to resources is the most complex issue of threading.*

There are a large number of techniques you can use for thread synchronization and we don't have the scope to explore them all extensively in this chapter. I will just introduce the most common and simple options here.

Calling Synchronize

The first option is the one we have already used: the `Synchronize` method of the `TThread` class. The idea is simple: *there is some code that needs to be executed in the context of the main thread.* This is the case for UI-related code, as mentioned earlier. In general, if you need to make sure that code in multiple threads and main threads is not executed at the same time, this is a simple solution.

The drawback of this approach, though, is that if you have a lot of code, in the `Synchronize` method, it is serialized by losing any advantage of multithreading. The second big issue is that an incorrect use of this technique can lead to stalling the entire application with threads waiting on each other.

Again, for simple scenarios, this can be a good and handy technique. However, how does it really work?

In the classic scenario, you can add a method with no parameters in a `TThread` class and pass the procedure to the `Synchronize` method. In the modern scenario, you can pass an anonymous method, as in the previous demo.

Atomic operations

Another relatively simple solution (but one you can use only in some very specific scenarios) is to make sure an operation is executed entirely as a single piece of code that cannot be interrupted by a thread switch. Some of these atomic operations are provided by operating systems and are made available in the Delphi RTL as part of the `TInterlocked` class, which offers static class methods for core math operations:

- `Increment`
- `Decrement`
- `Add`
- `BitTestAndSet`
- `Exchange`
- `CompareExchange`

If these are the operations that multiple threads need to execute on a variable, using the `TInterlocked` class is a simple and effective solution.

Using a critical section

Another approach is to use a critical section, an instance of the `TCriticalSection` class. The idea of a critical section is to protect a block of code in a thread that can be executed only by one thread at a time. This makes sense when you plan on having more than one thread running at the same time.

To use a critical section, the key issue is declaring a shared variable (accessible by all threads), so you might want to use a global variable, even if local to a unit:

```
var
   CS: TCriticalSection;

initialization
   CS := TCriticalSection.Create;

finalization
   CS.Free;

// thread code
begin
   CS.Acquire;
   try
     // code you want to protect
   finally
     CS.Release;
   end;
```

Notice that it is fundamental that you protect the `Acquire/Release` combination with a `try/finally` block because, otherwise, in case of an exception, the critical section won't be released and no thread will be able to execute that code, blocking the program. I've added the same sample code to use a critical section in the `Threads101` project in a way that's pretty much useless with the primary goal of showing the syntax.

Using TMonitor

The last technique I want to cover in this chapter is the use of `TMonitor`. This is a core mechanism built into the entire Delphi RTL. Each object has an associated access lock that you can enable and disable to gain exclusive access to that object. The usage of `TMonitor` is somehow similar to that of a critical section but with the ability to automatically associate one to each object without the creation of an additional object – something that can be subject to threading conflicts as well. Notice that because there is a TMonitor in the UI library, you may have to prefix the type name with the name of the unit that defines it: the System unit.

This is a simple code example:

```
System.TMonitor.Enter(FIntList);
try
  // use FIntList
finally
  System.TMonitor.Exit(FIntList);
end;
```

Again, using a try/finally block is fundamental to avoid leaving an infinite lock on the resource in case of an exception in the code processing it.

The features of TMonitor are fairly extensive. You can use TryEnter to check whether the resource is available, you can use Wait on a resource, and call the TMonitor methods (Pulse and PulseAll) to awaken waiting threads. Additionally, TMonitor uses so-called **spin-locking**, which means it waits by consuming CPU cycles and continuously checking on the lock status to provide immediate continuation of the code with no delay due to thread context switching – while it defaults to blocking the thread in a standard Wait operation after some time.

Overall, TMonitor is a very complex synchronization mechanism, worth studying with care and using in a large number of scenarios.

> **Note**
>
> If you want to learn more about threading and synchronization in Delphi, the recommended read is *Delphi High Performance* by Primož Gabrijelčič, also published by Packt.

Exploring the Parallel Programming Library

On top of this core foundation, Delphi offers the more abstract **Parallel Programming Library** (**PPL**). This library allows you to express your application logic in a way that is less tied to the actual hardware and the capabilities of the CPU the program is running into. To clarify, the core element of the PPL is the TTask class; this is conceptually similar to a thread but abstracted from the hardware. For example, if you create 20 threads, you are making requests to the operating system and the CPU. If you create 20 tasks, the PPL will create some threads in a pool, depending on the CPU multicore capabilities, and assign tasks to those threads, without overloading the CPU. Also, reusing threads saves time, as thread creation is a heavy operation at the operating system level.

The very first thing to do in order to use the PPL is to add the `System.Threading` unit to the `uses` clause of your program. As mentioned, on behalf of the app, the library maintains a self-tuning pool of threads that are used to execute tasks.

In the following sections, we'll look at the high-level features that PPL offers to Delphi developers.

Parallel loops

The easiest concept to grasp in the PPL is the parallel `for` loop. This is useful when calculations for different values of a control variable are independent and it is not important in which order they are executed. A good example of this use case comes from ray tracing algorithms used in computer graphics. To generate an image, we need to calculate the color of each pixel that makes up the resulting image. This is done by calculating the path of each ray of light in space. Calculating the color of a given pixel is completely independent of other pixels and can be performed simultaneously to generate the resulting bitmap faster.

Instead of implementing a ray tracer here, let's create a truly simple demo that will allow us to observe how much faster a parallel loop would execute compared to a traditional loop. Instead of calculating pixel colors in each iteration of the loop, we will just call the `Sleep` procedure, which will make the current thread sleep for a given number of milliseconds and then it will continue to run.

Let's create a complete example using a parallel loop from scratch. First, create a new multi-device project in Delphi. Next, drop two buttons on the form and write the following code; in the caption of each button, this will display how much time it took to execute the loop. To calculate the elapsed time, we are using a `TStopWatch` record type from the `System.Diagnostics` unit. This is the code used to perform a slow operation:

```
function TForm1.DoTimeConsumingOperation(Length: integer): Double;
begin
  var Tot := 1.0;
  for var I := 1 to 10_000 * Length do
    // some random slow math operation
    Tot := Log2(Tot) + Sqrt(I);
  Result := Tot;
end;
```

Now, let's write a regular `for` loop using this slow operation and check how much time it takes:

```
procedure TForm1.btnForLoopRegularClick(Sender: TObject);
var
  SW: TStopwatch;
begin
  SW := TStopwatch.StartNew;
  for var I := 0 to 99 do
    DoTimeConsumingOperation(10);
```

```
    SW.Stop;
    (Sender as TButton).Text :=
      SW.ElapsedMilliseconds.ToString + 'ms';
  end;
```

By comparison, this is the same code using a parallel `for` loop:

```
procedure TForm1.btnForLoopParallelClick(Sender: TObject);
var
  SW: TStopwatch;
  I: Integer;
begin
  SW := TStopwatch.StartNew;
  TParallel.For(0, 99, procedure(I: integer)
  begin
    DoTimeConsumingOperation(10);
  end);
  SW.Stop;
  (Sender as TButton).Text :=
    SW.ElapsedMilliseconds.ToString + 'ms';
end;
```

The `TParallel.For` class method we are using in the preceding code has many overloaded versions. In this example, it takes the starting index, ending index, and an anonymous procedure that takes an `integer` parameter for the index.

On my Windows PC, for a 64-bit application, the regular `for` loop takes about half a second (425 milliseconds, on average) while the parallel version takes only 35 milliseconds, about one-tenth of the time. While the absolute speed depends on your CPU power, the difference between the two timings depends on the number of cores available to your CPU.

By comparison on my Android phone, the same app compiled for 64-bit takes 2,814 milliseconds for the regular loop and only 670 milliseconds for the parallel version. Your time will vary depending on the device, but the difference between the two versions should remain significant (unless you run on virtualized hardware with only a few available cores).

Using tasks

One of the key use cases for multithreading code is to keep the user interface responsive while performing some long-running operation, such as downloading data from the internet or performing calculations. The main thread of the application (the one where the user interface runs) should not be busy with those time-consuming operations. They should be executed in the background thread to keep the user interface responsive.

Now, you can add two more buttons to the form and enter the following code in their OnClick events:

```
procedure TForm1.btnNonResponsiveClick(Sender: TObject);
begin
  DoTimeConsumingOperation(3_000);
  (Sender as TButton).Text := 'Done';
end;


procedure TForm1.btnResponsive1Click(Sender: TObject);
var
  ATask: ITask;
begin
  ATask := TTask.Create(procedure
  begin
    DoTimeConsumingOperation(3_000);
  end);
  ATask.Start;
  (Sender as TButton).Text := 'Done';
end;
```

When you click the first button, the form freezes for a few seconds. When you click on the second button, the form stays responsive because the time-consuming operation is executed in a different thread and the main app thread can process user events normally. In fact, the Done message is displayed almost immediately because the main thread continues to execute just after it starts the task. If you would like to display the Done text on the button after the task is complete, you would need to do it from inside the background thread. You can only manipulate the user interface from the main app thread, which is why the call to change the button's Text property needs to be synchronized:

```
procedure TForm1.btnResponsive2Click(Sender: TObject);
var
  ATask: ITask;
begin
  ATask := TTask.Create(procedure
  begin
    DoTimeConsumingOperation(3000);
    TThread.Synchronize(nil,
      procedure
      begin
        (Sender as TButton).Text := 'Done';
      end);
  end);
  ATask.Start;
end;
```

Now, the label doesn't change immediately, but after a few seconds, when the operation completes. A task is a bit like an anonymous procedure. You can declare it, but it only starts to execute when it is told to. You need to call the `Start` method, and only then will the task start.

The beauty of futures

The PPL also provides the notion of a "future." This is a specialization of a task generally tied to calculations or mathematical operations. A future is a task that returns a value. In the case of a task, you call its `Start` method to execute. In the case of a future, you can just declare it and assign it to a variable. The PPL will execute the code when it has a thread available. When you try to retrieve the value of this variable, if the future has already been executed, the value is returned; if the future is still pending, it is executed as soon as possible and the program will wait for its completion. In any case, when you access the value of the future, you'll read the value.

There are some interesting use cases when futures are used. For example, you may want to calculate something based on values of two or more parameters that need to be calculated first. Instead of calculating these parameters sequentially, we could perform these calculations in parallel.

For this demo, let's reuse the calculations done earlier and read the resulting value. Let's assume we have to calculate the value for three different parameters and add them at the end.

Let's first have a look at how we could implement this functionality without futures. Here is an example using standard code (I've omitted the lines for timing and for displaying results):

```
var
   First, Second, Third: Double;
begin
   First := DoTimeConsumingOperation(200);
   Second := DoTimeConsumingOperation(300);
   Third := DoTimeConsumingOperation(400);

   var GrandTotal := First + Second + Third;
```

`GrandTotal` has to be computed by performing all the previous calculations first; on my PC, this code takes about 389 milliseconds.

You can implement the same functionality using futures. In this case, the code will look like this:

```
var
   First, Second, Third: IFuture<Double>;
begin
   First := TTask.Future<Double>(function: Double
   begin
     Result := DoTimeConsumingOperation(200);
   end);
```

```
Second := TTask.Future<Double>(function: Double
begin
  Result := DoTimeConsumingOperation(300);
end);

Third := TTask.Future<Double>(function: Double
begin
  Result := DoTimeConsumingOperation(400);
end);

var GrantTotal: Double :=
  First.Value + Second.Value + Third.Value;
```

This code wraps each of the three operations in a future by providing the corresponding code in an anonymous method. At the end, you need to read the result of that calculation using the Value property of each TFuture<Double> variable.

Executing this code on the same PC requires about 176 milliseconds. This is about half and it's possibly the time it takes for the slowest of the three calculations: the one with 400 as a parameter.

So, what's the difference between a task and a future? A task is an operation or a procedure that you want to be executed in a thread. A future is a calculation or a function that you want to be executed in a thread.

Summary

In this chapter, we have focused on one of the most important and most complex features of modern computing: multithreaded applications and parallel programming. We had room only for an overview to get you started in this area.

In particular, we delved into Delphi's Parallel Programming Library. With constructs such as parallel for loops, tasks, and futures, we can really make our Delphi apps faster and more responsive. However, keep in mind that you need to be careful in terms of resource access and synchronization, and for this reason, we introduced some of the key concepts in this space, from critical sections to TMonitor and the intrinsic operations.

If you want to learn more about threading and parallel programming, I fully recommend reading books and articles by Primoz Gabrijelcic, particularly his recent book, *Delphi High Performance* by Packt (ISBN: 9781805125877).

Now that we have looked into the foundations of the Delphi language and touched on some important and common use RTL features, it's time to start looking into the FireMonkey framework and its architecture.

Part 2: Going Mobile

Now that we have gone over the foundations of Delphi, its IDE, language, and RTL building blocks, it's time to jump into the main focus area of this book: developing mobile applications with Delphi.

As usual, we are going to proceed in steps, starting with a broad overview of the FireMonkey UI library and its key architectural elements. We'll look into the support for 3D graphics, and we'll dive deep into the main architectural feature of FireMonkey and its styling model. This part of the book ends with a deep dive into specific mobile device capabilities supported by Delphi and touches briefly on desktop development and how desktop and mobile apps can work together.

We'll do this by building a large number of small apps, all available in the book GitHub repository, but also a couple of larger ones to help you understand how to organize apps with multiple screens and a number of course code files.

This part has the following chapters:

- *Chapter 5, Playing with FireMonkey*
- *Chapter 6, FireMonkey in 3D*
- *Chapter 7, Building User Interfaces with Style*
- *Chapter 8, Working with Mobile Operating System*
- *Chapter 9, Desktop Apps and Mobile Bridges*

5
Playing with FireMonkey

First of all, Delphi development is great fun. The best way to learn how to build mobile apps is to start by creating a few small apps. In this chapter, we are going to build a simple *Game of Memory* application using primitive components such as layouts, shapes, effects, and animations. We are also going to learn how to deliver an advanced mobile user experience with touch, multi-touch, and gestures.

This chapter will cover the following topics:

- Drawing in code
- Get moving with timers
- The power of parenting
- Touching the screen
- Game of Memory
- Working with images
- Designing the user interface
- Building the game's main form

The objective of this chapter is to learn the basics of **FireMonkey programming**. To do so, we'll build a simple but complete game in the last part of this chapter.

Technical requirements

The examples in this chapter work in any version of Delphi. The complete source is available at https://github.com/PacktPublishing/Expert-Delphi_Second-edition.

Drawing in code

The key to FireMonkey's cross-platform support is its rendering architecture. When you create a new multi-device project with Delphi, on the first page of the wizard, you can choose an application type. Effectively, this selects the type of the first form to add to a new app. For this, you can choose **Blank Application**. This will add a form inherited from TForm to the project, which is a basic two-dimensional form. The second choice is **3D Application**. This will add a form inherited from TForm3D. All other choices give you a TForm descendant with some additional controls already added.

If you decide to add more forms to the project, then you'll come across the real choice: **HD Form** or **3D Form**. Here, HD stands for high-definition and is just a different name for 2D. Depending on the chosen platform, FireMonkey forms are rendered using different graphics APIs, such as OpenGL or DirectX. These are the same APIs that many developers use to implement graphically intensive games.

In the FireMonkey library, the TForm class inherits from the TCustomForm class, which, in turn, derives from the TCommonCustomForm class and implements the IScene interface. The key method of this interface is GetCanvas, which returns an instance of TCanvas. The TCanvas class is the main abstraction for 2D drawing in FireMonkey. It is an abstract class that defines a common denominator for writing cross-platform drawing code. It has different implementations for different targets. If we look into the Delphi source directory, we will find that there are units with different Tcanvas implementations, depending on the platform. If we compile our app for Windows, we will be using a TCanvas implementation based on Windows Direct2D graphics defined in the FMX. Canvas.D2D unit. The same app compiled for other targets will use OpenGL graphics and the TCanvas implementation from FMX.Canvas.GPU. This is a typical pattern in FireMonkey. A base abstract class provides an interface for programmer code and its implementation is platform-specific.

FireMonkey is based on vector graphics; so, a programmer can easily scale, rotate, and transform user interface controls without losing graphics fidelity! At the lowest level, we can just use TCanvas methods to write cross-platform drawing code.

If we want to draw on the FireMonkey form using Canvas directly, we can use the TPaintBox control. It has an OnPaint event that provides access to a Canvas object as its parameter. Typically, code that is responsible for drawing on the canvas is enclosed within BeginScene and EndScene calls so that all of the painting operations are executed as a single batch at the end (for faster performance and to avoid flickering).

Here is the structure of the code you can use:

```
procedure TForm1.PaintBox1Paint(Sender: TObject; Canvas: TCanvas);
begin
  Canvas.BeginScene;
  try
    // access "Canvas" methods and properties here
  finally
```

```
    Canvas.EndScene;
  end;
end;
```

The TCanvas class has many methods for drawing lines, ellipses, rectangles, and other geometries. Any actual drawing call uses the currently active brush and other properties of a canvas. For this reason, you need to set these properties before a call to draw something.

Let's draw a simple scene with a blue sky and a beautiful yellow Sun.

To do this, you can create a new Delphi multi-device project:

1. Select **Blank Application** as the project type.
2. Save the form's unit as uFormSunCodeStatic and the project as SunAppCodeStatic.
3. Drop a TPaintBox component onto the form and align it with the client area.
4. Double-click on the OnPaint event of the control and enter the following code.

However, before we start coding, we can define some constants we are going to use, to avoid intermixing actual values in the code:

```
const
  DEFAULT_OPACITY = 1;
  POS_X = 150;
  POS_Y = 150;
  SUN_RADIUS = 50;
  RAY_COUNT = 12;
  RAY_LENGTH = 100;
```

With these values available, let's look at the actual code of the paint box's OnPaint event handler. In the first part of the code, we paint the sky and the sun:

```
procedure TFormSunCodeStatic.PaintBox1Paint(Sender: Tobject;
  Canvas: TCanvas);
begin
  Canvas.BeginScene;
  try
    // draw blue sky
    Canvas.Fill.Color := TAlphaColorRec.Skyblue;
    Canvas.FillRect(PaintBox1.BoundsRect, 0, 0, [],
      DEFAULT_OPACITY);
```

```
    // draw yellow sun solid circle
    Canvas.Fill.Color := TAlphaColorRec.Yellow;
    Canvas.Fill.Kind := TBrushKind.Solid;
    var X := POS_X;
    var Y := POS_Y;
    var R := SUN_RADIUS;
    var ARect := RectF(X-R, Y-R, X+R, Y+R);
    Canvas.FillEllipse(aRect, DEFAULT_OPACITY);
```

Using a square as a base structure, the ellipse we are drawing is a circle. The second part of the method's code draws the sun's rays around the sun:

```
    // prepare stroke for drawing sun rays
    Canvas.Stroke.Color := TAlphaColorRec.Yellow;
    Canvas.Stroke.Kind := TBrushKind.Solid;
    Canvas.Stroke.Thickness := 5;

    // draw sun rays
    for var I := 0 to RAY_COUNT-1 do
    begin
      var Angle := I * Pi * 2 / RAY_COUNT;
      var A := PointF(X, Y);
      var B := PointF(
        X + RAY_LENGTH * Cos(Angle),
        Y + RAY_LENGTH * Sin(Angle));
      Canvas.DrawLine(A, B, DEFAULT_OPACITY);
    end;
  finally
    Canvas.EndScene;
  end;
end;
```

Each of the sun's rays is a line starting from the center. As you can see, the code uses some trigonometric functions to calculate the initial and final position of each line in a `for` loop. If we run the app, we should see a beautiful Sun shining on a blue sky. This can be seen in *Figure 5.1*, which shows the app running on Windows:

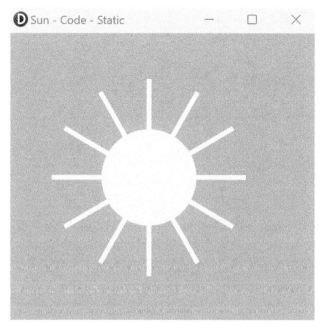

Figure 5.1: The Sun and the sky drawn on the canvas by the SubAppCodeStatic app

The code for drawing lines and filling rectangles can be simplified by defining functions that embed some of the operations in a simplified way. Adding those functions to a class inherited from the TCanvas class would be simple, but it would require us to make changes in FireMonkey so that the library can create our custom canvas class instead of the default one. Another option would be to use global functions. This would be effective, but far from clean.

An alternative option is to write a class helper for the TCanvas class. So, instead of calling a global function and passing a Canvas object as a parameter, we can apply our new methods directly to the library's TCanvas class. The advantage of the calling code is that we only need to write one more abstract call instead of writing three or four lines of code.

This is the definition of the helper class:

```
type
  TFmxCanvasHelper = class helper for TCanvas
    procedure Linc(A, D: TPointF; AColor: TColor;
      AThickness: Single = 1);
    procedure SolidRect(aRect: TRectF;
      AColor: TColor = TAlphaColorRec.White);
    procedure SolidCircle(A: TPointF; R: Double; AColor: TColor);
  end;
```

The preceding code is very similar to what we'd write in a regular class. The first method paints a solid rectangle, as shown in the following code:

```
const
  DEFAULT_OPACITY: Double = 1;

procedure TFmxCanvasHelper.SolidRect(ARect: TRectF;
  AColor: TColor);
begin
  Fill.Color := AColor;
  FillRect(ARect, 0, 0, [], DEFAULT_OPACITY);
end;
```

Notice how we can directly access other elements of the helped class (TCanvas), such as the Fill property. It is possible to use self.Fill for more clarity, but this won't matter for the compiler or most developers. The second method draws a line with a specific line configuration:

```
procedure TFmxCanvasHelper.Line(A, B: TPointF; AColor: TColor;
  AThickness: Single);
begin
  Stroke.Color := AColor;
  Stroke.Kind := TBrushKind.bkSolid;
  Stroke.Thickness := AThickness;
  DrawLine(A, B, DEFAULT_OPACITY);
end;
```

Finally, the third method draws a solid circle:

```
procedure TFmxCanvasHelper.SolidCircle(A: TPointF; R: Double;
  AColor: TColor);
begin
  var ARect := RectF(A.X-R, A.Y-R, A.X+R, A.Y+R);
  Fill.Color := AColor;
  Fill.Kind := TBrushKind.Solid;
  FillEllipse(ARect, DEFAULT_OPACITY);
end;
```

Now, we can just add this unit to the uses clause of the form that we want to draw on a FireMonkey canvas and use simplified code. We'll see this in the next section.

> **Warning!**
> When defining helpers for some fundamental library classes, always make sure that no helper is already defined – any given type can only have one helper applied to it.

Get moving with timers

Let's go a step further – instead of having a static scene, we'll add some animation. It is a normal thing for the Sun to ascend in the morning. To achieve the effect of sunrise, the form must be repainted. We are going to change the Y coordinate that is used for painting the Sun's circle and rays. To do this, we'll add a private member called FSunPosY: double to our TFormSun class that will store the current vertical position of the Sun.

The simplest way to change our scene over time is with the TTimer component. To do so, drop a timer on the form. It has only one event, OnTimer. The frequency of this event is controlled by the Interval property, which specifies the number of milliseconds between firing the OnTimer event. The default value of the Interval property is 1000, which means that the timer fires its event every second. For a smooth animation, this is too slow. Change the Interval property to 20 and double-click on the OnTimer event. Here, we want to constantly increment the FSunPosY field that we will be using in the OnPaint event. We also want to force the form to repaint itself. This can be done by *invalidating* the form's canvas. Here is the updated drawing code, which uses our timer to achieve the animation effect. We are also using a canvas helper to simplify the code that's used for drawing.

Let's start with the complete declaration of the form class:

```
type
  TFormSunCodeAnim = class(TForm)
    PaintBox1: TPaintBox;
    Timer1: TTimer;
    procedure PaintBox1Paint(Sender: TObject;
      Canvas: TCanvas);
    procedure Timer1Timer(Sender: TObject);
    procedure FormCreate(Sender: TObject);
  private
    FSunPosY: Double;
  end;
```

When the program starts and when the timer fires, we change the Sun's position. This can be seen in the following code:

```
const
  END_SUN_POS_Y = 150;

procedure TFormSunCodeAnim.FormCreate(Sender: TObject);
begin
  FSunPosY := self.Height + 150;
end;

procedure TFormSunCodeAnim.Timer1Timer(Sender: TObject);
```

```
begin
  if FSunPosY > END_SUN_POS_Y then
    FSunPosY := FSunPosY - 10;
  Invalidate;
end;
```

Finally, this is the new version of the `OnPaint` event handler, which uses the constants and the class helper we defined earlier. Again, the first part of the event handler code draws the background and the Sun's circle, but this time with simplified code:

```
procedure TFormSunCodeAnim.PaintBox1Paint(Sender: Tobject;
  Canvas: TCanvas);
begin
  Canvas.BeginScene;
  try
    // draw blue sky
    Canvas.SolidRect(PaintBox1.BoundsRect,
      TAlphaColorRec.Skyblue);

    var X := POS_X;
    var Y := FSunPosY;

    // draw yellow sun solid circle
    Canvas.SolidCircle(PointF(X, Y),
      SUN_RADIUS, TAlphaColorRec.Yellow);
```

The second part of the event handler code draws the Sun's rays, as we did previously:

```
    for var I := 0 to RAY_COUNT-1 do
    begin
      var Angle := I * Pi * 2 / RAY_COUNT;
      var A := PointF(X, Y);
      var B := PointF(
        x + RAY_LENGTH * Cos(Angle),
        y + RAY_LENGTH * Sin(Angle));
      Canvas.Line(A, B, TAlphaColorRec.Yellow, 5);
    end;
  finally
    Canvas.EndScene;
  end;
end;
```

This technique of drawing on the canvas gives you a lot of flexibility in terms of the graphical effects that you can achieve. However, the code becomes difficult to maintain.

Precise timing

The TTimer component cannot be used for very precise timing as it relies on the operating system and the workload in the application message queue. If your animation code is time-sensitive when you are using a physics engine, for example, it needs the exact amount of time that elapsed from the last timer event. In this case, you could use the TstopWatch record type from the System. Diagnostics unit. This record makes it easy to read precise time information from the underlying operating system clock in a cross-platform way. The TstopWatch data structure needs to be initialized, so, somewhere, such as in the OnCreate event of the form, you need to call its StartNew method. The GetTimeStamp method returns the current number of underlying operating system ticks, which is the most precise available timing information. Luckily, there is also a Frequency method, which gives us the number of ticks per second. By dividing these two values, we can get the low-level reference to time in seconds.

Let's create a simple test app. Declare an FLastTime: double private field in the form's class. Drop a timer component and implement the OnTimer event. The default value for the Interval property is 1 second, but as we will see, it is never exactly 1 second between every two OnTimer events. To test this, in the form's OnCreate event handler, we can initialize a TStopWatch data structure:

```
procedure TFormTiming.FormCreate(Sender: Tobject);
begin
  TStopwatch.StartNew;
  Log('Stopwatch Frequency = ' +
    TStopwatch.Frequency.ToString);
end;
```

When the timer fires (the OnTimer event), we log details about the time that's elapsed using a custom function to calculate the ratio:

```
function TFormTiming.GetRawReferenceTime: double;
begin
  Result := TStopwatch.GetTimeStamp / TStopwatch.Frequency;
end;

procedure TFormTiming.Timer1Timer(Sender: TObject);
var
  T, Elapsed: double;
begin
  T := GetRawReferenceTime;
  Elapsed := T - FLastTime;
  FLastTime := T;
  Log('T=' + T.ToString + '   Elapsed=' + Elapsed.ToString);
end;
```

If we run this app, we will see the precise difference in seconds between the timer events. This can be seen in *Figure 5.2*.

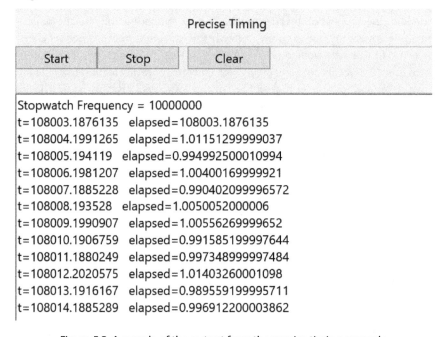

Figure 5.2: A sample of the output from the precise timing example

This technique can be useful if you need very precise timing in your next high-end game written in Delphi. Even in an almost empty app, the timer has accuracy up to a few milliseconds. In a more complex app, the differences could be bigger.

The power of parenting

One of the nicest things about FireMonkey's architecture is **parenting**. Essentially, any FireMonkey component can contain or "be a parent" to other components. What's cool about this is that all children inherit different properties of their parents, such as position, scale, and rotation. This also provides a lot of possibilities when it comes to building user interfaces since we can create composite controls without having to declare completely new classes.

Shapes

A lot of low-level drawing code can be avoided by using different controls from the **Shape** category on the palette. There are lines, circles, ellipses, rectangles, pies, paths, and more. They encapsulate drawings on the canvas, so you don't need to write much code.

Let's try to recreate our Sun visualization with shapes to better compare these two possible approaches to drawing. Add a new **Form HD** element to the project. Drop a TRectangle component on the form and align it with the **Client** area. Then, change its Name property to RectSky. Expand its Fill property and change its Color to Skyblue. Now, drop a TCircle component on the form and name it CircleSun. Change its Width and Height properties to 100 to make it bigger and its Position.X and Position.Y properties to 100 to move it toward the top-left corner of the screen. Next, change its Fill.Color and Stroke.Color properties to Yellow.

So far, we have been changing the color, position, and dimension of FireMonkey shapes, but we can also scale them horizontally and vertically, rotate them using the RotationAngle and RotationCenter properties, and change their Opacity values. This gives us a lot of possibilities to show off our artistic skills while designing user interfaces with FireMonkey.

Now, it's time to add some Sun rays! Make sure that the Sun's circle is selected on the form; then, drop a TLine component on it and rename it LineRay01. Change its LineType property to Top so that it is horizontal and not diagonal. Then, change its Width and Height properties to 100, Stroke.Color to Yellow, and Thickness to 5.

Now comes the important part: make sure that the line component *belongs* to the circle. In the **Structure** tree view, it should be a child (or leaf) of the circle. We will be adding more lines to the circle, and they all need to be children of the Sun, as shown in *Figure 5.3*:

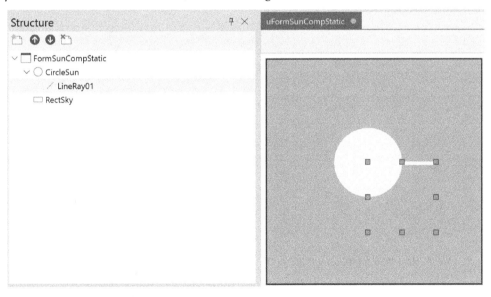

Figure 5.3: Adding a child Sun ray line under the Sun circle object

Child properties are set relative to their parents. This is very powerful because changes to parent properties automatically propagate to children. Make sure that the Position.X and Position.Y properties of the line component are both set to 50 so that the ray starts exactly in the center of the Sun. If we were to change the position of the circle, the line would go with it. Again, this is the parent-child relationship between controls and it is one of the most important and powerful aspects of FireMonkey's architecture.

Next, we will add the remaining rays by copying the first ray and changing their rotations. Right-click on the line and select **Copy** from the **Edit** context menu. Click on the circle to select it. Right-click again and select **Paste**. A copy of the line will be added to the form. Now, in the **Structure** tree view, drag the new line onto the circle so that it becomes its child. Change its `Position.X` and `Position.Y` properties to `50` to make sure it starts exactly at the center. Now, we want to rotate the second ray. Change the `RotationAngle` property to `30` degrees. Note that this is not exactly the rotation that we wanted to achieve. By default, shapes rotate around their center, but we want the line to rotate around its top-left corner. How can we do that? There is also the `RotationCenter` property with default values of `X=0.5` and `Y=0.5`. These properties control the rotation's center relative to the dimensions of the control. Just half and half means the center. If we change both values to `0`, we will achieve the desired rotation.

Now, paste 10 more lines onto the form, setting the same position and rotation center for each of them, but incrementing the rotation angle by 30 degrees. As shown in *Figure 5.4* (notice the `RotationAngle` property value), we should have a beautiful Sun with 12 rays.

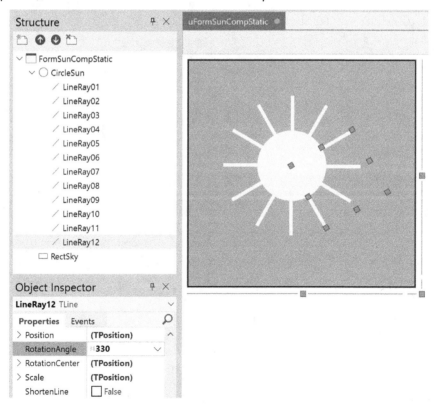

Figure 5.4: The configuration for additional Sun rays

Notice that we have achieved the same graphical result that we did previously, but this time, we have not written a single line of code. Everything has been done visually, at design time. You don't even need to run the app to see what it is going to look like.

Animations

When it comes to animations, there's no coding, just shapes.

The next step is to recreate the animation of the rising Sun in the new app, which is made up of components only. The easiest way to add animation is to use special *animation* components. In the **Tool Palette** area, there is a separate category for **Animations**. There are different animation components for animating the values of different types over time. There is TFloatAnimation for changing float values, TColorAnimation for changing colors, and so on.

Instead of dropping an animation component on the form, we can create one directly from inside the **Object Inspector** area. For our demo, we would like to change the Position.Y property of the circle component. Just expand this property in the **Object Inspector** area, as shown in *Figure 5.5*, and select the **Create New TFloatAnimation** option:

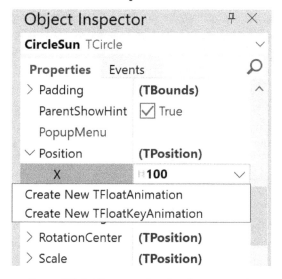

Figure 5.5: Adding an animation for a property

Animation components make it very easy to change the values of different properties over time in background threads without having to use timer components. When we create an animation from the **Object Inspector** area, it is already parented under the component. In this case, the property that the animation is going to manipulate is already implicitly set.

An animation is just a component, so we can adjust its properties at design time with **Object Inspector**. Set Duration to 2 seconds, set Enabled to True, set StopValue to 100, and set StartValue to 600. We might want to set the StartValue property in code to accommodate different display heights. We want the Sun to start ascending from outside the border of the screen. To obtain this effect, you can add just one line of code to the OnCreate event of the form:

```
procedure TFormSunCompAnim.FormCreate(Sender: TObject);
begin
  FloatAnimation1.StartValue := RectSky.Height + 150;
end;
```

The last property we can optionally adjust is Interpolation. By default, it is set to Linear, which means that the value changes linearly from StartValue to StopValue for the duration of the animation. Change Interopolation to Sinusoidal for a slightly more interesting visual effect.

Our animation is Enabled at design time, which means that it will start as soon as our app starts to run. It is also possible to do animations in code. Instead of using animation components, we can animate the properties of different objects with the TAnimator class.

So far, we have focused on generating great graphics, but with no user interaction. Great apps are all about great user experience. To get some feedback from apps, users are usually busy touching their screens in all manner of ways.

Touching the screen

FireMonkey forms provide support for handling simple **touch**, **multi-touch**, and **gesture** events. You can use standard and interactive gestures, such as zoom and rotation, to make your apps more dynamic and interactive.

Touch

FireMonkey forms are used for building both mobile and desktop applications. It is just a matter of changing the selected **Target Platform** and recompiling the project. Certain concepts exist on desktops that do not exist on mobile platforms and vice versa. For example, on mobile devices, there is no concept of a mouse, but this exists on desktops. FireMonkey forms provide different mouse events that are fired in response to simple touch events on mobile platforms. When the end user touches the screen, the OnMouseDown event is fired. Other events, such as OnMouseUp and OnMouseMove, are fired when the user stops touching the screen, or when the touch point changes. For individual controls, there are also two additional events, OnMouseEnter and OnMouseLeave.

If a scene is built in code, then we can just implement mouse events on the form itself. In FireMonkey, it is more common to create visualizations with shapes and complex controls. Higher-level components, such as TButton, offer events such as OnClick that centralize touch support. When we're building a scene with only shapes, we need to understand how touch events work.

Every shape component derives from the TControl class. In this class, all user interactions, including touch, are handled. If a control does not need to respond to touch events, we can set its HitTest property to False. This can be important when we are combining different primitive shapes into a more complex thing. Typically, we just want the parent shape to receive touch events.

Let's modify our Sun app so that the end user can change the position of the Sun. This involves handling the OnMouseDown and OnMouseUp events. In the OnMouseDown event, we just set a Boolean flag that states we are in the process of *moving* and store the initial X and Y coordinates of the touch event. In the OnMouseUp event, we do the actual *move* operation and reset the Moving flag.

There is also our initial *Sun rising* animation, which is played when the app starts. We do not want the user to move the Sun before it is in its target position on the form. That's why we are also adding the FReady: Boolean private field to the form; this is set to False in the OnCreate event of the form and set to True in the animation's OnFinish event.

Double-click on the OnMouseDown and OnMouseUp events of the form and add the following code to the events. However, before we do that, let's declare new fields in the form class itself:

```
type
  TFormSunMove = class(TForm)
    // ...
  private
    FReady: Boolean;
    FDown: TPointF;
    FMoving: Boolean;
  end;
```

Here's the code that controls the FReady status:

```
procedure TFormSunMove.FormCreate(Sender: TObject);
begin
  FReady := False;
  FloatAnimation1.StartValue := RectSky.Height + 150;
end;

procedure TFormSunMove.FloatAnimation1Finish(Sender: TObject);
begin
  FReady := True;
end;
```

The most important portion of the code for this app is in the mouse event handler. On mouse down, we initiate the `moving` process:

```
procedure TFormSunMove.FormMouseDown(Sender: TObject;
  Button: TMouseButton; Shift: TShiftState; X, Y: Single);
begin
  if FReady then
  begin
    FDown := PointF(X, Y);
    FMoving := True;
  end;
end;
```

When the mouse is released, we apply the changes if the `FMoving` flag has been set:

```
procedure TFormSunMove.FormMouseUp(Sender: TObject;
  Button: TMouseButton; Shift: TShiftState; X, Y: Single);
begin
  if FMoving then
  begin
    CircleSun.Position.X := CircleSun.Position.X + (X - FDown.X);
    CircleSun.Position.Y := CircleSun.Position.Y + (Y - FDown.Y);
    FMoving := False;
  end;
end;
```

If we run the app now, movement does not work. Touch events do not reach the form, which is completely occupied by the sky rectangle. If we change its `HitTest` property to `False`, then the app will work as expected.

With that, we've made our form interactive!

Gestures

Another standard way to interact with a mobile app is to use more than one finger at a time. FireMonkey supports handling standard and interactive gestures. Let's add support for interactive rotation to our Sun demo app.

Make sure that the form is selected in the **Object Inspector** area and expand its **Touch** property. Check the `Rotate` gesture under the **Interactive Gestures** sub-property, as shown in *Figure 5.6*:

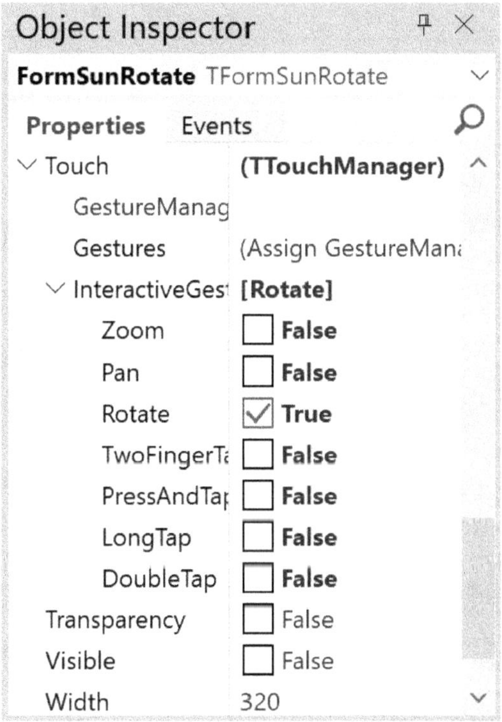

Figure 5.6: Configuring an interactive gesture for the app

Now, we can respond to selected gestures. Double-click on the `OnGesture` event of the form. In the generated event handler, there are two parameters. The first parameter is `EventInfo:` `TGestureEventInfo` and contains all information about the gesture that was detected. Inside the `FMX.Types` unit, we can find the declaration of the `TGestureEventInfo` record and its corresponding types:

```
type
  TInteractiveGestureFlag = (gfBegin, gfInertia, gfEnd);
  TInteractiveGestureFlags = set of TInteractiveGestureFlag;

  TGestureEventInfo = record
    GestureID: TGestureID;
    Location: TPointF;
    Flags: TInteractiveGestureFlags;
    Angle: Double;
    InertiaVector: TPointF;
    Distance: Integer;
    TapLocation: TPointF;
  end;
```

```
TGestureEvent = procedure(Sender: TObject;
  const EventInfo: TGestureEventInfo;
  var Handled: Boolean) of object;
```

The first field, GestureID, identifies what gesture it is, while the remaining fields give information about the location of the gesture and other properties. An interactive gesture occurs over time. The Flags field is a set of TInteractiveGestureFlag values that can be used to process a gesture differently when the gesture has just started or just ended.

In our OnGesture event handler implementation, first, we will check if it is a Rotate gesture. If this is the case, then we will change the RotationAngle property of the Sun's circle. We will also need a new FLastAngle: double private field in the form's class to store the last rotation angle. Here is the actual code:

```
procedure TFormSunGestures.FormGesture(Sender: TObject;
  const EventInfo: TGestureEventInfo; var Handled: Boolean);
begin
  if EventInfo.GestureID = igiRotate then
  begin
    if (TInteractiveGestureFlag.gfBegin in EventInfo.Flags) then
      FLastAngle := CircleSun.RotationAngle
    else if EventInfo.Angle <> 0 then
      CircleSun.RotationAngle := FLastAngle -
        (EventInfo.Angle * 180) / Pi;
  end;
end;
```

If we run the app now, we can verify that the Sun is now responding to rotation gestures. We can make these on a multi-touch device (not a regular computer) by touching the screen with two fingers and rotating them.

There are also other gestures that we can handle in FireMonkey. Inside the Touch property of the form, we are instructed to use **Gesture Manager**. Drop TGestureManager onto the form and point the GestureManager1 property to the newly added component. Notice that next to the Gestures property, there's a plus sign; now, it is possible to check which standard gestures we would like to handle. The Object Inspector area will look similar to the following:

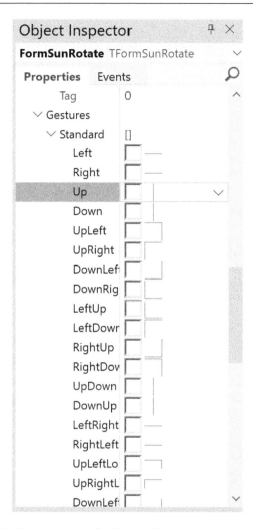

Figure 5.7: Assigning gestures to the Gesture Manager area of a FireMonkey app

> **Need more gestures?**
> There are 34 standard gestures that we could add to our demo app.

Multi-touch

Sometimes, users touch the app with multiple fingers at the same time. With multi-touch, we can provide a nice user experience.

Let's create a new multi-device Delphi project. Drop `TPaintBox` onto the form and align it with `Client`. Save the app as `TouchApp` and the form as `uFormTouch`. Instead of drawing directly on the paint box canvas, we can also draw on the offline bitmap and draw the whole bitmap in one operation. To implement this, we can add an `FBitmap: TBitmap` field to the form. This setup can be useful if we wish to achieve more complex animations. In the following code, we're creating the bitmap and using it to paint on the screen:

```
procedure TFormTouch.FormCreate(Sender: TObject);
begin
  FBitmap := TBitmap.Create;
  FBitmap.SetSize(self.ClientWidth, self.ClientHeight);
  FBitmap.Clear(TAlphaColors.White);
end;

procedure TFormTouch.PaintBox1Paint(Sender: TObject;
  Canvas: TCanvas);
var
  R: TRectF;
begin
  R := TRectF.Create(0, 0, FBitmap.Width, FBitmap.Height);
  PaintBox1.Canvas.DrawBitmap(FBitmap, R, R, 1, True);
end;
```

Now, double-click on the `OnTouch` event of the form in the **Object Inspector** area to generate an empty event handler. As a parameter to this event, we are getting a dynamic array of locations of individual touchpoints. Let's draw some lines that connect all the touchpoints using the FireMonkey canvas helper we defined earlier:

```
procedure TFormTouch.FormTouch(Sender: TObject;
  const Touches: TTouches; const Action: TTouchAction);
var
  Count: Integer;
begin
  FBitmap.Canvas.BeginScene;
  try
    FBitmap.Clear(TAlphaColors.White);
    Count := Length(Touches);
    if Count > 1 then
    for var I := 0 to Count-2 do
      FBitmap.Canvas.Line(
        Touches[i].Location,
        Touches[i+1].Location,
        TAlphaColorRec.Red);
  finally
```

```
    FBitmap.Canvas.EndScene;
  end;
  PaintBox1.Repaint;
end;
```

When you run the app, it will show the touchpoints connected with red lines. *Figure 5.8* shows red lines painted across four touchpoints by the TouchApp demo running on an Android phone:

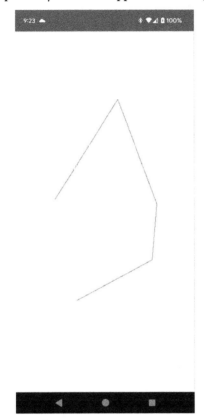

Figure 5.8: The lines painted across touchpoints by TouchApp

It is not the most useful multi-touch demo, but it is intentionally simple to illustrate how to handle multi-touch information.

Game of Memory

Let's put together what we have learned about the FireMonkey architecture so far and build a complete but simple game. In the process, we will look at how to handle images with the TImageList component and some basics of building FireMonkey 2D user interfaces.

Designing the game

Game of Memory is a board game. A player is presented with a grid of tiles. Every tile has an image on it, but all images are initially hidden. When a user touches a tile, its image is revealed. When the next tile is touched, the image of the currently visible tile is made hidden again, and the image of the new tile is shown. This means that at any one moment during the game, only one image is shown. The number of tiles has to be even because every image is used twice. The objective of the game is to remove all the tiles in the shortest possible time by touching tiles with the same image one after another. If a user touches another tile with the same image as the currently visible tile, both tiles are removed from the grid. To get a better idea, an image of the game in action has been provided (*Figure 5.11*, later in this chapter). This process continues until there are no more tiles in the grid and the game ends. The score is the time that elapsed from the beginning of the game to the moment when the last two tiles were removed. The shortest time is the best.

To make our game more interesting, we are going to let the player choose the initial size of the grid – from a small one that should only take a couple of seconds to complete to bigger ones that will take longer. We are also going to keep track of the top scores for each grid size.

We started building this game in *Chapter 2*. There is a main form called `FormMain` that we are going to use to display game tiles. We will also add buttons to control starting, pausing, and stopping the game. The second form is called `FormSettings` and is displayed from within the main form. This form is created lazily – that is, not when the app starts but at the moment a player clicks on the settings menu button for the first time. On this form, we are going to change the current difficulty level and display the best times for each grid size.

Before we start coding the game logic, let's start by working on displaying images, given that's one of the core elements of the app.

Working with images

The key assets in our game are the images to be used on the back of every tile. There will be at least as many images as the number of pairs at the highest difficulty level, plus two additional images. The first image in the list will be completely white and will be used for tiles that have been removed. The second special image will be used as a cover for every hidden tile. Before every new game is started, we are going to randomly assign image pairs to tiles. This will ensure that the game is different every time the user plays it.

FireMonkey comes with the `TImageList` component, which has been designed to efficiently manage all images that are used across the whole app. It is good practice to put images and all other global game assets on the dedicated data module. In this way, we can easily access them from all app forms, or even reuse them across different projects.

Add a new data module to the game project. Save the file as `uDMGameOfMem` and change its `Name` property to `DMGameOfMem`. A naming convention that you might want to follow is starting the names of data modules with `DM` and their unit names with `uDM`. Every programmer has a different naming scheme, but once you adopt one, you should try to use it consistently.

This data module will always be needed by all the other forms in the app, so we are not going to create it lazily. However, we will make sure that it is always created before all the other forms in the app. Select **Options** in the **Project** menu and, in the **Forms** tab, drag the data module to the top of the list of auto-created forms.

Drop TImageList onto the data module and change its Name property to ImageListMain. In short, the TImageList component has two collections of images defined in the component: Source and Destination. The Source list contains all images added to the image list components. They can be in different formats, such as BMP, PNG, JPEG, GIF, TIFF, and a few others. The images from this collection are used to construct images available in the Destination collection, which are used across the application. If you double-click on the image list component, you will be presented with the image list editor, which you can use to work with both lists of images. Images in the Destination list can be created by combining different parts of images from the Source list using layers and transparent colors. The most frequently used images are stored in the built-in buffer for faster access, as shown in *Figure 5.9*:

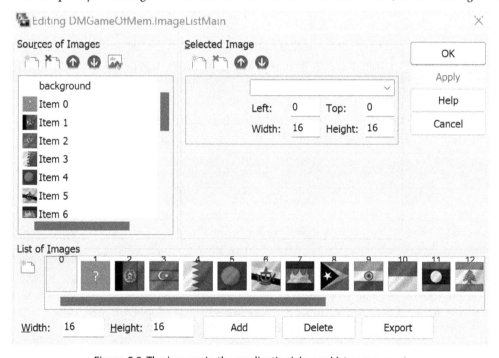

Figure 5.9: The images in the application's ImageList component

I have added 18 randomly chosen images of national flags downloaded from the public domain. They are all roughly 80 x 80 pixels large. The list at the top left contains *sources*, while the list at the bottom contains *destinations*. First, you need to add images to **Sources of Images** and then add the currently selected images in **Sources of Images** to **Destinations**. The first two images in the list are special. The first image is completely white. It is the same color as the background of the main form, so we can display it where a tile has been removed. The second image contains the back of the tile and is displayed for all hidden images. It has a white question mark on it.

Image lists are very flexible and can be very useful where different visual FireMonkey controls need to display many small images efficiently.

Designing the user interface

We now have a set of images ready to be used in the visual part of the app. In this section, we'll start building the main form for *Game of Memory*. This is where the end user will be spending most of their time un-hiding tiles and removing them from the grid.

> **Designing for multi-device**
>
> The key consideration in building mobile user interfaces with FireMonkey is the fact that our app can be compiled for different targets and it should run properly on displays with different sizes and orientations. There are different strategies to handle different screen sizes. The most powerful approach is to organize different visual controls on the form in such a way that they always work properly on screens of all possible sizes, from small mobile phones to large tablets.

Aligning, anchoring, and margins

We have already used the `Align` property a lot. Regardless of a given control size, we can instruct it to align itself with a portion or the whole area of its visual container. This is where FireMonkey parenting comes into play. When designing user interfaces, we have to decide which visual components should act as containers for other components. The relative position of the children components can be controlled with the `Align`, `Anchors`, and `Margins` properties.

`TAlignment` is an enumerated type with many values, but in practice, most of the time, we just use alignment to `Client`, `Top`, `Bottom`, `Left`, and `Right`.

The `TAnchors` property is a set of `Top`, `Bottom`, `Left`, and `Right` Boolean values that can be used to *snap* a given side of the control to its visual container. By default, a control is anchored to the top and left-hand sides of its parent. Anchors control how a visual component reacts to the resizing of its visual container. For example, if we set the `Right` anchor to `True` and make the container wider, the child control will get wider as well, preserving the original distance between the right-hand side of the control and its container. Setting just the `Bottom` and `Right` anchors to `True`, and the others to `False`, can be useful for buttons in dialog screens, where we want them to always be at the bottom-right corner of the form, regardless of their size.

The `TMargins` property has `Top`, `Bottom`, `Left`, and `Right` values that can be used to indicate the distance between a given side of the control and its visual container. It is typically used when a child control is aligned with its parent container.

Layouts

When designing the user interface in FireMonkey, we typically group controls in visual containers. FireMonkey comes with different components in the **Layouts** category in the **Tool Palette** area (you can see a list of these components in *Figure 5.10*). These controls do not have a visual representation at runtime; their sole purpose is to act as containers for other visual and non-visual controls:

Figure 5.10: FireMonkey – Layouts

The most generic is the `TLayout` component. It is just a simple container for other controls and is the most commonly used to organize FireMonkey user interfaces.

Building the main form of the game

In our game, we have a visual grid of tiles. The most natural component to use in this context is the `TGridLayout` component. Drop it on the main form of our app, change its **Name** property to `GridLayoutTiles`, and align it with `Client` so that it occupies the whole screen of the main form under the toolbar. Now, we can add other visual controls to the grid layout. The size of each item in the grid layout can be controlled with its `ItemHeight` and `ItemWidth` properties.

We are going to use the `TGlyph` component to display bitmaps from our image list in the data module. There is also the `TImage` component, which we could have used, but in this case, we would need to load bitmaps directly to every `TImage`, which is not as effective as using just one set of bitmaps. Let's get started:

1. Change the background color of the main form to white. Expand `Fill`, then change `Color` to `White` and `Kind` to `Solid`.

2. Add the `uDMGameOfMem` unit to the uses clause of the form and drop the `TGlyph` control onto the grid layout. Point its **Images** property to `DMGameOfMem.ImageListMain` and `ImageIndex` to `1`. Now, we should see the second image from the **Destination** collection of the image list displayed in the glyph control, which symbolizes a hidden tile. Change all four margins of the `Glyph` control to 2 so that there is some distance between different tiles in the grid.

3. Drop a speed button component onto the toolbar, change its `Name` property to `SpdbtnPlay`, align it to the left, and change its `StyleLookup` property to `playtoolbutton`. Resize the button horizontally to make it smaller. This should resize its width so that it will be fixed and the same as its height. Now, drop a `TLabel` component onto the toolbar. Change `Name` to `LblScore`, `Text` to `Game of Memory`, and then align it with `Client`.

4. Drop a `TComboBox` component onto the toolbar. Align it to the right. Here, we are going to control the size of the grid. Change the `Name` property of the combo to `CmbbxLevel`. In its `Items` property, enter eight levels of difficulty, starting from 4 pairs up to 18 pairs, as shown in *Figure 5.11*. We don't want this list to be too long, so difficulty levels are incremented by two pairs:

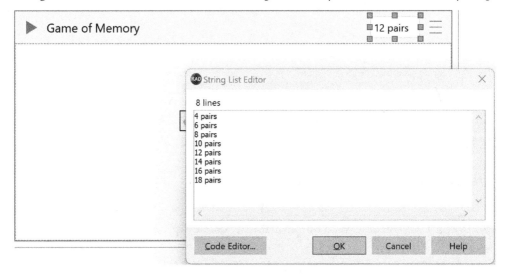

Figure 5.11: Entering the value of the combo box in the main form for Game of Memory

5. Change the `ItemIndex` property of the combo box to 4 so that the initial selection will be 12 pairs. Later, we are going to store the currently selected difficulty level in a configuration file,

so it would be handy to define a property on the form class called `CurrPairsCount` that could be used to set and get the current selection in the difficulty level combo.

This is how you can add the `CurrPairsCount` property to the form:

```
type
  TFormMain = class(TForm)
  private
    procedure SetCurrPairsCount(const Value: integer);
    function GetCurrPairsCount: Integer;
    property CurrPairsCount: Integer
      read GetCurrPairsCount write SetCurrPairsCount;
```

The following code shows how to implement the property's getter and setter methods:

```
function TformMain.GetCurrPairsCount: Integer;
begin
  Result := 4 + CmbbxLevel.ItemIndex * 2;
end;

procedure TformMain.SetCurrPairsCount(const Value: integer);
begin
  CmbbxLevel.ItemIndex := (Value - 4) div 2;
end;
```

We need a way to calculate the time that's elapsed from when the game started. Drop a `TTimer` component onto the form and change its name to `TimerGame`. Then, change `Interval` to `50`. When the timer is enabled, the game is running; when it is not enabled, the game is stopped. In the `Score` label, we will be displaying the time of the game. We will need a function to nicely format the elapsed time. Add a new unit to the project, save it as `uGameUtils`, and enter the following code in the interface section:

```
function GameTimeToStr(Value: TTime): string;
```

The actual code is in the implementation section. The `GameTimeToStr` function uses a second one for formatting:

```
function Pad3Zeros(Value: string): string; inline;
var
  I: integer;
begin
  I := Length(Value);
  if I = 3 then
    Result := Value
  else if I = 2 then
```

```
      Result := '0' + Value
    else if I = 1 then
      Result := '00' + Value
    else
      Result := '000';
  end;
```

Here is the code of the actual GameTimeToStr function:

```
function GameTimeToStr(Value: TTime): string;
var
  H, Min, Sec, Msec: Word;
  S: string;
begin
  DecodeTime(Value, H, Min, Sec, Msec);
  S := 'Time: ';
  if H > 0 then
    S := S + H.ToString + 'h ';
  if Min > 0 then
    S := S + Min.ToString + 'min ';

  S := S + Sec.ToString + '.' + Pad3Zeros(Msec.ToString) + 's';
  Result := S;
end;
```

Now, let's add a new private field called FGameStart: TTime to the form class that will store the time when the game started. Add the following code to the OnTimer event:

```
procedure TFormMain.TimerGameTimer(Sender: TObject);
begin
  var Delta := Now - FTimeStart;
  var S := GameTimeToStr(Delta);
  LblScore.Text := S;
end;
```

Now, we are going to implement the heart of the game logic. First, delete the specific glyph that we have added to the grid layout; we are going to add all the glyphs in the code.

Let's implement a GameStart method that will be called when the player touches the **Start** button and a corresponding GameEnd method:

```
procedure TFormMain.SpdbtnPlayClick(Sender: TObject);
begin
  if not TimerGame.Enabled then
    GameStart
  else
```

```
    GameEnd;
  end;
```

We will read the current number of pairs and dynamically add an appropriate number of tiles to the grid. We will also need an `OnGlyphClick` event handler; this will be attached to every glyph control so that it can react to end user touches. For this, every glyph needs to have its `HitTest` property set to `True`. We will also need a way to associate a given tile with its image. For this, we will use the `Tag` property; this is an integer value and is available for all descendants of the `TComponent` class. It can be used by programmers in situations like this. The FireMonkey library does not use the `Tag` property at all.

The first two indices in the underlying image list component are reserved for displaying either a removed or hidden tile. Depending on the number of tiles, we can create a local dynamic list of indices and write some code to randomize their order.

In the form class, we will also need a counter that specifies the number of pairs of tiles left on the board. We will also need a reference to the currently visible glyph component. The initial part of the `GameStart` method, which is the code that's executed to configure and start the game, has some configuration settings:

```
procedure TFormMain.GameStart;
const
  SHUFFLE_TIMES = 10;
var
  Indices: array of integer;
begin
  // remove all glyphs from the grid,
  // if there are any left
  GrdltTiles.DeleteChildren;

  var PairsCount := CurrPairsCount;
  var TilesCount := PairsCount * 2;

  FVisibleGlyph := nil;
  FPairsLeft := PairsCount;
```

Next, the `GameStart` method initializes the list of indices, randomizes it, and adds an offset of 2:

```
  SetLength(Indices, TilesCount);
  for var I := 0 to PairsCount-1 do
  begin
    Indices[I] := I;
    Indices[I + PairsCount] := I;
  end;
```

```
// randomize indices list
for var I := 0 to SHUFFLE_TIMES - 1 do
  for var J := 0 to TilesCount - 1 do
  begin
    var K := Random(TilesCount);
    var Temp := Indices[K];
    Indices[K] := Indices[J];
    Indices[J] := Temp;
  end;

// add "2" to every index
// because "0" and "1" are special
for var I := 0 to TilesCount-1 do
  Indices[I] := Indices[I] + 2;
```

After this step, the GameStart method creates the tiles:

```
for var I := 0 to TilesCount-1 do
begin
  var G  := TGlyph.Create(GrdltTiles);
  g.Parent := GrdltTiles;
  g.Images := DMGameOfMem.ImageListMain;
  g.ImageIndex := 1; // hidden tile
  g.Tag := indices[i]; // image index
  g.HitTest := True;
  g.OnClick := OnGlyphClick;
  G.Margins.Top := TILE_MARGIN;
  g.Margins.Left := TILE_MARGIN;
  g.Margins.Bottom := TILE_MARGIN;
  g.Margins.Right := TILE_MARGIN;
end;
```

At this point of the GameStart method, we are almost done and only need to reset some flags and buttons:

```
AdjustTileSize;

FTimeStart := Now;
TimerGame.Enabled := True;
SpdbtnPlay.StyleLookup := 'stoptoolbutton';
CmbbxLevel.Enabled := False;
```

When one of the images is clicked, the code checks various conditions and determines if we have a new match. If not, it keeps the last image as the current selection:

```
procedure TFormMain.OnGlyphClick(Sender: TObject);
begin
  if Sender is TGlyph then
  begin
    var G := TGlyph(Sender);

    if G.ImageIndex > 0 then // it is not a "removed" tile
    begin
      // if clicked on currently visible tile, do nothing
      if G <> FVisibleGlyph then
      begin
        G.ImageIndex := G.Tag; // show touched tile

        if FVisibleGlyph <> nil then // another visible tile
        begin
          // there is match, remove both tiles
          if G.Tag = FVisibleGlyph.Tag then
          begin
            G.ImageIndex := 0;
            FVisibleGlyph.ImageIndex := 0;
            FVisibleGlyph := nil;

            Dec(FPairsLeft);
            if FPairsLeft = 0 then
              GameEnd;
          end
          else // there is no match, hide previously visible tile
          begin
            FVisibleGlyph.ImageIndex := 1;
            FVisibleGlyph := G;
          end;

        end
        else
          FVisibleGlyph := G; // first tile, make this current

      end;
    end;
  end;
end;
```

When the number of pairs left reaches zero, the game ends:

```
procedure TFormMain.GameEnd;
var
  BestTime: TTime;
  S: string;
begin
  TimerGame.Enabled := False;
  var GameTime := Now - FTimeStart;
  DisplayGameTime(GameTime);
  SpdbtnPlay.StyleLookup := 'playtoolbutton';
  CmbbxLevel.Enabled := True;

  if FPairsLeft = 0 then // game was completed
  begin
    BestTime := DMGameOfMem.ReadScore(CurrPairsCount);
    if (BestTime > 0) and (GameTime > BestTime) then
      S := 'GAME FINISHED!' + sLineBreak +
        'Your time: ' + GameTimeToStr(GameTime)
    else
    begin
      S := 'YOU WON! BEST TIME!' + sLineBreak +
        'New best time: ' + GameTimeToStr(GameTime);
      DMGameOfMem.SaveScore(GameTime, CurrPairsCount);
    end;
    ShowMessage(S);
  end;
end;
```

A nice thing about using glyphs is that they scale easily. Once all the tiles have been loaded into the grid, we need to adjust their sizes. First of all, there could be a different number of image pairs and we could be running our game on different display sizes. The logic to calculate the size of the glyph has been implemented in a separate `AdjustTileSize` method that is also called from the `OnFormResize` events. On mobile targets, this event is fired when the end user changes the orientation of the screen, while on desktops, the form's size changes every time. Here is the code of the `AdjustTileSize` method:

```
procedure TFormMain.AdjustTileSize;
const
  ADJUST_FACTOR = 0.9;
begin
  // adjust the size of every tile in the grid
  var TileArea := GrdltTiles.Width * GrdltTiles.Height /
    CurrPairsCount / 2;
```

```
  var TileSize := (sqrt(TileArea) - 2 * TILE_MARGIN)
    * ADJUST_FACTOR;
  GrdltTiles.ItemHeight := TileSize;
  GrdltTiles.ItemWidth := TileSize;
end;
```

This code helps the app adapt the display to the device's size (and orientation).

Storing the game's configuration

The last part is to implement the functionality to remember the currently selected difficulty level and to keep track of top scores. We are going to add private `FIniFile: TIniFile` fields from the `System.IniFiles` unit to the game's data module. In the `OnCreate` event of the data module, we will instantiate this class and free it in the `OnDestroy` event. The constructor of the `INI` file object requires us to specify the path and filename. In our case, this will be the `Documents` folder on a given target platform.

Storing app configuration information in an `INI` file is very convenient. The `TIniFile` class has read and write methods for getting and setting values of different types, such as strings, numbers, time, and so on. An `INI` file is a plain text file with key-value pairs organized into sections.

We are going to declare two public methods in the data module class for reading and writing the top times for different difficulty levels. If there is no top score, we will enter `-1` as a special value. We will also use the `ClearAllScores` method to remove all top scores:

```
type
  TDMGameOfMem = class(TDataModule)
    ImageListMain: TImageList;
    procedure DataModuleCreate(Sender: TObject);
    procedure DataModuleDestroy(Sender: TObject);
  private
    FIniFile: TIniFile;
  public
    procedure SaveScore(GameTime: TTime; APairsCount: Integer);
    function ReadScore(APairsCount: Integer): TTime;
    procedure ClearAllScores;
    procedure SaveCurrLevel(aPairsCount: Integer);
    function ReadCurrLevel: Integer;
  end;
```

The last two methods will be for remembering the currently selected difficulty level, so the end user doesn't need to change it every time the app is started. To implement these methods, we need some constant values:

```
const
  StrSCORES = 'SCORES';
  StrLEVEL = 'LEVEL';
  StrSETTINGS = 'SETTINGS';
  StrCURRLEVEL = 'CURR_LEVEL';
```

When the data module starts up, we create the `FIniFile` object, which is later cleared in the `OnDestroy` event handler:

```
procedure TDMGameOfMem.DataModuleCreate(Sender: TObject);
var
  Filename: string;
begin
  Filename := TPath.Combine(TPath.GetDocumentsPath,
    MEM_GAME_CONFIG);
  FIniFile := TIniFile.Create(Filename);
end;


procedure TDMGameOfMem.DataModuleDestroy(Sender: TObject);
begin
  FIniFile.Free;
end;
```

To save the scores or read them, all we have to do is write to the INI file or read from it:

```
procedure TDMGameOfMem.SaveScore(GameTime: TTime;
  APairsCount: Integer);
begin
  FIniFile.WriteTime(StrSCORES, StrLEVEL +
    APairsCount.ToString, GameTime);
  FIniFile.UpdateFile;
end;


function TDMGameOfMem.ReadScore(APairsCount: Integer): TTime;
begin
  Result := FIniFile.ReadTime(StrSCORES, StrLEVEL +
    APairsCount.ToString, -1);
end;
```

The data module also offers methods to clear all scores (resetting the INI file's content) and to save and read the current level:

```
procedure TDMGameOfMem.ClearAllScores;
begin
  FIniFile.EraseSection(StrSCORES);
  FIniFile.UpdateFile;
end;

procedure TDMGameOfMem.SaveCurrLevel(APairsCount: Integer);
begin
  FIniFile.WriteInteger(StrSETTINGS, StrCURRLEVEL, aPairsCount);
  FIniFile.UpdateFile;
end;

function TDMGameOfMem.ReadCurrLevel: Integer;
begin
  Result := FIniFile.ReadInteger(StrSETTINGS, StrCURRLEVEL, 4);
end;
```

Changes to an INI file are kept in memory. To save them in the file, we need to call the `UpdateFile` method every time, as shown in the preceding code.

In the main form's `OnCreate` event, we are going to add code to read the last used difficulty level, while in the combo box's `OnChange` event, we are going to save the currently selected difficulty level:

```
procedure TFormMain.FormCreate(Sender: TObject);
begin
  CurrPairsCount := DMGameOfMem.ReadCurrLevel;
end;

procedure TFormMain.CmbbxLevelChange(Sender: TObject);
begin
  DMGameOfMem.SaveCurrLevel(CurrPairsCount);
end;
```

With this code, we can manage scores and keep them persistent across subsequent executions of the app.

The game's settings form

Our game is almost complete. We are storing top scores for different levels, but there is no place to see them. This is the purpose of the game's settings form:

1. Drop a label component on the `FormSettings` toolbar and align it with `Client`. Change its `Text` property to `Top Scores`.

2. Now, drop a `TButton` component onto the toolbar and align it to the right. Change its **Name** property to `BtnClear` and its **Text** property to `Clear All`.

3. Drop a `TComboBox` property onto the form. Align it to **Client**. Then, change its **Margins** property to 8 so that there is a nice border around it. Right-click on the list box and select the **Add TListBoxItem** option to add the first item to the list box. Change its **StyleLookup** property to `listboxitemrightdetail`. Expand the **ItemData** property and enter 4 Pairs in the **Text** property. The **Detail** property is where we are going to display the best time for a given difficulty level. Right-click on the list box item and select **Copy** from the **Edit** menu. Paste the list box item seven times into the list box and adjust the **Text** property of every item. Change their names so that they correspond with the number of pairs: lbi04, lbi06, lbi08, and so on until lbi18.

> **Note**
>
> List boxes are great for all kinds of static information. You can easily set them up at design time. For dynamic information, such as that coming from a database, it is much better to use `TListView` components.

4. Add the `uDMGameOfMem` unit to the uses clause of the **Settings** form. Implement a `ReadTopScores` private method in the form class to display all top scores in the list box. Double-click on the `OnShow` event of the form and enter a call to the `ReadTopScores` method. In the `OnClick` event of the button, we will call the method to clear all scores:

```
uses
  uFormMain, uDMGameOfMem, uGameUtils;


procedure TFormSettings.FormShow(Sender: TObject);
begin
  ReadTopScores;
end;


procedure TFormSettings.btnClearClick(Sender: TObject);
begin
  DMGameOfMem.ClearAllScores;
  ReadTopScores;
end;


procedure TFormSettings.ReadTopScores;


procedure ShowScore(Lbi: TListBoxItem; Level: integer);
begin
  var T: TTime := DMGameOfMem.ReadScore(Level);
  if T > 0 then
```

```
      Lbi.ItemData.Detail := GameTimeToStr(T)
    else
      Lbi.ItemData.Detail := '';
  end;

begin
  ShowScore(lbi04, 4);
  ShowScore(lbi06, 6);
  ShowScore(lbi08, 8);
  ShowScore(lbi10, 10);
  ShowScore(lbi12, 12);
  ShowScore(lbi14, 14);
  ShowScore(lbi16, 16);
  ShowScore(lbi18, 18);
end;

procedure TFormSettings.SpdbtnBackClick(Sender: TObject);
begin
  FormMain.Show;

end;
```

Figure 5.12 shows what the game looks like on Windows with a regular wide layout:

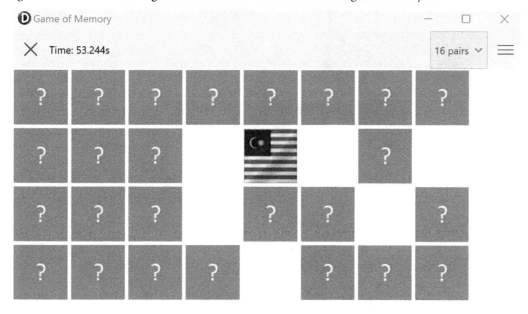

Figure 5.12: Game of Memory running on Windows

In contrast, *Figure 5.13* shows the same app running on an Android device with a vertical layout:

Figure 5.13: Game of Memory running on Android

That's it! We've just implemented our first mobile game in Delphi. Congratulations!

Summary

In this chapter, we learned some of the fundamentals of FireMonkey 2D programming. Starting from writing low-level code for drawing on the canvas, we quickly learned the fundamentals of rapid app development with reusable shapes, animations, and timers. This is where Delphi shines! At this point, you are on your way to becoming a developer superhero who writes less code to achieve better results.

In the next chapter, we are going to add an additional dimension to what we have seen so far and dive into the realm of FireMonkey 3D.

6

FireMonkey in 3D

FireMonkey user interface controls offer a powerful multi-platform and multi-device development solution based on a single source code, with Delphi offering you the ability to build a native app for each target operating system. There are other solutions in this space, some of them more popular, even if not as powerful. What is unique to Delphi is having a component library, similar to the 2D one, for 3D programming. With FireMonkey, we can create fully cross-platform GPU-powered GUIs, based on a specific 3D API on each platform.

In this chapter, we are going to add the third dimension to our FireMonkey projects. We will cover the following points:

- Cross-platform 3D rendering
- Direct use of Context3D
- Ready-to-use 3D objects
- Mixing 3D and 2D

The objective of this chapter is to learn FireMonkey 3D programming and how to build interactive cross-platform 3D GUIs. As usual, we'll do this by going over demos – showcasing different approaches.

Technical requirements

The examples in this chapter work in any version of Delphi. Their complete source is available at the following link: `https://github.com/PacktPublishing/Expert-Delphi_Second-edition`

Cross-platform 3D rendering

Similar to the 2D side, abstracting away the underlying 3D API from the programmer is the foundation of FireMonkey 3D graphics architecture. On top of this basis, there is the second pillar: rapid application development with components. The FireMonkey framework comes with pre-built reusable 3D components that make it easy to write complex 3D applications.

In FireMonkey, it is very easy to create sophisticated, GPU-powered 3D user interfaces using reusable visual components that let you focus on your business application logic instead of spending time on writing low-level 3D API code.

There are different 3D APIs available on different operating systems supported by the FireMonkey library. The standard API for rendering 3D graphics on mobile targets is a cut-down version of the **OpenGL** library, called **OpenGL ES**. On desktop targets, FireMonkey supports DirectX on Windows and full OpenGL on Mac. All these APIs have different interfaces and abstractions, but the FireMonkey library provides one common denominator for writing cross-platform 3D apps using just one code base.

The key abstraction in FireMonkey 3D graphics is the `TContext3D` class, which declares virtual drawing methods that are implemented differently on different targets. This is a similar architecture to FireMonkey 2D rendering, where the abstract `TCanvas` class has different implementations on each of the supported operating systems.

Writing 3D apps is considered a domain for professional developers because it involves understanding low-level 3D mathematics and interacting with the **Graphics Processing Unit (GPU)**. The component-based development of Delphi hides the underlying complexity of 3D coding and you can create highly interactive and visually rich 3D apps with very little to no coding at all.

FireMonkey provides a 3D material system that is based on GPU shader programs. You do not have to be an expert in writing DirectX HLSL or OpenGL shader code to create high-performance 3D graphics applications. In the FireMonkey framework, applying a different shading model is a matter of using a dedicated material component that can be just attached to a 3D object control that represents a specific geometry.

Direct use of Context3D

Similar to FireMonkey 2D architecture, there are two possible approaches to 3D rendering. We can render in code or use reusable components. The first path is what is used by many other programming languages and development environments, and it is what we are going to cover in the first part of this chapter. The main issue is that the more complex and sophisticated our 3D visualization is, the more complex our 3D rendering code becomes.

Using **rapid application development** with components very quickly pays off as we typically do not need to write too much code to build a great user experience with interactive 3D worlds. This is what we are going to focus on later in the chapter.

As mentioned, the main interface for calling 3D APIs in a cross-platform way in FireMonkey is the `TContext3D` class. For this reason, let's start by building a simple project that is going to use the `TContext3D` class directly in code.

The starting point is to create a new Delphi multi-device project and select **3D Application** as the application template. As usual, save the main form unit as `uFormCubeInCode` and the whole project as `CubeInCode`. Finally, change the `Name` property of the form to `FormCubeInCode` and press **Save All** again.

If you look into the source of the form, you'll see that this time the main form class is derived from TForm3D and not TForm:

```
type
  TFormCubeInCode = class(TForm3D)
  . . .
```

One of the best things about Delphi is that we can quickly inspect the source code of classes and types that come with it. Just right-click on the TForm3D identifier and select **Find Declaration**. You will jump to the FMX.Forms3D unit where this class is defined. The ancestor of the 3D form class is TCustomForm3D, which implements the IViewport3D interface. This interface among other members has the Context : TContext3D property. We can use this property to access the underlying 3D context of the form in our code. An even more straightforward way to access the 3D context is to use the OnRender event of the TForm3D class, which receives the context as one of its parameters.

To proceed in this direction, just double-click on the OnRender event of the 3D form. Remember, we need to enclose all rendering code with calls to BeginScene and EndScene. For this reason, the base structure of the event handler should look like the following code block:

```
procedure TFormCubeInCode.Form3DRender(Sender: TObject;
  Context: TContext3D);
begin
  Context.BeginScene;
  try
    // access context 3D methods and properties here
  finally
    Context.EndScene;
  end;
end;
```

If you right-click on the Context3D parameter and select the option to find its declaration, you can inspect the available operations. This time, we'll navigate to the FMX.Types3D unit, in which we can find the TContext3D class. It is defined as an **abstract** class because it serves as the interface to the functionality that is implemented by different platform-specific classes inherited from it that override its abstract virtual methods. There are quite a number of low-level functions for drawing different geometries and dealing with states, shaders, materials, and more. It has to be like this because 3D APIs, such as OpenGL and DirectX, are relatively complex. Luckily, we generally do not need to write code at such a low level. Only if we want to do something beyond what FireMonkey 3D classes provide, we can do it here; most of the time, we will be dealing with higher-level abstractions for working in 3D.

Within the TContext3D class public methods, there is a section with higher-level drawing primitives, indicated by the { drawing } comment. These include methods such as DrawTriangles, DrawLines, and DrawPoints, but also FillCube, DrawCube, and FillPolygon, to mention just a few.

We can use them to quickly render typical geometries such as lines, rectangles, polygons, or cubes in 3D. To start, let's draw a cube. Enter this line of code between the BeginScene and EndScene lines in the OnRender event of the form:

```
Context.DrawCube(Point3D(0,0,0), Point3D(10,10,10),
    1, TAlphaColorRec.Black);
```

If we run the application with this code only, there will be just an empty white space (or actually, a tiny cube at the form's upper-left corner). This is because the OnRender event has not been called with the form at its actual resolution. We need a mechanism to call it and we can use a TTimer component. Add one to the project and its OnTimer event will just call the Invalidate method of the form to force its re-rendering, as in the following code block:

```
procedure TFormCubeInCode.Timer1Timer(Sender: TObject);
begin
  Invalidate;
end;
```

If we kept the default timer's Interval value of 1000 milliseconds, the black wireframe cube (see *Figure 6.1*) should show up just exactly one second after the app starts and will get refreshed after we resize the form.

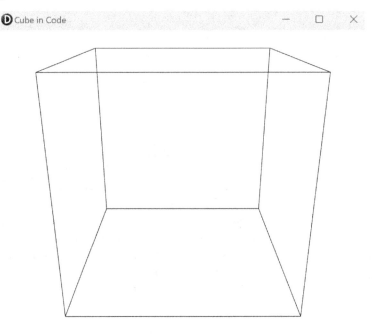

Figure 6.1: A 3D cube drawn with a single line of code

Now that we have seen how to create a cube with direct API calls, let's do the same using a component.

Using a cube component

Although we want to focus this first part of the chapter on direct coding, let's do a quick experiment to show the alternative approach offered by FireMonkey. Let's create a new 3D app, which I'm going to call CubeWithComp. In this case, we won't add any code. Just drop a TStrokeCube component on the form. Change its Color property to Black and its Width, Height, and Depth properties to 10. The form at design time in the Delphi IDE should look like *Figure 6.2*.

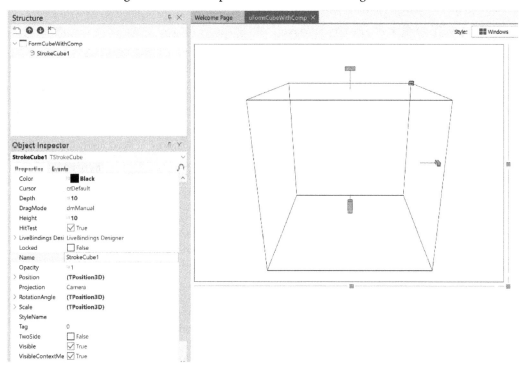

Figure 6.2: A 3D cube at design time

If we run the app, we should see exactly the same wireframe of a cube as the previous example, but this time without writing any code. In fact, we are using a component that encapsulates the call to the DrawCube method of the 3D context. We can make sure this is the case by jumping to the declaration of the TStrokeCube class, navigating to its Render method, and seeing it implemented almost identically to our custom code in the previous app, as you can see here:

```
procedure TStrokeCube.Render;
begin
  Context.DrawCube(
    TPoint3D.Zero,
    TPoint3D.Create(Width, Height, Depth),
```

```
      AbsoluteOpacity, FColor);
  end;
```

Using components for 3D rendering makes you a more productive programmer, given you only have to configure some properties rather than write a large amount of fairly complex code. However, before we get deeper into the components, we want to improve our understanding of how FireMonkey 3D works by delving into its details a bit more.

A custom wireframe component

The source code of FireMonkey is very helpful in understanding how the library works, but we can also use it as a template to build our own custom components. Rendering a cube doesn't require a lot of code, but using a similar approach, we could create a custom wireframe component similar to TStrokeCube. All we need to do is to implement the Render method differently and paint arbitrary lines, using coordinates stored internally within our component.

To do this experiment, create a new Delphi multi-device application and select **3D Application** as the application type. This time, save the main form unit as uFormWireframe and the whole project as WireframeTest. Rename the form FormWireframe and save all files.

To better structure the code, add a new unit to the project and save it as uWireframe. Here, we are going to implement a custom component called TWireframe that, similar to TStrokeCube, inherits from the TControl3D class and renders an arbitrary wireframe by drawing lines.

Drawing a wireframe is based on just two data structures. We need a list of vertices, which are points in the 3D space, and a list of edges, which represent lines to be drawn. Each edge contains two indices in the list of vertices, with the index of the starting and ending points of the line. Let's start by defining these two data structures in the uWireframe unit with the following code:

```
uses
  System.Math.Vectors, // TPoint3D
  System.Generics.Collections; // TList<T>

type
  TPoints3D = class(TList<TPoint3D>);

  TEdge = record
    A, B: Integer;
  end;

  TEdges = class(TList<TEdge>)
    procedure AddEdge(PStart, PEnd: Integer);
  end;
```

The `TEdges` list class has a convenience method, `AddEdge`, for simplifying code that adds a new edge to it:

```
procedure TEdges.AddEdge(PStart, PEnd: Integer);
var
  Edge: TEdge;
begin
  Edge.A := PStart;
  Edge.B := PEnd;
  Add(Edge);
end;
```

Next, we need to declare a new `TWireframe` class derived from `TControl3D`. It will have two properties for the points and the edges, based on the data types just declared, `TPoints3D` and `TEdges`. These are read-only public properties for accessing the wireframe, as you can see in the following class declaration:

```
type
  TWireframe = class(TControl3D)
  private
    FDrawColor: TAlphaColor;
    FEdges: TEdges;
    FPoints3D: TPoints3D;
    FDisplayed: Boolean;
  public
    constructor Create(AOwner: TComponent); override;
    destructor Destroy; override;
    procedure Render; override;
    property DrawColor: TAlphaColor
      read FDrawColor write FDrawColor;
    property Points3D: TPoints3D read FPoints3D;
    property Edges: TEdges read FEdges;
    property Displayed: Boolean read FDisplayed write FDisplayed;
  end;
```

In the constructor, we need to instantiate these lists and free them in the destructor, as in the following code:

```
constructor TWireframe.Create(AOwner: TComponent);
begin
  inherited Create(AOwner);
  FPoints3D := TPoints3D.Create;
  FEdges := TEdges.Create;
```

```
    FDrawColor := TAlphaColorRec.Red;
    FDisplayed := True;
  end;


destructor TWireframe.Destroy;
begin
  FEdges.Free;
  FPoints3D.Free;
  inherited;
end;
```

The actual drawing happens in the overridden virtual `Render` method. In the `for..in` loop of this method, we draw all lines defined in the `Edges` list using a color defined by `DrawColor` property:

```
procedure TWireframe.Render;
var
  Edge: TEdge;
begin
  if Displayed then
    for Edge in Edges do
      Context.DrawLine(Points3D[Edge.A],
        Points3D[Edge.B], 1, DrawColor);
end;
```

Now, we need to test whether this class is actually working. Instead of creating a new package, installing this component in the IDE, and so on, we can quickly test the wireframe class by declaring it as a field in the main form of our app, `TFormWireframe`, as you can see in the form class declaration here, which includes an additional `CreatePyramid` method to define the specific wireframe 3D points:

```
type
  TFormWireframe = class(TForm3D)
    procedure Form3DCreate(Sender: TObject);
    procedure Form3DDestroy(Sender: TObject);
  private
    FWireframe: TWireframe;
    procedure CreatePyramid;
  end;
```

We can create and free the wireframe component instance in the form's OnCreate and OnDestroy events. Remember that in order to properly display this control, we need to assign its Parent property to the form itself:

```
procedure TFormWireframe.Form3DCreate(Sender: TObject);
begin
  FWireframe := TWireframe.Create(Self);
  FWireframe.Parent := Self;
  FWireframe.RotationAngle.Point := Point3D(75, 10, 15);

  CreatePyramid;
end;


procedure TFormWireframe.Form3DDestroy(Sender: TObject);
begin
  FWireframe.Free;
end;
```

As mentioned, the specific data for the 3D wireframe is set up in the CreatePyramid method:

```
procedure TFormWireframe.CreatePyramid;
begin
  with FWireframe do
  begin
    Points3D.Add(Point3D(-2,-2,0)); // 0
    Points3D.Add(Point3D(2,-2,0));  // 1
    Points3D.Add(Point3D(-2,2,0));  // 2
    Points3D.Add(Point3D(2,2,0));   // 3
    Points3D.Add(Point3D(0,0,6));   // 4

    Edges.AddEdge(0,1);
    Edges.AddEdge(1,3);
    Edges.AddEdge(3,2);
    Edges.AddEdge(2,0);
    Edges.AddEdge(0,4);
    Edges.AddEdge(1,4);
    Edges.AddEdge(2,4);
    Edges.AddEdge(3,4);
  end;
end;
```

We need to create four points (numbered 0 to 3 in the comments) for the four corners of the pyramid base and one point for the top (4). Next, we need to draw edges connecting the four base corners on each side and finally four edges from each of the four corners of the base to the top. You need all of this complicated code to build a simple pyramid wireframe, as you can see in *Figure 6.3*.

Figure 6.3: A wireframe component showing a pyramid

Notice that in the OnCreate event handler, there is an extra line of code executed after the wireframe is created. This is used to slightly rotate it by setting its RotationAngle property, so it looks better on screen.

Ready-to-use 3D objects

In the first part of this chapter, we looked into some of the low-level and direct APIs for building 3D apps in FireMonkey. Now let's start looking in more detail into the ready-to-use components.

There are different 3D objects that we can use in our Delphi FireMonkey apps, from really simple ones, such as TStrokeCube or TGrid3D, that just render a few lines in 3D space, to more complex components that maintain their own vertex and index buffers for drawing complex geometries with triangles. This is a typical approach for rendering arbitrary geometries in 3D apps such as mobile games and it requires quite a lot of coding.

At the lowest level, all 3D objects inherit from the TControl3D class, which introduces location and transformations in 3D space. This class also adds interactivity to all 3D controls by implementing different *mouse* events that are translated to *touch* events on mobile targets. These user events have different parameters that provide the application code information about where such an event happened in 3D space.

The `TShape3D` class inherits from the `TControl3D` class, adding support for material components. All classes derived from a 3D shape have the `MaterialSource` property, which can be used to connect any component that inherits from the `TMaterialSource` class. Material components implement different shading models used for rendering. Specific classes such as `TText3D`, `TPath3D`, `TEllipse3D`, or `TRectangle3D` inherit from `TShape3D` and can work with materials.

You can find a complete class hierarchy of the 3D classes and components (and all other classes and components) in FireMonkey at `https://docwiki.embarcadero.com/RADStudio/en/ FireMonkey_Component_Library`.

The Moving Earth app

We are going to start with something simple and create an interactive 3D visualization of the rotating Earth in deep space. To make it interactive, we will implement a 3D touch event to move Earth closer and further from the viewer. This first example will be as minimal as possible to demonstrate how quickly you can build a 3D app with FireMonkey.

Create a new Delphi multi-device project and select **3D Application** as the application type. Save the form unit as `uFormEarth` and the project as `MovingEarth`. Change the `Name` property of the form to `FormEarth` and its `Color` to `Black`.

The next step is to add a `TDummy` component to the form. This component acts as a container for other 3D components and is very useful for applying a common transformation to a group of 3D objects. It does not have any visual representation at runtime. In the FireMonkey 2D world, the `TLayout` component plays a similar role. Like in 2D, in the world of FireMonkey 3D the concept of **parenting** is also very important. Most FireMonkey components can *own* other components, and owned components inherit different properties from their owners, including geometrical transformation, such as moving, scaling, and rotations. For this reason, it is a common pattern to use a `TDummy` component as a parent for all other visual and non-visual 3D objects. In this way, we have one central point for manipulating the 3D scene as a whole, changing its position, rotation, and so on.

Getting back to the steps for building the demo, drop the `TDummy` component on the form. Change its `Name` property to `DummyScene`. Next, drop a `TSphere` component on the form and make sure that it belongs to the root dummy control. Rename the sphere to `SphereEarth`. Let's make the Earth bigger. Select the root dummy component in **Object Inspector**. Expand its `Scale` property and change all three `X`, `Y`, and `Z` values to 5. Notice that the contained sphere changed its size. In this way, we control the scale, rotation, and position of all 3D objects that make up the scene.

Now drop a `TTextureMaterialSource` component on the form and connect it with the sphere using the `MaterialSource` property of the `SphereEarth` object. Click on the ellipsis button next to the `Texture` property (see *Figure 6.4*) and click on **Edit**.

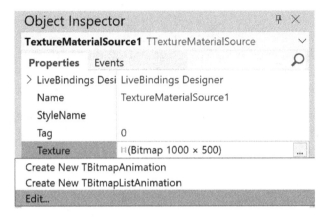

Figure 6.4: Selecting a file to use as a material

This will show a dialog box where we can load a bitmap to be used as texture. There are some free textures of Earth available for download on the internet. I have downloaded one from `http://visibleearth.nasa.gov/` and saved it locally as `Earth.jpg`.

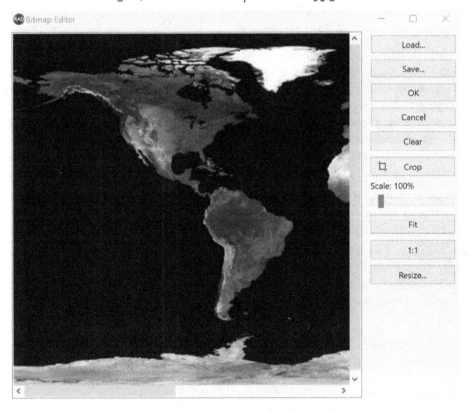

Figure 6.5: Selecting the image for the 3D sphere

Click on the **Load...** button, select the texture image (as you can see in *Figure 6.5*), and click on **OK**. You should now see the sphere object with a nice Earth texture applied, as in *Figure 6.6*.

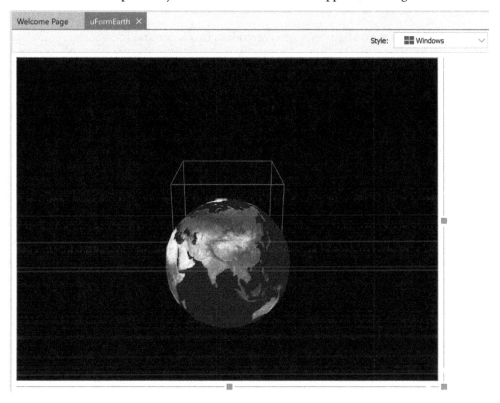

Figure 6.6: The bitmap applied to the 3D sphere at design time in Delphi

It already looks nice, but let's add some movement and interactivity to this visualization.

Drop a `TFloatAnimation` component on the form. In the **Structure** view, drag it onto the `EarthSphere` component, as visible in *Figure 6.7*.

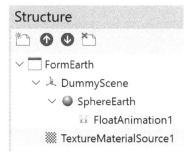

Figure 6.7: Adding a FloatAnimation as a child of the sphere object

Now expand its `PropertyName` property and you will see all float properties that belong to the `TSphere` class. Select the `RotationAngle.Y` property, because we want Earth to rotate around its vertical axis.

Make sure that the float animation is selected in **Object Inspector** and then change some of its properties. Set `Enabled` and `Loop` to `True`. Change `Duration` to 5 seconds (that's the time for a complete rotation) and `StopValue` to `-360`. Save all and run the application. We now have a spinning Earth and so far we have not written a single line of code!

The last step will be adding some basic interactivity to our app. When the end user touches the Earth on the screen, it will move either closer or further in space. By default, when we drop 3D objects onto the 3D view, their position is at the beginning of the coordinate system. In FireMonkey, the X axis increases to the right side of the screen, the Y axis increases down the screen, and Z goes into the screen. We will be changing the `Position.Z` property in the code to move the object closer or far. If you change the `Position.Z` property of the sphere to `-1`, the Earth moves closer. If we change it to a positive value, it would go further.

To implement this, double-click on the sphere's `OnClick` event. This will be translated to a touch event on a mobile target. In order to achieve a better visual effect, we will not be changing the Z position immediately, but with an animation. Enter the following code into the `OnClick` event handler:

```
procedure TFormEarth.SphereEarthClick(Sender: TObject);
begin
  if SphereEarth.Position.Z < 0 then
    TAnimator.AnimateFloat(SphereEarth, 'Position.Z', 1, 0.2)
  else
    TAnimator.AnimateFloat(SphereEarth, 'Position.Z', -1, 0.2);
end;
```

This is another way of using animations in FireMonkey. We can use an animation component or we can use one of the different `Animate` class methods of the `TAnimator` class and specify the object and its property we want to animate, the final value, and the duration of the animation. This class is declared in the `FMX.Ani` unit, but it was already automatically added to the `uses` clause of our form because we added a `TFloatAnimation` component earlier.

You can now run the application. If you touch the spinning Earth, it will move either further away from or closer to you. We can now deploy this app to an iOS device and an Android device (as you can see in *Figure 6.8*) to verify that it works as expected on these target platforms as well.

Figure 6.8: The Moving Earth app on an Android phone

This is the power of cross-platform FireMonkey 3D development. We have quickly created an interactive 3D app with a custom texture, with almost no coding. This app can be compiled as a native application for all supported mobile and desktop platforms.

Building an interactive 3D scene

In the first example, we wanted to keep things simple. This time, we are going to build an interactive visualization of three 3D arrows marking the beginning and orientation of the 3D coordinate system used in FireMonkey. For this, we will just use some cylinder and cone 3D objects, color materials, lights, and an explicit TCamera component. We will also see how to implement looking at the scene from different points of view and distances.

Create a new Delphi multi-device project. This time, make sure to select the **Blank Application** template and not **3D Application**. Save the form unit as uFormArrows3D and the project as Arrows3D. Change the Name property of the form to FormArrows3D.

Now drop a TViewport3D component on the form and align it to Client. This component can be found in the special **Viewports** category in **Palette**.

This approach represents another way of building 3D visualizations. We can use either a 3D form that directly implements the IViewport3D interface or we can use a TViewport3D component placed on a traditional 2D form. This second approach is more common and offers more flexibility. Specifically, the TForm3D class does not support multi-touch and gesture events, which are critical for delivering a proper user experience on mobile targets.

Another change is that this time we are going to use an explicit TCamera component that will allow us to view the scene from different locations. This requires a few steps:

1. Drop a TDummy component on the form and change its Name to DummyCamera.

2. Drop a TCamera component on the form and change its Name property to CameraZ.

3. In the **Structure** view, drag the camera component onto the DummyCamera component.

4. By default, a camera component has position 0, 0, -5 and looks along the Z axis. Change the camera's Position.Z property to -10 to move it closer to the edge of the form.

    Now by changing the RotationAngle of the dummy component that the camera belongs to, we will be changing the location of the camera in 3D space and it will be constantly looking at the beginning of the coordinate system where we are going to place our scene. By changing the Z position of the camera, we will be able to look at the scene from a closer or further distance, effectively making the visualization appear smaller or bigger. It is a kind of "selfie stick" that our camera is attached to. When the user is going to move their finger horizontally across the screen, we will be changing the DummyCamera rotation angle along the Y axis. Moving the touch point vertically will change the rotation along the X axis. The interactive zoom gesture will increase and decrease the Position.Z property of the camera.

5. Drop a TLight component on the form and drag it onto the camera in the **Structure** view. It is a common practice to put at least one light component onto the camera, so it is always in the same position as the camera. There are three different light types that can be used. We will keep the default LightType property as Directional. The other two possible values are Point and Spot.

In general, there could be more than one camera component. The one that is used for rendering needs to be connected to the Camera property of the viewport or the 3D form. There is also a built-in design camera that we have used so far.

1. Set the UsingDesignCamera property of the viewport to False and change its Camera property, so it is pointing to our explicit camera component.

   Now we are going to build the scene.

2. Drop a TDummy component on the form and change its name to DummyScene.

3. Let's add three colored arrows representing three space dimensions. Drop a TCylinder component on the form. Make sure that it belongs to the dummy scene component. Change its Name to CylX.

4. We need to make it a bit longer and thinner and correctly orientate in space. Change its Height property to 4 and its Width and Depth values to 0.1.

5. Change its RotationAngle.Z property to 270, so it is located along the X axis.

6. Now drop a TCone component on the form and make sure it belongs to the CylX component. Change its Name to ConeX. Change its Height property to 0.5 and its Width and Depth properties to 0.2. Set the Position.Y property to 2 and RotationAngle.X to 180. Now we have a really nice arrow!

7. Make sure that the CylX component is selected on the form and copy and paste it into the DummyScene component. Rename the cylinder to CylY and the cone to ConeY.

8. Change the RotationAngle.X property of the new cylinder to 180 and its Z part to 0. We have the second arrow.

9. Now paste the cylinder with the cone one more time into the dummy scene component. Change the names of both new components to CylZ and ConeZ and change the RotationAngle.X property of the cylinder to 90.

   We have the geometry right, but all components are red. We need to attach some materials to 3D objects. Every arrow will have a different color.

10. Drop three TLightMaterialSource components on the form. Change their names to MaterialSourceX, MaterialSourceY, and MaterialSourceZ.

11. Change the DiffuseColor property of the first one to Red, the second one to Green, and the third one to Blue. Now set the MaterialSource properties of cylinders and cones to their respective materials. Immediately we should see that our arrows now have different colors. That looks much better, as you can see in *Figure 6.9*!

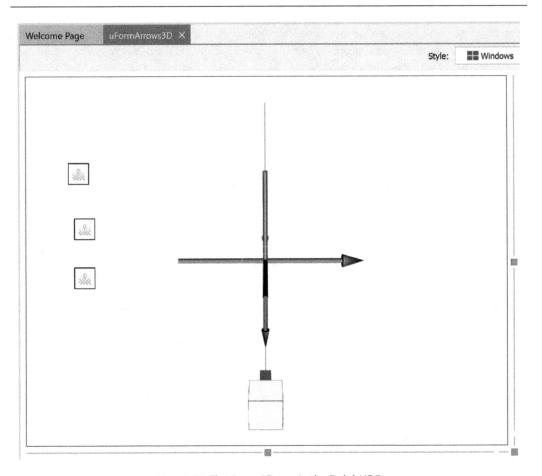

Figure 6.9: The Arrow3D app in the Delphi IDE

After all of these steps, you should see in the **Structure** view of Delphi the component hierarchy of *Figure 6.10*. You can compare your code to that of the Arrows3D project on GitHub.

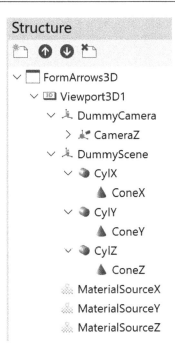

Figure 6.10: The hierarchy of FMX objects in the Arrow3D app

The last step is to add code to move the camera. We are going to use the OnMouseDown and OnMouseMove events to achieve the illusion of rotation. In fact, the scene will remain in the same position, but we will be changing the position of the camera in 3D space. We can do this by doing the following steps:

1. Add an FDown: TPointF private field to the form class. Here we are going to store the location of the last touch point on the screen.

2. Double-click on the OnMouseDown and OnMouseMove events of the viewport component. Enter the following code into event handlers:

```
const
  ROTATION_STEP = 0.3;

procedure TFormArrows3D.Viewport3D1MouseDown(Sender: TObject;
  Button: TMouseButton; Shift: TShiftState; X, Y: Single);
begin
  FDown := PointF(X, Y);
end;

procedure TFormArrows3D.Viewport3D1MouseMove(Sender: TObject;
  Shift: TShiftState; X, Y: Single);
```

```
begin
  if (ssLeft in Shift) then
  begin
    DummyCamera.RotationAngle.X :=
      DummyCamera.RotationAngle.X - ((Y - FDown.Y) *
      ROTATION_STEP);
    DummyCamera.RotationAngle.Y :=
      DummyCamera.RotationAngle.Y + ((X - FDown.X) *
      ROTATION_STEP);
    FDown := PointF(X, Y);
  end;
end;
```

Now you can save all and run the application. The orientation of arrows changes when we use the mouse on Windows or touch on a mobile target, as you can see in *Figure 6.11*.

Figure 6.11: The Arrow3D app running on Windows

The very last thing to implement is zooming. This feature works differently on desktop and on mobile. On desktop, we can use the OnMouseWheel event, and on mobile an interactive zoom gesture.

Let's centralize the actual zooming code in one method that we are going to call from different event handlers, depending on the platform. The method is called DoZoom:

```
const
  ZOOM_STEP = 2;
```

```
  CAMERA_MAX_Z = -2;
  CAMERA_MIN_Z = -102;


procedure TFormArrows3D.DoZoom(AIn: Boolean);
var
  NewZ: Single;
begin
  if AIn then
    NewZ := CameraZ.Position.Z + ZOOM_STEP
  else
    NewZ := CameraZ.Position.Z - ZOOM_STEP;

  if (NewZ < CAMERA_MAX_Z) and (NewZ > CAMERA_MIN_Z) then
    CameraZ.Position.Z := NewZ;
end;
```

The CAMERA_MIN_Z and CAMERA_MAX_Z constants are used to avoid moving the camera into positive Z values or too far away from the scene.

The implementation of the mouse wheel event is very straightforward. We either zoom in or out, depending on the wheel move direction:

```
procedure TFormArrows3D.Viewport3D1MouseWheel(Sender: TObject;
  Shift: TShiftState; WheelDelta: Integer; var Handled: Boolean);
begin
  DoZoom(WheelDelta > 0);
end;
```

On mobile platforms, there is niether a mouse nor a scroll wheel. The most natural way of handling zoom is through an interactive gesture event. As one of the event parameters, we will get the distance between the two touch points. If this distance decreases, we want to zoom in, otherwise we will zoom out. That's why we will need a new private field declared in the FLastDistance: Integer form class where we are going to store the last distance to compare the current one and decide whether it is a zoom in or out.

To configure this part, we have to expand the Touch property of the form in **Object Inspector** and check the Zoom event that we want to handle in our code. Next, double-click on the OnGesture event of the form and enter the following code:

```
procedure TFormArrows3D.FormGesture(Sender: TObject;
  const EventInfo: TGestureEventInfo; var Handled: Boolean);
var
  Delta: integer;
begin
  if EventInfo.GestureID = igiZoom then
  begin
```

```
    if (not (TInteractiveGestureFlag.gfBegin in EventInfo.Flags))
      and (not (TInteractiveGestureFlag.gfEnd in EventInfo.Flags))
      then
    begin
      Delta := EventInfo.Distance - FLastDistance;
      DoZoom(Delta > 0);
    end;
    FLastDistance := EventInfo.Distance;
  end;
end;
```

You can save all and run on both Windows and a mobile target to verify that rotation and zooming work as expected.

We have just built an interactive 3D visualization using the "camera on a selfie stick" approach. This code is a good starting point for interactive display of arbitrary geometries. You can remove all 3D objects from DummyScene and replace them with any other geometries that you want to display in 3D.

Using 3D models

Until now, we have been using different out-of-the-box 3D objects that come with built-in geometries. The FireMonkey library also provides a TModel3D component that makes it possible to use geometries defined outside of Delphi, typically using 3D modeling software and importing mesh data using one of the supported 3D file formats.

FireMonkey supports importing 3D models from OBJ, DAE, and ASE file formats. These are standard formats supported by many 3D modeling software packages.

If you have 3D modeling artistic skills, then you can create your own models. Many programmers don't, so they need already existing models for their 3D apps. There are many websites offering free and commercial 3D models. One of them is www.turbosquid.com, where I found a nice royalty-free OBJ model of a medieval helmet that you can see in *Figure 6.12* (https://www.turbosquid.com/3d-models/free-3ds-model-medieval-helmet/681191). That's what we want to import in a 3D Delphi app.

Figure 6.12: A 3D model of a helmet

Instead of rebuilding the 3D visualization logic, copy the source code of the Arrows3D demo into a new HelmetApp folder. Open the project and rename it as HelmetApp. Save the main form as uFormHelmet and change the form's Name property to FormHelmet. Delete all material components from the form and also cylinders and cones from the DummyScene component. We have a clean slate; we just have the 3D visualization code and an empty scene.

Now drop a TModel3D component on the form and make sure that it is parented under the DummyScene object in the **Structure** view. In Object Inspector, click on the ellipsis button next to the MeshCollection property to display **Mesh Collection Editor**. Click on the **Load** button and select the Helmet.obj downloaded file. The helmet should show up inside the scene. Change the X, Y, and Z sub-properties of the DummyScene.Scale property to make the helmet bigger. Now change the OrientationAngle.X property value to 180, so that the helmet is initially not upside down.

You should now see the geometry and rotate and zoom it, but it is all red, without any materials applied. To fix this, drop a TLightMaterialSource component on the form and change its Diffuse color to Slategray.

Unfortunately, the TModel3D component does not have a MaterialSource property that we could use to connect the material component. We need to do it in code by double-clicking on the OnCreate event of the form and entering the following code , which will assign our new light material to every mesh in the model's mesh collection:

```
procedure TFormHelmet.FormCreate(Sender: TObject);
begin
  for var Mesh: TMesh in Model3D1.MeshCollection do
    mesh.MaterialSource := LightMaterialSource1;
end;
```

If we run the app now, we should see that it looks much better now with the helmet properly shaded, as you can see in *Figure 6.13*.

Figure 6.13: The Helmet app at runtime

Different 3D modeling software packages output different types of information into exported files. The `TModel3D` component imports just the basic geometry information necessary to build its internal vertex and index buffers.

The support for importing different file formats is implemented in different `FMX.*.Importer` units that you might need to include in the project's `uses` clause, if you want to load the model from a file in code and not at design time like we did.

A starfield simulation

In this section, we will be looking into building efficient 3D visualizations that are using multiple geometries. We will create a starfield simulation using the `TSphere` and `TObjectProxy` components for sharing mesh data.

If we look into the source code of the `TSphere`, `TCone`, `TCylinder`, and other components in the `FMX.Objects3D` unit, we will see that their vertices and indices are hard coded. If we want to build a 3D scene with many different objects, every object will occupy quite a lot of space in memory.

FireMonkey comes with a special `TProxyObject` 3D object. This object does not store its geometry. Instead, it has a `SourceObject` property, which can be used to connect to any other 3D object. In this way, we have just one copy of geometry data in memory and multiple objects available for rendering at different 3D positions and with different settings.

To illustrate this concept, let's build a starfield simulation, with many sphere objects moving in space, similar to a classic Windows screensaver. We will just use one instance of a `TSphere` component and all other spheres will be rendered using proxy objects:

1. To create this app, start with a new Delphi multi-device application and select **Blank Application** from the application templates gallery. Save the form's unit as `uFormStars` and the project as `Starfield`. Change the `Name` property of the main form to `FormStars` and save everything.

2. Now drop a `TViewport3D` component on the form, align it to `Client`, and change its `Color` to `Black`. This is the deep space.

3. Next drop a `TCamera` component on the viewport and a `TLight` component on the camera. Connect the `Camera` property of the viewport to point to the `Camera1` component and set its `UsingDesignCamera` property to `False`.

4. Drop a `TDummy` component on the viewport and change its `Name` to `DummyScene`.

5. Now drop a `TSphere` component on the dummy scene component. Change its `Name` to `SphereStar`. It will serve as the main holder of the sphere geometry. Change its `Position.Z` property to `-10`, so it is behind the camera and therefore not visible.

6. Drop a `TLightMaterialSource` component on the form and set the sphere's `MaterialSource` property to point to the material component. We should see the sphere turning from red to nice shades of gray, as you can see in *Figure 6.14*. The screenshot also includes the **Structure** view with the hierarchy of components used in this demo app.

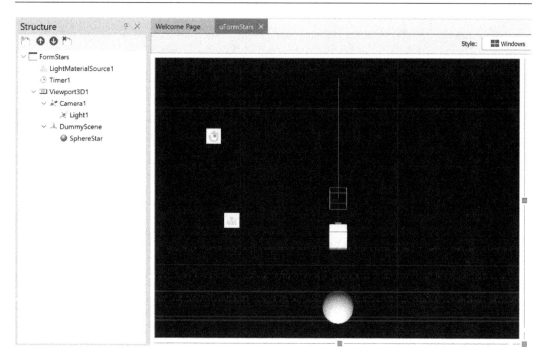

Figure 6.14: The Starfield app at design time in Delphi

7. This time, instead of moving the camera, we will be moving the Z position of all stars using a timer component. Drop a TProxyObject component on the form and set its SourceObject property to point to SphereStar. You should see the second sphere on the form.

8. You can now safely delete the TProxyObject component from the form. We will be creating proxy spheres in code. First let's implement a method for getting a random location within a cube defined by MAX_X, MAX_Y, and MAX_Z constants. This is the code we can use:

```
function TFormStars.RandomLocation: TPoint3D;
const
  MAX_X = 50;
  MAX_Y = 50;
  MAX_Z = 200;
begin
  Result.X := -MAX_X + Random * 2 * MAX_X;
  Result.Y := -MAX_Y + Random * 2 * MAX_Y;
  Result.Z := Random * MAX_Z;
end;
```

9. Double-click on the form's OnCreate event in **Object Inspector** and enter there the following code, which will create 100 spheres in random locations in front of the camera:

```
procedure TFormStars.FormCreate(Sender: TObject);
const
  STARS_COUNT = 100;
var
  Star: TProxyObject;
begin
  Randomize;
  for var I := 0 to STARS_COUNT-1 do
  begin
    Star := TProxyObject.Create(DummyScene);
    Star.SourceObject := SphereStar;
    Star.Parent := DummyScene;
    Star.Position.Point := RandomLocation;
  end;
end;
```

If you save and run the application, you should see a starfield, like in *Figure 6.15*.

Figure 6.15: The Starfield app running on Windows

10. Now we need to add movement. Drop a TTimer component on the form. Set its Interval property to 50 milliseconds. In the OnTimer event, we will be decreasing the Z position of

3D objects contained in the DummyScene component. If the value gets smaller than 0, the object is moved again to a random place within a virtual cube. This is the code we can use:

```
procedure TFormStars.Timer1Timer(Sender: TObject);
const
  DELTA_Z = 2;
var
  Ctrl: TControl3D;
  Obj: TFmxObject;
begin
  for var I := 0 to DummyScene.ChildrenCount-1 do
  begin
    Obj := DummyScene.Children[I];
    if Obj is TControl3D then
    begin
      Ctrl := TControl3D(Obj);
      Ctrl.Position.Z := Ctrl.Position.Z - DELTA_Z;

      if Ctrl.Position.Z < 0 then
        Ctrl.Position.Point := RandomLocation;
    end;
  end;
end;
```

If you now run the application, you'll see a moving starfield (something we cannot really visualize in a book!). The actual app shows the illusion of moving through the starfield in space.

Mixing 3D and 2D

In FireMonkey, you can mix 2D with 3D. In a 3D form, we can use 2D user interface controls, or we can embed the special TViewport3D component in a standard FireMonkey 2D form to do some 3D rendering.

In this example, we are going to add some special visual effects by building a 2D user interface in the 3D space. This will allow the user to interact with the app in a traditional way, but we could do some extra things such as rotating or moving the whole user interface in 3D space for a surprising user experience.

On the **Tool** palette, we can find the **3D Layers** category with different 3D controls for using normal 2D controls. In this demo, we will use the TLayer3D component to pretend that the user interface is 2D, but at any moment in time, we can do something in 3D.

These are the steps for building the app:

1. Create a new multi-device Delphi project and select **Blank Application** as the application type.

2. Save the main form's unit as `uFormTwistMe` and the whole app as `TwistMe`. Change the Name property of the form to `FormTwistMe`.

3. Drop a `TViewport3D` component on the form and align it to `Client`.

4. Drop a `TLayer3D` component on the viewport, change its `Projection` property from `Camera` to `Screen` and its `Align` property to `Client`.

5. Drop a `TButton` component on the layer and change its `Text` property to **Click me to twist!**, as you can see in *Figure 6.16*.

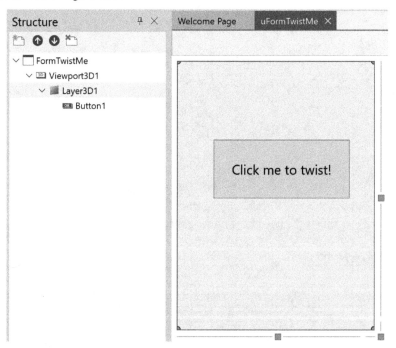

Figure 6.16: The TwistMe app in Delphi

6. When the user touches the button, the whole layer will be animated in 3D space. To accomplish this, add the `FMX.Ani` unit to the `uses` clause of the form, double-click on the button, and enter the following code inside the `OnClick` event handler, which will animate the `RotationAngle.X` property of the `Layer3D1` component:

```
procedure TFormTwistMe.Button1Click(Sender: TObject);
begin
  TAnimator.AnimateFloat(Layer3D1, 'RotationAngle.X', 360, 1);
end;
```

When the user touches the button, the whole form makes a full rotation around the X axis, as you can see in *Figure 6.17*, which shows the app running on a phone.

Figure 6.17: The TwistMe app running on Android

This is a simple example that just shows the possibilities of using 3D in 2D user interfaces for building interesting visual effects, with very little code.

Summary

In this chapter, we have explored the world of FireMonkey 3D programming.

With components, FireMonkey parenting architecture, and cross-platform rendering, it is possible to build stunning 3D interactive visualizations with little or no code that can be compiled for all major mobile and desktop platforms. That's a unique capability in the market today!

In the next chapter, we are going back to 2D controls, and we'll delve into one of the most important aspects of FireMonkey architecture: styling!

7

Building User Interfaces with Style

If you would need to choose one single most important concept to understand in Delphi cross-platform programming, then it would probably be the concept of **styles**. Styling is the cornerstone of cross-platform FireMonkey architecture. Styles are used at different levels. There are built-in styles, which are specific to a platform that you use when you create a multi-device project and switch between in the form designer. The FireMonkey controls on a form have a StyleLookup property, which can be used to use a specific style for a given component. You can also apply a custom style using a TStyleBook component. Finally, with the built-in style editor, you can visually customize a given style item in the stylebook as easily as you would customize a component on the form. The goal of this chapter is to give you a solid understanding of FireMonkey styles for building stunning **graphical user interfaces** (**GUIs**).

This chapter will cover the following points:

- Working with built-in styles
- Using custom styles
- Customizing styles
- Using frames
- Working with inherited views
- Previewing forms on devices

The objective of this chapter is to understand how to create great-looking **user interfaces** (**UIs**) with custom styling.

Working with built-in styles

The look and feel of every FireMonkey control depends on the style. There is only one code base of your app, but when you compile it for a given platform, there is a different style used to render any control. In this way, magic is possible. The same app running on iOS will look like a regular iOS app, and when compiled for Android, it will look like an Android app. You can also compile the project for desktop targets and then an appropriate Windows or Mac style will be used.

Delphi comes with built-in styles. When you create a new multi-device application, during the design time, you can preview how a given form will look with a different style applied.

Let's give it a try. Create a new multi-device blank application. Save the main form unit as uFormStylesTest and the whole project as StylesTest. Above the form designer area, there is a **Style** combo box where you can change the style that is used to preview the form you are working with, as you can see in *Figure 7.1*.

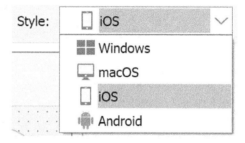

Figure 7.1: The Style selection combo box in FireMonkey Form Designer

The selection of a style in the **Style** combo box applies a different style to the form we are working with, so we can see how a given form will look when it is compiled for the selected platform. Let's do an experiment:

1. Drop a TToolBar component on the form and then a TSpeedButton control on the toolbar.
2. Align the speed button to Left and make it slightly wider, so that the whole caption is visible.

When we change the style in the **Style** combo box from **Android** to **iOS**, we can see that the look and feel of the speed button changes accordingly to match the selected platform design guidelines. In *Figure 7.2* you can see how the speed button looks with the iOS and Android styles selected.

Figure 7.2: A TSpeedButton control with iOS style (top) and the Android style (bottom)

Within a style, there could be more than one definition of how a given control could look. FireMonkey controls have a StyleLookup property that we can use to apply a different style definition. Click on the drop-down button next to the StyleLookup property in **Object Inspector** to see different styles that can be applied to a TSpeedButton control. Depending on the selected platform, the choices can be different.

In *Figure 7.3*, you can see the choices for Android styles for the TSpeedButton control.

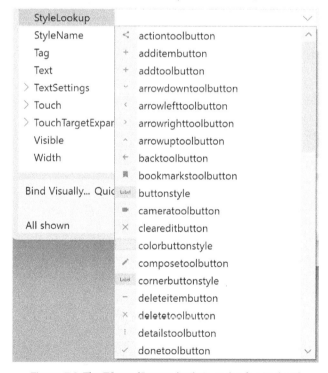

Figure 7.3: The TSpeedButton built-in styles for Android

If the selected style in the Form Designer is iOS, then the choices are different, as you can see in *Figure 7.4*.

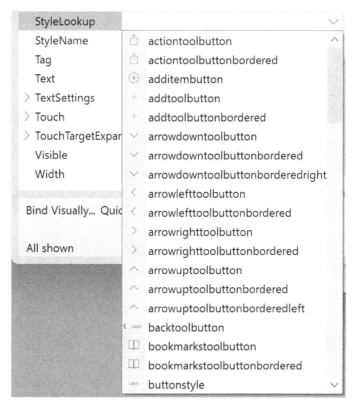

StyleLookup		
StyleName		actiontoolbutton
Tag		actiontoolbuttonbordered
Text		additembutton
> TextSettings		addtoolbutton
> Touch		addtoolbuttonbordered
> TouchTargetExpar		arrowdowntoolbutton
Visible		arrowdowntoolbuttonbordered
Width		arrowdowntoolbuttonborderedright
		arrowlefttoolbutton
Bind Visually... Quic		arrowlefttoolbuttonbordered
		arrowrighttoolbutton
All shown		arrowrighttoolbuttonbordered
		arrowuptoolbutton
		arrowuptoolbuttonbordered
		arrowuptoolbuttonborderedleft
		backtoolbutton
		bookmarkstoolbutton
		bookmarkstoolbuttonbordered
		buttonstyle

Figure 7.4: TSpeedButton built-in styles for iOS

If you select `drawertoolbutton` from the list of available choices for the `StyleLookup` property, you can notice that the size of the speed button changes, and it is now a square. Now, it looks like a proper "menu" button familiar to many mobile apps! If we now switch between styles in the **Style** combo box, we can see what our app would look like on the Android and iOS targets. In *Figure 7.5*, you can see the same `drawertoolbutton` style applied to a `TSpeedButton` control, but on iOS.

Figure 7.5: A TSpeedButton with the drawertoolbutton style on Android (top) and iOS (bottom)

Obviously, everything here also applies to desktop platforms, but we are focusing on mobile development in this book, which is why only iOS and Android styles are demonstrated.

Adding more controls

Let's add some more controls to the form to play with:

1. Drop a TLabel component on the toolbar, align it to Client, and change its StyleLookup property to toollabel.

2. Add a TTabControl component to the form and align it to Client.

3. Right-click on the tab control and click on the **Add TTabItem** option from the context menu three times to add three tabs to the form.

4. The tab control is one of the most useful UI elements and something that end users find very intuitive to use. It also illustrates differences in how styles are handled across different platforms. On iOS, tabs are located at the bottom of the screen, whereas they are placed at the top of the screen on Android. This is because of the different design guidelines on different platforms. FireMonkey elegantly handles these differences. If you really want to have the tabs either at the bottom or at the top, regardless of the platform, you can change the TabPosition property. By default, it is set to PlatformDefault, but you can make it Top or Bottom. There is also the ability to not display tabs at all and change the currently visible tab in the code, which in many scenarios can be useful.

If we expand the TabPosition property, we see PlatformDefault listed in the combo, as you can see in *Figure 7.6*.

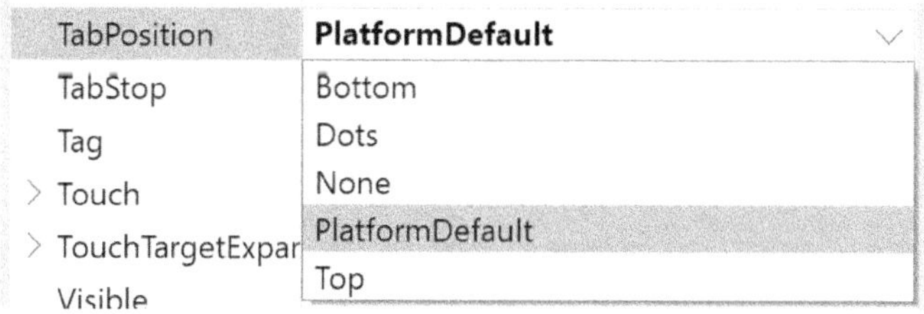

TabPosition	**PlatformDefault**	⌄
TabStop	Bottom	
Tag	Dots	
› Touch	None	
› TouchTargetExpan	PlatformDefault	
Visible	Top	

Figure 7.6: The TabPosition property choices for the TTabControl component

It is important to be aware of the differences in the look and feel of a given control on different platforms. For example, the styling for individual tab items is quite different on iOS and Android. On iOS, there are many different style lookup choices, and on Android, there are hardly any. Make sure that **iOS** is the currently selected style in the Form Designer and change the StyleLookup properties of individual tabs to styles that you like, for example, to tabitemfeatured, tabitemhistory, and tabitemmore. Luckily, if we select a style lookup for a tab on iOS, it will simply not have any effect on Android. The style engine will try to find the matching style specified in the StyleLookup property and if it fails, the built-in style will be used.

Adding the dials

The next step in building our demo application is to add three dial controls, which we'll style differently to investigate different options offered by the library. Here are the steps you can follow to rebuild the demo:

1. Now drop a TArcDial control on the first tab. Change its Height and Width properties to 100.

2. Copy and paste this control two times, so there are three arc dial controls next to each other on the form.

3. In order to have a sample of different controls, also drop the TCheckBox, TSwitch, and TButton components on the form.

In *Figure 7.7*, you can see how our form looks with the **iOS** style selected.

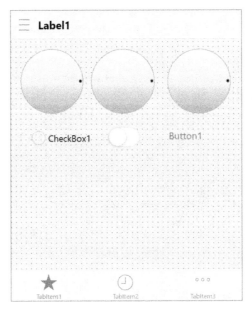

Figure 7.7: A form with sample controls with the iOS style

In *Figure 7.8*, you can see the same form but previewed with the **Android** styling. The initial version of the project we are building in this chapter is available in the code StylesTest1.

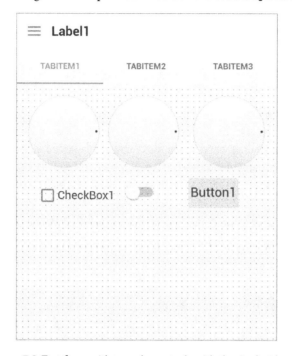

Figure 7.8: Test form with sample controls with the Android style

In this section, we have seen how you can use different built-in styles for an application, depending on the platform and the specific controls. FireMonkey also offers the ability to use custom styles, as we'll see next, and even the ability for a developer to create a new style, as we'll see later in this chapter.

Using custom styles

If we do not want to use a built-in style, we can always use a custom style. Delphi installation comes with a number of custom styles. In Delphi, FireMonkey custom styles are installed by default in the C:\Users\Public\Documents\Embarcadero\Studio\NN.0\Styles directory (where NN is the internal product version number). FireMonkey styles are files with *.style extension. If we preview a FireMonkey style file with a text viewer, we will see that its content looks very much like a form file we design with Form Designer inside the IDE.

It is good practice not to put non-visual components such as a stylebook directly on the form but rather on a dedicated data module. To do this, select **File | New | Data Module** to add a new data module to the project.

Save the unit as uDMStyles. Change the Name property of the data module to DMStyles. Make sure that the data module is created before the application main form. You can do it in the **Forms** tab in the **Options** dialog for the current project, by moving the DMStyles to the top of the list of auto-created forms. At this point, add the new data module to the implementation uses clause of the application main form.

Now drop a TStyleBook component on the data module. It can be used to load custom styles for different platforms.

Double-click on the stylebook component. This will open integrated FireMonkey Style Designer. Click on the second button at the top-left corner of the style designer and load the Transparent.style file. Save and close the editor by answering **Yes** in the dialog message that asks whether to save changes to the stylebook. Change the name of the stylebook component to StyleBookTransparent. Add another TStyleBook component to the form. Load into it the AquaGraphite style and rename the component to StyleBookAquaGraphite. In order to apply a custom style to the form, we need to connect the stylebook component with StyleBook property of the form.

Pointing this property to a given stylebook component will immediately load the style.

It would look like *Figure 7.9*. You can find this code in the StylesTest2 project.

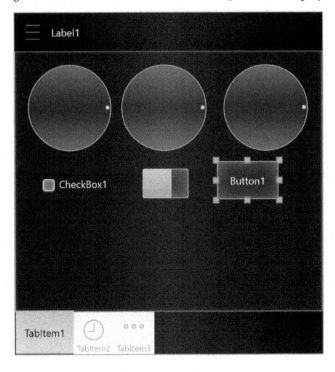

Figure 7.9: The FormStylesTest form with the Transparent iOS style

This is how our form will look after loading the `Transparent` style on iOS, while in *Figure 7.10* you can see how it looks on Android.

Figure 7.10: The FormStylesTest form with the Transparent Android style

I really like it. It has a nice gradient and the controls look more like the dashboards of spaceships in science fiction movies.

Why is it a good practice to put a stylebook component on a dedicated data module? The reason for this is that this way, we can have multiple forms in the app reusing the same styles, and also, we can possibly reuse this data module across different projects.

Another option to load a custom style is to use the `TStyleManager` class defined in the `FMX`. `Styles` unit directly. The class has different public class methods for loading styles from a file or a resource. The advantage of this approach is the fact that a style is loaded globally for the whole application and applied to all forms, but the disadvantage is the added complexity of deploying a custom style file with the mobile app. This can be done either by compiling the style into the app as a resource or deploying it as a separate file with the Deployment Manager.

Embedding styles as resources

Let's have a look at the process of embedding custom style into an app as a resource. Using custom resources is not limited to embedding. We can embed arbitrary files, such as video, audio, custom graphics, data, or anything.

Remove the data module with stylebook components, because now we are going to load a custom style differently. In order to verify that custom is loaded globally for all forms, we are going to add an additional form to the `StyleTest` app:

1. Add an empty **FireMonkey HD** form to the project.

2. Save the form's unit as `uFormExtra` and change the `Name` property of the new form to `FormExtra`.

3. Add the new form to the `uses` clause of the main form.

4. In the `OnClick` event of the menu speed button of the main form, add one line of code to display the new form. This code will display `FormExtra` when an end user clicks on the button:

    ```
    uses
      uFormExtra;

    procedure TFormStylesTest.SpeedButton1Click(Sender: TObject);
    begin
      FormExtra.Show;
    end;
    ```

We will leave the form completely blank. A form itself will have a custom `backgroundstyle` applied. If we preview the `Transparent` style definition from the previous example, we will see that the `backgroundstyle` definition is just a rectangle with a custom gradient fill.

In the **Project** menu, click on the **Resources and Images** option. This will display the **Resources** dialog. Click on the **Add** button in the dialog and choose the file with a custom style that you want to embed. In the dialog, we need to enter an identifier in the **Resource identifier** field. Using this identifier, we can reference individual resources in code.

This could be anything. For example, we can add the `Transparent.style` file as a resource and use `TransparentStyle` as **Resource identifier**. This is visible in *Figure 7.11*.

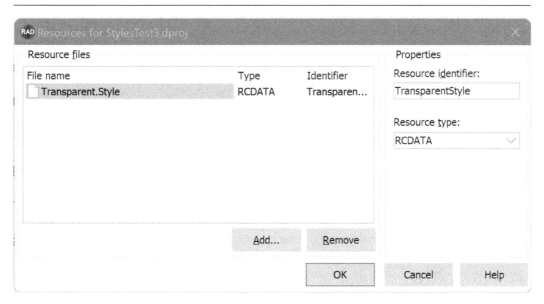

Figure 7.11: The Transparent style added to the project as a resource

After you click on **OK** to close the **Resources** dialog, the next step is to write code that will read the custom style from the resource and set it as a style for the whole application. Because this is global to all forms, that is why a logical place to enter this code is in the project file itself.

If you click on the **View Source** menu item in the **Project** menu, Delphi will open the project source code file. Add FMX.Styles to the project's uses clause and add a call to the TStyleManager class to try to load a custom style from the resource. The project code should look like the following:

```
program StylesTest3;

{$R *.dres}

uses
  System.StartUpCopy,
  FMX.Styles,
  FMX.Forms,
  uFormStylesTest in 'uFormStylesTest.pas' {FormStylesTest},
  uFormExtra in 'uFormExtra.pas' {FormExtra};

{$R *.res}

begin
  TStyleManager.TrySetStyleFromResource('TransparentStyle');
  Application.Initialize;
```

```
    Application.CreateForm(TFormStylesTest, FormStylesTest);
    Application.CreateForm(TFormExtra, FormExtra);
    Application.Run;
  end.
```

Adding a custom resource to a file has added some additional files to the project, linked with the `{$R *.dres}` compiler directive (a directive automatically added to the project file).

You can build the app and deploy it to iOS and Android devices to verify that a custom style has been globally loaded for all forms in the application.

Customizing styles

FireMonkey styling gives us a lot of flexibility. One option you have is to use built-in styles. Within a built-in style, there could be multiple style definitions for a given control. There is also the possibility of using a custom style. But what if we want to have a really special look for our styled control? We can go one step further and customize a built-in or custom style.

On our test form, there are three `TArcDial` components. If we right-click on any styled control at the bottom of the context menu, there will be two options: one to edit the custom style and one for editing the default style.

- If we select **Edit Default Style**, we will be modifying the default style used by all controls of a given type in the app

- If we select **Edit Custom Style**, we will only change the style for the specific control, without changing the style of all other controls of the same type

To see this in action, right-click on the `ArcDial1` control and select **Edit Custom Style** from the context menu. This will open **Style Designer** and in the **Structure** view, we can see the individual components that are used to define a `TArcDial` control. It feels very much like editing a form, with a designer and **Object Inspector**, but we are editing a style instead. **Object Inspector** can be used to modify properties of all sub-elements of a style and we can also modify them visually in the designer.

Let's change something to see the effect in the running app. For example, let's change the size and color of the indicator ellipse. Change its `Width` property to `30` and its `Height` property to `10`. Now it is bigger. Expand its `Brush` property and change the `Color` property to `Cornflowerblue`. You can see this scenario in *Figure 7.12* and the sample project `StylesTest4`.

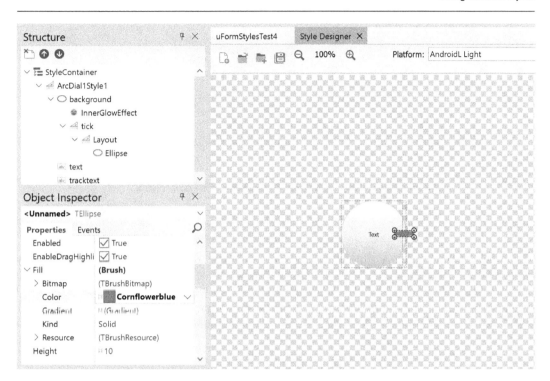

Figure 7.12: Editing a custom style in Style Designer

Now you can close **Style Designer**. You will get a prompt if you want to save changes made to the style. Click on **Yes** and you'll save the changes and go back to the form.

There are few things to notice now. First, a new `TStyleBook` component has been added to the form. It contains the `ArcDial1Style1` style definition and this value is also already set in the `StyleLookup` property of the `ArcDial1` control. If we expand the `StyleLookup` property of any of the `TArcDial` on the form, we can now see the additional choice that we could use to change the style of any of the other `TArcDial` controls on the form to match the one we have customized. This way we can apply this style to other controls as well, as you see in *Figure 7.13*.

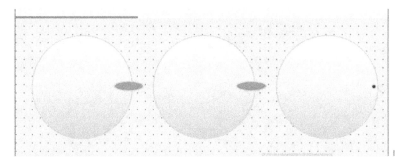

Figure 7.13: A custom style applied to a second ArcDial control

If we expand the `StyleBook1` component in the **Structure** view, we will see that the style that we have created is for `iOS` only. There are only the **Default** and **iOS** options. If we change the current style for the form from **iOS** to **Android**, our custom indicator will not show up. If we want to be truly cross-platform, we need to make sure that our custom style has an **Android** version, too. To obtain this, make sure that **Android** is selected in the **Style** combo box and double-click on the stylebook component. We are back in **Style Designer**. Now, a new **Android Light** option has been added to values that were listed earlier, **Default** and **iOS**. You can also consider adding **iOS Dark** and desktop platforms.

We can now make the same or similar modifications to the Android version of the custom `ArcDial1Style1` style. When we close **Style Designer**, we can see that there is also an Android version of our custom style applied.

What happens if we choose to edit the **Default** style? Right-click on any of the `TArcDial` controls on the form and select the **Edit Default Style** option from the context menu. The **Style Designer** window opens again. In the **Structure** view, there is a new node. This time, we are modifying the `ArcDialstyle` style definition.

This is a naming convention that the FireMonkey styling system uses. The default style for a given class is the name of the class, without the preceding `T`, but with the word "style" appended at the end. If such a style is found, then it is applied if there is no style specified in the `StyleLookup` property.

Let's now introduce some modifications to the default style for the `TArcDial` controls. Change the `Width` and `Height` properties of the indicator ellipse to `10` and its `Brush.Fill` color to `Cadetblue` for both Android and iOS styles. Save and close the style editor. Now, the `ArcDial3` control is using the new style, applied automatically to add controls without a custom style. Go to the `StyleLookup` property for `ArcDial1` and `ArcDial2` and clear their `StyleLookup` properties. Notice that now all three controls are using the modified default `ArcDialstyle`, as you can see in *Figure 7.14*, and the `StylesTest5` demo project.

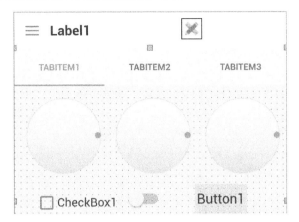

Figure 7.14: The ArcDial controls using a new default style

As you have seen, there is a difference between editing the custom and default styles. Which of the two approaches you want to use depends on the specific app that you are building. If you just want to modify a given control, it makes sense to edit a custom style and apply it to this one control. If you prefer to customize the look and feel of all controls of a given type on the form (or the entire app), it is easier to just modify the default style, which is automatically used by all controls.

Styles are core to the FireMonkey architecture, but they are not the only feature you can use in terms of the architecture and structure of the UI of your application. Frames offer an additional interesting opportunity to have a cleaner architecture and avoid having multiple copies of the same UI element.

Using frames

At times, you might want to define a group of controls working together in a certain way and reuse them multiple times. This can be done using frames.

Developer productivity often relies on being able to reuse previous work. Delphi projects consist of forms, data modules, and source code units. If you have an existing unit, it can always be added to a new project. At a smaller scale, there are occasions in which it would be desirable to reuse a certain combination of components. This is where frames come in. If you have a few controls working together that you would like to reuse multiple times in the same or multiple forms, then you can use frames.

Frames cannot exist on their own in the final application. They always need to be embedded in a form. They can contain controls and code, like a regular form.

Let's consider address information. Imagine we are designing a form with different controls for storing contact data. Our "contact" can have a home and office address. We can simplify our form and make it more user friendly by defining a custom frame for address information and by using it twice in the same form.

Let's see this in practice:

1. Create a new Delphi multi-device project.

2. Save the main form as `uFormContact` and the whole project as `Contacts`. Change the `Name` property of the form to `FormContact` and save all.

3. Now click on **File** | **New** | **Other** and inside the **New Items** dialog, select the **Delphi Files** category and double-click on the **FireMonkey Frame** icon.

4. Save the new unit as `uFrameAddress` and change the `Name` property of the new frame to `FrameAddress`.

At first, the frame looks very much like a form. If we look into the source code, we will see that `TFrameAddress` is not derived from the `TForm` class, but from the `TFrame` class. The process of designing the frame is the same as that of a form:

1. Drop five edits and six labels on the frame.

2. In the **Structure** view, drag five labels onto edits so that they become their children.

3. Place a label above the top left corner of each edit of the form. In this way, when we move edits, labels will go with them. The structure of the frame is visible in *Figure 7.15* along with the frame in the designer:

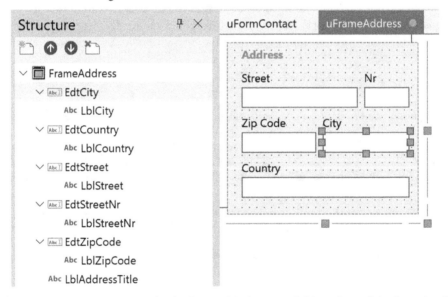

Figure 7.15: The Structure view for the frame with the controls hierarchy and the frame itself in the designer

Using the *Ctrl* key along with the mouse, you can select more than one component at a time. In **Object Inspector**, we can see that three items are selected. In one operation, we can change the properties of multiple components. That's a very useful trick! If you select components of different types, then only their common properties are listed in **Object Inspector**.

4. Rename the edits to `EdtStreet`, `EdtStreetNr`, `EdtZipCode`, `EdtCity`, and `EdtCountry`. Make the frame as small as possible so that the controls occupy most of its space. We can use anchors to automatically adjust the widths of all edits when the frame is resized.

In order to make our frame easy to use in code, we can define the `Street`, `StreetNr`, `ZipCode`, `City`, and `Country` properties to read and write from corresponding edit components. In this way, even if the internal structure or names of components change, the code of the form using the frame would remain unchanged. This is the frame class definition:

```
type
  TFrameAddress = class(TFrame)
    EdtStreet: TEdit;
    LblStreet: TLabel;
    EdtStreetNr: TEdit;
    LblStreetNr: TLabel;
    EdtCity: TEdit;
    LblCity: TLabel;
    LblAddressTitle: TLabel;
    EdtCountry: TEdit;
    LblCountry: TLabel;
    EdtZipCode: TEdit;
    LblZipCode: TLabel;
  private
    procedure SetCity(const Value: string);
    procedure SetCountry(const Value: string);
    procedure SetStreet(const Value: string);
    procedure SetStreetNr(const Value: string);
    function GetCity: string;
    function GetCountry: string;
    function GetStreet: string;
    function GetStreetNr: string;
    procedure SetZipCode(const Value: string);
    function GetZipCode: string;
  public
    property Street: string read GetStreet;
    write SetStreet;
    property StreetNr: string read GetStreetNr;
    write SetStreetNr;
    property ZipCode: string read GetZipCode;
```

```
    write SetZipCode;
    property City: string read GetCity;
    write SetCity;
    property Country: string read GetCountry
    write SetCountry;
  end;
```

The code of these property reader and writer methods are all very simple. Here is a sample one:

```
function TFrameAddress.GetCity: string;
begin
  Result := EdtCity.Text;
end;

procedure TFrameAddress.SetCity(const Value: string);
begin
  EdtCity.Text := Value;
end;
```

It is worth noting that frames do not have an OnCreate and OnDestroy event. Their initialization and finalization code need to go into the corresponding event handlers of a form that contains them.

Now that our frame is ready, this is how we can use it:

1. In order to place the frame on the form, we need to select the first item in the first tab of **Tool Palette**, **Standard**. Click on **Frame** and select the frame you want to add from the list of frames contained in the project. In our case, we have only one frame, as you can see in *Figure 7.16*.

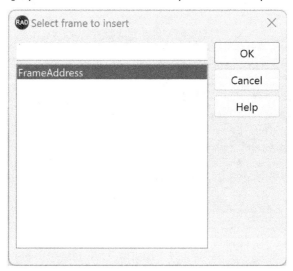

Figure 7.16: Selecting a frame to add to a form

2. Drop two frames on the contact form.

3. Change their names to `FrameAddressHome` and `FrameAddressOffice`. Change the `Text` property of `lblTitle` on each frame to `Home Address` and `Office Address`.

4. In order to make our form more realistic, let's also add a toolbar with a label and two edits with two labels for the contact's `Firstname` and `Lastname` to the form.

If we now switch the form style from Windows to iOS or Android, we will see that the vertical distances between edit boxes on frames are too small and that the labels overlap with the edits above them. We have two choices here. We can either modify the positions and sizes of controls directly on the form or go back to the frame and change them there. The advantage of this second approach is that the change is automatically propagated to all frame instances already embedded in forms. If we want to change all frames, it is easier to do it once in the frame itself.

If we want to adjust just one specific frame, we can do it directly on the form. Once we change a property of a component in a frame that is already on the form, this change overrides any change made in the frame definition itself. As an example, let's go to the frame design and change the font color or the title label from `Black` to `Red`. If we now switch to the form, we will see that the title labels on both frames are now `Red`. The change has propagated to both of them.

If we now change the color of `lblAddress` on `FrameAddressHome` to `Blue`, then any subsequent changes to the font color on the frame itself will not be propagated. The connection has been broken. The local value for the font color property overrides the inherited value. There is an option, however, to restore the connection by using the **Revert to Inherited** option of the control local menu.

In *Figure 7.17* you can see how the form with two address frames looks in the Form Designer, with the iOS style applied.

Figure 7.17: A form with two frames with the iOS style

With frames, we can be more productive, because we can reuse big portions of a form design across the same form, in multiple forms in the same project, or even across different projects. Not only can the visual design be reused, but also the logic; that is, the code behind the form. We could easily add some logic to the form to look up the city using a backend service based on the value entered into the ZIP code edit.

Frames offer a lot of flexibility in terms of customizing portions of a form. Another customization feature is the ability to have a slightly different UI depending on the target platform. This is what you can accomplish using inherited views.

Working with inherited views

When we design a form, it is the same for all platforms, form factors, and orientations. While you can use layouts, alignments, and anchors to make the form flexible, the differences in screen resolution and layout between different devices are generally very significant and had to accommodate.

By changing the platforms of a FireMonkey form, we can preview what the form is going to look like on different platforms, but the design remains the same. To address this problem, the FireMonkey Form Designer allows us to define inherited views that are specific to a given platform and the form factor. Next to the **Style** combo box at the top of the Form Designer, there is another combo box called **View**. Using it, we can add additional form files to our form that are specific to a given platform or a specific form factor.

Every form always has a built-in **Master** view. From the list, we can add additional views, as you can see in *Figure 7.18*.

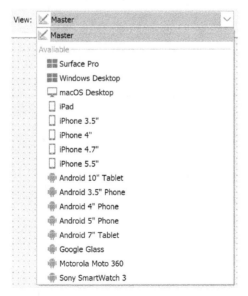

Figure 7.18: Available views in the FireMonkey Form Designer

For example, let's add the **iPhone 4** and **Android 7' Tablet** views to the FormContact design. The selected choices will be now listed in the **Created** category, as you can see in *Figure 7.19*.

Figure 7.19: The Available and Created views in the FireMonkey Form Designer

Inherited views are similar to frames. Instead of reusing a part of a form, now we are reusing the whole form. Changes made to the main form are propagated to inherited views unless they are locally overridden on a given view-specific form.

If we now switch to the Code Editor, we will see that there are two new additional compiler directives for compiling into the executable new device-specific form files.

Beyond the standard {$R *.fmx} directive that connects the **Master** view, there are two new ones, which we have just added from the combo box, as you can see in this code snippet:

```
var
  FormContact: TFormContact;

implementation

{$R *.fmx}
{$R *.iPhone4in.fmx IOS}
```

```
{$R *.LgXhdpiTb.fmx ANDROID}
{$R *.NmXhdpiPh.fmx ANDROID}
```

While resource files are generally included in the executable, in this case, the compiler offers an optimization. If we have views defined for multiple platforms, only views for a specific platform will be compiled into the resulting executable for the given platform. In our case, the **Android 7** view will not be included if we build for iOS, and vice versa.

When we use frames, we have both a form file and a unit with source code. In the case of inherited views, there is only one source code file for a form and multiple form files with the configuration of the components. These inherited views can be used to adjust the form to a given form factor. In our case, we could, for example, modify the location of the address frames so that they are one on top of another.

On the right side of the **View** combo box, there are buttons to remove the added view, switch between portrait and landscape views, and hide or show the custom image of a device that is displayed by default for an inherited view.

We can also preview the current form on all different form factors and devices inside the **Multi-Device Preview** tab in the top right corner of the IDE. In the default layout, this view is located under **Project Manager** and it has content similar to *Figure 7.20* (here with two Android form factors).

Figure 7.20: Selecting available views in Multi-Device Preview

This is very useful because we can quickly see how the current form is going to look on screens of different sizes. By default, created views are checked in the list of forms to preview, but we can also see additional forms, even though there is no inherited view created for them. These form factors that have inherited views are marked with a check icon in their top-left corner, as you can see in *Figure 7.21*.

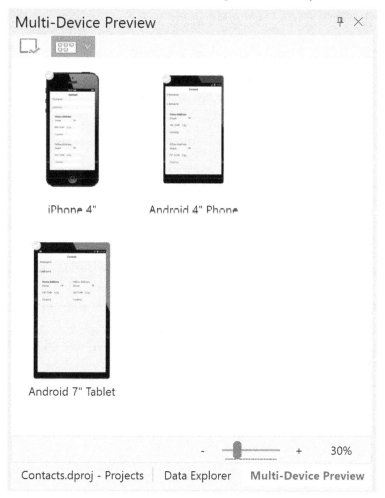

Figure 7.21: Multi-Device Preview in action

If you have more screens, it is probably a good idea to move the **Multi-Device Preview** pane to a secondary screen to constantly preview the form you are designing on different devices.

Depending on the app that we are designing, it could be useful to be able to specify that our design, for example, works in the **Portrait** orientation only. Or maybe we are building an arcade game and we only want to support the **Landscape** orientation.

In **Project Options**, there is a special **Orientation** tab that we can use to specify custom orientations of our app. This information is then stored in a manifest file that the IDE generated for different supported platforms and embedded in the final executable file.

Previewing forms on devices

Delphi form designer gives us a "what you see is what you get" functionality, but we can go one step further and use Delphi's built-in functionality to preview the form we are designing live on a physical device. For this, we will have to build from the Delphi samples and deploy them to our device, or download a special app published by Embarcadero Technologies and called **FireUI App Preview** from an online store.

With the **FireUI App Preview** app, you can preview the app as you are designing it live on a physical device. The Form Designer broadcasts the current form, with any changes applied by the developer, to all connected devices in real time. This app uses the **App Tethering** technology available in Delphi, where arbitrary apps written in either Delphi or C++Builder, desktop or mobile, can communicate with each other over a Wi-Fi network or using Bluetooth.

In this scenario, the Delphi IDE runs on a Windows desktop and communicates with a remote app running on any of the supported platforms. Installers for Windows and Mac versions of **FireUI App Preview** are available in the **LivePreview** directory in the main install folder of Delphi. For mobile, you can either get the app from the mobile stores or it is possible to build it directly from source code, which is provided as part of Delphi installation in the `source\Tools\FireUIAppPreview` folder.

To enable this feature, in the Delphi Options dialog (available from the **Tools** menu) there is a special tab under **Environment Options | Form Designer | FireUI Live Preview**. In this tab, we can see all currently connected devices, the name under which the IDE is broadcasting, and an optional password to protect the communication between the IDE and the preview devices, as you can see in *Figure 7.22*.

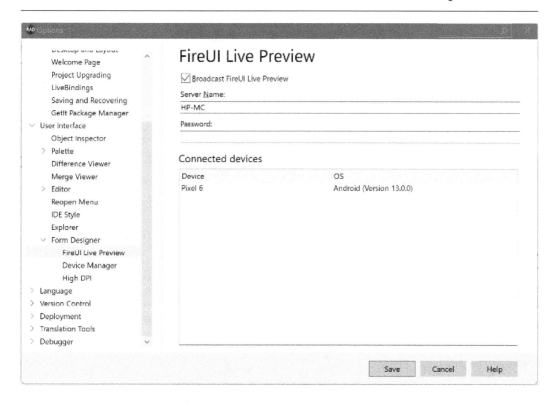

Figure 7.22: The FireUI Live Preview configuration in the Tools Options dialog

Notice that you can also toggle **Live Preview** using **View | Broadcast** to device menu item. The feature is disabled by default because in some scenarios it can slow down the IDE startup.

Once you start the **FireUI Live Preview** app, it searches the local network for the Delphi IDE and offers to connect, as you can see in *Figure 7.23*. If the app does not see the IDE, it could be related to the wireless network configuration or the fact that the device and the computer or VM the IDE is running on are not on the same network and subnet. In fact, App Tethering uses UDP broadcasting for making the connection, and this requires both apps to be running in the same subnet.

Figure 7.23: Connecting the FireUI Live Preview app to the Delphi IDE

After establishing the connection to the IDE, the mobile app preview shows the form that is currently being designed inside of the Form Designer, as you can see in *Figure 7.24*. In this case, I'm using the StylesTest4 demo program described earlier in this chapter. The form itself is interactive, so, for example, if you have an edit, you would be able to enter a value into it, but the logic connected through events is not available through broadcasting. In other words, the preview is only for the designer, not for the source code you need to compile.

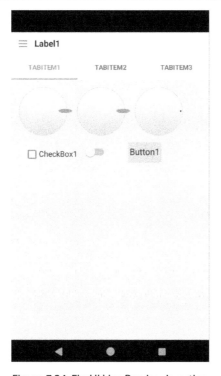

Figure 7.24: FireUI Live Preview in action

The end goal is to preview the UI design and not the application logic. At any moment, we can just run the app we are designing on the device itself. The nice thing about **FireUI Live Preview** is the fact that it can broadcast the form to many different devices simultaneously in real time, so we can preview the UI design instantly.

Summary

Building GUIs with the Delphi and FireMonkey libraries requires an understanding of the concept of a style. Styles in FireMonkey UI design play a similar role to cascading style sheets in web development.

Every FireMonkey app uses a style. This could be a built-in style or a custom style loaded from the TStyleBook component or an embedded resource. Integrated FireMonkey Style Designer lets us modify existing styles as easily as designing a form.

We have learned a lot about building UIs with FireMonkey. In the next chapter, we will go deeper into the rich world of different frameworks and components available on iOS and Android operating systems, and how FireMonkey helps us write cross-platform code that abstracts away the differences between different APIs.

8

Working with Mobile Operating Systems

In this chapter, we are going to move from playing with FireMonkey to building useful cross-platform apps that access mobile hardware and operating system features with high-level components, abstracting away the underlying mobile APIs.

This chapter will cover the following topics:

- James Bond's toy
- What am I running on?
- The life of an app
- Sensing the world
- Taking photos
- Using share sheets
- Camera, action!
- Notify me!
- Navigating the web
- Delphi language bridges

The objective of this chapter is to learn how to create native cross-platform apps that use different frameworks and functionality provided by mobile operating systems.

James Bond's toy

Contemporary mobile hardware does not significantly differ in capabilities from secret agent James Bond's gadgets from just a few years ago. Your mobile phone is equipped with all kinds of sensors that you can use in your mobile apps, including for location, orientation, motion, and ambient light, along with a microphone, speakers, camera, and plenty of other hardware you can control.

An app is immersed in the given operating system it runs on, which is in charge of every aspect of an app's execution. In your code, you can respond to different app life cycle events such as startup, switching to background execution, moving back to the foreground, and app termination. Ultimately, this interaction is about responding to different events sent by the operating system and invoking operating system APIs. The FireMonkey library encapsulates access to common mobile operating system functionality through specialized types, classes, and components, but there is nothing that can stop you from invoking arbitrary platform APIs directly in your code. Sometimes this could be the only way to achieve certain things, such as, for example, making your phone vibrate. Luckily most of the time, you can use cross-platform components and libraries that generalize common functionality, including accessing maps or contacts, embedding web browsers, and sharing data with other apps and services.

Different mobile operating systems provide functionality that might not exist on other platforms or older versions of the same system. In such cases, we might want to write code against a specific feature on a specific platform. In this chapter, we are going to see how to invoke mobile APIs through Delphi language bridges. We will also see how to deal with features unique to iOS or Android, such as using and creating Android services.

What am I running on?

Building apps for multiple operating systems from the very same source code imposes unique challenges. Your code might be running on iOS or Android. It only takes two mouse clicks to recompile your app for a different target. Certain features might exist on a given platform and not be there on other platforms. Going further, new functionality is constantly being added to platforms, so you may want to know on which platform and operating system version your app is being executed.

This can be done with the `TOSVersion` record type defined in the `System.SysUtils` unit. This record has a class constructor that instantiates all of its fields. The `TOSVersion` record defines the internal `TArchitecture` and `TPlatform` enumerated types and corresponding public class properties to read the current operating system architecture, platform, name, and major and minor numbers.

We can very quickly build a simple app that will log in a memo all of the information from the `TOSVersion` record, as follows:

1. Create a new blank, multi-device project, saving the main form as `uFormOSVer` and the whole project as `OSVersion`.

2. Drop a toolbar on the form and add a label with a nice title, such as What am I Running On?. Change the TextSettings.HorzAlign property of the label to Center and its Align property to Client.

3. Drop a TMemo component on the form, align it to Client, and rename it MemoLog.

4. In order to simplify the conversion of the TArchitecture and TPlatform enumerated types to strings, we can provide helper classes for these types. Add a new unit to the project and save it as uOSVerHelpers. In there, enter the following class helper declarations:

```
type
  TOSArchHelper = record helper for TOSVersion.TArchitecture
    function ToString: string;
  end;

  TOSPlatHelper = record helper for TOSVersion.TPlatform
    function ToString: string;
  end;
```

In terms of implementation, these helper methods have case statements returning a descriptive string for each possible value. The preceding is one of the two; the other is very similar, as you can see in the following complete project source code:

```
function TOSArchHelper.ToString: string;
begin
  case self of
    arIntelX86: Result := 'IntelX86';
    arIntelX64: Result := 'IntelX64';
    arARM32: Result := 'ARM32';
    arARM64: Result := 'ARM64';
  else
    Result := 'Unknown OS Architecture';
  end;
end;
```

5. Add this unit to the uses clause of the main form.

6. We can additionally define in the form class a simple Log(S: string) method that will just display a given string in the memo:

```
procedure TFormOSVer.Log(S: string);
begin
  MemoLog.Lines.Add(S);
end;
```

7. Now, in the `OnCreate` event of the form, we can log all OS version information in the memo, as in the following code:

```
procedure TFormOSVer.FormCreate(Sender: TObject);
begin
  Log('OS Version Summary: ' + sLineBreak +
    TOSVersion.ToString);

  Log('OS Architecture: ' + TOSVersion.Architecture. ToString);
  Log('OS Platform: ' + TOSVersion.Platform.ToString);
  Log('OS Name: ' + TOSVersion.Name);
  Log('OS Build: ' + TOSVersion.Build.ToString);
  Log('Version: ' + TOSVersion.Major.ToString + '.' +
    TOSVersion.Minor.ToString);
end;
```

You can see the top portion of the application running on Android in *Figure 8.1*.

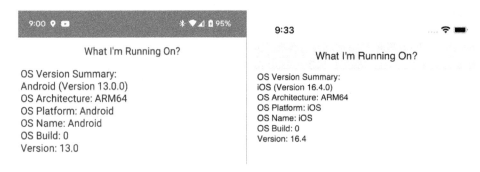

Figure 8.1: The OSVersion app running on an Android phone and on the iOS Simulator

This could be a useful piece of code for troubleshooting apps running on unknown or exotic mobile devices, but the core information can also be used to adapt the behavior of the code to a different operating system or a different version of the same operating system. This is generally accomplished by using one of the overloaded versions of the `TOSVersion.Check` method.

The second and more common approach for dealing with different underlying operating systems is to use conditional compilation (with the `$IF` or `$IFDEF` compiler directives). Somewhere deep in the FireMonkey source, there must ultimately be places where there is different code accessing different operating systems. A typical pattern is to have one header unit, with type declarations in the `interface` section and then platform-specific `implementation` units enclosed with `IFDEF` directives listed in the `uses` clause of the implementation section of the unit.

Let's consider the `FMX.Platform` unit. It has a number of interface and class declarations in its interface section, while its implementation section has the following structure:

```
unit FMX.Platform;

// ...

implementation

uses
{$IFDEF IOS}
  FMX.Platform.iOS
{$ENDIF IOS}

{$IFDEF ANDROID}
  FMX.Platform.Android
{$ENDIF}

// and so on
```

This is a very common pattern used in the FireMonkey library. The main unit provides an interface to the cross-platform application code, and specific units ending with the operating system name contain the platform-specific implementation code.

More specifically, in the `FMX.Platform` unit there is a `TPlatformServices` class that is used as the common access point to different platform services. The `TPlatformServices` class provides the `Current` class property that is used to query whether a given service is available or not.

If a given service is implemented via a hypothetical `IFMXAService` interface, then we could use the following code snippet to check whether it is available and access it:

```
var
  AFMXAService: IFMXAService;
begin
  if TPlatformServices.Current.SupportsPlatformService(
    IFMXAService, IInterface(AFMXAService)) then
  begin
    // call methods defined in the IFMXAService:
    // AFMXAService.AMethod;
  end
  else
    // IFMXAService is not supported
```

In this way, we have clean code for cross-platform access to the common services provided by the FireMonkey library.

Knowing the platform an app is running on is important when writing single-source, multi-device applications because you might need to have specific code for a single platform. As we have seen in this section, there are multiple techniques you can use to provide platform-specific behavior to a FireMonkey app. We'll see more cases throughout the rest of this chapter. For the time being, let's focus on another key element, which is the sequence of operations that determine the status of an app over time.

The life of an app

An app is not a lonely island. It is always executed by the operating system within the bounds that it imposes. Depending on the type of the app, we could be interested in responding to different application life cycle events that the operating system sends to it. Every operating system has a slightly different app life cycle model, but in the case of mobile platforms, the trickiest part is properly handling the situation when our apps move from foreground execution to the background and back again.

FireMonkey provides a common abstraction for handling the application life cycle through different types of application events defined in the FMX.Platform unit, as shown in the following code:

```
type
  TApplicationEvent = (FinishedLaunching, BecameActive,
    WillBecomeInactive, EnteredBackground, WillBecomeForeground,
    WillTerminate, LowMemory, TimeChange, OpenURL);
```

If we want to receive the app life cycle events, we need to pass the reference to our event handler function to the SetApplicationEventHandler method available as part of the IFMXApplicationEventService. First, we need to check whether this service is available from the TPlatformServices class using the blueprint described earlier. Our event handler can be any method that takes a TApplicationEvent and a TObject parameter and returns a Boolean value.

Let's create a test app that will display app life cycle events on different platforms:

1. Select the new **Multi-Device Application – Delphi** option in the IDE and choose the **Blank Application** template.

2. Save the main form unit as uFormLifecycle and the whole project as AppLifecycle, and change the main form's Name property to FormLifecycle. Click **Save All**.

3. Drop a TToolbar and a TMemo control on the form.

4. Rename the memo to MemoLog and align it to Client. Declare a Log(S: string) method in the form's class to output a message to the memo.

5. Now we have a generic skeleton for the app. It's time to do something about app life cycle events. Add the `FMX.Platform` unit to the `uses` clause in the interface section of the form and implement the event handler method to log app life cycle events:

```
function TFormLifecycle.HandleAppEvent(
  AappEvent: TapplicationEvent;
  Acontext: Tobject): Boolean;
begin
  case AappEvent of
    TApplicationEvent.FinishedLaunching:
      Log('App event: Finished Launching');
    TApplicationEvent.BecameActive:
      Log('App event: Became Active');
    TApplicationEvent.WillBecomeInactive:
      Log('App event: Will Become Inactive');
    TApplicationEvent.EnteredBackground:
      Log('App event: Entered Background');
    TApplicationEvent.WillBecomeForeground:
      Log('App event: Will Become Foreground');
    TApplicationEvent.WillTerminate:
      Log('App event: Will Terminate');
    TApplicationEvent.LowMemory:
      Log('App event: Low Memory');
    TApplicationEvent.TimeChange:
      Log('App event: Time Change');
    TApplicationEvent.OpenURL:
      Log('App event: Open URL');
  else
    Log('Unknown app event');
  end;
  Result := True;
end;
```

6. The last step is to register the `HandleAppEvent` method with the app life cycle service so it gets invoked by the operating system when important things happen to the app. A good place to do so is in the `OnCreate` event of the form:

```
procedure TFormLifecycle.FormCreate(Sender: TObject);
var
  AFMXApplicationEventService: IFMXApplicationEventService;
begin
  if TPlatformServices.Current.SupportsPlatformService(
      IFMXApplicationEventService, AFMXApplicationEventService) then
```

```
    aFMXApplicationEventService.
      SetApplicationEventHandler(HandleAppEvent)
  else
    Log('Application Event Service is not supported.');
  end;
```

Save everything and run the app. In *Figure 8.2,* you can see how the app looks on iOS.

Figure 8.2: The App Lifecycle project running on iOS

Figure 8.3 is a screenshot of this very same app running on Android.

Figure 8.3: The App Lifecycle project running on Android

When you switch to a different app on your phone or tablet, you will see that our app changes to background execution, and then when it is selected again it returns to the foreground.

Interestingly, the events on iOS and Android do not work exactly the same. For example, on Android the very first app life cycle event received is **Finished Launching**, while on iOS this is never received. It seems that **Became Active** and **Entered Background** are good choices for cross-platform handling of switching between the background and foreground.

There are also other interesting platform services that can be useful: for example, the IFMXSaveStateService interface is also surfaced as the event of a FireMonkey form. A mobile operating system may decide to suddenly kill your app, and this could be a good place to preserve your app execution state.

Finally, notice that this app would make little sense on desktop platforms, which have a much simpler application life cycle without a background mode. On desktop platforms, in fact, applications only start and terminate, there is no other special status.

 Now that we have looked into platform detection and app lifecycles, let's jump into the main topic of this chapter, which is the use of device sensors to let an app interact with the physical world.

Sensing the world

Unlike desktop computers, mobile devices have a rich set of sensors. They obviously have cameras, but they also generally have **Global Positioning System** (**GPS**), a compass, a gyroscope, possibly light detectors, a torch light, at times humidity and pressure sensors, and even more.

Delphi comes with a System.Sensors unit, where all kinds of possible sensors are defined. Similar to the FMX.Platform unit, the System.Sensors unit also has IFDEF compiler directives in its implementation uses clause for different platforms, including Android and iOS.

In the library, there is the main TSensorManager class that acts as a gateway to all sensor information. The class has a class property called Current: TSensorManager, which is used to expose a global object including all sensor information.

At the top of the System.Sensors unit you can find a TSensorCategory enumerated type, which provides the top-level categorization of all possible types of sensors:

```
type
    TSensorCategory = (Location, Environmental, Motion, Orientation,
       Mechanical, Electrical, Biometric, Light, Scanner);
```

Within each category, there are different sensor types, so each category has its own enumerated type as well.

All specialized sensor classes derive from an abstract TCustomSensor class, which provides basic functionality that is common to all sensors, such as the Start and Stop methods. In order to get access to individual sensors in your project's source code, you need to call the GetSensorsByCategory method of the TSensorManager class. This method takes as a parameter a sensor category and returns a dynamic array of available custom sensors of the given category. It's not uncommon to have a device with multiple sensors of the same family.

At a higher level of abstraction, there is also a System.Sensors.Components unit, which defines a generic TSensor class derived from TComponent and parameterized by the TCustomSensor type. This is a base class that provides core functionality, such as maintaining a reference to the TSensorManager, calling its GetSensorsByCategory method, and access to the specific properties made available in a given TCustomSensor descendant type.

In practical terms, you don't use this generic class. In fact, there are nine `TSensor` descendant components, all implemented in this unit, one for every value of the `TSensorCategory` enumeration. However, only three of them are actually registered with the IDE and appear on the Tool Palette in the **Sensors** category, as you can see in *Figure 8.4*.

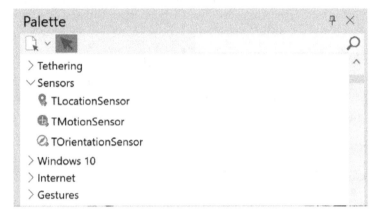

Figure 8.4: The sensor components in the Tool Palette

Using the location

A lot of mobile apps depend on location information. The GPS sensor is a standard part of typical smartphones and tablets. With the `TLocationSensor` component, it is very easy to add location awareness to an app.

There is nothing like building a test app and giving sensor components a try! Follow these steps to build a test app:

1. Create a new multi-device Delphi app, select the **Blank Application** template, and save the main form unit as `uFormSensors` and the project as `Sensors`. You can also change the `Name` property of the form to `FormSensors`.

2. Locate the **Sensors** category in the Tool Palette and add a `TLocationSensor` component to the form, or just use IDE Insight to search for the component by name.

3. As the next step, we need to switch the sensor on. To do this, there is an `Active` property that needs to be set to `True`. Drop a `TCheckBox` component on the form and align it to `Top`. Change all its `Margin` sub-properties to 8 to add some margin space before the border of the form.

4. Change its `Name` to `ChkbxLocSensor` and its `Text` property to `Location Sensor Active`.

5. In the checkbox's OnChange event, enter the following lines of code:

```
procedure TFormLoc.ChkbxLocSensorChange(Sender: TObject);
begin
  LocationSensor1.Active := ChkbxLocSensor.IsChecked;
end;
```

6. The next step is to respond to location change events. Readings from sensors are typically real numbers, so, before we proceed, let's implement a small DblToStr convenience function that will convert these float numbers to strings, to avoid calling ToString methods that would display fourteen digits after the decimal point. We only need a few decimals:

```
uses
  System.Math; // for IsNan

function TFormSensors.DblToStr(Value: Double): string;
begin
  if not IsNan(Value) then
    Result := Format('%3.5f',[Value])
  else
    Result := 'NaN';
end;
```

Add a TLabel component to the form. Align it to Top and change its Name to LblLocation. Expand its TextSettings property in the Object Inspector and change the HorzAlign property to Center. Change its Text property to (Location).

7. Double-click on the OnLocationChange event of the location sensor and enter the following code to display the current geographical coordinates read from the GPS sensor on our device:

```
procedure TFormLoc.LocationSensor1LocationChanged(Sender:
TObject;
  const OldLocation, NewLocation: TLocationCoord2D);
begin
  lblLocation.Text := DblToStr(NewLocation.Latitude)
    + ' : ' + DblToStr(NewLocation.Longitude);
end;
```

Save all files and run the app. Let's run it on iOS first. So, the moment we touch the checkbox to enable the location sensor, we should see the confirmation dialog from iOS asking whether we want to allow our app to have access to location information.

Click on **Allow** and you should see current latitude and longitude in the label.

Figure 8.5: The iOS system confirmation to allow the app to access location information

In the case of Android, for older versions of the operating system, access to different services is configured in the **Project Options**. There are two options for **coarse** and **fine** location information, and they are checked by default, so we do not need to do anything. For other services, it could be necessary to adjust **Uses Permissions**. With this model, the required permissions were communicated to the user and accepted by them when the app was installed.

More recent versions of Android, however, have moved to a model similar to iOS, with permissions explicitly requested by the app on execution before accessing the given service. If you try to use the location without asking for permission first (or if the user doesn't grant the app the requested permission), the event won't fire and you'll see no information.

To ask for permission on Android, we need to change the code used when the checkbox is activated. We ask for permission every time, but depending on the user choice, the same app might not really ask for permission again. The following code refers to a permission by string name and asks for it by using an anonymous method to do the follow-up action after the dialog is closed by the user:

```
procedure TFormSensors.ChkbxLocSensorChange(Sender: TObject);
const
  PermissionAccessFineLocation =
    'android.permission.ACCESS_FINE_LOCATION';
begin
{$IFDEF ANDROID}
  PermissionsService.RequestPermissions(
    [PermissionAccessFineLocation],
    procedure(const APermissions: TClassicStringDynArray;
      const AGrantResults: TClassicPermissionStatusDynArray)
    begin
      if (Length(AGrantResults) = 1) and
          (AGrantResults[0] = TPermissionStatus.Granted) then
        LocationSensor1.Active := ChkbxLocSensor.IsChecked
```

```
    else
    begin
      ChkbxLocSensor.IsChecked := False;
      TDialogService.ShowMessage(
        'Location permission not granted');
    end;
  end);
{$ELSE}
  LocationSensor1.Active := ChkbxLocSensor.IsChecked;
{$ENDIF}
end;
```

When you run this code the first time, the operating system will display a dialog requesting permission on behalf of your app, as shown in *Figure 8.6*.

Figure 8.6: The Android system confirmation to allow the app to access location information

Once permission has been granted, you'll see the latitude and longitude of the current position in the display label, as shown in *Figure 8.7*.

Figure 8.7: The location information in the Sensors app on Android

As you can see, the app can display the position of a device in latitude and longitude coordinates, which can also be used to determine a street address using reverse geocoding. Knowing the position of a device (that is, of the person using the app) is a powerful feature – and for good reason, this is protected in terms of requiring permissions for privacy reasons.

Using the orientation and motion sensors

In the **Sensors** category on the Tool Palette, we also have the `TMotionSensor` and `TOrientationSensor` components. Unlike the `TLocationSensor` component, they don't provide change events and it is up to the application code to access their readings from time to time. A common solution to this problem is to schedule regular checks. Let's continue building our Sensor app as follows:

1. Drop a `TTimer` component on the form so we can periodically update the user interface with the current information. Sets its `Enabled` property to `True`.

2. Drop `TMotionSensor` and `TOrientationSensor` components on the form.

3. They both have `Active` properties that need to be activated to enable the reading of information. Let's create two more sections on the form for motion and orientation information, which are similar to location. Add two more checkboxes and two more labels to the form. Align all of them to `Top` and adjust their margins, giving you something like *Figure 8.8*.

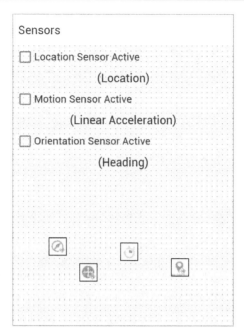

Figure 8.8: The Sensors project's main form in the Delphi Form Designer

4. Now we need to add OnChange event handlers to the two new checkboxes to enable or disable the respective sensors, depending on the value of the IsChecked property.

5. In the OnTimer event, if the sensors are active, we will update the labels with readings from specific properties of sensor components:

```
procedure TformSensors.Timer1Timer(Sender: Tobject);
begin
  if Assigned (MotionSensor1.Sensor) then
  begin
    LblLinearAccel.Text :=
      DblToStr(MotionSensor1.Sensor.AccelerationX) + ', '
      + DblToStr(MotionSensor1.Sensor.AccelerationY) + ', '
      + DblToStr(MotionSensor1.Sensor.AccelerationZ);
  end;
  if Assigned (OrientationSensor1.Sensor) then
  begin
    LblHeadingXYZ.Text :=
      DblToStr(OrientationSensor1.Sensor.HeadingX) + ', '
      + DblToStr(OrientationSensor1.Sensor.HeadingY) + ', '
      + DblToStr(OrientationSensor1.Sensor.HeadingZ);
  end;
end;
```

The result on Android is an app similar to *Figure 8.9*.

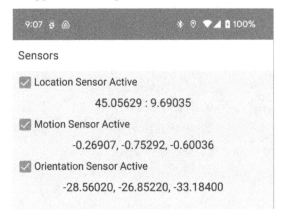

Figure 8.9: The Sensors app on Android

With the location, motion, and orientation sensors under our belts, we have explored the most common device sensors. By leveraging these sensors, you can create more powerful apps that are aware of the physical position and movement of the device. As indicated earlier, there are other applications of device sensors, the most relevant of them being cameras. Let us explore that in the next section.

Taking photos

There are many occasions when it is useful to be able to take a photo from an app. The programming model is very easy, but it is not the `TCamera` component that you need to use. In FireMonkey, taking photos is achieved by executing a special **take photo from camera** action. The following steps take you through building a demo based on that action:

1. Create a new blank multi-device FireMonkey application. Save the main form's unit as `uFormCam` and the project as `CamApp`, and change the `Name` property of the form to `FormCam`.

2. Change the **Style** setting in the combobox above the form to **iOS** or **Android**.

3. Drop a `TImage` component on the form, rename it to `ImagePhoto`, and align it to `Client`.

4. Add a `TToolBar` component and drop a `TSpeedbutton` onto the `ToolBar1` control. Change its `Name` to `SpdbtnTakePhoto` and the button's `Stylelookup` property to `cameratoolbutton`, align it to `Left`, and adjust the width so it becomes a square.

5. Drop a `TActionList` component on the form and double-click on it to display the **Action List Editor**. Right-click on the editor and select the **New Standard Action** option from the context menu. Now expand the **Media Library** category and double-click on the **TakePhotoFromTheCamera** action to add it to the list of actions, as you can see in *Figure 8.10*.

Figure 8.10: The TakePhotoFromCameraAction in the Standard Action Classes dialog box

There are all kinds of interesting actions here. We will have a look at more of them later. Actions are just regular components with properties and events. Any action can be executed via code by calling its `Execute` or `ExecuteTarget` methods. A simpler way to invoke the action from a visual control is to attach it to the `Action` property. In this way, we do not need to write any code.

With the code configured so far, when the end user taps the button, the mobile device will display the view that would normally be displayed when clicking on the integrated camera app. The next step is to do something in the code with the photo that is taken with the camera. The `TakePhotoFromCameraAction1` component that was added to the form has different events, including an `OnDidFinishTaking` event that we can handle.

Double-click on the `OnDidFinishTaking` event. The generated event handler has an `Image` parameter of type `TBitmap`, which contains the bitmap with the photo that was just taken. We can do anything with it, including, for example, display it in the image component already on our form. Enter the following code to display the bitmap:

```
procedure TFormCam.TakePhotoFromCameraAction1DidFinishTaking(
  Image: TBitmap);
```

```
begin
  ImagePhoto.Bitmap.Assign(Image);
end;
```

The first time you run the app on iOS, after tapping the camera button, you will be presented with a message stating that your app wants to access the camera. Click **OK** and take the photo. It is now displayed in the form.

On Android, again, things are a bit more complex – and we need to ask for permission both to use the camera and to store a temporary file with the image. If we fail to do so, the app will show an error as in *Figure 8.11*.

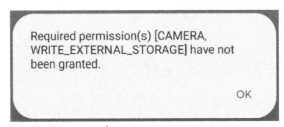

Figure 8.11: The error displayed by the CamApp app on Android
if we fail to ask for permission to use the camera

To address this issue, we need to write some code similar to our previous location-sensor use case. In this case, we need to ask for the two required permissions and check that both have been granted, enabling the toolbar button in the positive case. The following code asks for permission using the PermissionService and determines what action to take depending on the result of the request:

```
procedure TFormCam.FormCreate(Sender: TObject);
const
  PermissionCamera = 'android.permission.CAMERA';
  PermissionExtStorage =
    'android.permission.WRITE_EXTERNAL_STORAGE';
begin
{$IFDEF ANDROID}
  PermissionsService.RequestPermissions(
    [PermissionCamera, PermissionExtStorage],
    procedure(const APermissions: TClassicStringDynArray;
      const AGrantResults: TClassicPermissionStatusDynArray)
    begin
      if (Length(AGrantResults) = 2) and
         (AGrantResults[0] = TPermissionStatus.Granted) and
         (AGrantResults[1] = TPermissionStatus.Granted) then
        TakePhotoFromCameraAction1.Enabled := True
      else
```

```
        TakePhotoFromCameraAction1.Enabled := False;
    end);
{$ENDIF}
end;
```

When the permissions are granted, the app allows a user to capture a photo, as you can see in *Figure 8.12* (in this case, a photo of the Delphi software box).

Figure 8.12: Displaying a photo of the Delphi 1 box in an image control with the CamApp app on Android

---

The CamApp in Android 14

The way the FireMonkey library requests permission for the CamApp application file sharing worked fine in old versions of Android. If you use Android 14, you'll have to recompile the app with Delphi 12 to make it work without modifications. In Delphi 11.3, you'll see an error message.

In this section, we have seen how we can use the phone camera to take pictures within an application. This is a very nice feature, but it can be further extended by adding the ability to share these pictures with other apps, as covered in the next section.

Using share sheets

Our app is coming along nicely, but it is not very useful. The photo is displayed in the form, but goes away when we stop the app or take another photo. It is a typical functionality in mobile operating systems to be able to share things with other installed apps. For example, we might want to share a photo on social media or send it by email. This can be achieved through *share sheets* that are also available through actions.

The term *share sheet* refers to the ability of apps to share data with other apps, such as the common use case of sharing an image with a social network application. We can see this in action by extending our existing app from the previous section as follows:

1. Drop another `TSpeedButton` on the toolbar. Rename it to `SpdbtnSharePhoto`, change its `StyleLookup` property to `actiontoolbutton`, adjust its width, and align it to `Right`.

2. Expand its `Action` property in the Object Inspector, and through the context menu, add the `TShowShareSheetAction` standard action from the **Media Library** category.

    This is a faster way of adding actions, directly from the Object Inspector without having to display the **Action List Editor** and then hooking the action to a control.

    The speed button will take care of executing the action, but we need to write some code to share this particular photo that we have just taken with the camera and that is now stored in the image component on the form.

3. Select the `ShowShareSheetAction1` component in the Object Inspector. It has a `Bitmap` property. It is the bitmap that is going to be shared with other apps. In the **Events** tab, double-click on the `OnBeforeExecute` event and enter the following code that assigns the bitmap from the image to the action:

    ```
    procedure TFormCam.ShowShareSheetAction1BeforeExecute(
      Sender: TObject);
    begin
      ShowShareSheetAction1.Bitmap.Assign(ImagePhoto.Bitmap);
    end;
    ```

    With this change, we have built a much more useful app. We are just missing a nice title and we can consider it ready.

4. Drop a `TLabel` component on the toolbar and align it to `Client`. Expand its `TextSettings` property and change `HorzAlign` to `Center`. Enter `Delphi Camera` into its `Text` property, as shown in *Figure 8.13* (the app itself at runtime was already shown in *Figure 8.12*).

Figure 8.13: The main form of CamApp in the Form Designer

Save the source code and run the app on a device. Now we can take photos and share them through other apps installed on the device, as shown in *Figure 8.14*.

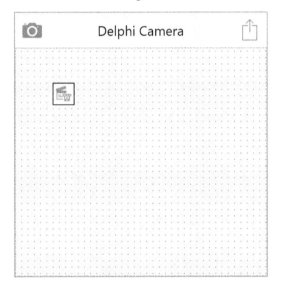

Figure 8.14: The Save to Drive configuration in the share sheet dialog on Android

Two lines of code (plus a few more for the permissions) for a fully functional cross-platform camera mobile app? Not bad at all! This demo shows the power of FireMonkey, but also of the actions architecture, and the rapid development that is possible thanks to predefined actions.

In the previous two sections, we have seen how we can use the phone camera to take pictures within an application and share them with other apps. The camera, however, can also be used to display or record full videos, as covered in the next section.

Camera, action!

If we can take photos with action components, as we have done in the previous sections, then what is the purpose of the TCameraComponent component that can be found in the **Additional** category on the Tool Palette? A quick answer could be that it is the way to switch on and off the flashlight that most phones are equipped with. A more elaborate answer would be that it can be used to take videos.

The FireMonkey library has generic support for handling the many types of cameras available across different hardware. The actual access to the underlying video hardware is done through the non-visual TCaptureDeviceManager class defined in the FMX.Media unit.

The programming model follows the same pattern as in other platform services. The class itself is abstract, but it has a Current public class property that returns a reference to the actual TCaptureDeviceManager implementation on a given platform. The TCaptureDeviceManager class has a Devices array property where we can access all available capture devices, but there are also the following ready-to-use properties:

- DefaultAudioCaptureDevice: TAudioCaptureDevice
- DefaultVideoCaptureDevice: TVideoCaptureDevice

While we could have implemented video recording in the app by directly accessing DefaultVideoCaptureDevice, TCameraComponent provides as more convenient interface to this same functionality.

Creating a demo application for managing the camera and displaying a video is simple. The following are the steps to build it:

1. Create a new blank multi-device application. Save the form's unit as uFormVideo and the whole project as VideoApp.

2. Drop a TToolbar on the form.

3. Drop a TCameraComponent on the form.

4. Drop a TImage component on the form, align it to Client, and rename it to ImgVideo.

5. Now drop another TCheckbox component on the Toolbar1. Change its Name to ChkbxCamera and its Text to Camera Active, and align it to Left. In its Margin. Left property enter 8, so that the checkbox is not exactly at the edge of the form.

6. In the OnChange event of the checkbox, add the following code to activate the camera:

```
procedure TFormVideo.ChkbxCameraChange(Sender: TObject);
```

```
begin
  CameraComponent1.Active := ChkbxCamera.IsChecked;
end;
```

In order to access video information from the camera, we need to handle its `OnSampleBufferReady` event, which is fired when there is a new image from the camera available in the buffer. The `TCameraComponent` class provides a specific `SampleBufferToBitmap` method that can be used to easily display the contents of the buffer:

1. Enter the following code for the `OnSampleBufferReady` event handler:

    ```
    procedure TformVideo.CameraComponent1SampleBufferReady(
      Sender: Tobject; const ATime: TMediaTime);
    begin
      CameraComponent1.SampleBufferToBitmap(ImgVideo.Bitmap, True);
    end;
    ```

2. Save all the source code files and run the app on a device. You'll see something like that shown in *Figure 8.15*.

Figure 8.15: Capturing a video of my blog with the phone camera on Android

The process is just as simple as taking photos in Delphi. Notice that making an **Augmented Reality (AR)** app is just one step away. Before we put the bitmap from the sample buffer into the image on the form, we could have done some preprocessing, such as checking the orientation of the device in 3D space and drawing on the bitmap things that only exist in AR.

Notify me!

One of the most common ways of attracting a mobile device user to a particular app is to display a notification. When a new email arrives or a friend posts something on social media, we are typically alerted with a notification. Clicking on it displays the app that sent the notification.

Delphi provides a TNotificationCenter component that can be used to display and react to notifications. A very common use case is displaying a number next to the app icon for the count of new notifications. This can also be used for unread emails and missed calls:

1. Create a new, blank, multi-device app. Save the main form as uFormNotify and the project as NotifyMe.

2. Add a toolbar with a label aligned to Client with text reading Delphi Notifications.

3. Now drop a TNotificationCenter component on the form. As a side effect, the System. Notification unit will be added to the form's uses clause.

4. The first class defined in this unit is TNotification, which is used as a lightweight object that represents a notification. If we want to display a notification, we first need to call the CreateNotification method of the TNotificationCenter class, which returns a new TNotification object. At this point, we need to configure the public fields of the notification. The last step is to pass the notification object to one of the methods of TNotificationCenter to display the notification immediately or to schedule it to be displayed in the future or in given time intervals. There are also methods to cancel an already scheduled notification.

5. Drop a button on the form. Change its Name to BtnNotify and its Text to Notify Me.

6. Double-click on the button and enter the following code to display a test notification from the app:

```
procedure TFormNotify.BtnNotifyClick(Sender: TObject);
var
  N: TNotification;
begin
  N := NotificationCenter1.CreateNotification;
  try
    N.Name := 'MY_APP_NOTIFICATION_1';
    N.Title := 'Notify Me App';
    N.AlertBody :=
       'This is an important notification from Delphi!';
    NotificationCenter1.PresentNotification(N);
```

```
  finally
    N.Free;
  end;
end;
```

The result of this code is a notification like the one shown in *Figure 8.16*. Selecting it activates the app, even if the app has been closed by the user.

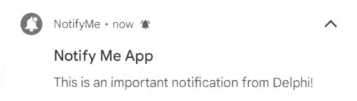

Figure 8.16. A notification displayed by a Delphi app

The Name field of the notification object is used to uniquely identify it within an application. It is used, for example, to cancel a specific notification.

If we had added another button named BtnCancel to the form, we could cancel the notification with the following code:

```
procedure TFormNotify.BtnCancelClick(Sender: TObject);
begin
  NotificationCenter1.CancelNotification('MY_APP_NOTIFICATION_1');
end;
```

Notifications are very important for apps, as they attract the attention of the device user to some specific event and display relevant information as part of the device notifications list. This is important to improve the value of an app and increase user interactions.

Another key feature of many apps is the ability to not live in isolation, but access external resources on the internet. The simplest way to access remote information is via the use of an integrated web browser component.

Navigating the web

The debate about whether natively compiled or JavaScript-based web mobile apps are better seems to be over. Native mobile apps such as those built with Delphi, C++Builder, or Xcode are the most common choice for developers. However, sometimes it makes a lot of sense to combine these two different worlds and create a hybrid solution where an app is still native, but also embeds a web browser.

Luckily in FireMonkey, there is a special `TWebBrowser` component that makes it easy to embed web-browsing functionality in your app:

1. Create a blank multi-device application. Save the form as `uFormWebBrowser` and the project as `WebBrowserApp`.

2. Drop a toolbar component on the form. Drop a `TEdit` component on the toolbar and rename it to `EdtURL`. It will contain a URL for the web browser component to navigate to. For convenience, you can already put a valid URL into the `Text` property of the edit, so it is faster at runtime to check that our app is working correctly. This could, for example, be the web address of the Embarcadero blog site at `http://blogs.embarcadero.com`.

3. Now drop a `TSpeedButton` on the toolbar. Change its `Name` property to `SpdbtnGo`, its `Stylelookup` to `refreshtoolbutton`, and its `Align` property to `Right`.

4. Drop two more speed buttons on the toolbar. Change their `Name` properties respectively to `SpdbtnBack` and `SpdbtnForward`. Change their `Stylelookup` properties to `arrowlefttoolbutton` and `arrowrighttoolbutton`. Align them both to `Left`.

5. Now change the `Align` property of the URL edit to `Client` and its `Margin.Top` property to 8, so there is a distance between the edit and the top of the form.

6. Drop a `TWebBrowser` component on the form and align it to `Client`. Now double-click on each speed button and enter the following simple code for web browser navigation, invoking actions including `GoBack`, `GoForward`, and `Navigate`:

```
procedure TFormWebBrowser.SpdbtnBackClick(Sender: TObject);
begin
  WebBrowser1.GoBack;
end;


procedure TFormWebBrowser.SpdbtnForwardClick(Sender: TObject);
begin
  WebBrowser1.GoForward;
end;


procedure TFormWebBrowser.SpdbtnGoClick(Sender: TObject);
begin
  WebBrowser1.Navigate(EdtURL.Text);
end;
```

Save everything and run your work on iOS and Android devices. We have just created a fully functional cross-platform mobile web browser app, as you can see in *Figure 8.17*.

Figure 8.17: Using a web browser in an app

This is all that is needed for a simple app that offers web-browsing capabilities along with native code. The ability to merge compiled app features and web content is a very powerful element of FireMonkey and should be leveraged whenever it will reduce the development effort.

To conclude this chapter, let's now move to a more advanced topic: the ability to call platform-specific features not surfaced by the FireMonkey framework.

Delphi language bridges

So far, we have seen how to access cross-platform implementations of services including sensors, address books, maps, and other features we have covered so far in this chapter. All of them come out of the box with Delphi. Luckily, Delphi comes with the source code, so it is possible to inspect how Delphi itself is accessing the underlying mobile APIs on Android and iOS. All supported operating systems are different and there are different ways of accessing their raw APIs.

The Delphi language offers "bridges" to call native platforms APIs on all supported platforms, although the technique varies for each target operating system. While in most cases, this is not required, it's important to know that unlike other cross-platform development tools that offer only a subset of the underlying platform features, with Delphi you have the full power of the device and the entire API available to you. Only, programming for the API takes a bit more effort and requires a good understanding of the API itself.

Let's consider a simple example of making your mobile device vibrate via code. That is not something that Delphi provides out of the box, but we will use this case to analyze the process of accessing any functionality that is not readily accessible in Android and iOS.

Vibrating on Android

Android is based on Linux and Java. Accessing Android APIs requires being able to call Java code from Object Pascal. This is the role of the Object-Pascal-to-Java language bridge, and this is how FireMonkey gets access to Android's functionality. Before we can access certain functionality in Android, we need to review the documentation and know what Java class we want to access and what methods we want to call. Vibrations on Android are accessible through the `Vibrator` class declared in the `Android.os` namespace and derived directly from the `java.lang.object` base class. The online documentation of this class can be found at the following URL:

`https://developer.android.com/reference/android/os/Vibrator.html`

In the `source\rtl\Android` folder, under the Delphi installation, we can find a number of Object Pascal units with names that start with `Android.JNI`. These are files already imported into Object Pascal. In the `Android.Jni.Os` unit, we can find the Object Pascal interfaces for different Java classes imported from the `Android.os` namespace, including `JVibrator`. That's the one we need, but how do we use it in code?

Browsing through the source code, we can find two interface declarations: `JVibratorClass` and `JVibrator`. The first interface represents the `class` methods of the given Java type and the second is for `instance` methods. The `TJVibrator` class derived from the generic `TJavaGenericImport` class glues these interfaces together. The `TJavaGenericImport` class is defined in the `Androidapi.JNIBridge` unit and provides the base functionality for importing all kinds of Java classes. This is the definition in the Delphi unit:

```
type
  TJVibrator = class(
    TJavaGenericImport<JVibratorClass, JVibrator>)
  end;
```

What we want to do is to call the `Vibrate` method declared in the `JVibrator` interface, but how do we get access to it? Different Java classes can be accessed through the `SharedActivityContext` procedure defined in the `Androidapi.Helpers` unit that returns the Java application context. The documentation says that we need to call the `GetSystemService` method and pass `VIBRATOR_SERVICE` as an argument. The `TJavaGenericImport` class declares the handy `Wrap` method that lets us typecast from a raw pointer into the proper interface type.

In this way, we can make our Android device vibrate using the following code. It has to be surrounded by `IFDEF`s for Android. In this case, an inline variable comes in very handy:

```
uses
  Androidapi.JNI.Os, Androidapi.JNI.GraphicsContentViewText,
  Androidapi.Helpers, Androidapi.JNIBridge;

. . .
  var AVibrator: JVibrator := TJVibrator.Wrap(
    (SharedActivityContext.GetSystemService(
       TJContext.JavaClass.VIBRATOR_SERVICE) as
         ILocalObject).GetObjectID
  );
  // Vibrate for 500 milliseconds
  AVibrator.Vibrate(500);
```

This is just a simple example. There are also Java classes without already imported Object Pascal interfaces. In these cases, you can use the **Java2OP** command-line tool available in the `bin\converters\java2op` sub-directory in the Delphi installation (or a similar tool) to generate the appropriate Delphi-to-Java mapping code.

Let's now see how we can tackle our vibration use case on iOS.

Vibrations on iOS

Making an iOS device vibrate requires completely different steps compared to Android. Vibrations on iOS are available as part of the `AudioToolbox` framework. To make an iOS device vibrate, we need to call the `AudioServicesPlaySystemSound` API function, which is documented at the following URL:

`https://developer.apple.com/reference/audiotoolbox/system_sound_services`

Similarly to Android, there are already a few pre-imported units with interfaces to the iOS APIs in the `source\rtl\ios` directory. The model is similar. Different frameworks have their own import units with names starting with `iOSapi`. There is also a generic class for importing arbitrary Objective-C classes defined in the `Macapi.ObjectiveC` unit, called `TOCGenericImport`, that serves a similar role as `TJavaGenericImport` in Android.

The Delphi installation comes with a number of iOS frameworks already imported. Go to the **Tools** dialog and find **SDK Manager**. Scroll down through the list. Unfortunately, the `AudioToolbox` framework is not present in Delphi out of the box, so it is not listed as an available framework and there is no `iOSapi.AudioToolbox` unit in the source directory.

If we want to write code that uses a certain framework functionality, we need to first import it into Delphi. Look for the **AudioToolbox** framework in the main list, select it, and enable it by editing its configuration and pressing the **OK** button as shown in *Figure 8.18*.

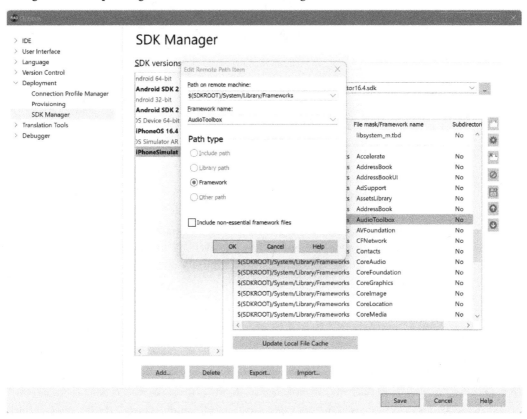

Figure 8.18: Configuring the AudioToolbox

With this done, how do we call the `AudioServicesPlaySystemSound` function from the imported framework?

In the `bin` directory of Delphi is the **SdkTransform** tool that can help with importing Objective-C frameworks into Object Pascal. This was done to generate the code used by the demo application to call the framework function (you don't need to repeat this step if you are using the companion source code).

Once we know the signature of our API method, we can call it in the code. Again, the following code should be surrounded with `IFDEFs` for iOS to be able to compile it:

```
uses
  IOSapi.MediaPlayer, IOSapi.CoreGraphics, FMX.Platform,
  FMX.Platform.IOS, IOSapi.UIKit, Macapi.ObjCRuntime,
  Macapi.ObjectiveC, iOSapi.Cocoatypes, Macapi.CoreFoundation,
  iOSapi.Foundation, iOSapi.CoreImage, iOSapi.QuartzCore,
  iOSapi.CoreData;

const
  libAudioToolbox =
'/System/Library/Frameworks/AudioToolbox.framework/AudioToolbox';
  kSystemSoundID_vibrate = $FFF;

procedure AudioServicesPlaySystemSound(
    inSystemSoundID: integer); cdecl;
  external libAudioToolbox name _PU +
    'AudioServicesPlaySystemSound';

procedure Tform1.Button1Click(Sender: TObject);
begin
  AudioServicesPlaySystemSound(kSystemSoundID_vibrate);
end;
```

In this and the previous section, we have seen how to add native capabilities to Android and iOS apps, which allows you to call APIs not directly available in the library. Luckily, Delphi and FireMonkey come with most of the commonly used functionalities already available in the form of components and libraries, so we rarely need to extend to such low-level programming.

Summary

In this chapter, we have learned how to work with different platform functionalities provided by the two mobile operating systems, Android and iOS. While the two are quite different, most of the core concepts are the same. We can use high-level components in the FireMonkey library and their cross-platform abstractions. This way, we can just recompile our projects for both OSs with the same source code.

Toward the end of the chapter, we also explored what you need to do to call platform APIs not wrapped by the FireMonkey library. This is significantly more work, but it's important to realize that it is possible, unlike in cross-platform mobile development tools, which offer a defined set of features without the ability to add others.

While the focus on mobile is particularly relevant, in the next chapter, we'll spend a little time focusing on desktop, as FireMonkey also supports Windows, macOS, and even Linux (via an add-on library). We'll cover some tips for developing apps for desktop and for both desktop and mobile and also focus on building desktop and mobile apps that interact one with the other.

9

Desktop Apps and Mobile Bridges

Although, in this book, we are primarily focused on building mobile apps with Delphi and FireMonkey, this chapter touches on the development menu of desktop applications and on the development of applications that work seamlessly on desktop and mobile, with a single source code base. The chapter will offer specific tips and recommendations for Windows, macOS, and Linux, and it will focus on what Delphi offers to create desktop and mobile applications that interact directly, using a technology called app tethering.

Given that FireMonkey is a great library for desktop development, it is important to focus on this area of the library, besides covering iOS and Android support. A significant advantage of FireMonkey is its ability to target desktop and mobile with a single source code, and the goal of this chapter is to help you understand this powerful feature while exploring specific examples.

This chapter will cover the following points:

- Single source for mobile and desktop
- Using the MultiView control
- Using data grids
- Using layout controls
- Building desktop apps for Windows, macOS, and Linux
- App tethering

The objective of this chapter is to learn how to build FireMonkey applications that are truly multi-device and not just mobile.

Technical requirements

The source code for the demos in this chapter is available at `https://github.com/PacktPublishing/Expert-Delphi_Second-edition`.

Single source for mobile and desktop

The beauty of building applications using FireMonkey is that you can compile them for each of the supported platforms and they just work, adapting automatically to the platform controls' style and look and feel. Additionally, as we have seen, you can adapt the UI to each of the platforms you want to target, by creating specific views in the FireMonkey form designer in the Delphi IDE.

Therefore, it is possible to build a single app for multiple platforms. We have focused on building native apps for Android and iOS, seamlessly. However, within the desktop world, there are additional considerations to take into account. One of them is the fact that screens tend to be wide, and applications tend to stretch horizontally, unlike in the mobile world. Also, most visual interaction is through the mouse rather than through the touch of a finger. This affects the entire UI design.

There are many other differences for desktop applications, and I won't be able to cover them all in detail in this chapter. There is some possible desktop integration, which is very different depending on the platform. There are menus that users interact with, including system menus. There are pop-up menus on right-click, but that is very Windows-specific. You should take into consideration keyboard shortcuts, something that doesn't exist on mobile.

FireMonkey comes with ready-to-use solutions to help you add all of these features. However, in this chapter, I want to focus primarily on the layout of applications, using different controls. These general techniques are not only useful for desktop but also mobile, and they can help you build an app that works across both paradigms.

We'll explore user-interface techniques, starting with the MultiView control, a very powerful and flexible FireMonkey control container that is fairly complex to use.

Using the MultiView control

A very peculiar control in FireMonkey is the **MultiView** control, which can be used to offer a flexible set of commands or menus, easily adaptable for mobile and desktop applications. It offers an implementation of the so-called *hamburger menu* (a button with three horizontal lines), with a drawer that can overlap the content or push it to the side. The MultiView control associates a master pane (with the application menu or controls elements) with a details pane, generally showing the actual application content and data.

In this case, I want to build a general app that can change the behavior of the MultiView control, by switching its *mode* at runtime. Let's look at the display options (or *modes*) for this control:

- Drawer mode has a master pane that is hidden and can slide to overlap the details pane

- Panel mode has independent panels, with the master docked on the side of the detail pane

- Popover mode has the master pane in a pop-up window

- Navigation mode has an initially minimized master pane, which expands on request

- PlatformBehaviour mode offers automatic behavior, depending on the device type and orientation, with different defaults for a phone or tablet in landscape or portrait orientation

- Custom mode offers the user the ability to create a custom container class for the master pane (a setting I'm going to ignore in this demo)

How do we create a demo application to understand the behavior of the MultiView control? Let's follow these steps:

1. Create a new multi-device application. Save the form unit as `MultiViewDemo_Form` and the application as `MultiViewDemo`.

2. Change the form name to `MViewForm`.

3. Add a `TMultiView` control to the form.

4. Place in the MultiView control a `TLayout` control (a visually neutral controls container) and set its `Align` property to `Top`.

5. In this layout control, add `TSpeedButton`, align it to the left, set its four `Margins` subproperties (`Left`, `Top`, `Right`, and `Bottom`) to 8, and select as `StyleLookup` the `addtoolbutton` value.

6. Now, add in the same Layout control a `TLabel`, `Align` it to `Client`, change its `TextSettings.Font.Size` setting to 16, and change its text setting to `Add Item`.

7. Now, repeat the preceding steps, adding a second `TLayout`, also aligned to `Top`, and add to it another `TSpeedButton` aligned to `Left` with proper margins, and a `TLabel` aligned to `Client`. Set their properties as previously, but this time, set the `StyleLookup` speed button to `infotoolbutton` and the `Text` label to `Information`.

8. Add a `TPanel` to the form, which we'll use as the detail panel, and set its `Align` property to `Client`. In the `MultiView1` control, set the `TargetControl` property to `Panel1`. This associates the two sides of the MultiView control.

9. Add to the panel `TToolBar`. This is aligned to `Top` by default. Add to the toolbar a `TSpeedButton`, and change its name to `BtnDrawer`. Align it to `Left`, and select for the `StyleLookup` property the `drawertoolbutton` value.

10. Associate this button to the MultiView control using the `MasterButton` property of `MultiView1`, by setting the property to `BtnDrawer`.

11. Now, add a TComboBox control to the toolbar, and set its `Align` property to `Client`. Set its four `Margins` sub-properties to 8. Set its `Items` property to the following list of values, which need to be in the same order as the underlying enumerated data type:

```
PlatformBehaviour
Panel
Popover
Drawer
Custom
NavigationPane
```

12. This is all we need in terms of component configuration. Now, we need to add some code to a few event handlers. First, add an `OnChange` event handler to the combo box we just added:

```
procedure TMViewForm.ComboModeChange(Sender: TObject);
begin
  if ComboMode.ItemIndex >= 0 then
    MultiView1.Mode := TMultiViewMode(ComboMode.ItemIndex);

  Caption := 'MultiViewDemo (' +
    ComboMode.Items [ComboMode.ItemIndex] + ')';
end;
```

13. To initialize the status, also add this code to the `OnCreate` event handler of the form:

```
procedure TMViewForm.FormCreate(Sender: TObject);
begin
  MultiView1.Mode := TMultiViewMode.PlatformBehaviour;
  ComboMode.ItemIndex := 0;
end;
```

14. You can also add an event handler with a simple message to the `OnClick` event of the information button.

Now, we can run the application and see how it behaves. By default, it shows the MultiView control with the platform configuration for desktop (in this case, Windows), as shown in *Figure 9.1*.

Figure 9.1: The default appearance of MultiViewDemo on desktop

When you click on the drawer button, the side panel expands, overlapping the empty detail view and visibly obscuring it, as you can see in *Figure 9.2*.

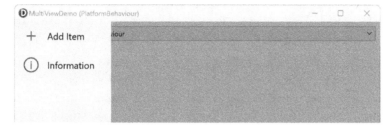

Figure 9.2: MultiViewDemo once you click the drawer button

If you now select the other MultiView control modes in the combo box, you can see the different configurations. By picking **Panel**, you'll have a fixed size side panel pushing the content to the side (rather than overlapping it). By picking **Drawer**, the master pane disappears, leaving more room for the detail pane, and it becomes enabled only when you click the drawer button. Once expanded, the drawer is configured (in this case) to reduce the detail pane rather than overlapping it, as shown in *Figure 9.3*.

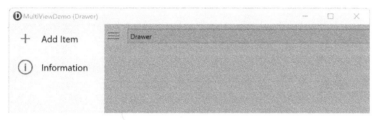

Figure 9.3: The MultiViewDemo in Drawer mode

Finally, **Popover** mode has a hidden master pane that pops up in a separate panel on top of the form once the drawer button is clicked. It's difficult to add images for all of the various configurations, and even more difficult to explain the animations and effects. I recommend you experiment with the demo by running it to see it in action.

What's important to note here is the fact that this UI can nicely adapt to mobile. I'm going to show you the mobile version of it in *Figure 9.5*, but first, I want to add some content to its detail pane by introducing another family of controls, called grids. These are more commonly used on desktop rather than mobile applications.

Using data grids

Every time you need to display complex, structured information to a user, you can use the **grid**, one of the most common UI controls. We'll read more about grids in the next chapter, when covering database apps. However, I want to introduce grids now, as they are even more common on desktop applications.

Let's see how TStringGrid works in FireMonkey. Let's get back to our MultiViewDemo example and place a string grid control on the detail panel called Panel1. Align this grid to Client. Now, select the grid and right click on it, or view the commands at the bottom of the Object Inspector and open its **Items Editor** window. In the combo box on the side, make sure that TStringColum is selected (as we want to have a grid of strings), and press **Add Item** five times. You should have now added five columns, as shown in *Figure 9.4*.

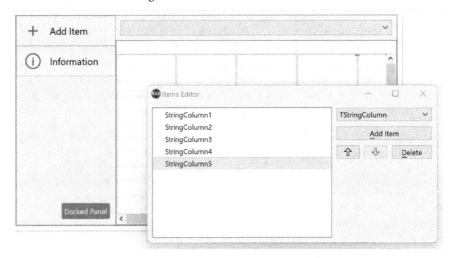

Figure 9.4: Adding columns to a string grid at design time

Close this dialog, and set the RowCount property of the string grid to 20. Now, we have a grid with 5 columns and 20 rows. We can add some strings to it, by adding the following code to the OnCreate event handler of the form, which sets column headers first and then fills the grid with content:

```
for var J := 0 to StringGrid1.ColumnCount - 1 do
  StringGrid1.Columns[J].Header := 'Col ' +
    (J+1).ToString;
for var I := 0 to StringGrid1.RowCount - 1 do
  for var J := 0 to StringGrid1.ColumnCount - 1 do
  begin
    StringGrid1.Cells[J, I] := Format (
      '%d, %d', [I+1, J+1]);
  end;
```

Note that the code is written to be independent from the number of columns and rows in the string grid.

Finally, we can implement the **Add Item** speed button in the MultiView control with the following code, which adds a new row by increasing the row count and fills the new row with data:

```
procedure TMViewForm.SpeedButton1Click(Sender: TObject);
begin
  StringGrid1.RowCount := StringGrid1.RowCount + 1;
  var I := StringGrid1.RowCount - 1;
  for var J := 0 to StringGrid1.ColumnCount -1 do
  begin
    StringGrid1.Cells[J, I] := Format (
      '%d, %d', [I+1, J+1]);
  end;
end;
```

The net effect of this code is filling the grid with values. In *Figure 9.5*, you can see this application but this time running on Android, with the platform default configuration of the MultiView control.

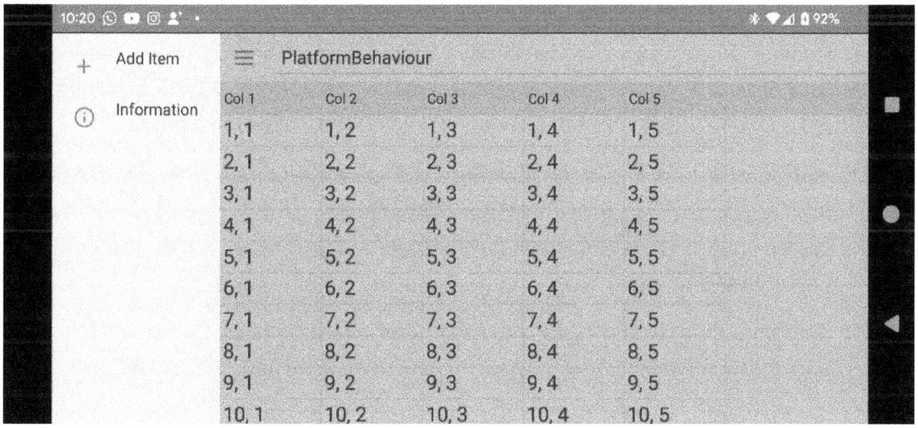

Figure 9.5: MultiViewDemo with the populated string grid running on Android in a landscape orientation

FireMonkey grids are way more powerful than just string grids. First, you can have columns of many different types:

- TCheckColumn, with a checkbox to display Boolean values
- TCurrencyColumn, displaying currency values
- TDateColumn, displaying dates
- TGlyphColumn, displaying small graphical elements
- TImageColumn, displaying a full image

- `TPopupColumn`, with the ability to create a custom pop-up pane

- `TProgressColumn`, showing a progress bar

- `TStringColumn`, holding a string (as we did in the previous demo)

- `TTimeColumn`, displaying a time

The second reason grids can be powerful is that they offer support for Live Bindings to data sources, either in the form of a list of objects or a database table, as we'll see in *Chapter 10*.

While this chapter only covered string grids with one example, grids are a very common element of a FireMonkey application UI, particularly on desktop applications. Now that we have looked at the MultiView control and grids, we can move to another fundamental tool for FireMonkey UI developers, which is the use of layouts to help adapt the UI to different screen sizes.

Leveraging layout controls

Layout controls are a fundamental tool to define an adaptive and flexible UI for FireMonkey apps.

If you want to create a flexible and fluid UI that adapts to different device sizes, you should not position your controls at absolute points. In most of the previous demos, we used alignments and nested controls to allow the actual controls to adapt to the hosting surface and window. In the MultiViewDemo example, for example, I used a layout with a speed button and a label with specific alignments.

The `TLayout` control is the base layout. It's an empty and invisible container. By invisible, I mean it has no visible elements in the UI, but the control itself needs to be visible for a user to see the controls it hosts. The `TLayout` control can use absolute positioning or alignment with margins, like any other FireMonkey container control.

However, there are a number of inherited layout classes that offer specialized behavior. If you search layout in the **Palette** pane in the Delphi IDE, you'll see a list, as shown in *Figure 9.6*.

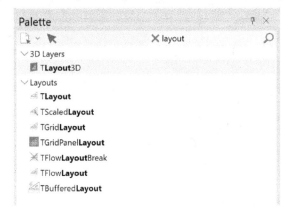

Figure 9.6: The layout controls available in FireMonkey

Each of these layout controls has a specific role. However, they do have things in common – they are container controls without a specific UI, and they determine the positioning of the child controls, each with a different rule. Rather than providing a general description of each available layout, I'm going to cover some of them while including them in a demo. Let's start by creating the core infrastructure.

1. Create a new multi-device application, but this time, pick the **Tabbed** template. Select a target folder. Rename the project, using the **File | Save Project As** menu item, to LayoutsDemo. Rename the main form unit, using the **File | Save As** menu item, to LayoutsDemo_Form.

2. The main form of the demo should have a toolbar, called HeaderToolBar, hosting a label called ToolBarLabel. Change the text of this label to Layouts Demo.

3. The form also has TTabControl with four TTabItem objects. You can remove and add more tabs using the **Items Editor** window (see *Figure 9.7*) of TabControl1, available at the bottom of the Object Inspector or by right-clicking on the control itself, in the Structure view. Change the text of each of the tabs to describe the layout they are going to contain – Flow, Grid, Scaled, and Grid Panel (also shown in *Figure 9.7*).

Figure 9.7: Editing the tabs of TabControl

Now, let's start analyzing each of these layouts one by one.

Flow layout

A **FlowLayout** control is a fairly simple layout. Child controls are positioned in a flow, one after the other, and they are moved to a new line when they don't fit in the host layout (often aligned to the container window). The position properties of the control are ignored, as it is the layout's job to determine the position.

Let's continue building our demo by adding this layout to the first tab:

1. Select the first tab of the `TabControl1` component, and place a `TFlowLayout` control in it. Set its `Align` property to `Client`.

2. Select the `Padding` property, and set each of the four elements (`Top`, `Right`, `Bottom`, `Width`) to 4. This provides some spacing inside the layout so that internal controls don't get aligned to the border but, instead, a few pixels inside.

3. Given we are going with the defaults, we can leave the `Justify` property as `Left`, `JustifyLastLine` as `Left`, and `FlowDirection` as `LeftToRight`. These are critical properties, as the flow can be left to right, top to bottom, right to left, or even bottom to top.

4. Now, start adding a number of buttons inside the `FlowLayout1` control. Once this is done, select them all in the Structure view, set the four sub-properties of the `Margins` property to 4, and set `Size.Width` to `120` and `Size.Height` to `40`.

5. You can have a set of controls over a few lines. Tweak the size of some of the controls to make them different. You can see how they are arranged in the demo project, as design time, in *Figure 9.8*. Some buttons are wider than others, and one is taller.

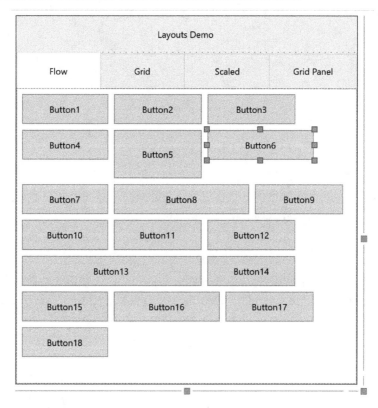

Figure 9.8: The sizes of the buttons in FlowLayout in the LayoutsDemo project, at design time

If you run the application and change the size of the form, you'll see the buttons shift up and down in the rows, fitting the available space. A static image doesn't do this behavior justice, but you can see what happens with a wider form in *Figure 9.9*.

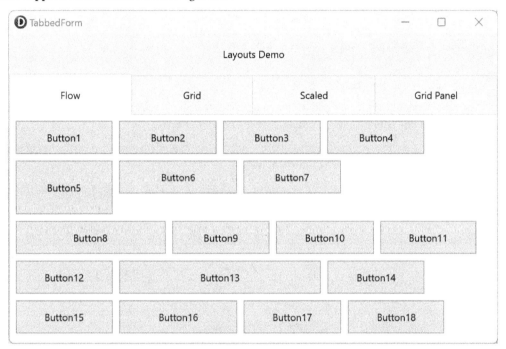

Figure 9.9: How FlowLayout adapts to the available space

The flow layout is handy and offers more flexibility than absolute positioning. However, in terms of adapting to the available space, if controls have different sizes, they can end up almost anywhere on the screen with a confusing UI. The fact is, you don't have control over the actual position of each control.

There is one specific way to customize how elements are displayed in the flow layout, which is by using the TFlowLayoutBreak control. This component adds a *line break* to the flow so that the next control will be on a new line, regardless of the position of the others.

Note that, instead of individual controls, you can add to the flow layout other nested layouts as containers of controls that need to stay together. You can create building blocks (or even use frames), and each of them is a portion of the flow, moving to a new line if space isn't sufficient.

Grid layout

The grid layout offers a more consistent form of UI. In a grid control, each element is positioned according to a grid and flows to the first available position. The main difference from the flow layout is that the space available for each control is the same, and the gird cells act as containers of controls, which are automatically aligned to the cell surface. Again, it's often recommended to add an internal layout hosting the controls in each cell:

1. Select the second tab of `TabControl1`. Add `TGridLayout` to it, and set its `Align` property to `Client`.

2. Set the four `Padding` sub-properties of the layout to 4.

3. Set the `ItemHeight` property to 80 and the `ItemWidth` property to 120. These are the sizes of each cell of the grid.

4. Now, add some buttons to the grid. Cells get added automatically, with new rows being created once the first one is full. In my example, I added seven buttons.

5. Set the four `Margins` sub-properties of each button to 4, but add a variation by changing one of them to 8 (just to see how the button behaves).

The grid layout in the FireMonkey designer, at this point, should look like the one in *Figure 9.10*.

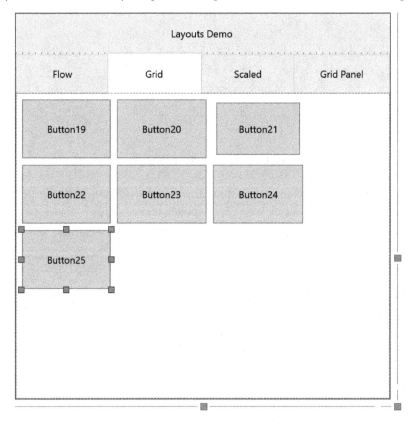

Figure 9.10: GridLayout in LayoutsDemo in the Delphi IDE

If you run the application and extend its window horizontally slightly, the buttons will rearrange themselves, as shown in *Figure 9.11*.

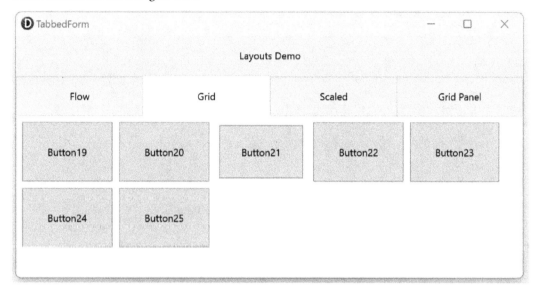

Figure 9.11: GridLayout in LayoutsDemo at runtime

Is using `TGridLayout` effective? While this is a handy layout to use in combination with others, it's a bit limited. We'll see later that FireMonkey offers a similar alternative with `TGridPanelLayout`, which is much more flexible and powerful.

Scaled layout

The next layout we are going to look at, the `TScaledLayout` component, works in a totally different way. FireMonkey offers the ability to scale the content of a form, using various scaling properties and methods. The advantage of this layout is that it applies scaling automatically, without the need to write any code. You can position the controls with the standard absolute position and size, and the controls will adapt to the form size:

1. Select the third tab of `TabControl1`. Add `TScaledLayout` to it, and set its `Align` property to `Client`.

2. Set the four `Padding` sub-properties of the layout to 4, as usual. There are not many properties to configure in this layout.

3. Add seven buttons to the layout, and place them in a way similar to the grid layout in *Figure 9.10*, while keeping their size as the platform default.

If you run the application and make the form larger, the buttons will increasse in size, as you can see in *Figure 9.12* (which is scaled down in the book to fit in the page, but you can see the font difference between the tabs and the buttons in the screenshot).

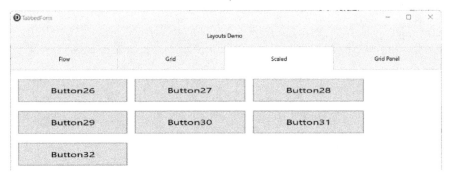

Figure 9.12: ScaledLayout in LayoutsDemo at runtime

As you can see in the screenshot, the ability to resize the elements of the UI to adapt to the available space can be handy, and it allows you to adapt to phones of different resolutions (and pixel density), but such a full-screen application on a 4K desktop monitor would not look right.

Grid panel layout

The last layout I want to cover in this section and in the `LayoutsDemo` application is probably the most interesting and powerful one. `TGridPanelLayout`, in fact, offers you the ability to define the size of the grid elements in different ways, by letting you configure the size of each row and column, using absolute values of percentages (which is better for adapting to different sizes). The content can also extend to multiple adjacent cells, like what happens in an HTML grid. Again, let's see this in practice in our demo application:

1. Select the last tab of `TabControl1`. Add `TGridPanelLayout` to it, and set its `Align` property to `Client`.

2. Set the four `Padding` sub-properties of the layout to `4`, as usual.

3. Open the **ColumnsCollection** property editor, and make sure that the two columns are set to each take up 50% of the grid, as shown in *Figure 9.13*.

Figure 9.13: Editing the ColumnsCollection of the GridPanelLayout

4. Add two more rows to `RowCollection`, and set each of the row heights to `25%`. This can be tricky, as the control recalculates the relative percentage to the total. If you persist for a few times, it should work.

5. Add a number of buttons; in my demo, I added seven buttons to this page. Align each of them to `Client`, and set their four `Margins` sub-properties to `4`.

6. In the Structure view, open the `ControlCollection` node under the grid layout, select one of `TControlItem` elements, and change its `ColumnSpan` setting to `2`, as shown in *Figure 9.14*. You can change the column and row span properties to experiment with this layout.

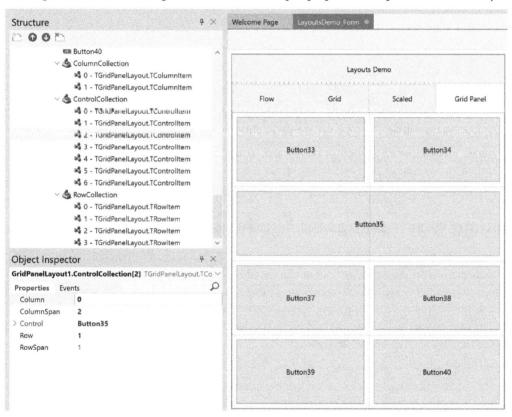

Figure 9.14: In GridPanelLayout, you can have items spanning multiple cells

The result is a very flexible layout, displayed at a smaller scale at runtime, as shown in *Figure 9.15*. This layout offers a very large degree of flexibility and configuration, and you can make the same changes also at runtime in code, depending on the actual screen and window size.

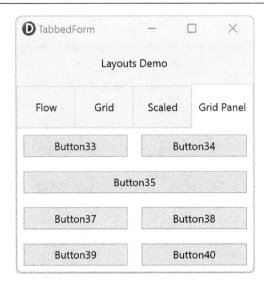

Figure 9.15: GridPanelLayout at a small scale at runtime

While this section only scratched the surface of using layouts in FireMonkey, the goal was to help you understand the basics and encourage you to experiment. A good use of layouts is fundamental to creating a nice UI with the library and apps that works smoothly on both desktop and mobile apps.

Building desktop apps for Windows, macOS, and Linux

Besides mobile apps for Android and iOS, Delphi and FireMonkey offer you the ability to build native applications for the desktop, as we saw in the previous sections. While this book is focused on mobile, in this chapter I want to add some quick notes regarding the desktop platform, offering a bit of specific advice and steps to build applications for Windows, macOS, and even Linux (if you own the Enterprise edition of Delphi or RAD Studio). This won't be a deep dive; I will only highlight some core considerations for Windows development.

We have built Windows applications in this chapter as well as previous chapters of this book. The reason is simple – the Delphi IDE runs on Windows, and it should be no surprise that Delphi offers the best platform support in terms of tooling for Windows. For all other platforms, Delphi has a cross-compiler, a compiler that runs on Windows and produces a binary for different operating systems, possibly a different CPU family. To deploy an application, it first needs to be copied to a different computer or device, and debugging happens via a remote debugger, connecting the Delphi IDE to the target platform, with a debug engine running on that platform.

On Windows, the compiler is local instead; the application can just be executed directly on the local machine, and debugging is also local. The Windows platform offers the faster compile-deploy-debug experience, and in many cases, even if you are exclusively targeting mobile with an application, doing some initial testing on Windows (possibly ignoring the UI) generally provides a better experience and a quicker turnaround.

Also, Delphi and FireMonkey can be used to create very nice and powerful Windows applications. By default, the library maps the rendering code to DirectX, and it's quite fast. In addition, Delphi offers a deep integration of the Windows platform APIs, so you can easily extend an application by embedding native calls.

In this section, I want to highlight a nice FireMonkey feature specifically for desktop platforms that provides direct support in a component for drag-and-drop operations, using the TDropTarget control. We can build a simple demo showing this feature with the following steps:

1. Create a new FireMonkey Blank Application, and save the project as DropTarget and the main unit as DropTarget_Form. Change Caption of the main form to Drop Target.

2. Add a TDropTarget object to the form, and set its Align property to Top. Set its four Margins sub-properties to 8.

3. In this component, indicate which files you want to accept in the Filter property. If you want to receive any file, just enter *.*.

4. Change its Text property to something like Drop Files Here.

5. Add a TMemo component to the form. Set its Align property to Client and its four Margins subproperties to 8.

6. Finally, add an event handler for the OnDropped event of the TDropTarget object, and enter the following code:

```
procedure TFormDrop.DropTarget1Dropped(Sender: TObject;
  const Data: TDragObject; const Point: TPointF);
begin
  for var AFile in Data.Files do
    Memo1.Lines.Add (AFile);
end;
```

The preceding code allows you to drag multiple files at once; they'll all get listed in the memo. Build and run the application on Windows, and you'll get an output like *Figure 9.16*, after dragging a few files to it.

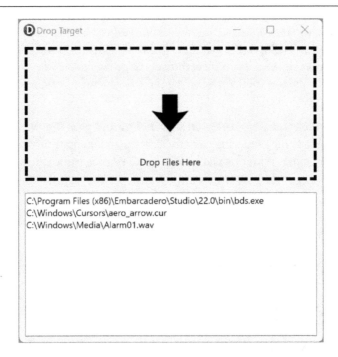

Figure 9.16: The DropTarget demo project on Windows

This is a simple example of a Windows application with a desktop-specific feature. Let's now see how a similar app can adapt to other desktop platforms.

Creating apps for macOS

Apple macOS is likely the second most popular desktop platform after Windows. While the Delphi IDE cannot run on Windows, many developers who prefer using a Macrun the IDE on a Windows VM.

As you certainly know, the macOS platform has undergone a radical transformation in recent years, abandoning the Intel CPUs in favor of ARM CPUs. While Intel applications built with Delphi (or other development tools) run on the newer ARM CPUs thanks to the Rosetta emulation layer, it's fully recommended to migrate applications to the new ARM target. Note that an ARM binary won't run on Intel Macs.

Delphi offers support for building native ARM and native Intel applications for macOS (see *Figure 9.17*), and it also has the ability to combine them in a single binary (called a Universal binary) for store distribution. Note that both macOS target platforms are 64-bit platforms, as Apple has ended support for 32-bit applications on all of its operating systems.

∨ ▦ **DropTarget**
    > ⚙️ Build Configurations (Debug)
    ∨ ◯ Target Platforms (macOS ARM 64-bit)
        > 🤖 Android 32-bit - Android SDK 25.2.5 32-bit
        > 🤖 Android 64-bit - Android SDK 25.2.5 64-bit
        > ▢ iOS Device 64-bit - iPhoneOS 16.4 - M1 profile
        > ▢ iOS Simulator ARM 64-bit - iPhoneSimulator 16.4 - M1 …
        🐧 Linux 64-bit
        > 🖥️ macOS 64-bit - M1 profile
        > 🖥️ **macOS ARM 64-bit - M1 profile**
        > ⊞ Windows 32-bit
        > ⊞ Windows 64-bit
    ∨ 📄 DropTarget_Form.pas
        🖼️ DropTarget_Form.fmx

Figure 9.17: Delphi offers native compilers for macOS ARM and macOS Intel

Can we rebuild the `DropTarget` demo for macOS and leverage the same feature? Yes, that's certainly an option, but I wanted to add one small extra feature to the demo first to cover a specific FireMonkey feature for macOS:

1. Reopen the `DropTarget` demo, and add a `TMainMenu` component to it. Configure the menu with a simple **Help** menu and an **About** item, as shown in *Figure 9.18*.

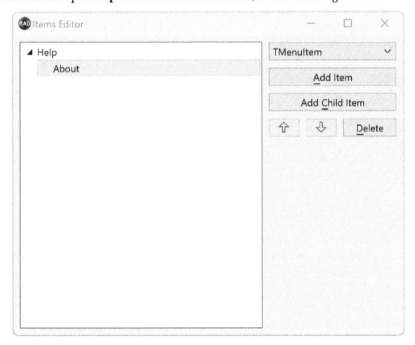

Figure 9.18: Adding a menu to the DropTarget application

2. Add an event handler for the **About** menu item, with a simple `ShowMessage` call that displays an informative message.

Now, run the program on Windows, and you'll see a regular menu added to the form, under the title bar. Run the program on a Mac, and you'll see a platform menu at the top of the screen, as shown in *Figure 9.19*.

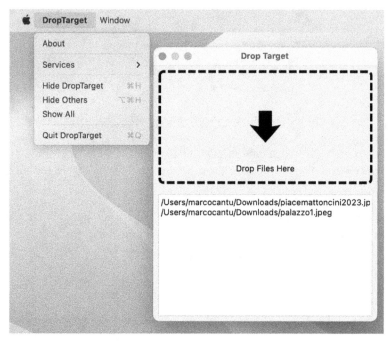

Figure 9.19: The main menu in a macOS application

This is a neat example of how FireMonkey applications adapt to the specific UI requirements of different target platforms.

What about targeting Linux?

Lastly, I want to touch briefly on the development of Linux client applications. The Enterprise version of Delphi includes a native compiler for the Linux Intel 64-bit platform. While FireMonkey doesn't include Linux in its options, Embarcadero licenses and distributes the FMXLinux add-on, a library that brings together all of the features of FireMonkey to Linux. This library is available in the Delphi IDE GetIt Package Manager. Just open **GetIt** (from the **Tools** menu or the **Welcome** page), search for `Linux`, and you'll see the package, which you can install easily, as shown in *Figure 9.20*. Note that there is also a second GetIt package with specific FMXLinux demos.

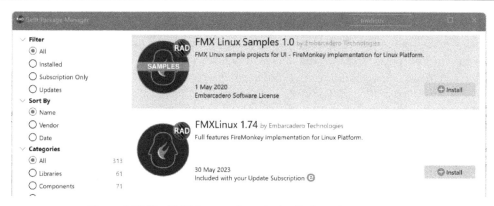

Figure 9.20: The FMXLinux package in the GetIt package manager

Before you can build an FMXLinux application, you need to configure building applications for the Windows target. The first step is configuring the Linux computer with the proper tools. There are detailed steps at `https://docwiki.embarcadero.com/RADStudio/en/Linux_Application_Development`.

The preceding web page also includes the steps required to install PAServer on Linux. Once this is done, you can add a Linux SDK to the Delphi IDE configuration, similar to how it is done for all other platforms.

Once you have the Linux platform configured and FMXLinux installed, you can start PAServer on the Linux machine, build the app, and deploy it directly there. The UI will be executed on the Linux box.

You can see this in action in *Figure 9.21*. It shows a very specific configuration, with Ubuntu running on Windows Subsystem for Linux (WLS 2.0). In this case, the application can be used seamlessly alongside with Windows applications, as the Windows Linux Subsystem hosts it in a Windows frame. In the following screenshot, you can see the console, with PAServer and the client app in a separate window.

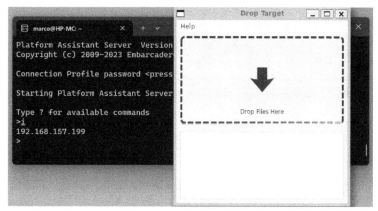

Figure 9.21: The app running on Linux

There is, of course, much more to say in terms of building and running Delphi UI apps on Linux, as well as on Windows and macOS. This section of this chapter was offered as a short introduction, and I hope it served its purpose. Next, we want to explore an interesting technology that Delphi offers to let desktop and mobile apps communicate, called app tethering.

App tethering

App tethering is a unique feature of Delphi that can be used to set up communication between different types of applications, such as mobile or desktop, running on any of the supported platforms using FireMonkey. It can also be used in the Windows-specific VCL library. The original use case for app tethering was to be able to *extend* existing desktop apps to mobile and easily create mobile *companion* apps. Instead of trying to re-implement existing desktop apps on mobile, the idea was to be able to either control a desktop app from a mobile app or to be able to easily exchange data between the two.

For example, we could have an existing desktop application written in Delphi that help doctors keep track of patients' data and possibly control some medical instruments. There is nothing wrong with this desktop application; it has stood the test of time and is very useful. However, mobile has brought new possibilities. It would be cool to use a mobile device with a camera and send images to the existing desktop app. With app tethering, such a use case is very easy to achieve.

By the way, the Delphi IDE itself uses app tethering for the **Live Preview** feature, which gives you the ability to immediately see the UI of an app on a mobile device, while you are changing it in the FireMonkey designer window in the Delphi IDE. In this scenario, the IDE, which is a good example of a Delphi desktop app, communicates with a Live Preview app running on iOS or Android.

Using app tethering in your apps is relatively straightforward. Both apps that need to communicate with each other need to have two app tethering components on the form – `TTetheringManager` and `TtetheringAppProfile`. These two components work together. The `TTetheringAppProfile` component has the `Manager` property, which is used to connect the associated `TTetheringManager`.

App tethering can use either Wi-Fi or Bluetooth for communication. The `TTetheringManager` component has an `AllowedAdapters` property, with which we can specify communication protocols to be used. By default, the tethering manager component is set to `Network`, which means using standard TCP/IP network protocol for communication, but we can also choose `Bluetooth`. It is also possible to specify more than one communication protocol, separating their names with the `|` or `;` character.

Communication in app tethering starts by discovering other tethering managers available in the network or via Bluetooth. The app that acts as a client needs to call the `DiscoverManagers` method on the app tethering manager component. There are different overloaded variations of this method. We can specify the discovery timeout and also a list of targets, if we want to connect to a specific manager. When the discovery process is finished, the `OnEndDiscovery` event is triggered, and a list of discovered managers is passed to this event in the `ARemoteManagers` parameter of type `TTetheringManagerInfoList`.

The next step is to *pair* a remote manager. In order to do this, we need to call the `PairManager` method of the `TAppTetheringManager` class, passing as a parameter a reference to one of the discovered managers from the list. When the *pairing* process is finished, the library executes the `OnEndProfileDiscovery` event. Again, a list of remote profiles is passed in the `ARemoteProfiles` event parameter of type `TTetheringProfileInfoList`.

The last step is to establish a connection with a remote profile component. This can be done by calling the `Connect` method of the `TTetheringAppProfile` component, passing as a parameter a reference to a selected remote profile from the list.

When a connection is established, we can either send data to a remote application or execute remote actions on the server application. This second option is useful in scenarios where we use app tethering to implement a *remote control* app in an existing desktop app. On the server, or the controlled application, we need to decide which actions should be exposed to remote applications. The `TTetheringAppProfile` component has an `Actions` collection property. For every exposed regular action, there should be an item added to the `Actions` property, which has an `Action` property that needs to be connected to the actual action component to be executed. These action items in the `Actions` collection in the tethering app profile have a `Name` property that is used to identify an action to be executed. The *remote controller* app can execute remote actions by calling the `RunRemoteAction` method of the tethering app profile component, passing the reference to a remote profile and the action name.

I know the steps involved can be confusing, but the net result is fully worth the effort. Let's have a look at app tethering by implementing a simple system. In this use case, there will be a mobile app that will take photos and a second app that could be run on a desktop app, and its job will be to display a received photo.

First, let's implement the app to take and send photos:

1. Create a new Delphi multi-device Blank Application, and save the main form as `uFormPhotoTake` and the whole project as `PhotoTake`. Change the Name property of the form to `FormPhotoTake`.

2. Drop a `TToolbar` component on the form, and drop `TSpeedButton` on the toolbar. Change its Name property to `SpdbtnSendPhoto` and its `Align` property to `Right`.

3. Drop another `TSpeedButton` component on the form. `Align` it to `Bottom`, and change its Name property to `SpdbtnTakePhoto`.

4. Now, drop a `TImage` component on the form, align it to `Client`, and change its Name property to `ImagePhoto`. The UI is ready.

5. Drop a `TActionList` component on the form. Double-click on it, and add a `TakePhotoFromCameraAction` action to it. Change the `CustomText` property of the action to `Take Photo`.

6. Double-click on the `OnDidFinishTaking` event of the action, and enter a line of code to display the photo from the camera in the image on the form:

```
procedure TFormPhotoTake.
  TakePhotoFromCameraAction1DidFinishTaking(Image: TBitmap);
begin
  ImagePhoto.Bitmap.Assign(Image);
end;
```

7. Select the `SpdbtnTakePhoto` component in the Object Inspector, and connect the button's `Action` property to the `TakePhotoFromCameraAction1` action. At this point, the UI of the form should look like *Figure 9.22*.

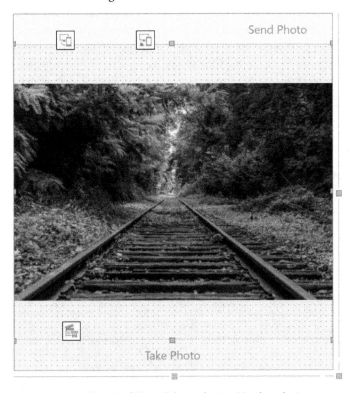

Figure 9.22: The UI of PhotoTake in the FireMonkey designer

8. Now that we have the logic to take a photo, the next step will be to send it to another app with app tethering technology. Drop `TTetheringManager` and `TTetheringAppProfile` components on the form, and set their names to `TetherMng1` and `TetherProf1`, respectively. Set the `Manager` property of the `TetherProf1` component to the `TetherMng1` value from the drop-down list.

9.   To avoid connecting to random tethering apps that are visible to our app in the network, we are going to provide a password for both applications. In the `Password` property of `TetherMng1`, enter an arbitrary password.

10. Now, implement the `OnRequestManagerPassword` event to use the password stored in the `Password` property, using this code:

```
procedure TFormPhotoTake.TetherMng1RequestManagerPassword(
  const Sender: TObject; const ARemoteIdentifier: string;
  var Password: string);
begin
  Password := TetherMng1.Password;
end;
```

11. Add a new action to the action list. Change its `Name` property to `ActSendPhoto` and its `CustomText` property to `Send Photo`. Attach this action to the `SpdbtnSendPhoto` component, and implement its `OnExecute` event, as shown in the following code, which starts the tethering process if a picture is available:

```
procedure TFormPhotoTake.ActSendPhotoExecute(
  Sender: TObject);
begin
  if not ImagePhoto.Bitmap.IsEmpty then
    TetherMng1.DiscoverManagers(1000)
  else
    ShowMessage('Take a photo before sending');
end;
```

12. In the preceding code, if there is a bitmap to be sent, we initiate communication with the receiver app through a call to the `DiscoverManagers` method, specifying the timeout of one second. When remote managers are discovered, the `OnEndManagersDiscovery` event is executed. In our demo, this event handler has the following code:

```
procedure TFormPhotoTake.TetherMng1EndManagersDiscovery(
  const Sender: TObject;
  const ARemoteManagers: TTetheringManagerInfoList);
begin
  if aRemoteManagers.Count > 0 then
    TetherMng1.PairManager(ARemoteManagers[0])
  else
    ShowMessage('Cannot find any photo receiver app.');
end;
```

13. With this code, we just pair with the first manager on the list. When pairing is done, the
OnEndProfilesDiscovery event is executed. In its handler, we connect to the first profile
in the list, and if the connection is successful, we send the bitmap to the remote app profile
using the SendStream method:

```
procedure TFormPhotoTake.TetherMng1EndProfilesDiscovery(
  const Sender: TObject;
  const ARemoteProfiles: TTetheringProfileInfoList);
var
  Memstr: TMemoryStream;
begin
  if ARemoteProfiles.Count > 0 then
  begin
    if not TetherProf1.Connect(ARemoteProfiles[0]) then
      ShowMessage('Failed to connect to remote profile.')
    else
    begin
      Memstr := TMemoryStream.Create;
      try
        ImagePhoto.Bitmap.SaveToStream(Memstr);
        if TetherProf1.SendStream(
            ARemoteProfiles[0], 'Photo', Memstr) then
          ShowMessage('Image sent')
        else
          ShowMessage('Failed to send image');
      finally
        Memstr.Free;
      end;
    end;
  end
  else
    ShowMessage(
      'Cannot find any remote profiles to connect to.');
end;
```

The nice thing about app tethering is the fact that the whole discovery process reduces a lot of the
complexity typically involved with network communication. We do not need to specify remote host
addresses and port numbers. However, it is also possible to specify the exact IP address of the machine
where the server app is running. By default, the network discovery is done through **User Datagram
Protocol** (**UDP**) broadcasting, which is the reason that both apps need to be running in the same
subnet to be properly discovered.

The photo receiving app is even simpler than the one used for sending the photos, as it needs to listen for a communication request and receive the information sent. You can recreate this behavior by following these steps:

1. Add to the existing project group a new multi-device blank Delphi app, and save the main form unit as uFormPhotoDisplay and the project as PhotoDisplay.

2. Drop TToolbar on the form and a TLabel on top of it. Align the label to Client, and change its HorzAlign property in TextSettings to Center. Enter Photo Display in its Text property.

3. Now, drop TImage on the form, align it to Client, and rename it ImageDisplay.

4. Again, drop TTetheringManager and TTetheringAppProfile components on the form, and name them TetherMng1 and TetherProf1, respectively. Connect the two components using the Manager property of the app profile component.

5. In the Password property of TetherMng1, enter the same password that was entered in the PhotoTake app, and pass the password to the component in the OnRequestManagerPassword event.

6. The final step is to handle the OnResourceReceived event of the TetheringAppProfile1 component. This event has an AResource parameter of type TRemoteResource that contains received information. In our case, we know that this is a stream with bitmap data, so we can just access the AsStream information and directly load it into the image by calling the LoadFromStream method, by writing the following code:

```
procedure TFormPhotoDisplay.TetherProf1ResourceReceived(
  const Sender: TObject; const AResource: TRemoteResource);
begin
  ImageDisplay.Bitmap.LoadFromStream(
    AResource.Value.AsStream);
end;
```

This is all we need to do. Now, we can run the PhotoTake app on a mobile device equipped with a camera, take a photo, and send it over with app tethering to a remote app, running on another mobile or a desktop machine.

Before deploying to mobile, it is always good to test both apps on Windows. Typically, you won't have a camera on Windows, but you can load a test image into ImagePhoto at design time and just try out the actual sending. This scenario is shown in *Figure 9.23*.

Figure 9.23: The two sides of the app tethering photo app running on Windows

As you saw in this section, using app tethering is fairly simple, given the ready-to-use components provided by Delphi. At the same, it is a very powerful technique for peer-to-peer communication across apps on the same local network, including the common scenario of communicating across mobile and desktop apps.

Summary

This chapter focused on desktop applications, taking a slight detour from the main focus of this book, which is building mobile apps. The beauty of FireMonkey is that the same application can run on desktop and mobile platforms, although it takes some extra effort to create a UI that adapts to both. In this chapter, we covered some of the scenarios, but there is more you can explore. We also touched on specific elements of desktop apps and built a macOS and Linux app.

We also focused on app tethering, which is a very powerful set of components to connect desktop applications with mobile companion apps. The app tethering framework allows two arbitrary Delphi apps to exchange data over Bluetooth or TCP/IP, with almost no coding required.

The ability to create desktop applications can certainly come handy for you in many cases, as the power of Delphi is in its ability to target both desktop and mobile apps, and by learning to use FireMonkey, you'll be able to create applications in both spaces.

In the next chapter, our focus will return to mobile apps, and we will learn how to embed a database on a mobile device and use it from a Delphi FireMonkey app.

Part 3:
From Data to Services

No app is an island. Your apps will need to store data locally, with more powerful options than using files. That's why we start the last part of the book by looking into on-device database support. Modern applications, however, rarely need only a local database. Using web services and reaching out to cloud features is extremely common these days. Leveraging mobile backends is also critical, but with Delphi you can also build mobile backends, becoming a Delphi full-stack developer.

Throughout the last part, we'll be building many different versions of a todo application, reusing its code, and leveraging the same abstraction layer for local databases, cloud storage, and multitier apps.

This part has the following chapters:

- *Chapter 10, Embedding Databases,*
- *Chapter 11, Integrating with Web Services*
- *Chapter 12, Building Mobile Backends*
- *Chapter 13, Easy REST API Publishing with RAD Server*
- *Chapter 14, App Deployment*
- *Chapter 15, The Road Ahead*

10
Embedding Databases

The majority of mobile apps work with data. Building database applications has always been one of the strongest Delphi features. In this chapter, we are going to learn how to build data-driven mobile **user interfaces** (**UIs**) in FireMonkey, how to use the FireDAC database access framework, and how to embed databases on mobile devices.

While mobile apps rely on data from the internet, building a fast and responsive app always requires caching some data locally. For this reason, using a database in your mobile app is very important, and this chapter will help you understand how to do it. As an example, we are going to build a simple mobile app for managing a todo list.

This chapter will cover the following points:

- Data-driven apps
- Modeling data
- Choosing a database
- Accessing databases with FireDAC
- Building a data-driven UI
- Using visual live bindings
- Fast UI prototyping

The objective of this chapter is to learn how to build a data-driven **Graphical User Interface** (**GUI**) from the ground up.

Technical requirements

The source code for the examples covered in this chapter can be found at https://github.com/ PacktPublishing/Expert-Delphi_Second-edition.

Data-driven apps

In this chapter, we are going to go through the steps of building a simple mobile app with an embedded database for managing a list of todo items. Before jumping into coding, let's first look into the overall application architecture. The more complex the system we want to build, the more important it is to properly structure it.

The typical approach is to divide and conquer; break a big problem into smaller problems that are simpler to solve. The most common approach in software development is to break the whole system into clearly separated tiers. In a data-driven app, we should be able to identify at least two logical parts: the UI and data access logic. Clear separation of these two tiers enables a plugin architecture, where the UI can connect to different data access blocks in a standard way and the UI can be replaced without touching the underlying data access layer.

In the context of a Delphi app, we can split our project into three independent entities, as shown in *Figure 10.1*:

- One or more visual forms that will serve as the GUI

- One or more data modules with non-visual components for working with a database

- One or more standalone units, with common types and utility functions used by both tiers of the application

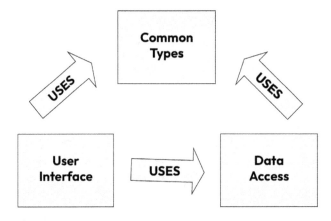

Figure 10.1: The overall architecture of a simple database app

Let's now build this structure in Delphi:

1. Create a new multi-device, blank Delphi project. Save the main form unit as uFormToDo and the whole app as ToDoList. Change the Name property of the form to FormToDo.

2. Select **File | New | Data Module** from the Delphi main menu. Change the data module `Name` property to `DMToDo` and save it as `uDMToDo`.

3. Now select **File | New | Unit** from the Delphi main menu to a blank unit for the project. Save it as `uToDoTypes`.

You should now have a project with the structure of *Figure 10.2*.

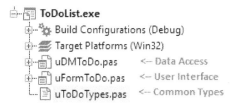

Figure 10.2: The structure of the project of a simple database app in Delphi

Our project consists of three different units that represent three major building blocks of our data-driven app. Now, let's create dependencies between these three units. The unit `uToDoTypes` does not depend on any other unit in the project, so nothing to add to its `uses` clauses. This unit needs to be used by both the UI and data access logic. Using the **File** and **Use Unit** command, add the `uToDoTypes` unit to the `uses` clauses in the interface parts of the form and of the data module. Now, add the data module `uDMToDo` to the `uses` clause in the implementation part of the main form's unit. This should match what we saw in *Figure 10.1*.

This is the starting point of the app that we'll keep building in the following sections of this chapter. In this section, we started creating the overall application structure, in terms of code, and now we can start looking into each of the areas we need to develop.

Modeling data

The `uToDoTypes` unit is where we can add data types that are shared between the UI and the data access module. To achieve a proper level of separation between the UI and the data access logic, we should define the interface for communication between the two tiers of the application. The data module will implement it and the main form of the application should use this interface as the only way to communicate with the data module. In this way, we have true plugin architecture. The UI can be developed independently, and we can provide different implementations of data access logic without affecting the rest of the application. Our data-driven app could be using different types of embedded databases and different data access frameworks, or maybe later we would want to switch to storing our data in a plain file or cloud storage.

The `ToDoList` app will be dealing with todo items, so it makes perfect sense to declare in the common types unit a type that will represent a single todo item. We need to decide if this type should be a record or a class. With records, we do not need to worry about memory management, and typically records have better performance than objects. On the other hand, defining our "data wrapper" type as an object is also a good option. Record types cannot be inherited. In more complex scenarios, the flexibility that comes from using objects could justify using them rather than records.

What attributes should a todo item should have? To keep the demo simple, let's just add a `Title` and a `Category` string field. In databases, it is also handy to have an identifier for any given item; typically, this is an integer value.

Here is how we could represent a todo item in code, in the `uToDoTypes` unit:

```
type
  TToDo = record
    Id: integer;
    Title: string;
    Category: string;
  end;
  TToDos = TList<TToDo>;
```

Notice that we have also implemented a generic list of todo items. It will be very useful to return the list of all todo items from the data module.

The next step is to define the standard operations that the data module should provide. In the database world, this is typically referred to as **CRUD** operations. This abbreviation stands for **Create**, **Read**, **Update**, and **Delete**. We just have one entity in our data model, so these operations should be implemented by four different methods. A fifth method we want to add is the ability to list the records.

To abstract these operations, let's declare a new interface type called `IToDoData`, which will define what functionality our data module should offer:

```
type
  IToDoData = interface
    function ToDoCreate(AValue: TToDo): Integer;
    function ToDoRead(Id: Integer; out AValue: TToDo): Boolean;
    function ToDoUpdate(AValue: TToDo): Boolean;
    function ToDoDelete(Id: Integer): Boolean;
    procedure ToDoList(AList: TToDos);
  end;
```

This is a fairly common way of representing CRUD operations. The `ToDoCreate` function takes the `TToDo` item, optionally checks if the data is correct, and returns the identifier of the new item in the underlying data store. If the operation is not successful, it returns a special value, for example, `-1`. The identifier for the new data item could be generated by the underlying database or created in code.

The `ToDoRead` function could return the item as the function result, but it is also practical to return it as the `out` parameter and indicate with a Boolean value if it contains valid data. The `Update` and `Delete` functions are self-explanatory.

The last procedure for retrieving all items takes the list as a parameter. The underlying code would check if the pointer to the list is not `nil`, optionally clear it, and populate the list with the underlying data.

The data module class in our app needs to implement this interface. We are going to do this in the coming section after we decide which database to use and how to access it.

Choosing a database

As mentioned before, the majority of mobile apps work with data. If you are not building a calculator app or an arcade game, the ability to store the data that your app is using can be very valuable. When designing your app, you need to make some architectural choices upfront. Where and how is my data stored? One obvious solution is to store your data in the cloud. This approach is the most common, but what if you do not have network access? You still want to be able to work with your app, and with the latest version of your data. This is the main reason why you also want to store your data locally on the device.

In simple cases, storing data as plain files, text, or binary is sufficient. However, it is also possible, and generally better, to embed a complete database system locally on the device. There are many relational and non-relational embedded databases available. If we think about an arbitrary database as just another mobile framework available from the mobile operating system, then it should be possible to integrate your Delphi mobile app with pretty much any database. However, that could require a deep understanding of the inner workings of your particular database. In most cases, we just want to have the job done, and it is the most productive approach to use databases that Delphi already provides support for. The key database access framework for mobile Delphi apps is FireDAC. The FireDAC data access layer provides connectivity to all major databases and also includes support for working with embedded databases. There are two main databases that you can embed on mobile:

- InterBase
- SQLite

Depending on your app, you may want to choose one or the other.

InterBase is the SQL relational database management system from Embarcadero (`https://www.embarcadero.com/products/interbase`). It is one of the best available SQL databases on the market and is very popular, primarily in embedded applications. InterBase Developer Edition is installed as part of the Delphi installation and comes with a development license. InterBase runs on all major platforms, both mobile and desktop. It has a very light footprint, it is self-tuning, and it requires almost no administration. Internally, it is based on unique, transactional multi-generational architecture. It provides very high performance and referential integrity. The database file format is the same across different platforms, so the same database file can be used in the standalone installation and an embedded mobile app.

For working with InterBase, I recommend using the IBConsole application that ships with InterBase and is available directly in RAD Studio if you include the InterBase Developer Edition in your installation.

There are two mobile-embedded variants of InterBase:

- **IBLite**: This is a free SQL engine, and a database file can be up to 100 MB in size. It lacks encryption and the **Change Views** support. A license to distribute IBLite for all supported platforms is included in Delphi (and RAD Studio).

- **IBToGo**: The commercial, embedded IBToGo version has no database size limits and it has the very important feature, especially on mobile, of providing strong (AES) database, table, and column-level encryption.

With an embedded database engine, only one application at a time is allowed to connect to the database, as the application exclusively locks the database file. However, this application is allowed to make multiple connections to the database, so a multi-threaded application can make a single connection or multiple connections and access the database simultaneously.

To embed the InterBase database within your app, you need to additionally deploy the database engine library and the database file with your application. For this purpose, you can use Delphi **Deployment Manager**, select the **Add Features Files** button, and pick the proper configuration for embedded InterBase (it is called InterBase ToGo, and it also works for IBLite). This results in the files already visible in the background in *Figure 10.3*.

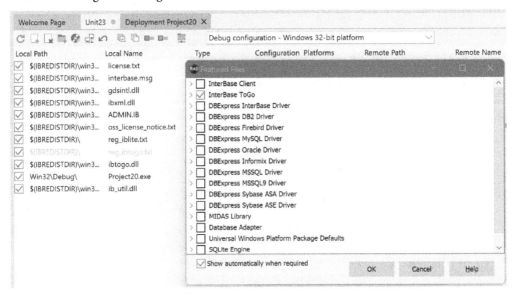

Figure 10.3: Configuring the deployment of an InterBase ToGo-based app

A simpler, although less powerful, alternative to InterBase is SQLite (`https://www.sqlite.org/`). It is a relational database engine that belongs to the public domain and is managed by Hwaci (Hipp, Wyrick & Company, Inc.). The deployment of apps that are using SQLite is very simple because the engine itself is already installed on both the iOS and Android operating systems.

SQLite does not have all the power of InterBase and does not provide referential integrity. In fact, with SQLite, you do not need to deploy anything with your mobile Delphi app, because the database and its structure can be created by the application on the fly. SQLite does not have a separate server process like most database engines do. SQLite basically reads and writes the data directly to disk files, which is unique to a single application. It is, however, a complete SQL database. Notice also that the SQLite file format is portable across different operating systems and processor architectures similar to InterBase.

There are many tools you can use for working with SQLite. One I can recommend is SQLite Expert, available at `https://www.sqliteexpert.com/`.

Accessing databases with FireDAC

Now that we have a database, we need a way to access it, reading and writing data via SQL commands. The best way to do it in a Delphi application is to use FireDAC, a very powerful data access library, which has been a part of the product for many years and offers access to a dozen different database engines with native and specific drivers.

To keep the demo app simple, we are going to use SQLite as the database engine and our *ToDo List* app will have just one database table called `ToDos`. SQLite has a simple type system and effectively a column can store null, integer, real, text, or blob values.

In our design, we are going to use an integer `Id` value as the primary key. We will also need the `Title` and `Category` text fields. The key FireDAC component that we will need is a FireDAC database connection. There will also be query components connected to the database connection.

Let's see how we can add a data access layer to our sample app:

1. Drop a `TFDConnection` component onto the data module. Change its `Name` property to `FDConnToDos`.

2. Now double-click on the connection component to display the **FireDAC Connection Editor** window. Select `SQLite` in the `Driver ID` combo box. This should display the list of different parameters specific to working with SQLite.

3. Now, we have to enter the name of the database file. It is important to realize that the location of the database file on our development Windows machine, where we have Delphi installed, will be different from the location on a mobile device where our app will be deployed. During the development of our application, we will be running it on Windows for testing, and when the app is finished, we will deploy and run it on an Android or iOS device.

4. On your Windows machine, create a directory for the SQLite database file, for example, `C:\Users\Public\Documents\`. The name of the database file will be `ToDos.db`. The extension of the database file can be anything, and it is a matter of convention.

5. There is no need to enter a username and password; we can leave all default parameter values. The default `OpenMode` parameter is set to `CreateUTF8`. This means that the database file will be created automatically on the first attempt to connect to it. This simplifies the deployment to a mobile device because the database file can be created the first time the mobile app runs.

6. Click on the **Test** button in the **Connection Editor** window. Leave the password blank and you should get the message that the connection has been successful, as you can see in *Figure 10.3*. If you now go to the `C:\Users\Public\Documents\` folder, you should find a new, empty SQLite database file there.

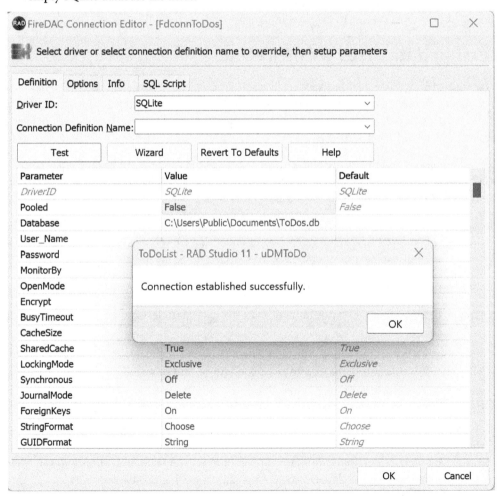

Figure 10.4: Testing the SQLite connection in the FireDAC Connection Editor

Connection Editor is very handy. On the second tab, there are different options that can control how FireDAC works. The third tab provides all kinds of information about the database connection. The last tab is called **SQL Script**, and it can be used to execute arbitrary SQL statements against the connected database.

SQLite has a nice SQL construct, CREATE TABLE IF NOT EXIST..., which can be used to create the database table directly after opening the database.

Let's continue building our application:

7. Click on the **SQL Script** tab and enter the following code into the query window to create the ToDos database table:

```
CREATE TABLE IF NOT EXISTS ToDos (
    Id INTEGER NOT NULL PRIMARY KEY,
    Title TEXT,
    Category TEXT)
```

8. Click on the green arrow button to execute the query. You should get the message that the query has been successfully executed, as you can see in *Figure 10.5*.

Figure 10.5: Running an SQL script for creating a ToDos table from the the FireDAC Connection Editor

9. At this point, we have the database file with the `ToDo` table created. There are two possible approaches to deploying the database to a mobile device. We could use **Deployment Manager** and add an existing database file to the list of files to be deployed. The other, simpler option is to create the database file and the database table on the fly.

The following steps add database initialization and connection to our app:

1. Change the `LoginPrompt` property of the connection component to `False`.

2. Double-click on the `OnBeforeConnect` event to generate matching event handlers. Before opening the database connection, we are going to specify the location and the name of the database file in the code. The only practical location on a mobile device is the `Documents` folder. The database file will be created when the app is executed for the first time:

```
function TDMToDo.IsMobilePlatform: Boolean;
begin
  Result := (TOSVersion.Platform = pfiOS) or
    (TOSVersion.Platform = pfAndroid);
end;

procedure TDMToDo.FDConnToDosBeforeConnect(Sender: Tobject);
begin
  if IsMobilePlatform then
    FDConnToDos.Params.Values['Database'] :=
      TPath.Combine(TPath.GetDocumentsPath, 'ToDos.db');
end;
```

3. Now, add an event handler for the `OnAfterConnect` event. After the connection is established and the database file is created, we are going to execute the SQL code to create the `ToDos` table if it does not already exist, as detailed in the following code:

```
procedure TDMToDo.FDConnToDosAfterConnect(Sender: Tobject);
const
  SCreateTableSQL = 'CREATE TABLE IF NOT EXISTS ToDos ('
    + 'Id INTEGER NOT NULL PRIMARY KEY,'
    + 'Title TEXT, Category TEXT)';
begin
  if IsMobilePlatform then
    FDConnToDos.ExecSQL(SCreateTableSQL);
end;
```

4. For convenience, the demo has a simple `IsMobilePlatform` function. Alternatively, we could use conditional compilation, but using the `TOSVersion` record for checking if the app executes on a mobile platform is more elegant.

5. Now, we can start implementing the functionality defined in the IToDoData interface. Add IToDoData to the class declaration of the TDMToDo ancestor class, which is TDataModule, and the copy signatures of methods of the interface to the public section of the data module class.

6. Now press the *Ctrl + Shift + C* key combination to invoke class completion and generate empty method implementations.

7. Drop six TFDQuery components on the form and change their names respectively to FdqToDoMaxId, FdqToDoInsert, FdqToDoSelect, FdqToDoUpdate, FdqToDoDelete, and FdqToDoSelectAll. The result should be similar to *Figure 10.6*.

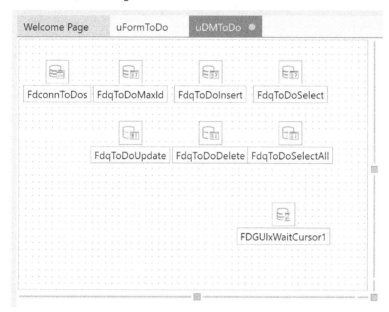

Figure 10.6: FireDAC components on the data module

8. The first method in the data access interface will be responsible for adding a new record to the table. In our data model, we have defined an Id integer primary key for storing identifiers. There are different strategies for generating unique identifiers. Some databases, for example, InterBase, provide generators that can efficiently generate primary keys. In our design, we are going to calculate the new value for an identifier by using an additional query that will return the maximum value stored in the Id column so far. The new identifier will be the maximum value increased by one. If there are no records in the table, we can return an arbitrary positive value that will serve as the starting point for consecutive inserts. For this purpose, I added a new private function called GetNewId to the private section of the data module.

9. At this point, the declaration of the `TDMToDo` data module class is complete. The following code listing includes the complete class declaration:

```
type
  TDMToDo = class(TDataModule, IToDoData)
    FdconnToDos: TFDConnection;
    FdqToDoInsert: TFDQuery;
    FdqToDoSelect: TFDQuery;
    FdqToDoUpdate: TFDQuery;
    FdqToDoDelete: TFDQuery;
    FdqToDoSelectAll: TFDQuery;
    FdqToDoMaxId: TFDQuery;
    FDGUIxWaitCursor1: TFDGUIxWaitCursor;
    procedure FdconnToDosBeforeConnect(Sender: TObject);
    procedure FdconnToDosAfterConnect(Sender: TObject);
  private
    function IsMobilePlatform: Boolean;
    function GetNewId: Integer;
  public
    // IToDoData
    function ToDoCreate(AValue: TToDo): Integer;
    function ToDoRead(Id: Integer;
      out AValue: TToDo): Boolean;
    function ToDoUpdate(AValue: TToDo): Boolean;
    function ToDoDelete(Id: Integer): Boolean;
    procedure ToDoList(AList: TToDos);
  end;
```

10. Now that we have defined the class, we need to continue working on the data mapping layer by implementing the various methods of the `TDMToDo` class:

11. Double-click on the `FdqToDoMaxId` query component. This will display the **Query Editor** window where we can enter the SQL code of the query, as you can see in *Figure 10.7*.

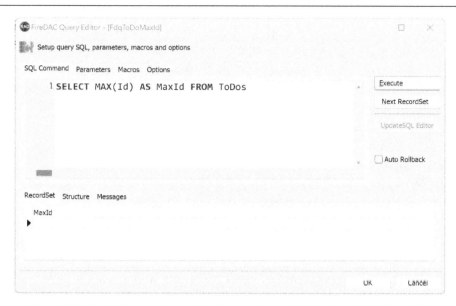

Figure 10.7: The SQL query for getting the maximum Id value from the ToDos table

12. Working with FireDAC is relatively simple. In **Query Editor**, there is also an **Execute** button that we can use to test our queries. At this stage, there are no records in the database, so this query will return an empty dataset. Still, by executing the query at design time, we can check if there are any errors in the SQL statement.

13. Before we move to implementing the creation of the new record, we need to take care of the Id generation. Enter the following code in the body of the GetMaxId method:

```
function TDMToDo.GetNewId: Integer;
begin
  FdqToDoMaxId.Open;
  try
    var Fld := FdqToDoMaxId.FieldByName('MaxId');
    if Fld.IsNull then
      Result := 1
    else
      Result := Fld.AsInteger + 1;
  finally
    FdqToDoMaxId.Close;
  end;
end;
```

14. The `Fld` local variable is here to simplify the code and make it more readable. Otherwise, we would need to make `FieldByName` call two times. It is also more efficient, too.

15. Double-click on the `FdqToDoInsert` query component. The `INSERT` statement will be responsible for the `Create` operation and adding a new todo item to the table, as in *Figure 10.8*.

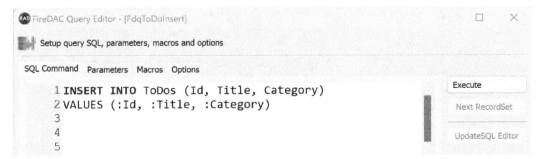

Figure 10.8: A parameterized SQL query for inserting a new record

16. In the second tab of **Query Editor** (*see Figure 10.9*), we need to specify parameter directions and their data types. All three parameters have a `ptInput` direction. The `ID` has the `ftInteger` type and `Title` and `Category` are both of the `ftString` type.

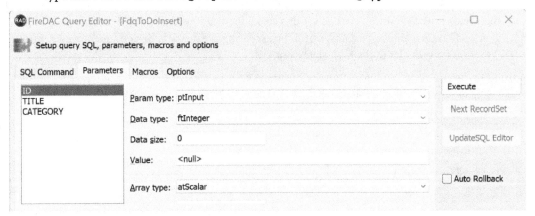

Figure 10.9: The management of the parameters in the FireDAC Query Editor

17. In the `ToDoCreate` method, we are going to calculate a new identifier for a todo record, assign values to parameters, execute the query, and return the new identifier if the query is successful or `-1` otherwise:

```
function TDMToDo.ToDoCreate(AValue: TToDo): Integer;
begin
  var Id := GetNewId;
  FdqToDoInsert.ParamByName('Id').AsInteger := Id;
  FdqToDoInsert.ParamByName('Title').AsString := AValue.Title;;
```

```
  FdqToDoInsert.ParamByName('Category').AsString :=
    AValue.Category;
  try
    FdqToDoInsert.ExecSQL;
    Result := Id;
  except
    Result := -1;
  end;
end;
```

18. The next method to implement in our **CRUD** list is reading a todo item. Double-click on the FdqToDoSelect query component and enter the following simple parameterized SQL statement:

```
SELECT Title, Category
FROM ToDos
WHERE Id = :Id
```

19. In the next tab, specify ptInput as the Id parameter type and ftInteger as the data type. The implementation of the ToDoRead method is relatively simple:

```
function TDMToDo.ToDoRead(Id: Integer;
  out AValue: TToDo): Boolean;
begin
  FdqToDoSelect.ParamByName('Id').AsInteger := Id;
  FdqToDoSelect.Open;
  try
    if FdqToDoSelect.RecordCount > 0 then
    begin
      Result := True;
      AValue.Id := Id;
      AValue.Title := FdqToDoSelect.FieldByName('Title').
        AsString;
      AValue.Category :=
        FdqToDoSelect.FieldByName('Category').AsString;
    end
    else
      Result := False;
  finally
    FdqToDoSelect.Close;
  end;
end;
```

20. The next method to implement is responsible for updating an existing todo record. Double-click on the FdqToDoUpdate query component and enter the following SQL code. On the second page, set types and data types of parameters in the same way as we did for the insert query:

```
UPDATE ToDos SET
Title = :Title,
Category = :Category
WHERE Id = :Id
```

21. The implementation of the update method is simple, as shown in the following:

```
function TDMToDo.ToDoUpdate(AValue: TToDo): Boolean;
begin
  FdqToDoUpdate.ParamByName('Id').AsInteger := AValue.Id;
  FdqToDoUpdate.ParamByName('Title').AsString := AValue.Title;;
  FdqToDoUpdate.ParamByName('Category').AsString :=
    AValue.Category;
  try
    FdqToDoUpdate.ExecSQL;
    Result := True;
  except
    Result := False;
  end;
end;
```

22. The method responsible for deleting a todo item is the simplest. Double-click on the FdqToDoDelete query component and enter the following SQL:

```
DELETE FROM ToDos WHERE Id = :Id
```

23. Set the Id parameter on the second tab in **Query Editor** as ptInput and ftInteger.

24. Again, the implementation of the corresponding method is not difficult at all, as you can see in the following code:

```
function TDMToDo.ToDoDelete(Id: Integer): Boolean;
begin
  FdqToDoDelete.ParamByName('Id').AsInteger := Id;
  try
    FdqToDoDelete.ExecSQL;
    Result := True;
  except
    Result := False;
  end;
end;
```

25. The last method of the data module is going to return the list of all todo items in the database. Double-click on `FdqToDoSelectAll` and enter the following SQL code:

```
SELECT * FROM ToDos
ORDER BY Id DESC
```

26. Enter the following code in the body of the `ToDoList` method to run the select query, go over each record, and add its identifier and title to a list of todo objects:

```
procedure TDMToDo.ToDoList(AList: TToDos);
var
  Item: TToDo;
begin
  if AList <> nil then
  begin
    AList.Clear;
    FdqToDoSelectAll.Open;
    try
      while not FdqToDoSelectAll.Eof do
      begin
        Item.Id := FdqToDoSelectAll.FieldByName('Id').AsInteger;
        Item.Title :=
          FdqToDoSelectAll.FieldByName('Title').AsString;
        Item.Category :=
          FdqToDoSelectAll.FieldByName('Category').AsString;
        AList.Add(Item);
        FdqToDoSelectAll.Next;
      end;
    finally
      FdqToDoSelectAll.Close;
    end;
  end;
end;
```

In the `ToDoList` method, we check first if the `aList` parameter is not `nil` and then we populate the list with todo items retrieved from the table.

At this point, we have finished building the data access layer of our application with the database access code. The next and final step is to create the UI.

Building a data-driven UI

We can now build the GUI of the app, using the services provided by the data access layer we just built.

The data access logic has been implemented and it is available through the `IToDoData` interface. This should be the only way for the UI logic to access data. That is, we are going to implement the `GetToDoData` method in the main form's unit that will return the reference to the data access interface. The following is the code for that:

```
uses uDMToDo;

function TFormToDo.GetToDoData: IToDoData;
begin
  if DMToDo = nil then
    DMToDo := TDMToDo.Create(Application);
  Result := DMToDo;
end;
```

In this way, we have achieved true plugin architecture. If we decide to change the underlying database access logic, the database access framework, or the database platform, we only need to make sure that the new class implements the `IToDoData` interface, which is available to the GUI code through the `GetToDoData` method:

1. The UI for the database will be simple. Drop the `TTabControl` component on the form, align it to `Client`, and rename it `TbctrlMain`.

2. Right-click on the tab control and add two tabs. The first tab will contain the list of all todo items and the second one will be used for editing the selected todo item.

3. Drop two `TToolBar` components, one on each tab.

4. The navigation between tabs will be happening in code, so we do not want to see the tabs. For this, change the `TabPosition` property of the tab control to `None`.

5. Rename the individual tabs `TbiList` and `TbiEdit` respectively.

6. Drop a `TActionList` component on the form, double-click on it, and add two `ChangeTabActions` components. Change their names to `CtaList` and `CtaEdit` and connect their `Tab` properties to the correct tabs.

7. Double-click on the `OnCreate` and `OnDestroy` events of the form. Here, we are going to create and free a global list of all todo items. Declare a generic list of to do items as a private field in the class declaration of the form. We are going to pass it to the `ToDoList` method of the data module to get all records. Additionally, in the `OnCreate` event, we are also making sure that the tab with the list is always displayed at the start of the application. There is also a call to the `RefreshList` method, which is responsible for displaying all todo items as you can see in the following code block:

```
procedure TFormToDo.FormCreate(Sender: Tobject);
begin
  FToDos := TtoDos.Create;
  TbctrlMain.ActiveTab := TbiList;
```

```
      RefreshList;
   end;


   procedure TFormToDo.FormDestroy(Sender: Tobject);
   begin
      FtoDos.Free;
   end;
```

8. The best control for displaying a list of data in FireMonkey is `TListView`. Drop a `TListView` component on the first tab, rename it `LstvwToDos`, and align it to `Client`. The `TListView` component is very flexible and offers good performance. It has been designed for building data-driven UIs and has a number of properties that control the layout of data and how this control operates. The form you've built should be similar to *Figure 10.10*.

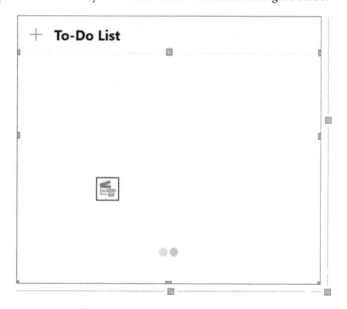

Figure 10.10: The first tab of the form of the ToDoList app

9. Expand the `ItemAppearance` node under `LstvwToDos` in the **Structure** view and click on the `Item` node. Here, we can see the elements that will make up a single row in the list view. There are also separate nodes for setting the header, footer, and additionally the layout of the item in **Edit mode**.

    By default, the `Apperance` property of a list view item is `ListItem` and the height of a single row is `44`. The default `ListItem` appearance will display just a line of text and the `>` sign at the right side of the item as an *accessory*. By selecting different elements of the list view in the **Structure** view, we can easily adjust their properties in **Object Inspector**.

10. In our app, a single todo item consists of `Title` and `Category`. Change the `Appearance` property of a list view item to `ListItemRightDetail`. Notice that changing the `Appearance` property changes the number of items under the `Item` node. Suddenly, we have not only `Text` but also a `Detail` element inside the individual item.

11. The default properties of `Text` and `Detail` could have been good for our app, but we want a more powerful approach. The most flexible `Appearance` option is `DynamicApperance`, where we don't need to select from the list of predefined appearances, but we can add our own elements and control their arrangement with the integrated list view designer.

12. Let's give it a try and change the `Appearance` of the `Item` node to `DynamicApperance`.

13. In **Object Inspector**, we now have the + sign at the bottom of the property list, where we can add visual elements of different types available from the drop-down list. By default, we already have one text element called `Text1`. Let's add one more text object and an accessory to indicate that touching a row would allow the editing of a single todo item.

14. This list is very dynamic. Change the `AppearanceObjectNames` to `Title, Category` for the text item, and `More` for the accessory item. We will be able to use these names in code. See the image in *Figure 10.11* for the elements of the `TListView` in the **Structure** view.

Figure 10.11: The structure of the TListView of the ToDoList app

15. Now, let's adjust the layout of a todo row. Change the `Height` property of an item to `64` and click on the **Toggle DesignMode** in **Object Inspector**. Alternatively, we could switch to **Design Mode** from the list view context menu.

16. The list view control in the form designer has changed and now we can design the layout of the individual list view item. Initially, all three elements are in the middle of the row, all of them on top of one another. Carefully reposition them and adjust their sizes. It is up to your artistic preferences. The `Title` item can be displayed on top of the row in bold and the category in italics, just below it.

Figure 10.12: The TListView appearance in Design Mode

When we are done with designing an item, we can switch back to the normal view by unchecking the **Toggle DesignMode** option from the context menu.

We can now implement the `RefreshList` method that will be responsible for reading data from the underlying database and displaying them in the list view. The method cycles over each of the todo item objects and, for each of them, it adds a listview item with the proper display data:

```
procedure TFormToDo.RefreshList;
begin
  GetToDoData.ToDoList(FToDos);
  LstvwToDos.BeginUpdate;
  try
    LstvwToDos.Items.Clear;
    for var Todo in FToDos do
    begin
      var Item := LstvwToDos.Items.Add;
      Item.Tag := Todo.Id;
      Item.Objects.FindObjectT<TListItemText>('Title').
        Text := Todo.Title;
      Item.Objects.FindObjectT<TListItemText>('Category').
        Text := Todo.Category;
    end;
  finally
    LstvwToDos.EndUpdate;
  end;
end;
```

Note that `FindObjectT` is a generic method that accepts the type of the element that we want to find inside the item.

Let's add the functionalities to add, delete, and edit the todo items from the list using the following steps:

1. Drop a `TSpeedButton` component on the toolbar on the first tab where the list view is located. Rename it `SpdbtnAdd`, change its `StyleLookup` property to `Addtoolbutton`, and its `Align` property to `Left`.

2. Now drop a `TLabel` component on the toolbar, change its `Text` property to `To-Do List`, its `StyleLookup` property to `Toollabel`, and its `Align` property to `Client`.

3. On the second tab, we are going to provide a way for the user to add, save, or delete a single todo item. Drop three speed buttons and one label on the toolbar.

4. Change the `StyleLookup` of the first button to `Arrowlefttoolbutton` and its `Name` property to `SpdbtnBack`. Align it to `Left`. Set its `Action` property to point to the `CtaList` change tab action.

5. Change the `Name` property of the second speed button to `SpdbtnSave`, its `StyleLookup` property to `Composetoolbutton`, and align it to `Right`.

6. The third speed button will be responsible for deleting items. Change its Name property to SpdbtnDelete, its StyleLookup property to Thrashtoolbutton, and align it to Right. Change the Text property of the label to To-Do Edit and align it to Client.

7. Add two edits and two labels to the tab. Change their names to EdtTitle and EdtCategory. Check the akRight option in the Anchors property of both edits so they will automatically adjust their width to different screen sizes. The result should be similar to *Figure 10.13.*

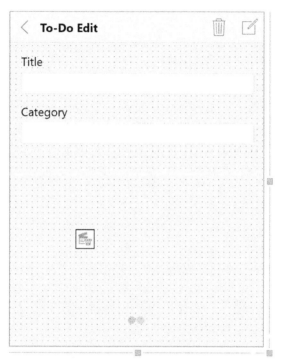

Figure 10.13: The second tab of the main form of the Todo app

The functionality of the **Save** button will depend on the current operation the user is doing. It can be either Insert for a new element or Update in case of changes to an existing item.

These are the steps to implement it:

1. Let's declare an FCurrentId private integer field of type Integer in the form class to indicate if we are adding or editing a todo item. If this value is -1, then it means that we are adding a new item, otherwise it will contain the identifier for the currently edited item.

2.   Double-click on the action list component and add two actions with the **New Action** option. Rename the first one to `ActAdd` and the second one to `ActDelete`. Connect both actions to corresponding speed buttons on both toolbars through their `Action` properties. Now, double-click on the `ActAdd` action to implement its `OnExecute` event handler:

```
procedure TFormToDo.ActAddExecute(Sender: TObject);
begin
  FCurrentId := -1;
  EdtTitle.Text := '';
  EdtCategory.Text := '';
  CtaEdit.ExecuteTarget(self);
end;
```

3.   Let's add another action to the action list. Rename it `ActSave` and in its `OnExecute` method, write the following code:

```
procedure TFormToDo.ActSaveExecute(Sender: TObject);
var
  Todo: TToDo;
begin
  Todo.Title := EdtTitle.Text;
  Todo.Category := EdtCategory.Text;
  if FCurrentId < 0 then
    GetToDoData.ToDoCreate(Todo)
  else
  begin
    Todo.Id := FCurrentId;
    GetToDoData.ToDoUpdate(Todo);
  end;
  RefreshList;
  CtaList.ExecuteTarget(self);
end;
```

4.   Right after inserting or updating a todo item, we refresh the list and jump back to the first tab with the list of all todos. Connect the `ActSave` action to the `SpdbtnSave` speed button through its `Action` property.

5.   The last functionality to implement is deleting the item. Double-click on the `OnExecute` event of the `ActDelete` action and enter the following code:

```
procedure TFormToDo.ActDeleteExecute(Sender: TObject);
begin
  if FCurrentId > 0 then
  begin
    GetToDoData.ToDoDelete(FCurrentId);
```

```
      RefreshList;
    end;
    if TbctrlMain.ActiveTab <> TbiList then
      CtaList.ExecuteTarget(self);
  end;
```

It only makes sense to delete an existing todo if we are in the middle of adding it. If the current identifier is negative, then there is nothing to delete. We just switch to the list tab. The last `if` is here to check if we are not in the list tab. This is because we are also going to provide a way to delete items directly from the list view. It is a common mobile UI feature to be able to swipe to delete. This functionality is built into the list view component.

6. There is a `CanSwipeDelete` property set to `True` by default and the `DeleteButtonText` property with the default `Delete` value. Double-click on the `OnDeleteItem` event and enter the following code:

```
procedure TformToDo.LstvwToDosDeleteItem(
  Sender: TObject; AIndex: Integer);
begin
  FCurrentId := FToDos[AIndex].Id;
  ActDelete.Execute;
end;
```

Before executing the delete action, we need to make sure that the `FCurrentId` field has the correct value of the todo item to be deleted.

7. The very last thing to implement is navigation between the list and the edit tab. Double-click on the `OnItemClick` event of the list view and type in the following code:

```
procedure TformToDo.LstvwToDosItemClick(
  const Sender: TObject; const AItem: TListViewItem);
var
  Todo: TToDo;
begin
  FCurrentId := AItem.Tag;
  GetToDoData.ToDoRead(FCurrentId, Todo);
  EdtTitle.Text := Todo.Title;
  EdtCategory.Text := Todo.Category;
  CtaEdit.ExecuteTarget(self);
end;
```

8. As a final touch, which isn't strictly required, you can place a `TFDGUIxWaitCursor` component on the data module and change its `Provider` property to `FMX`.

That's it! You can now try out the app by running it on Windows as you can see in *Figure 10.14*.

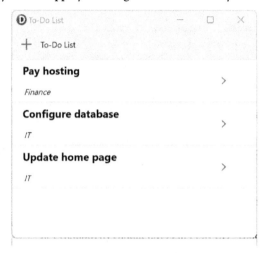

Figure 10.14: The first tab of the Todo app running on Windows, with the overall list

If it works OK, you can switch to one of the mobile targets and deploy the app to a mobile device, as you can see in *Figure 10.15* (which includes only the top part of the app on an Android phone).

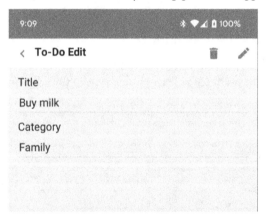

Figure 10.15: The second tab of the Todo app, with the details of one item, running on Android

The app architecture we have built up to now in this chapter is very sound. There is a true separation between the UI and the database access logic. We have created a data layer, the database mapping, and in this last section, the GUI.

We had to write quite a lot of code to wire the UI controls to the data, something Delphi can significantly simplify by using Live Bindings, the topic of the next section.

Using visual live bindings

There are many tools for developers on the market. What makes Delphi one of the most productive development environments is the Rapid Application Development paradigm, where you can use reusable components and very quickly assemble them together to create working applications. In Delphi, there is hardly a prototyping phase of the project. When you are building an app, it very quickly starts to look like the final product. Most applications work with data. The GUIs that we design typically display information coming from a database or a service in the cloud. In Delphi, you can preview the data at design time.

There are two visual frameworks in Delphi for building GUIs. There is the **Visual Component Library** (**VCL**), which is arguably the best library for building native applications for Windows. There is also the FireMonkey multi-device library for building cross-platform GUIs for all supported mobile and desktop operating systems. The VCL has a concept of data-aware controls that can be connected with a TDataSource component to a non-visual dataset component representing a database query, table, or stored procedure.

In FireMonkey, instead, there is no concept of data-aware controls. If you want to quickly build data driven GUIs in FireMonkey, you can use visual live bindings. This technology is much more capable than just connecting controls to data. Visual live bindings are components themselves and can be used to connect properties of arbitrary two objects. It should be noted that visual live bindings are not limited to FireMonkey and can be used in VCL and even in console applications.

Let's start, as usual, with a very simple example of connecting properties of visual controls on the form:

1. Create a new multi-device, blank Delphi project. Save the main form's units as uFormVLB and the whole project as VLBTest. Change the Name property of the form to FormVLB and save all.

2. Drop a TEdit and a TLabel component on the form. Right-click on the label component and select the **Bind Visually** option from the context menu. That will display the **LiveBindings Designer** window. Alternatively, we could have displayed this window from the **Tool Windows** menu in the **View** main menu option.

   In **LiveBindings Designer**, we can visually create live bindings between different properties so they can be automatically synchronized. Let's connect the Text properties of both controls so that when we change the text in the edit box, it gets automatically updated in the label.

3. Click on the Text property of the Edit1 control. Try to drag this property onto the other property that you wish to connect to. This will automatically create a binding between these two properties, as you can see in *Figure 10.16*.

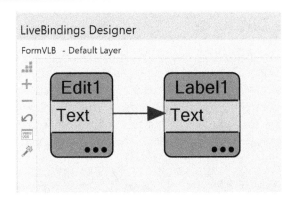

Figure 10.16: Connecting an edit and a label in the LiveBindings Designer

Notice that a `BindingList1` component has been automatically added to the form. This is where all bindings are stored. If you double-click on this component, you can preview all existing bindings (*see Figure 10.17*), which are just regular components with properties and events that can be set with **Object Inspector**.

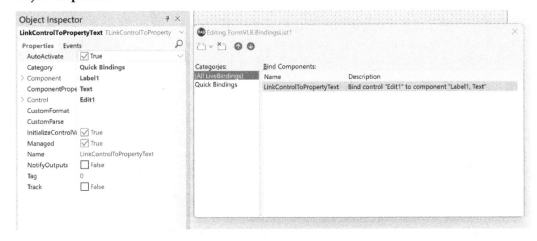

Figure 10.17: The editor of the BindingsList component

LiveBindings Designer automatically creates a `TLinkControlToProperty` binding, but there are other types of bindings that you can use to connect different types of properties and objects together.

There is also **LiveBindings Wizard**, which can be invoked from the `TBindingsList` component or using the magic wand button at the bottom of the menu in the **LiveBindings Designer** window. **LiveBindings Wizard**, shown in *Figure 10.18*, offers a large number of alternatives and features, and covering it in detail is beyond the scope of this book. We want to understand the key ideas of live bindings, but not delve deeply into the internal implementation. With **LiveBindingsWizard**, you can automatically create bindings and optionally add new objects.

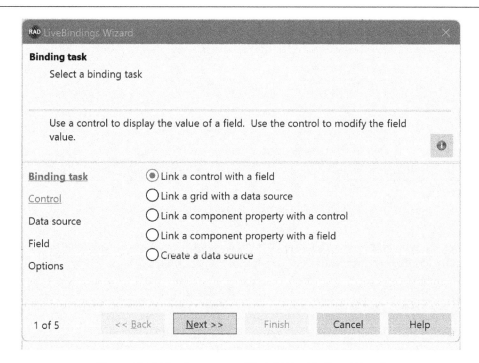

Figure 10.18: The first screen of Delphi LiveBindings Wizard

If we run our test app at this stage, we can see that the value of the label gets updated with the text of the edit every time we change the text in the edit and press *Enter* to confirm the input. Let's make two further changes:

1. Select the `LinkControlToPropertyText` object in the list of bindings (in the editor of *Figure 10.16* or the **Structure** view) and set its `CustomFormat` property to the value `'Hello ' + Text`, including the quotes. This is an expression made from concatenating two strings, a constant one plus the value of the `Text` property in the source control, the edit. What powers visual live bindings is Delphi's sophisticated **run-time type information** (**RTTI**) and reflection support.

2. Add an event handler for the `OnKeyUp` event of the edit, triggering a refresh of the associated controls. To make this happen, we can notify the live bindings system that the `Text` property of the `Edit1` control has changed, with the following code:

```
procedure TFormVLB.Edit1KeyUp(Sender: TObject; var Key: Word;
  var KeyChar: Char; Shift: TShiftState);
begin
  BindingsList1.Notify(Edit1, 'Text');
end;
```

You can see the resulting application in action in *Figure 10.19*, after typing a name in the edit. For each keystroke, the text is immediately reflected in the label, with the extra text added at the beginning.

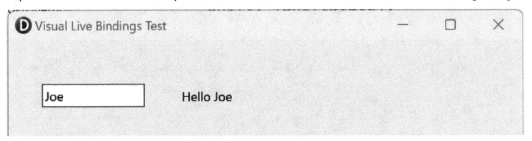

Figure 10.19: The VLBTest application on Windows

As we have seen in this section, we can build complex UIs with multiple controls connected to each other with live bindings and no coding (or very little coding if required).

Fast UI prototyping

Live bindings are not limited to string properties. You can bind different simple and complex data types. One of the really cool components that you can use to quickly design a data-driven UI is `TPrototypeBindSource`. This component can emulate a data table and generate test data for display. In this way, we can very quickly prototype GUIs.

Let's see how we could use live bindings to quickly prototype the UI of our ToDo List app:

1. Reopen the `ToDoList` project in the IDE, right-click on **Project Manager**, and select the option to add a new project to the project group.

2. Create a separate folder for the new project and save the main form's unit as `uFormToDoTest`, the project as `ToDoTest`, and the whole project group as `ToDoGrp`.

3. Change the `Name` property of the main form of the new project to `FormToDoTest`. Now, copy the list view control from the `FormToDo` form onto the `FormToDoTest`. We have our dynamic list view design in the new test form.

    Let's imagine that we have just started prototyping our app. It would be cool to preview what the ToDo list will look like without going through the process of implementing a proper data access logic.

4. Drop a `TPrototypeBindSource` component onto the form. Change its `Name` property to `PrototypeBindSourceToDo` and double-click on it. As you can see in *Figure 10.20*, we can add fields of different types to the source and preview sample test values that would be generated for us. In our case, we just need two fields with random string values. There are some interesting generators to create test contacts, *lorem ipsum* strings, bitmaps, or colors.

Figure 10.20: The Add Field dialog for the PrototypeBindSource component

5. Add one `BitmapNames` and one `ColorNames` field. Change the names of two test fields to `TestTitle` and `TestCategory`, as shown in *Figure 10.21*.

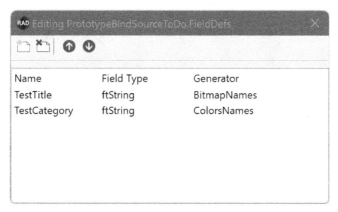

Figure 10.21: The fields added to the PrototypeBindSource1 component

6. Now, open the **LiveBindings Designer** window and make connections between the `Title` and `Category` fields in both components, the `TListView` and the `TPrototypeBindSource`, as you can see in *Figure 10.22*.

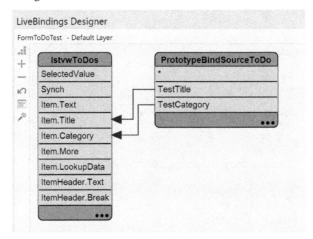

Figure 10.22: Visual LiveBindings connecting the list view with the prototype bind source

7. At this point, we can immediately see our list view populated with some test data, as you can see in *Figure 10.23*.

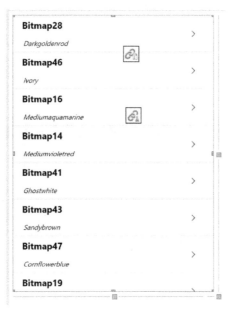

Figure 10.23: A list view populated with prototype data at design time

Visual live bindings technology is very powerful. It can be used to quickly prototype data-driven GUIs but it is also used as the underlying technology for building complete applications and to build interactive UIs even faster than in regular Delphi code.

A good example of a complete app that uses visual live bindings can be found as one of the multi-device project templates. Select the option to create a new Delphi multi-device project and instead of the usual **Blank** template, select the **Master-Detail** template. The generated project will have a list view and a prototype bind source emulating contact information. Have a look at the architecture and the live bindings used by this template app to get another example of this technology.

The ability to do fast prototyping is very important as a developer can use it to validate the concept and the UI of an application with very limited effort and later, if the customer approves it, they can do the actual database wiring and implementation to go from prototype to production. Without the ability to have a prototype the customer or end user can see, you have to make a much larger development effort only to make sure that what you are building matches the expectations.

Summary

In this chapter, we have learned how to build data-driven apps and embed databases on mobile devices. We have looked at creating the database, building a data mapping layer, and building a GUI associated with it. Database access is a critical feature for most apps given that you cannot always rely on local files in various formats, like we saw in terms of JSON and XML earlier in the book. A database offers better-structured storage, in most cases. Also, a database can be the local cache of a remote database you can access using various techniques for building cloud clients or multi-tier architectures, which are the topics of the following chapters.

In the next chapter, we are going to reuse the visual part of our ToDo List app and use cloud data storage as the underlying implementation of the `IToDoData` interface.

11
Integrating with Web Services

No mobile app is a lonely island. You can create a standalone mobile app with Delphi, but most of the time developers want to integrate with services to provide access to data and add the whole social dimension to the mobile user experience. In this chapter, we are going to have a tour of different technologies available in Delphi to integrate with mobile backends running in the cloud, including the HTTP native client library, accessing REST APIs, and using the Cloud API framework for integrating with cloud Web Services available on Amazon and Azure.

This chapter will cover the following points:

- Understanding Web Services
- Building a native HTTP client
- Consuming XML SOAP Web Services
- Integrating with REST Services
- Integrating with the cloud
- Using the AWS SDK for Delphi

The objective of this chapter is to learn how to build mobile HTTP clients and connect to Web Services and data in the cloud. This is a very broad topic. So we'll only be able to touch the surface of it.

Technical requirements

The code in this chapter uses external Web Services and cloud services and requires you to have accounts on the target systems. In most cases, a free account will be sufficient. In addition, the last demo uses the AWS SDK for Delphi, which is an add-on library. The examples in this chapter are available at https://github.com/PacktPublishing/Expert-Delphi_Second-edition.

Understanding Web Services

Not so long ago, and not in a galaxy far, far away, Sir Timothy John Berners-Lee invented the World Wide Web. In his vision for an information management system, individual documents should be hyperlinked with each other through special **Uniform Resource Locators** (**URLs**) and anyone reading a document in a web browser program should be able to jump directly to a referenced hypertext document. He was also the one who designed the **Hypertext Transfer Protocol** (**HTTP**) and implemented the first versions of web server and web browser programs, which used the HTTP protocol for communication. The fact that his ideas were – from the very beginning – open, public, and for everyone, contributed to the enormous, global success of the World Wide Web. At that time, it wasn't obvious that the web would become something that nowadays we take for granted, opening our favorite web browser and searching for information or reading the news.

HTTP is a simple protocol for exchanging text documents over the underlying TCP/IP infrastructure. It is very scalable because, due to its design, servers and clients do not need to maintain an active socket connection and every HTTP request is independent of any other. The HTTP specification defines different request types that a client can send to a server, sometimes referred to as *verbs*, that specify the type of action that a client wants to perform on a referenced "resource." There are many HTTP methods, but the most common ones are GET, HEAD, POST, PUT, and DELETE. An HTTP server performs requested actions and returns response codes and the requested data, if available. When a request is successful, the server returns the OK status code 200. Another popular standard HTTP response code is 404, which indicates a "not-found" error. You can find a very detailed list of HTTP status codes at https://en.wikipedia.org/wiki/List_of_HTTP_status_codes.

In the original WWW design from 1989, Tim Berners-Lee created HTML. Documents in this format can be displayed by web browsers. A few years later, the concept of Web Services was born from the realization that the HTTP protocol does not need to be limited to exchanging HTML documents. Any other document format can be returned from a web server and web client applications do not necessarily need to be web browsers. The first popular Web Services implementation was based on the **eXtensible Markup Language** (**XML**) document format. In this new format, the types of markup tags were not defined by a specification – anybody could define their own tags. XML-based Web Services defined a set of XML tags for encoding **Simple Object Access Protocol** (**SOAP**) messages that were exchanged between XML SOAP Web Service clients and servers. The key tag was envelope and Web Services request messages were sent by clients with information on what Web Service method needed to be invoked and the parameters. A web server would return an XML envelope with the results of a web method call.

Delphi 6 was the first developer tool on the market to support building SOAP Web Service servers and clients. This support is still there in current Delphi versions, but over time, the popularity of SOAP XML Web Services has decreased. Instead of SOAP and XML, it is now more common to use **JavaScript Object Notation** (**JSON**) as the document exchange format and **REprestational State Transfer** (**REST**) as the communication protocol. REST builds on the weaknesses of SOAP. In SOAP, the main focus is on the XML syntax of a request envelope and SOAP messages can be exchanged over any protocol, which doesn't need to be HTTP, although this is the most common implementation. RESTful Web Services are simpler and take full advantage of the underlying HTTP protocol, with its different request methods and response codes. The REST specification is not as formalized and rich as SOAP Web Services. The XML specification, over time, became very complex, and XML parsing is no longer a trivial process. As with many new technologies, the main adoption driver is simplification. REST Web Services typically use the simple JSON text format for exchanging data. REST became the main way to integrate with any remote functionality through a **REST Application Programming Interface (REST API)** exposed by the server.

Let's start examining how you can use Web Services in Delphi from the beginning, that is, making an HTTP call.

Building a native HTTP client

Arguably the most important network communication protocol is HTTP and its secure HTTPS version. Every operating system typically has its own HTTP client functionality built in. In the cross-platform world of Delphi programming, there is an HTTP client library, which provides uniform access to the HTTP client implementations available on different platforms.

Similar to other cross-platform libraries in Delphi, you can either work with HTTP entirely in code using types defined in the `System.Net.HttpClient` and `System.Net.URLClient` units, or you can rely on the ready-to-use components declared in the `System.Net.HttpClientComponents` unit and available in the **Net** category of **Tool Palette**.

Let's give it a try and build a simple app that will allow you to enter the URL into an edit box, download data using the HTTP GET request, and display the result in a memo component. These are the steps for building this demo:

1. Create a new blank Delphi multi-device project, saving the main form unit as `uFormHTTP` and the whole app as `HTTPApp`.

2. Change the `Name` property of the form to `FormHTTP`.

3. Drop a `TNetHTTPClient` component on the form.

4. Drop a `TToolbar` component on the form and drop a `TSpeedButton` and a `TEdit` component onto the toolbar.

5. Change the `Name` property of the speed button to `SpdBtnDownload`, its `StyleLookup` property to `arrowdowntoolbutton`, and the `Align` property to `Right`.

6. Change the `Name` property of the edit control to `EdtURL`. Expand its `Margins` property and enter 8 as the margin value for all four sides of the control. Now set `Align` to `Client`.

7. Drop a `TMemo` control on the form. Rename it to `MemoData` and align it to a `Client`. Add an 8-pixel margin to each of its sides, as we did for the `Edit` box.

8. The user interface is ready. As a nice twist, we can optionally set the `SystemStatusBar.Visibility` property of the form to `Invisible` to hide the system toolbar on iOS and have more space on the screen.

The `TNetHTTPClient` component has different methods for executing different types of HTTP requests that correspond to their names. For example, if we want to make a `GET` request, we need to use the `Get` method. For a `POST` request, there is the `Post` method, and so on.

Now, to fetch data from the server, double-click on the speed button and enter the following code in its `OnClick` event handler:

```
procedure TFormHTTP.SpdbtnDownloadClick(Sender: TObject);
var
  Memstr: TMemoryStream;
  Resp: IHTTPResponse;
begin
  Memstr := TMemoryStream.Create;
  try
    Resp := NetHTTPClient1.Get(EdtURL.Text, Memstr);
    if Resp.StatusCode = 200 then
      MemoData.Lines.LoadFromStream(Memstr)
    else
      ShowMessage(Resp.StatusCode.ToString + ': ' +
        Resp.StatusText);
  finally
    Memstr.Free;
  end;
end;
```

This is probably the simplest way of using the HTTP client component. Here we are assuming that the content in the response stream can be displayed as text in the memo. The response type can also be binary, like an image. Let's assume that we want to build a viewer for chemical molecules. In this case, we might want to download our app molecule information in the specific *PDB* text file format. In *Figure 11.1*, you can see the app displaying *Hemoglobin* data downloaded from the Protein Data Bank (www.rcsb.org). As you can see in the figure, this is just a text file.

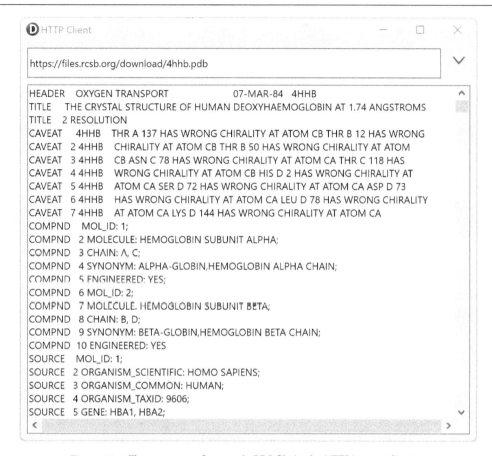

Figure 11.1: The contents of a sample PDB file in the HTTPApp application

The HTTP client library works with both HTTP and HTTPS protocols.

The library can also execute requests asynchronously. If you make a regular synchronous request and there is a lot of data to return from a server, the user interface gets temporarily frozen during the download. The app will start responding again only after the Get method is completed.

Let's modify our example to make the request asynchronously. First, we need to change the Asynchronous property of the HTTP client component to True.

If we execute our app again, after making this change, we will get an error. This is because the Get method would not block, but the execution would continue immediately to the next instruction, while the data from the response stream is not yet available.

When you set the Asynchronous property, the HTTP request will execute in a different thread, and when it is completed it fires an appropriate event. This is the OnRequestCompleted event of the HTTP client component.

For this reason, we need to modify the code of the OnClick event handler of the speed button, to only start the action:

```
procedure TFormHTTP.SpdbtnDownloadClick(Sender: TObject);
begin
  NetHTTPClient1.Get(EdtURL.Text);
  MemoData.Lines.Clear;
  MemoData.Lines.Add('Downloading...');
end;
```

Now handle the OnRequestCompleted event of the HTTP client component to process the response:

```
procedure TFormHTTP.NetHTTPClient1RequestCompleted(
  const Sender: TObject; const AResponse: IHTTPResponse);
begin
  if AResponse.StatusCode = 200 then
    MemoData.Lines.LoadFromStream(AResponse.ContentStream)
  else
    ShowMessage(AResponse.StatusCode.ToString + ': ' +
      AResponse.StatusText);
end;
```

With this change, the app will remain responsive and the UI can keep painting the screen even while the HTTP request is being executed because it happens in a different thread. Notice, though, that a user could click the button a second time while the HTTP operation is processing, starting a second request before the first is completed. You might want to disable the button when clicked and enable it again once the app receives a response.

The Delphi HTTP client library is the foundation for other specialized Web Service client library components, including SOAP, REST, and cloud API clients discussed in the following sections of this chapter. The next area we want to cover is using SOAP Web Services in client applications.

Consuming XML SOAP Web Services

The starting point for implementing a SOAP Web Service client is a **Web Services Description Language** (**WSDL**) document, which specifies the web methods a given Web Service implements, including the names and types of the expected parameters. Delphi provides a **WSDL Importer** wizard that takes as input a WSDL file and generates an Object Pascal unit with types and methods that correspond with the functionality exposed by a SOAP Web Service. The main application logic can use the generated classes in order to issue Web Service requests and receive results returned from a remote Web Services server app.

Let's have a look at the process of integrating with a SOAP Web Service on the example of a numeric processing service, capable of converting a number in its textual description. I found a free, open service, which is not terribly useful but is good for a demo. The WSDL file, if you want to take a look, is at `https://www.dataaccess.com/webservicesserver/NumberConversion.wso?WSDL`.

Let's create an example app around this service:

1. Create a new Delphi multi-device blank project. Save the main form as `NumbersAppForm` and the whole project as `NumbersApp`.

2. Change the `Name` property of the form to `FormNumbers` and save all.

3. Drop a `TPanel` control on the form and align it to `Top`.

4. Add a `TNumberBox` control to the panel, set `DecimalDigits` to 0, and the `Max` property to a large number, such as `100000`.

5. Add a `TButton` to the panel, set `Name` to `BtnConvert` and its `Text` property to `Convert`.

6. Add a `TMemo` on the form and align it to `Client`. Our simple user interface is now ready.

7. Now, go to the **File | New | Other** menu item and in the **New Items** dialog, click on the **Web Services** category in **Delphi Projects** and double-click on the **Import WSDL** wizard.

8. On the first page of the wizard, enter the WSDL file location, as shown in *Figure 11.2*.

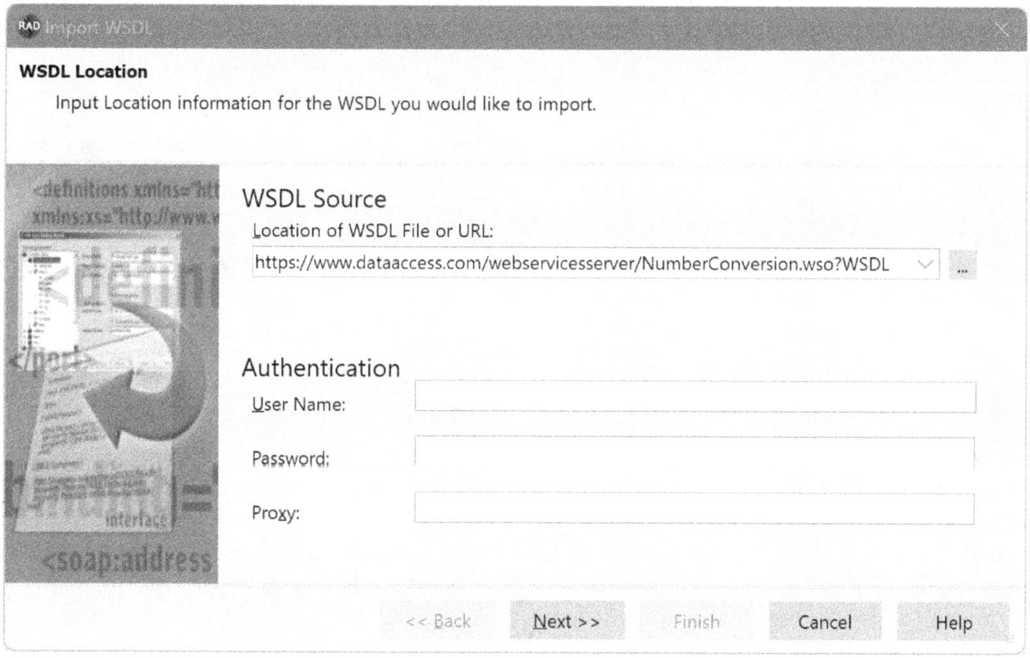

Figure 11.2: The WSDL Location tab of the Import WSDL wizard

9. On the following tabs of the wizard, just keep the default settings and close the wizard. The wizard will generate a new unit with a name derived from the Web Service and will automatically add it to the current project.

10. In our case, the name of the generated unit is `NumberConversion`. Select the main form and in the **File** menu select the **Use Unit** option and add the new unit to the `uses` clause in the implementation section of the main form unit.

11. The **Import WSDL** wizard generated, among other things, the interface type `NumberConversionSoapType`, which wraps the functionality of the imported Web Service. This is the source code of the interface:

```
type
  NumberConversionSoapType = interface(IInvokable)
  ['{A2E4D9CB-C96F-0965-87F0-E78269B29A8C}']
    function NumberToWords(const ubiNum: Int64):
      string; stdcall;
    function NumberToDollars(const dNum: TXSDecimal):
      string; stdcall;
  end;
```

12. In addition, the wizard also generates a global function – in this case, called `GetNumberConversionSoapType`, which returns the reference to this interface:

```
function GetNumberConversionSoapType(
  UseWSDL: Boolean=System.False; Addr: string='';
  HTTPRIO: THTTPRIO = nil): NumberConversionSoapType;
```

13. In the form code, we need to use the generated global function to obtain the Web Service interface reference and call the Web Service from it. Double-click on the button on the form and enter the following code in the `OnClick` event handler:

```
procedure TFormNumbers.BtnConvertClick(Sender: Tobject);
begin
  var SNumber := GetNumberConversionSoapType.NumberToWords(
    Trunc(NumberBox1.Value));
  Memo1.Text := Snumber;
end;
```

Very simple, isn't it? Now save all and run the app. You can enter an arbitrary number and get it converted to text, as in *Figure 11.3*.

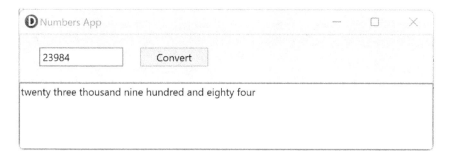

Figure 11.3: The text version of a number generated by a SOAP eb service

In this case, the code looks simple, but in real-world scenarios, the SOAP model can become extremely complex and, over the last few years, the SOAP model has lost some of its appeal. It is still relevant and used by public services in many countries, but in most common scenarios, SOAP has been replaced by REST. The use of REST Web Services is the next topic we are going to focus on.

Integrating with REST services

Technology does not like to stand still. It keeps evolving. Nowadays, SOAP Web Services are not as frequently used as compared to the early days, especially in comparison to REST.

Over time, the XML file format became harder and harder to process. The initially simple XML specification became more complex and the entire model has proven not flexible enough. In the meantime, the much simpler JSON became the most popular format for exchanging structured data.

The REST architecture for implementing Web Services is not as standardized as SOAP. There are several data structure and Web Service interface proposals, but none of them has gained a prominent position. The beauty of REST is that it fully adopts the underlying HTTP protocol (while SOAP is protocol agnostic) and it just uses HTTP request and response headers for structural information.

In REST, there is more freedom. Inside the REST server, there are different resources identified by their URL paths. Typically, these resources, or **endpoints**, can be accessed using different HTTP verbs, such as GET, POST, DELETE, and PUT. In many cases, these different verbs correspond to different CRUD operations on the underlying resource, such as for a database. The most common data format for returning information from REST services is JSON, but that could be XML or anything else. A REST Web Service can return a binary image, for example.

Delphi provides a number of components for integrating with REST services. They are available in the **Tool Palette** under the **REST Client** category and references with the name of **REST Client Library**. Internally, they are implemented using the HTTP client library discussed earlier in this chapter.

There are many free and paid, public and private REST APIs out there to integrate with. I like using the services of **APILayer**, an Embarcadero sister company, listed at https://apilayer.com/. Some of these services have limited free use, but they require a user identifier. For my demo, I'd like to use the **APILayer WeatherStack** service. To run this demo, you'd have to create a free account and get an API key at `https://weatherstack.com/`.

When integrating with a REST service, you need to know its base URL, the available endpoints, and any parameters needed. This is generally covered in detail in the service documentation. In this specific case, the base URL you have to use in every call is `http://api.weatherstack.com`, the endpoint we want to use is `current` (for the current weather), and the parameters needed are `access_key` and `query`. This last parameter is used to indicate the city or geographical location for which you want weather information.

If you want to make a test call, you can often use the web browser directly, given it's capable of passing query parameters and displaying the resulting JSON. It's much better, however, to use a specific tool to manage REST calls. Delphi comes with a tool called **REST Debugger** and it's available in the IDE **Tools** menu. In the **REST Debugger** tool, you should enter the preceding base in the URL edit box of the **Request** page, enter the endpoint and parameters on the second page, and you can click on the **Send Request** button to preview the results, as displayed in *Figure 11.4*.

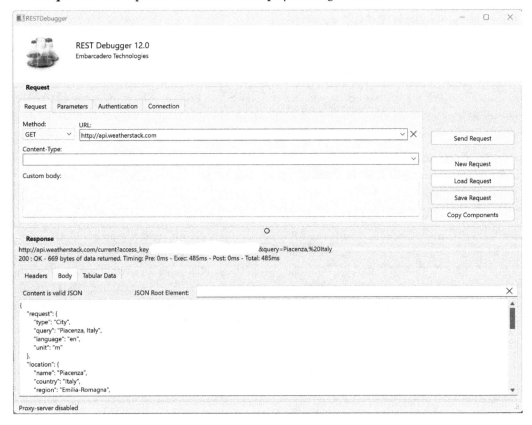

Figure 11.4: The REST Debugger tool showing weather information

The parameters are listed on the second page, and they are used to create the HTTP request you can see (with `access_key` omitted) above the resulting JSON in *Figure 11.4*.

You can preview the response as plain JSON, but you can also view it in tabular format. In most cases, this works better if you filter a portion of the JSON data structure, setting **JSON Root Element**. In this case, we are interested in the `current` section of the response, and we can display that in a tabular way as in *Figure 11.5*.

Figure 11.5: REST Debugger with filtered data in tabular format

Once you have configured **REST Debugger** and you are happy with the results, there are a couple of things you can do. First, you can save the configuration to a local file, so you can reload it in the future. Second, and a relevant reason for using this tool, you can copy the configuration in a set of components ready to be dropped in your Delphi application. For this, you have to use the **Copy Components** button.

Let's now build a simple app to try the weather service, leveraging this last capability:

1. Create a new Delphi multi-device application. Save the form file as `WeatherClient_Form` and the project as `WeatherClient`. Change the `Name` form to `FormWeather`.

2. Create a new data module, and add it to the project. Change the name of the data module to `DMWeather`. Save the data module unit as `WeatherClient_Module`.

3. In **REST Debugger**, copy the configured components. Open the designer of the data module and paste the components on it. You should not have three non-visual components on the form:

    - A `TRESTClient` component with `BaseURL` set to the REST server domain, `http://api.weatherstack.com`.

    - A `TRESTRequest` component with the `Resource` property set to `current` and two parameters, `access_key` and `query`.

    - A `TRESTResponse` component without any extra configuration.

4. Add to the data module a `TFDMemTable` component for the response data and a `TRESTResponseDataSetAdapter` component to map the response data to that table. In this adapter component, set the `Dataset` property to `FDMemTable1` and the `Response` property to `RESTResponse1`.

5. Right-click on the `TRESTRequest` component in the data module designer and call the `Execute` command of the local menu. This will run the HTTP request, and if everything is configured correctly (including the API access key!), you should see a **Response: 200 - OK** message. If not, you'll see an error message. In either case, you can select the response component and read the value of its `Content` property, which is going to have the resulting JSON data or a detailed error message. If the operation was successful, you can also select the memory table, pick the **Edit Data Set** option on the local menu, and see the JSON data loaded into the table fields as in *Figure 11.6*.

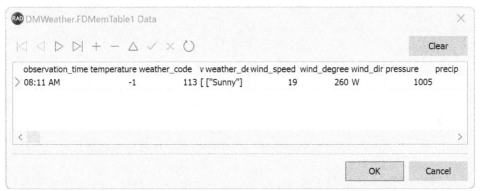

Figure 11.6: The in-memory table populated with JSON response data at design time

6. Let's now move on to the main form. Add a button, an edit box, and a label to the form. Name them respectively `BtnRefresh`, `EditLocation`, and `LabelTemp`. Set their font to be a bit bigger than the default. I've set `Size` to `20`. Set the edit text to a city name and the label text to `0` or `n/a`, as the initial status.

7. Now, in the `OnClick` event handler of the button, write the following code to set the location at the query request parameter, execute the request, and read the temperature field from the dataset:

```
procedure TFormWeather.BtnRefreshClick(Sender: TObject);
begin
  DMWeather.RESTRequest1.Params[1].Value :=
    EditLocation.Text;
  DMWeather.RESTRequest1.Execute();
  LabelTemp.Text := DMWeather.FDMemTable1.
    FieldByName('temperature').AsString;
end;
```

At this point, the app is complete. You can run it on Windows or any other target platform. Enter a city name, click on the button, and you should see the current temperature in that city. In *Figure 11.7*, you can see the app running on Windows.

Figure 11.7: The temperature information displayed by the WeatherClient app

While this is a nice and simple app, it has a significant issue running on mobile. The free account on the *WeatherStack* service allows you to use only HTTP and not HTTPS. However, recent operating system versions on mobile platforms prevent apps from using HTTP for security reasons. On Android, you can change the manifest file to request HTTP support with the following line (which is part of the project configuration on GitHub) under the `application` node:

```
android:usesCleartextTraffic="true"
```

The app will show a compatibility error message the first time it is executed on the most recent versions of Android, and it might not be accepted on the Google Play Store. This is not ideal, but sufficient for an initial experiment.

Now that we have seen the use of HTTP, SOAP, and REST client calls, let's move on to the final topic of this chapter, which is cloud computing.

Integrating with the cloud

Cloud computing is a fairly broad term referring to the global trend of moving in-house or on-premise servers and even servers owned by a company and hosted in a web farm to a fully hosted service solution. The difference between traditional hosting and cloud hosting is, in the first case, you manage hardware with an operating system and application software running on it, while in the cloud scenario, you use software services, regardless of the hardware infrastructure. In other words, rather than paying for hardware, electricity, web connectivity, and perpetual or yearly software licenses, you pay for a service per minute (or at times even millisecond) of use, by traffic volume, or by some use quota. The huge advantage of cloud services is the ability to scale them up very rapidly when there is more demand and scale them down when not needed so that you end up paying proportionally to the actual usage, rather than having to allocate a large amount of resources to account for a potential usage peak.

There are different cloud Web Service providers that offer all kinds of services. The main players in this arena are **Amazon Web Services (AWS)**, **Google Cloud Platform (GCP)**, and Microsoft Azure, but there are hundreds of other smaller players, often offering niche services and more competitive pricing.

Cloud services are typically accessible using the HTTPS protocol and, as such, they work like any other Web Service. So how can you access cloud services from Delphi? There are three different approaches:

- You can use the REST Client library we just covered in the last section. The difficulty here is that the security, encoding, and encryption rules required by the various platforms add some complexity to the work.

- You can use the Cloud API framework that Delphi has provided for a long time to access a few AWS and Azure services.

- You can use the AWS SDK for Delphi by Appercept, which is freely available in GetIt to Delphi Enterprise customers.

In this section, we'll focus briefly on the Delphi Cloud API covering Azure. In terms of AWS, we'll use it in a later section as we'll touch on the AWS SDK for Delphi.

The Delphi Cloud API

The **Delphi Cloud API** is defined in the `Data.Cloud.CloudAPI` unit, with specialized units with types and classes specific for working with selected services available from Amazon and Azure declared in `Data.Cloud.AmazonAPI` and `Data.Cloud.AzureAPI`.

As we discussed, the cloud features available in this library are fairly limited, but they are rather fundamental. The following table summarizes all currently supported services in the Cloud API framework.

	Amazon Web Services	**Microsoft Azure**
Storage	Simple Storage Service (S3)	Blobs Service
Table	Simple Database Service	Table Service
Queue	Simple Queue Service (SQS)	Queue Service

Table 11.1: AWS and Azure services available in the Delphi Cloud API

In this chapter, we are going to focus on the Azure Table service, while in the next chapter, we are going to look into AWS, but using a different API.

Moving the ToDo List app to Azure

In this section, we are going to focus on the Azure Table service. This is a NoSQL data storage service you can use to share data across multiple devices and even multiple applications. The goal of my demo application is fairly simple: update the *ToDo* app we wrote in the last chapter to use cloud-based storage rather than local database storage.

> **Note**
> You'll need to have an Azure account with the proper configuration to be able to run this demo application.

Before you can get started and test this app, you need to create a Microsoft Azure account (at the time I'm writing, it's possible to have a free account with some free limited use of the services). In the Azure portal, you'll have to go to **Storage accounts**, create or select a unique storage name (in my case, **marcocantu**), pick the **Tables** category, and create a new empty table. You can check the configuration I created for this project in *Figure 11.8*.

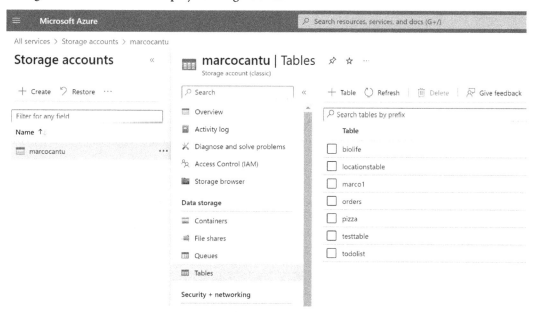

Figure 11.8: The configuration of Tables in the Azure Storage service

Notice that you don't need to define a table structure. As with any NoSQL database, each row or record can have different fields. There is another important element to know about to use Azure tables. Each row has two special fields, called `RowKey` and `PartitionKey` that are used as unique identifiers of each row. The two separate values can be changed to version data and in other scenarios. For our simple demo, we'll set both at the same value. Given the relevance of these two fields, you'll see that in the code of the following example, I've declared two constant strings for them:

```
const
  XML_ROWKEY = 'RowKey';
  XML_PARTITION = 'PartitionKey';
```

The code also has a third constant, with the name of the table:

```
const
   tablename = 'todolist';
```

We can now start the work to migrate the *ToDo List* app to use cloud storage. First, make a copy of the app we built in *Chapter 10*. If you remember, this was the app that was structured with a form unit with the UI, a data module for data access, and a unit defining an interface and in-memory objects to hold the data. The plan here is to keep the UI and the classes as they were in the previous version of the app, without touching them. All we need to change is the data module with the data access layer.

Let's convert the app with the following steps:

1. Locate the `ToDoList` source code files from the previous chapter and copy them to a new directory.

2. Save the project as `ToDoListAzure`.

3. The next step is to implement the `IToDoData` interface in the data module in the `DMToDoList` unit. In this data module, delete all FireDAC components and add a `TAzureConnectionInfo` component instead. There is generally no need to change any property of this component at design time unless you want to hardcode Azure access data.

4. To load the Azure configuration, it's better to use an external file. I've created an `azure.ini` file with an `azure` section and two entries for `AccountName` and `AccountKey`. The file is similar to this:

    ```
    [azure]
    AccountName=xyz
    AccountKey=1234567890
    ```

5. This `ini` file is loaded from the home path (on Windows, `C:\Users\<username>\AppData\Roaming`) when the data module is first created. From that file, we load the account name and key to the `TAzureConnectionInfo` component. This is the code of the event handler:

    ```
    procedure TDMToDo.DataModuleCreate(Sender: Tobject);
    var
       IniFile: TmemIniFile;
    begin
       var IniFilename := GetHomePath + PathDelim + 'azure.ini';
       if not FileExists (IniFilename) then
    ```

```
  raise Exception.Create('Missing Azure configuration');

IniFile := TMemIniFile.Create(IniFilename);
try
  AzureConnectionInfo1.AccountName :=
    IniFile.ReadString('azure', 'AccountName', '');
  AzureConnectionInfo1.AccountKey :=
    IniFile.ReadString('azure', 'AccountKey', '');
finally
  FreeAndNil (IniFile);
end;
```

6. In the same `OnCreate` event handler of the data module, we need to initialize a `TAzureTableService` object, declared as a field of the data module itself. We are going to use it extensively in the app. It can be created from the connection component with this code:

```
TableService := TAzureTableService.Create(
  AzureConnectionInfo1);
```

7. We are now ready to start writing the specific code to interact with the Azure table. Let's start with the code used to load the list of rows in the database table into the list of objects in memory. Notice that this code loads the data by iterating on the `RowsList` resulting from the call to the `QueryEntities` method of the `TableService` object. Additionally, in this loop, we also keep track of the maximum ID, information we'll need when creating a new row:

```
procedure TDMToDo.ToDoList(AList: TtoDos);
var
  Item: TtoDo;
  RowsList: Tlist<TcloudTableRow>;
begin
  MaxId := 0;
  if AList <> nil then
  begin
    Alist.Clear;
    RowsList := TableService.QueryEntities(tablename);
    try
      for var RowObj in rowsList do
      begin
        Item.Id := RowObj.GetColumn(XML_ROWKEY).
          Value.ToInteger;
        Item.Title := RowObj.GetColumn('title').Value;
        Item.Category := RowObj.GetColumn('category').Value;
        Alist.Add(Item);
```

```
      if Item.Id > MaxId then
        MaxId := Item.Id;
    end;
  finally
    RowsList.Free;
  end;
 end;
end;
```

8. Now the list won't show anything until we create a row in the table. So let's look at how we can create new rows. Before we can do that, however, we need to implement a local function calculating the ID for a new row:

```
function TDMToDo.GetNewId: Integer;
begin
  Inc (MaxId);
  Result := MaxId;
end;
```

9. Now we can create a new row. The ToDoCreate method receives as a parameter a TToDo object with the information the user entered in the second tab of the form. The main operation here is the InsertEntity call:

```
function TDMToDo.ToDoCreate(AValue: TToDo): Integer;
begin
  var Id := GetNewId;
  var RowObj := TcloudTableRow.Create;
  var ResponseInfo := TcloudResponseInfo.Create;
  try
    RowObj.SetColumn (XML_ROWKEY, Id.ToString);
    RowObj.SetColumn (XML_PARTITION, Id.ToString);
    RowObj.SetColumn('title',  Avalue.Title);
    RowObj.SetColumn('category',  Avalue.Category);
    TableService.InsertEntity(tablename,
      RowObj, ResponseInfo);
    if ResponseInfo.StatusCode = 200 then
      Result := Id
    else
      Result := -1;
  finally
    RowObj.Free;
    ResponseInfo.Free;
  end;
end;
```

10. Next, we need to be able to update the row, modifying the existing values, an operation done with the same tab of the user interface, but invoking the ToDoUdpate method, in case the row already exists. The core operation here is the UpdateEntity call:

```
function TDMToDo.ToDoUpdate(AValue: TToDo): Boolean;
begin
  var RowObj := TCloudTableRow.Create;
  var ResponseInfo := TCloudResponseInfo.Create;
  try
    RowObj.SetColumn (XML_ROWKEY, Avalue.Id.ToString);
    RowObj.SetColumn (XML_PARTITION, Avalue.Id.ToString);
    RowObj.SetColumn ('title', Avalue.Title);
    RowObj.SetColumn ('category', Avalue.Category);
    TableService.UpdateEntity(tablename,
      RowObj, ResponseInfo);
    Result := ResponseInfo.StatusCode = 200;
  finally
    RowObj.Free;
    ResponseInfo.Free;
  end;
end;
```

11. The next method we need to implement is ToDoDelete. The code deletes an existing row of the table, by calling the DeleteEntity method of the TableService object:

```
function TDMToDo.ToDoDelete(Id: integer): Boolean;
begin
  var RowObj := TcloudTableRow.Create;
  var ResponseInfo := TcloudResponseInfo.Create;
  try
    RowObj.SetColumn (XML_ROWKEY, Id.ToString);
    RowObj.SetColumn (XML_PARTITION, Id.ToString);
    TableService.DeleteEntity(tablename,
      RowObj, ResponseInfo);
    Result := ResponseInfo.StatusCode = 200;
  finally
    RowObj.Free;
    ResponseInfo.Free;
  end;
end;
```

12. Finally, we might want to be able to read a single row again, considering that another client working on the same data might have modified it:

```
function TDMToDo.ToDoRead(Id: Integer;
  out AValue: TToDo): Boolean;
begin
  var ResponseInfo := TcloudResponseInfo.Create;
  var RowObj := TableService.QueryEntity(
    tablename, Id.ToString, Id.ToString, ResponseInfo);
  if ResponseInfo.StatusCode = 200 then
  begin
    AValue.Title := RowObj.GetColumn('title').Value;
    AValue.Category := RowObj.GetColumn('category').Value;
    Result := True;
  end
  else
    Result := False;
end;
```

This is all of the code we need to add to ToDoList to move it from a local database application to a cloud-based one. The user interface remains identical, so I haven't added a specific screenshot here, as it will remain identical to those of the previous chapter.

The advantage of this solution is that if you run the app on Windows and enter some data, you can next deploy it on Android and see the same data, as the information lives on Azure. With this said, let's take a quick look at AWS, but we'll do it using a different approach, namely the AWS SDK for Delphi.

Using the AWS SDK for Delphi

If you prefer to use Amazon Web Services (AWS), rather than Azure, the Delphi Cloud API offers similar capabilities and integration. However, for AWS, there is a different, much expanded, client library you can use, the AWS SDK for Delphi by Appercept (see https://www.appercept.com/appercept-aws-sdk-for-delphi). This cloud client library is freely available in the Enterprise version of Delphi and can be downloaded from GetIt.

While based on the same concepts, this client library has more extensive coverage of the core APIs, but also offers a large number of additional AWS services, including (at the time of writing):

- Cognito (user pools)
- Cognito (identity pools)
- Polly
- Simple Email Service (SESV2)

- Simple Notification Service (SNS)

- Simple Queue Service (SQS)

- Simple Storage Service (S3)

- Textract

- Amazon Translate

- AWS Key Management Service (AWS KMS)

- AWS Secrets Manager

There is no room in this chapter to delve deeply into this rich and complex SDK. What I'm going to do, as usual, is create a small sample app to give you an idea of how this library is used. Specifically, the app I want to build is a **Simple Storage Server** *(S3)* client capable of listing files in a bucket and downloading and displaying images contained in those files.

The assumption, of course, is that you must have an AWS account and some data hosted in S3. In my case, I have a couple of demo buckets, as you can see in *Figure 11.9*.

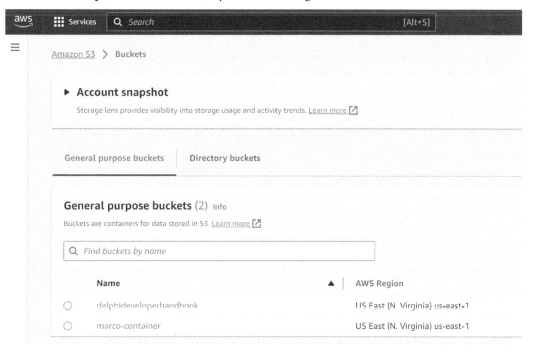

Figure 11.9: The configuration of S3 buckets in the AWS console

You also need the proper user account configuration. One of the options of the AWS SDK (any AWS SDK, not specifically the Delphi one) is to store the local account data in a `credentials` file in a `.aws` folder under the main user folder. So, in my case, the credential file is under `C:\Users\marco\.aws`. The file has the format of an INI file and entries such as the following:

```
[default]
aws_access_key_id=***
aws_secret_access_key=***
```

Before you build this app, you need to install the library. As mentioned, this is available in GetIt for free if you have an Enterprise version of Delphi. Once installed, it registers a few components and, more importantly, provides extensive Object Pascal interfaces to the AWS services listed.

To build this app, let's follow these steps:

1. Create a new Delphi multi-device app and save the main form unit as `S3SDKClient_MainForm` and the project as `S3SDKClient`.

2. Set the form name to `FormS3` and `Caption` to `S3SDKClient`.

3. Add a `TToolbar` control, aligned to a `Top`, and place a `TEdit` and a `TButton` on the toolbar. Set their `Name` properties to `EdBucketName` and `BtnList`, respectively.

4. Now add to the client area of the form a `TListBox`, aligned to `Left`, and a `TImage` aligned to `Client`. This is all we need for the user interface of the app.

5. Let's now move on to the code. First, we need to add the `AWS.S3` unit, installed with the AWS SDK, to the interface portion of the form unit.

6. We need to initialize a few objects to use over time and across methods. For this reason, add the following declarations to the `private` section of the `form` class, to store the S3 client interface and the response with the list of the elements in a bucket:

    ```
    private
      FS3Client: IS3Client;
      LResponse: IS3ListObjectsV2Response;
    ```

7. As you can see, most of the interaction is via interfaces, declared in the AWS SDK. We'll need to initialize each of these data structures. The initial client interface is configured with the programmatic start-up parameters, in the `OnCreate` event handler of the form. As with most AWS services, you need to associate the client with a specific region where the data is configured – in this case, `us-east-1`:

    ```
    procedure TFormS3.FormCreate(Sender: Tobject);
    begin
      var LOptions := TS3Options.Create;
      LOptions.Region := 'us-east-1';
    ```

```
    FS3Client := TS3Client.Create (Loptions);
  end;
```

8. Now we have the S3 client configured. When the button is clicked, we can use the name of the bucket from the edit box to initialize the request object (or type `IS3ListObjectsV2Request`) and call the `ListObjectsV2` method of the S3 client to fill the `IS3ListObjectsV2Response` with the actual data. We also want to use the data and fill the list box with the list of names (`Key`) of the objects in the bucket and their type:

```delphi
procedure TFormS3.BtnListClick(Sender: Tobject);
var
  LRequest: IS3ListObjectsV2Request;
begin
  LRequest := TS3ListObjectsV2Request.Create(
    EdBucketName.Text);
  LResponse := FS3Client.ListObjectsV2(LRequest);
  if LResponse.IsSuccessful then
    for var Item in LResponse.Contents do
      ListBox1.Items.Add (Item.Key + ' (' +
        Item.ContentType + ')');
end;
```

9. The last step is to handle the `OnDoubleClick` event of the list (although `OnTap` might also work on mobile) to download the selected element to a local file and display it in the image control:

```delphi
procedure TFormS3.ListBox1DblClick(Sender: Tobject);
begin
  var Item := Lresponse.Contents[ListBox1.ItemIndex];
  Item.DownloadFile(Item.Key);
  Image1.Bitmap.LoadFromFile(Item.Key);
end;
```

We can now run the application, which will result in a user interface similar to *Figure 11.10*, in which you can see the name of one of my buckets, its list of files, and the content of one of them, an image from *Chapter 1* of this book.

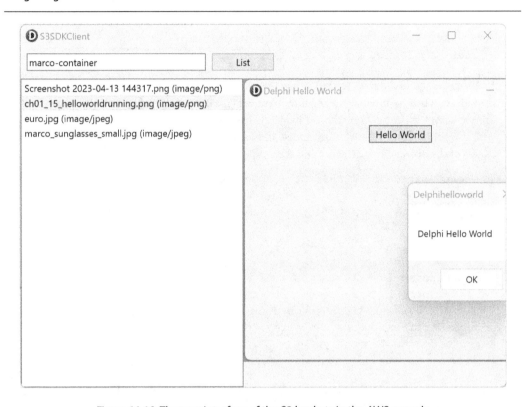

Figure 11.10: The user interface of the S3 buckets in the AWS console

What we've built is a very simple example of how you can use the AWS SDK to use the S3 service. As mentioned, this SSDK is much more extensive than what the Delphi Cloud API provides. More extensive demos of the AWS SDK for Delphi are available on GitHub at: `https://github.com/appercept/aws-sdk-delphi-samples`.

Summary

In this chapter, we have examined in some detail a number of different alternative techniques for building client applications that use Web Services. We looked into the HTTP, SOAP, and REST client libraries available in Delphi. We also examined the Delphi Cloud API and the AWS SDK for Delphi.

Overall, these techniques are very important, as most applications interact with remote data and Web Services these days. Which technique you use will depend on your specific needs – the reason we offered a broad overview of the many alternatives available in Delphi rather than focusing on a specific one.

In some cases, however, you might want to build both the client and the Web Service itself. That's the topic we'll cover in the next two chapters, starting with the foundations and progressing with more advanced features.

12

Building Mobile Backends

In the mobile development world, it is common to have dedicated developers and teams responsible for just building mobile **frontends** (the actual app running on the device) and **backends** (web services for accessing data and hosting some of the business logic). For this reason, we also want to wear the backend developer hat and use Delphi to build modern, scalable, secure, fault-tolerant REST API web services with full database access. This chapter will cover the following points:

- Delphi and multi-tier architectures
- Working at a low level with WebBroker
- Do-it-yourself with DataSnap

The objective of this chapter is to get you to understand the different choices for backend technologies in Delphi and gain practical knowledge on how to build web services. There is one further web service technology in Delphi called RAD Server, which will be the topic of the next chapter.

Technical requirements

As usual, all of the libraries covered in this chapter ship in Delphi, and most of them have been available for many releases. The DataSnap support, however, is available only in the Enterprise version of the product, not in the Professional and Community Editions.

The source code of the demos in this chapter can be found on GitHub at the following link: `https://github.com/PacktPublishing/Expert-Delphi_Second-edition`

Delphi and multi-tier architectures

In the previous chapter, we saw that you can use web services and cloud-hosted web APIs to create an information system where apps running on different devices can connect to the same data store. Not only you can use Delphi to integrate with existing web services, but you can also build your own.

Why would you build mobile backend services? Multi-tier architectures have a lot of benefits. But what exactly is a multi-tier solution? It's an architecture in which client apps communicate with server apps to access underlying resources. Compared to a client/server application, which has the **user interface** (**UI**), the business logic, and the database access all combined (even if possibly logically divided into different modules, as we did for the todo app in *Chapter 10*), in a multi-tier scenario where the database access lives on the server, along the core of the business logic, the client app has only the UI and the limited business logic required to support a better UI. These two different scenarios are depicted in *Figure 12.1*.

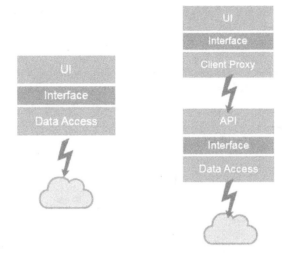

Figure 12.1: A representation of client/server and multi-tier application architectures

Additional tiers make the app architecture more complex, but they bring benefits such as improved scalability and security. They also provide the ability to build multiple clients (e.g., mobile, desktop, and even web clients) with a single, shared backend. The multi-tier approach simplifies change management because client apps are not tied to the underlying services and communicate with them through an abstraction layer provided by server APIs.

In multi-tier architectures, the actual server app is just one of the many pieces of the overall picture. It is very important how a server app is deployed. If scalability and high availability of services are our primary concerns, then we should think about using load-balancing technologies. Depending on the number of incoming HTTP requests, the auto-scaling infrastructure can start and stop instances of this virtual machine image, adapting to the current load.

In architectures like this, it is beneficial not to maintain the state of communication with a client app in the server tier, because different requests coming from the same client app might be received by different instances of the server. This is one of the reasons why using the HTTP protocol is so common for web services. The other technical element to consider for improved scalability and better cloud-deployment options is the use of Linux as a target platform, something Delphi supports only in the Enterprise Edition.

Now that we have covered the main reasons to consider adopting a multi-tier architecture, let's start with the first, foundation library offered by Delphi for building web services, called **WebBroker**.

Working at a low level with WebBroker

The most simple and generic web server development framework in Delphi is WebBroker. It is the underlying technology for many specialized web service types that you can build with Delphi, such as SOAP XML web services, DataSnap, and RAD Server. If you create a new web server app with the **New WebBroker App** wizard, you can implement arbitrary HTTP server functionality. In our case, that will be a simple web service that will provide REST API access to a new version of the Todo application.

Here are the steps to start building our first WebBroker server application:

1. Click on **File** | **New** | **Other** in the IDE and double-click on the **Web Server Application** wizard in the **Web** category.

2. On the first page of the wizard, titled **Platform**, you have the option to indicate the target platforms. Windows is required, and you can add Linux if you want. I recommend enabling it if your version of Delphi supports it.

3. On the second page of the wizard, titled **WebBroker Project type**, we need to decide how our project will integrate with a web server. WebBroker offers four options, but don't worry too much as your web service call remains independent of this selection and you can easily move to a new integration technology later on. There are four alternatives:

   - **Apache dynamic link module**: This is for integrating with the Apache web server on Windows or Linux

   - **Standalone console application**: This is a self-contained executable based on Indy web server technology with no GUI (and for this reason, it is better suited for the Linux target)

   - **Standalone GUI application**: This is also a self-contained executable based on Indy web server technology, but this time with a main form (it can be easier for debugging on Windows)

   - **ISAPI dynamic link library** (**DLL**): This is for integrating with Microsoft's IIS on Windows (this last option is not available if you select Linux on the first page)

One project, two targets

One possible solution is to create two WebBroker projects, one as an Apache module and the second as a standalone app, and add them to the same project group. Within this project group all units, except for those containing project sources, can be shared between both projects. During development, we can always select the **Build All** option to create test and production versions of the same web app.

Generating a standalone project

To start the development, let's generate a console-based WebBroker server:

1. For now, let's choose the **Standalone application console** option. Later on, we will add the second Apache project to the project group.

2. If we select a standalone option, on the last page of the wizard, titled **Port Number**, we can choose communication protocol, HTTP or HTTPS, and the

3. port to use, the default one being 8080. There is also a button to test whether the port is currently available as you can see in *Figure 12.2*. In the case of an Apache or IIS module, the wizard shows different pages where you can specify the version, name, and some of the integration parameters.

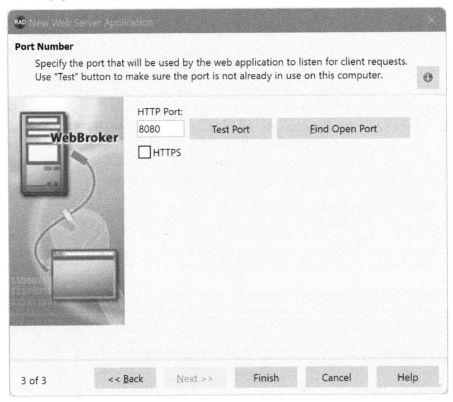

Figure 12.2: The Port Number page of the Web Server Application wizard

4. Click on the **Test Port** button to verify that the selected port is not in use and click **Finish** to generate the WebBroker server project.

Note

The default server generated by this wizard is configured to use port 8080 for HTTP communication, which is a common alternative port to the default one, which is 80. Only one server can listen to port 8080 at a time, so you might need to change this port to 8081 or any other value and update the client call accordingly. If you run a second server on the same port, you'll get an error message at the time the server opens the port, which tells you that it is already being used by another server on the same computer.

This is all we need to do to create a simple server that accepts HTTP requests. Next, we want to add an Apache module to the architecture.

The Standalone WebBroker server

Now that we have a project generated by the wizard, let's make sure we have a good folder structure to properly organize our two WebBroker projects, *Standalone* and *Apache*, before we proceed and test the project:

1. Create a new folder for the projects. Inside this folder, create three sub-directories: `apache`, `standalone`, and `shared`.

2. Click on the **Save All** button in Delphi. Save the `ServerConst1` unit into the `standalone` folder, the `WebModuleUnit1` into the `shared` folder, and save the project as `ToDoWebBrokerStandaloneHTTP`, making sure it is also saved in the `standalone` folder.

3. Run the web server project on Windows. You should see the console window prompting you to enter one of the options. Type in `start` to start the web server. If you see a message from the Windows Firewall, click on the **Allow** or **Allow Access** button (depending on your version of Windows) to let client apps communicate with the server.

4. If you now open your web browser and enter `localhost:8080` or `127.0.0.1:8080` in the address box, you should see the default web page of our server, as you can see in *Figure 12.3*. If you change the server port to a value other than `8080`, you'll have to adjust the URL accordingly.

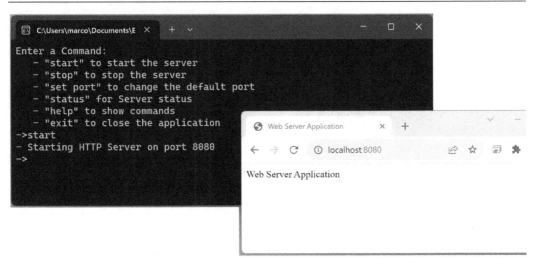

12.3: The default output from a blank WebBroker application

5. You can type `exit` in the web server console to stop the web server project.

6. It is not very convenient to have to enter `start` after the web server starts. Let's make a small modification in the main program file to start the server automatically.

7. Select **View Source** from the **Project** menu of the Delphi IDE. Scroll towards the end of the file. In the `RunServer` procedure, find the following line of code in the `while` loop:

```
StartServer(LServer)
```

8. Now, copy the line and paste it after the line with the assignment of the `LServer.DefaultPort` property and just before the `while True do` statement. In this way, we will not have to enter the `start` command manually, as the server will automatically start.

The main program file of the web server console app is more complex than a regular Delphi project file, but you seldom have to touch it. The Indy standalone web server will instantiate a web module using the class reference provided and will route to it the incoming URL for processing.

The real code of our web server app is encapsulated inside the `WebModuleClass` that is implemented in the `WebModuleUnit1` unit. The web module is a specialized form of a data module. You can put different non-visual components on this data module to implement the server logic.

The main structure of a WebBroker app is based around a collection of actions, which corresponds to different URL paths within the web server application. These actions are stored in the `Actions` collection property of the web module, as you can see in *Figure 12.4*.

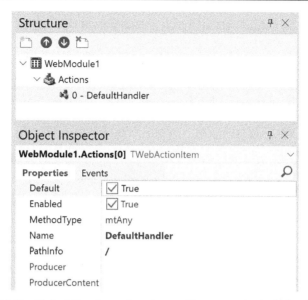

Figure 12.4: The DefaultHandler web action and its properties in Object Inspector

The wizard has generated a single action with the Default property enabled, which makes it the action that is called in response to any HTTP request that arrives at the server.

In the OnAction event of the web action item, we can enter the code that will be executed when the HTTP request arrives. This event has Request and Response parameters, providing us with information about the incoming web browser HTTP request (with fields providing the values of the HTTP headers and content) and allowing us to define the data and metadata of the HTTP response we want to send back to the web browser.

The response could be anything; it could be text data such as HTML or JSON, but also binary data such as JPEG or a Zip file. In the default scenario, the content that is sent back is HTML. We can modify the default handler to return the information that it is our ToDo REST API service.

Here is what the modified code looks like; it returns a bit of static HTML markup:

```
procedure TWebModule1.WebModule1DefaultHandlerAction(
  Sender: TObject;Request: TWebRequest;
  Response: TWebResponse; var Handled: Boolean);
begin
  Response.Content :=
    '<html>' +
    '<head><title>To-Do REST API</title></head>' +
    '<body>Delphi "To-Do List" REST API</body>' +
    '</html>';
end;
```

This is just a placeholder, so a simple HTML text is sufficient for now.

> **Note**
>
> Starting with Delphi 12, you can take advantage of the multi-line string literal support to write the HTML as a single string, rather than a series of strings concatenated with the + sign. This makes the THEML code much more readable.

Now that we have some understanding of the core structure of the app, let's add the Apache project. After that, we'll get back to writing the actual code of the demo.

Adding Apache support

Before starting to implement our web service, let's add the second project, the Apache module:

1. Right-click on the project group node in **Project Manager** and select the **Add New Project** option.
2. Double-click on the **New Web Server Application** icon, again.
3. On the first page of the wizard, select the option to add **Linux** support.
4. On the second page, make sure to select **Apache dynamic link module** as the project type.
5. On the last page of the wizard, you can specify the Apache version you want to support; in general, you'd want to leave the default values.
6. Click on the **Finish** button. The Apache project has been generated.
7. Now we need to carefully save it. Click on **Save All**, and save the web module unit as `WebModuleUnit2` in the `apache` folder and the project as `ToDoWebBrokerApache` in the same `apache` folder. Save the project group as `ToDoWebBrokerGrp`.
8. Now, we want both projects to use the same web module. Click on `WebModuleUnit1` in the **Project Manager** window and drag and drop it onto the Apache project node. A confirmation dialog will ask you if you want to add the selected unit to the project. Confirm that request.
9. Now, right-click on `WebModuleUnit2` in **Project Manager** and select the **Remove from project** option.

Now, both projects are using the same web module code, as you can see in *Figure 12.5*. Right-click on the **Project Group** node and select **Build All**. At any time, we can build our web server as a standalone app for testing and as the Apache module for deployment.

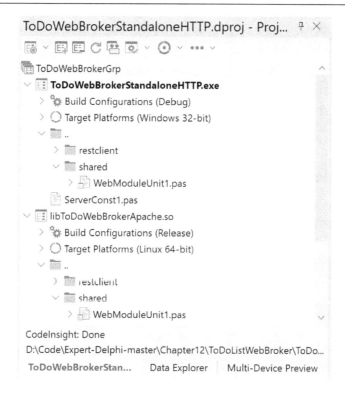

Figure 12.5: Both WebBroker projects in ToDoWebBrokerGrp share the same web module

This is all we need to do to create an Apache module based on the same code as the standalone WebBroker server.

Adding a client application

Let's add a client app project to the group, following these steps:

1. Create a new `restclient` folder in the previously created folder that already contains three other folders for both server projects.

2. Copy all files from the `ToDoListSQLite` project from *Chapter 10* to the newly created folder.

3. Right-click on the project group node in **Project Manager** and select the **Add Existing Project** option. Add the `ToDoListSQLite` project to the group.

4. Save the project as `ToDoListRESTClient`.

5. Save the main form unit as `uFormToDoRESTClient` and change the `Name` property of the form to `FormToDoRESTClient`.

6. Move the `uToDoTypes`, `uToDoUtils`, and `uDMToDo` units to the shared folder. Add them to both server projects.

7. Add the `uToDoTypes` and `uToDoUtils` units to the client project.

Now, right-click on the project and select **Build All**. All three projects should compile successfully.

Building the web module

There are different approaches for the architecture of a web service exposing a REST API. In our case, we want to expose the **CRUDL** operations on the underlying ToDo data. In our example, let's switch to `WebModule1` and add five more web action items to the `Actions` collection of the web module that will correspond to the underlying operations in our ToDo data. These are the operations that our REST server will expose using different URLs.

After adding new actions, rename them as `ActToDoCreate`, `ActToDoRead`, `ActToDoUpdate`, `ActToDoDelete`, and `ActToDoList`. You can see the structure of the actions in *Figure 12.6*, along with the configuration for one of them in **Object Inspector**.

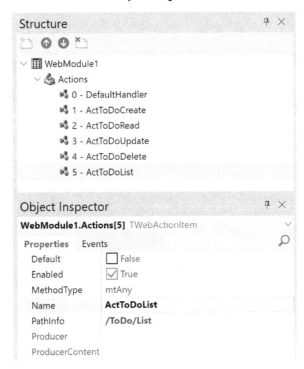

Figure 12.6: The Web Module action items in the "Structure View"

In the PathInfo property of the actions, enter /ToDo/Create, /ToDo/Read, /ToDo/Update, /ToDo/Delete, and /ToDo/List, respectively.

The first step to implementing their OnAction event handlers is to provide access to the underlying IToDoData interface exposed by the uDMToDo data module, which in turn uses SQLite for data storage. Add the uToDoTypes unit to the uses clause in the interface section of the data module, and uDMToDo and uToDoUtils to the implementation uses clause.

Now, declare a private FToDoData field of type IToDoData in the web module class declaration and a private GetToDoData function that will return the reference to the interface needed in the implementation of all web action items event handlers. This is the code of the function:

```
function TWebModule1.GetToDoData: IToDoData;
begin
  if FToDoData = nil then
    FToDoData := TDMToDoS3.Create(nil);
  Result := TToDoData;
end;
```

We'll use this function often to implement the various server operations.

Creating a new ToDo item

Now, double-click on the OnAction event of the ActToDoCreate web action item and enter the following code to add a new ToDo item in the underlying database storage:

```
procedure TWebModule1.WebModule1ActToDoCreateAction(
  Sender: TObject; Request: TWebRequest;
  Response: TWebResponse; var Handled: Boolean);
var
  AToDo: TToDo;
begin
  AToDo.Title := Request.QueryFields.Values['title'];
  AToDo.Category := Request.QueryFields.Values['category'];
  var Id := GetToDoData.ToDoCreate(AToDo);
  Response.Content := Id.ToString;
end;
```

Now that you can save the code, make sure that the standalone test web server project is active in **Project Manager** and run it. Now you can test it with a client, keeping in mind that the specific endpoint URL is as follows:

```
http://127.0.0.1:8080/ToDo/Create
```

You can use the **REST Debugger** utility available in Delphi. In this case, enter the preceding URL and in the **Parameter** tab, add **Title** and **Category** parameters with some test values. Click on the **Send Request** button. In the **Response** section, you should see the ID of the newly added ToDo item.

An alternative is to use a web browser, in this case adding the parameters directly to the URL using a query field, as in the following:

```
http://localhost:8080/todo/create?title=milk&category=food
```

Again, the result will be the number of the ID of the new item. Now we can similarly implement the remaining web action items.

Reading the data and other operations

In the `ActToDoRead` action, we are going to extract the `id` parameter from the request, invoke the underlying method of the data module, and return the `ToDo` item encoded as JSON (and we are setting the response `ContentType` property to `application/json` to send this encoding information back to the client):

```
procedure TWebModule1.WebModule1ActToDoReadAction(
  Sender: TObject; Request: TWebRequest;
  Response: TWebResponse; var Handled: Boolean);
var
  AToDo: TToDo;
begin
  var Id := Request.QueryFields.Values['id'].ToInteger;
  if GetToDoData.ToDoRead(Id, AToDo) then
    Response.Content := ToDoToStr(AToDo)
  else
    Response.Content := 'Failed';
  Response.ContentType := 'application/json';
end;
```

The core of the work is converting the single `TToDo` record to a JSON representation, an operation that is done in the `ToDoToStr` function we've added to the `uToDoUtils` unit:

```
function ToDoToStr(AToDo: TToDo): string;
var
  ASw: TStringWriter;
  AJtw: TJsonTextWriter;
begin
  ASw := TStringWriter.Create;
  AJtw := TJsonTextWriter.Create(ASw);
  try
    AJtw.WriteStartObject;
```

```
    WriteItem(AToDo, AJtw);
    AJtw.WriteEndObject;

    Result := ASw.ToString;
  finally
    AJtw.Free;
    ASw.Free;
  end;
end;
```

I don't want to get into the details of every other operation here, as once you've understood the idea, it is just fairly repetitive.

The updated web action is similar. We are extracting the three parameter values (Id, Title, and Category) and passing them to the underlying ToDoUpdate method of the data module. The same is done for the delete operation, which requires only the Id value of the record.

The last operation returns the list of all to do items. It does not expect any parameters, as it needs to fetch the data from the database and convert it to JSON using the ToDosToStr utility function:

```
    GetToDoData.ToDoList(aList);
    Response.Content := ToDosToStr(aList);
```

Our simple REST APIs based on WebBroker technology are ready. Right-click on the project group in **Project Manager** and select **Build All** to build test and deployment versions of our web server app.

A client for the REST API

Instead of communicating directly with the database, now we need to convert our REST client project, which is already in the project group, to invoke the REST APIs that we have just built. You can do this by following these steps:

1. Run the standalone version of the web server project and double-click on the ToDoListRESTClient project in **Project Manager** to active it.

2. Remove the uDMTo data module from the project and add a new data module.

3. Change the Name property of the data module to DMToDoWebBrokREST and save its unit as uDMToDoWebBrokREST.

4. Add the uToDoTypes unit to the uses clause in the interface section of the data module and the uToDoUtils unit in its implementation part.

5. Add the IToDoData interface to the class declaration of the data module.

    Copy the signatures of routines from the interface declaration to the public section of the data module class declaration and press the *Ctrl + Shift + C* key combination to invoke class completion.

6. In the main form class of the client application, change the name of the unit in the `uses` clause in the implementation section to use the new data module and modify the implementation of the `GetToDoData` method accordingly:

```
uses
  uDMToDoWebBrokREST;

function TFormToDoRESTClient.GetToDoData: IToDoData;
begin
  if DMToDoWebBrokREST = nil then
    DMToDoWebBrokREST := TDMToDoWebBrokREST.
      Create(Application);
  Result := DMToDoWebBrokREST;
end;
```

That's the beauty of the clear separation of application tiers we have implemented over the last few chapters: the UI and data access layers can be switched with limited effort. In this case, we have just plugged in a different implementation of the data access logic to the UI. Now, we have to finish implementing it.

7. Switch back to the uDMToDoWebBrokREST data module and drop the components needed to access the REST API onto it. You need a `TRESTClient` component, a `TRESTResponse` component, and five `TRESTRequest` components.

8. Rename the components of the data module respectively to `RClientToDo`, `RRespToDo`, `RReqToDoCreate`, `RReqToDoRead`, `RReqToDoUpdate`, `RReqToDoDelete`, and `RReqToDoList`, as you can see in *Figure 12.7*.

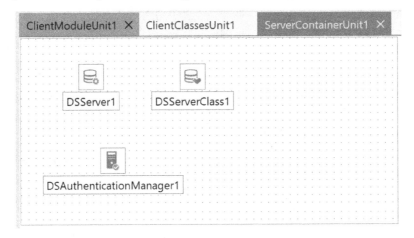

Figure 12.7: The REST client components on the data module

9. Set the Response property of the five request components to the same response object, RRespToDo.

10. In the REST client component, enter 127.0.0.1:8080 into the BaseURL property. This is for testing. In the final version of the client app, this value should be updated to the actual domain name or IP address of the server where our REST API web server app is running. Also, if you changed the server port to a value other than 8080, you'll have to adjust this value accordingly.

11. In the Resource property of the RReqToDoList component, enter the ToDo/List value.

    Now make sure that the test web server app is running. If this is the case, right-click on the RReqToDoList component and select **Execute** from its context menu. You should see the dialog form displayed with the message **Response: 200 - OK**. If you now click on the RRespToDo component and check its Content property, you should find the JSON data with the list of all ToDo items.

    We need to set up the properties of the remaining REST request components. In the RReqToDoCreate component, enter ToDo/Create as the Resource property. Add two parameters to the Params property and set their Name properties to title and category.

12. Do the same for all other components, resulting in a configuration like the one depicted in *Figure 12.8*.

Figure 12.8: The parameters of the various TRESTRequest components
in the data module of the client application

13. The last part of the work is to write the data module methods. Let's start with a simple one, the `ToDoCreate` method. We just need to assign the values of the parameter in the `RReqToDoCreate` component, call its `Execute` method, and return the result from the `Content` property of the REST response component. This is the function's code:

```
function TDMToDoWebBrokREST.ToDoCreate(
  AValue: TToDo): Integer;
begin
  RReqToDoCreate.Params[0].Value := AValue.Title;
  RReqToDoCreate.Params[1].Value := AValue.Category;
  RReqToDoCreate.Execute;
  Result := RRespToDo.Content.ToInteger;
end;
```

The `delete` and `update` operations are similar.

The implementation of the `ToDoRead` method, instead, requires the conversion of the JSON string received from the server to a `TToDo` record. To keep the code clean, this is done using a `StrToToDo` function to the `uToDoUtils` unit:

```
function StrToToDo(S: string): TToDo;
begin
  var ASr := TStringReader.Create(S);
  try
    var AJtr := TJsonTextReader.Create(ASr);
    try
      while AJtr.Read do
        if AJtr.TokenType = TJsonToken.StartObject then
        begin
          Result.Id := StrToInt(ReadStr(AJtr));
          Result.Title := ReadStr(AJtr);
          Result.Category := ReadStr(AJtr);
        end;
    finally
      AJtr.Free;
    end;
  finally
    ASr.Free;
  end;
end;
```

By using this function, we can now implement the `ToDoRead` method in a relatively simple way:

```
function TDMToDoWebBrokREST.ToDoRead(
  Id: integer; out AValue: TToDo): Boolean;
begin
  RReqToDoRead.Params[0].Value := Id.ToString;
```

```
    RReqToDoRead.Execute;
    Result := RRespToDo.Content <> 'Failed';
    if Result then
      AValue := StrToToDo(RRespToDo.Content);
  end;
```

The last method to implement is `ToDoList`. Here, we are using a `StrToToDos` utility method, similar to the one we've just seen, to convert the JSON representation of the list and populate the list passed in the `aList` parameter with received items:

```
procedure TDMToDoWebBrokREST.ToDoList(AList: TToDos);
begin
  AList.Clear;
  RReqToDoList.Execute;
  StrToToDos(RRespToDo.Content, AList);
end;
```

That's it. Click on **Save all** and run the REST client application. It should just work! Our modified client application will invoke the REST server built with WebBroker, which in turn uses a local database.

The WebBroker framework is the underlying technology for other types of web server apps such as the SOAP web server application or different DataSnap server project types hosted in a web server. It is the simplest form of an HTTP server that you can build with Delphi. So, let's now move to one of these higher-level server-side frameworks, DataSnap.

Do-it-yourself with DataSnap

WebBroker is good for a basic level HTTP server functionality, but the more complex the system you want to build, the more you look into complete Delphi multi-tier frameworks such as DataSnap (covered in this section) or RAD Server (covered in the next chapter). They provide a lot more high-level functionality than you can find in WebBroker. However, notice that the higher-level multi-tier solutions are available only in the Enterprise and Architect versions of Delphi, not in the Professional and Community Editions.

The DataSnap framework has been part of Delphi since its early days and has evolved over that time. Delphi 3 introduced the MIDAS technology to make it easy to build client/server database applications. In Delphi 6, this technology has been renamed to DataSnap, and in Delphi 2009, it has been completely rewritten. In this new architecture, remote methods published by a DataSnap server looked like database-stored procedures that a typical SQL relational database system exposes. The dbExpress database access framework has been reused and a special DBX driver has been built to provide connectivity between DataSnap clients and servers. The DBX model is still there in the current DataSnap implementation, but a newer REST-based model has been added. In DBX, you could have used TCP/IP or HTTP for communication between the client and server. In DataSnap, REST-based architecture, the only choice is to use HTTP or HTTPS.

When you open the **New Items** dialog in Delphi there are three different wizards in the **DataSnap Server** category to create new server projects:

- The **DataSnap REST Application** wizard generates a DataSnap web server project including web pages and JavaScript files to invoke server methods from a browser

- The **DataSnap Server** wizard supports creating old-style DBX-based DataSnap servers, which are not recommended

- The **DataSnap WebBroker Application** wizard generates a DataSnap server app hosted in a WebBroker web server

With this in mind, let's start building an actual server.

Building the DataSnap server

In the context of building backends for mobile apps, the last choice seems to be the most useful. Let's give it a try and build simple server and client projects to understand what the different building blocks of this framework are. You can follow these steps:

1. Select the **DataSnap WebBroker Application** wizard and click the **OK** button.

2. On the first page of the wizard, check the option to add **Linux** support.

3. On the third tab, we can choose which features will be added to a new project. Select all of them and click **Next**.

4. In the next tab, we can choose the base class for the `server methods` class. For simple projects, where we do not plan to use non-visual components in server implementation, we could choose **TComponent**. In most cases, it is best to choose **TDataModule**. The last choice can be ignored, given that the **TDSServerMethods** class is a specialized DBX-specific data module with support for building old-style client/server database apps using the `IAppServer` interface from the MIDAS era.

5. On the last tab, we need to specify the folder for the project files. The folder name needs to be a valid identifier for Delphi projects because the last part of the path will be used by the wizard to generate the project name.

6. Because we have selected `TDataModule` as the server methods ancestor class, we are presented with the dialog to confirm that we want to enable the VCL framework. Click on the **OK** button.

7. The wizard will generate the complete project for us. Click on **Save All** and accept default names for all new units.

The heart of the DataSnap server application is the `DSServer1` component, which you can find in `ServerContainerUnit1,` as you can see in *Figure 12.9*. It has the `AutoStart` property, which is set to `True`, so at the moment that the application starts, the web server starts to wait for incoming requests from clients.

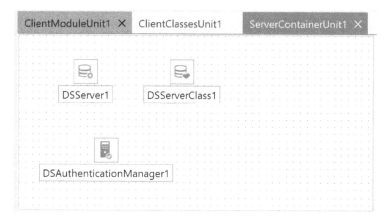

Figure 12.9: The DataSnap components on the ServerContainerUnit1 data module

ServerMethodsUnit1 holds the actual APIs of the server. All public and published methods declared in this class are callable by clients. The DSServerClass1 component in ServerContainerUnit1 connects the DSServer1 component with the server methods class. It has the Server property that points to DSServer1 and also an OnGetClass event that tells the DSServer1 components what the server class type is.

Notice that in the following code, we are assigning a class reference (the class itself) and not an instance, an object of that class:

```
procedure TServerContainer3.DSServerClass1GetClass(
  DSServerClass: TDSServerClass;
  var PersistentClass: TPersistentClass);
begin
  PersistentClass := TServerMethods3;
end;
```

Now that we have the structure of the project, let's focus on the actual code we need.

Implementing the DataSnap server functionality

In DataSnap architecture, a programmer does not write code to instantiate a server methods class inside the server app. The LifeCycle property of the DSServerClass1 component controls the lifecycle of the server class. This property can have the three different values:

- By default, it is set to Session, which means that for every connected client, there is one server methods class instance inside the server app. When a client connects, it is created, and when the client disconnects, it is destroyed.

- If this property is set to `Server`, then there is only one server class instance for all connected clients. In this case, the server method implementation should be thread-safe, because its methods could be called from different threads at the same time.

- The most scalable option for the `LifeCycle` property is `Invocation`. In this scenario, the server methods class is instantiated just for the duration of a server method call. It does not maintain state across server method calls.

DataSnap servers are usually hosting agnostic. This means that DataSnap servers can be implemented as a WebBroker web server, a console app, a VCL or FireMonkey forms application, or as a Windows Service.

The server wizard has generated the `TServerMethods3` class in `ServerMethodsUnit1`. It has just two sample server methods: `EchoString` and `ReverseString`. They take a string parameter and return a string. You can add other public methods to this class and they will automatically be available to clients. Note that the `METHODINFO` compiler directive enforces generating full RTTI information about methods belonging to a server methods class, which is needed by the DataSnap framework.

This is the complete class source code:

```
type
{$METHODINFO ON}
  TServerMethods3 = class(TDataModule)
  private
    { Private declarations }
  public
    { Public declarations }
    function EchoString(Value: string): string;
    function ReverseString(Value: string): string;
  end;
{$METHODINFO OFF}
```

In general, there could be more server methods classes in the DataSnap server. Each class would require its own `TDSServerClass` component pointing to the `DSServer1` returning in its `OnGetClass` event the data type (the class) of the server method class.

For now, let's keep the server project as is and build a client application for it.

Building a DataSnap client

Similar to building clients for XML SOAP Web Services, there must be a client access unit generated that mimics the functionality available on the server. In the case of SOAP Web Services, the starting point for generating client proxies is the WSDL document that is typically generated automatically from the running service. DataSnap client development is similar.

The DataSnap proxy generator needs to have access to a running server. It queries the server and generates a DataSnap client class that exposes the same methods available on the server. There are client proxy generators for multiple programming languages including Object Pascal, C++, PHP, JavaScript, C#, Java, and Objective C. Notice, however, that outside of Object Pascal and C++, the generators for other languages have not been maintained and are currently deprecated.

On the client, you just need to instantiate this DataSnap client class by passing the DataSnap connection component to the constructor. The DataSnap framework uses RTTI to provide serialization functionality for many simple and complex Delphi data types. Consequently, we do not need to manually convert parameter and result types from their native Delphi representation to strings and JSON. This is done for us, but the choice of parameter types is important in DataSnap. If the proxy generator does not support certain parameter types, it just ignores a given server method and the proxy is not generated for it.

Let's now build the client app:

1. The proxy generator will require access to the running server. Click on the **Run** button to start the DataSnap server.

2. Enter `start` in the console window and keep the server running. You can optionally enter the server URL in the web browser to verify that it listens on port `8080` as specified in the wizard, as in *Figure 12.10*.

Figure 12.10: The WebBroker DataSnap server running and a browser connected to it

3. Right-click on the project group node in **Project Manager** and select **Add New Project** from the context menu. Create a new Delphi multi-device blank application.

4. Save the main form unit as `uFormDSClient` and the project as `DataSnapClient`. Change the `Name` property of the main form to `FormDSClient`.

5. Now, we will use a wizard to generate the DataSnap client code. In the **DataSnap Server** category in the **New Items** dialog, double-click on the **DataSnap REST Client Module** icon.

6. On the first screen of the wizard, select **Remote Server** as the server location. At the end, our mobile DataSnap client will be accessing a remote server.

7. On the second screen of the wizard, we can specify the DataSnap server project type. Right now, we are building the client app against the standalone WebBroker server, but in production, we will most likely be using the DataSnap server built as an Apache module and deployed to a Linux machine. It is OK to specify the **Do not know** option here.

8. On the last screen, we need to enter the URL (or **Host Name**) of the server and test if the connection can be established. If the wizard cannot connect to the server, it will not be able to generate the DataSnap client code. Enter `127.0.0.1` as the host name and `8080` as the port number. Click on the **Test Connection** button to verify that we can connect with the server and click on the **Finish** button.

The wizard has generated two new units and added them to the client project: `ClientClassesUnit1` and `ClientModuleUnit1`. Click on the **Save All** button to save new units. You can see the project group architecture and the various units of the server and the client application in *Figure 12.11*.

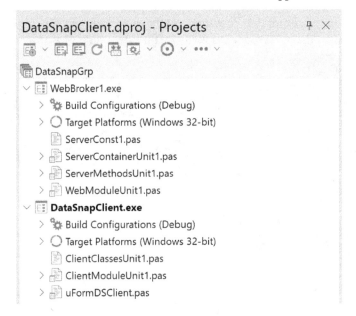

Figure 12.11: The DataSnap server and client projects in Project Manager

`ClientClassesUnit1` is the actual DataSnap proxy code. You will find there `TServer Methods3Client` class generated. It has the same name as the server methods class but with the `Client` word appended. It inherits from the `TDSAdminRestClient` class and has the same method declarations as the server. This is the complete code of the class:

```
type
  TServerMethods3Client = class(TDSAdminRestClient)
  private
    FEchoStringCommand: TDSRestCommand;
    FReverseStringCommand: TDSRestCommand;
  public
    constructor Create(
      ARestConnection: TDSRestConnection); overload;
    constructor Create(ARestConnection: TDSRestConnection;
      AInstanceOwner: Boolean); overload;
    destructor Destroy; override;
    function EchoString(Value: string;
      const ARequestFilter: string = ''): string;
    function ReverseString(Value: string;
      const ARequestFilter: string = ''): string;
  end;
```

The second unit, `ClientModuleUnit1`, is a data module with a `DSRESTConnection1` component already added. In its `Host` and `Port` properties, there are values entered on the last page of the wizard. Right-click on the connection component and select **Test Connection** from its context menu (see *Figure 12.12*) to verify that the server is still running.

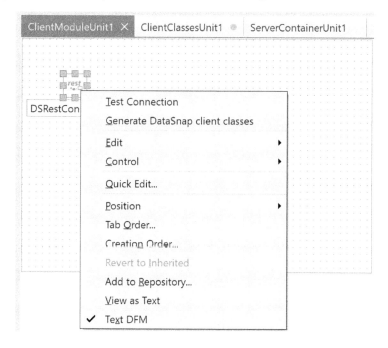

Figure 12.12: The Test Connection context menu option for the TDSRESTConnection component

The second option, **Generate DataSnap client classes**, is very useful when we want to regenerate client classes with the proxy generator. That needs to be done every time we add or change server method declarations.

The wizard has added the private FServerMethods3Client field to the client module class and added the GetServerMethods3Client public method that creates the TServerMethods3Client instance by passing the REST connection component to its constructor and then returns a ready-to-use class.

In the client app code, if we want to invoke any method of the remote DataSnap server, we can just call the corresponding method on the TServerMethods3Client class returned from GetServerMethods3Client and our call will be forwarded to a remote server for execution and the result received from the server will be returned. If a remote method throws an exception, then it is intercepted on the server and re-raised on the client side.

Let's complete the client application:

1. Go to the main form of the client app and add the ClientModuleUnit1 unit to its uses clause in the implementation part of the unit.
2. Drop a TButton and a TEdit control on the form.
3. Change the Name property of the button to BtnReverse and its Text to Reverse. Rename the edit to EdtTest and in its Text property enter any string, for example, Delphi.
4. Double-click on the button and enter just one line of code that will take the text from the edit, send it to the DataSnap ReverseString method, and display the reversed version of the original string in the edit:

```
uses
   ClientModuleUnit1;

procedure TFormDSClient.BtnReverseClick(Sender: TObject);
begin
   EdtTest.Text := ClientModule1.ServerMethods3Client.
      ReverseString(EdtTest.Text);
end;
```

Save the client app and run it. If you click on the button, you should see the original text from the edit reversed, as you can see in *Figure 12.13*.

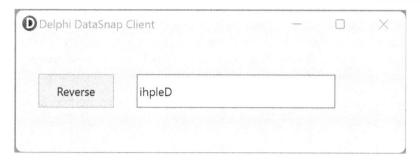

Figure 12.13: The DataSnap client app running on Windows

If you want to deploy this application to a mobile platform, for testing locally in your environment, you'd need to replace the value of the Host property of the DSRestConnection1 component in the ClientModule1 unit, so that it has the IP address of the computer on which you are running the DataSnap server. Also, if you want to run the client on Android, and you are using HTTP on your PC (and not HTTPS), you'll need to ask for an exception to the platform rule of using only HTTPS by adding the following line to the AndroidManifest.tempalte.xml file in your Delphi project folder:

```
android:usesCleartextTraffic="true"
```

DataSnap is a very powerful and rich framework. It is a very good choice for implementing systems with a relatively small number of concurrent clients. It also supports authentication and authorization, where access to certain server classes or methods can be restricted to a certain group of users. There is also support for communication filters, where you can provide custom modifications to the raw stream of bytes that are exchanged between clients and servers. Out of the box, there are compression and encryption filters available, but it is possible to implement a custom filter. Another interesting feature of DataSnap is **callback functionality**. Servers can notify selected or all connected client applications by sending the information that something interesting happened on the server to callback channels. There is also the FireDAC JSON Reflection framework that simplifies building client/server database applications. Data from multiple FireDAC datasets on the server can be combined into one object and sent to clients to be loaded into local TFDMemTable components for processing. All changes made to the data on the client can be sent in one operation to the server for updating the underlying database.

Summary

In this chapter, we have seen different options for building mobile backends with Delphi. There are many wizards to help you build all kinds of server apps, including simple WebBroker HTTP servers, SOAP XML web services, and DataSnap.

The DataSnap architecture was great when it was built, but it was never meant to be a backend for modern REST-style APIs. In fact, it started in the COM world and was extended to embrace HTTP.

If you want to fully embrace the REST model, creating a stateless and scalable architecture, with more ready-to-use out-of-the-box services, you might want to move to a new architecture Embarcadero added to Delphi, which is called RAD Server. This is covered in detail in the next chapter. RAD Server offers the best and most extensive solution as a backend for your mobile applications.

The next chapter will guide you in building a RAD Server web service and the matching client application, migrating our ToDo demo to this new technology, in a couple of different ways.

13
Easy REST API Publishing with RAD Server

Looking at the different options available for Delphi, the most feature-rich and powerful architecture for building mobile backends is **RAD Server**. Unlike other types of Delphi server applications, RAD Server is pre-built and includes core features out of the box.

In this chapter, we'll introduce the key elements of RAD Server, without going too deep into all of the features, as the features themselves would take an entire book. This is what we are going to cover:

- RAD Server setup
- Building RAD Server resources
- The ToDo list in RAD Server
- Creating a client app for RAD Server

The goal of this chapter is to introduce you to RAD Server and explain its core features and how you can write your own web service endpoints and call them in a client app. Of course, we'll do this by building practical demos as we usually do in this book.

Technical requirements

RAD Server is installed as part of Delphi Enterprise or Architect. RAD Server is designed as a scalable REST API publishing framework. Its functionality is extended through building Delphi BPL packages that are loaded into the RAD Server at its startup. It also requires access to the Embarcadero InterBase SQL database, where it keeps its system database. During the installation of Delphi, make sure to install the development version of InterBase. It comes with a special license for using it as a system database for RAD Server.

To summarize, the RAD Server support is available only in the Enterprise and Architect versions of the product, not in the Professional and Community editions.

The source code of the demos in this chapter can be found on GitHub at the following link: `https://github.com/PacktPublishing/Expert-Delphi_Second-edition`

RAD Server setup

As a starting point, make sure that InterBase is installed and running on your system. In the Windows Start menu, locate and run **InterBase Server Manager**. You can see the window of this utility app in *Figure 13.1*. If the server does not start, then run it. In the default installation, the InterBase instance name is `gds_db`. The name of the database instance will be needed during the RAD Server setup.

Figure 13.1: The InterBase Server Manager

Now go to the Windows command line and enter the `EMSDevServer` command. The Delphi `bin` directory is in the path after the installation, so RAD Server should start.

> **Note**
> Note that in many places you will see the word **EMS** when referring to RAD Server. It stands for **Enterprise Mobility Services** and it is the former name of RAD Server.

The very first time EMSDevServer is run, or when it is run with the -setup parameter, you will see the installation wizard (see *Figure 13.2*), which will create a RAD Server system database and the configuration ini file. Optionally, the setup wizard may also create a default user and a default group. Notice that you can use the -setup parameter, invoking the server from the Windows command line, to reset the configuration.

On the first page of the wizard, visible in *Figure 13.2*, we need to enter the instance name of InterBase Server where the RAD Server database needs to be created. In the default installation, it is gds_db. You can leave the default value for the other fields.

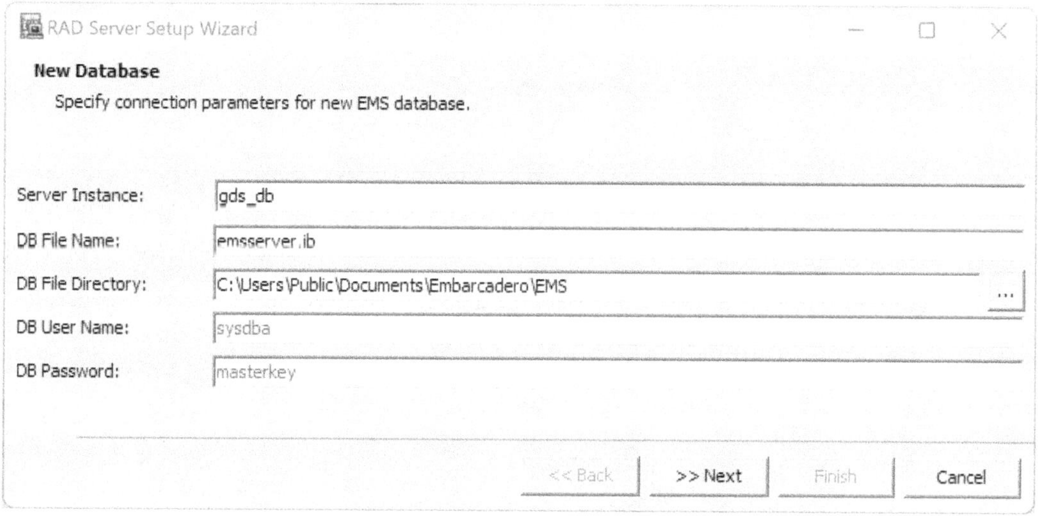

Figure 13.2: The New Database tab in the RAD Server Setup Wizard

In the second screen, leave default options to create sample users and groups.

On the next page of the RAD Server Setup wizard, we can specify a username and a password for accessing the EMS Console. The EMS Console is a separate EMSConsole.exe file that is located in Delphi's bin directory. It is used to manage users and groups and view REST API analytics.

The last page of the wizard provides the setup summary, as you can see in *Figure 13.3*. Click on the **Finish** button to run the RAD Server setup.

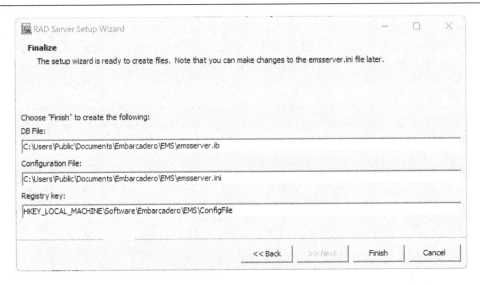

Figure 13.3: The Finalize tab of the RAD Server Setup Wizard

In the default installation, you just have the development RAD Server license, so it is OK to continue installation without a license at the following prompt. After a moment, you should see the information about operations performed by the setup. Click on **OK** and the EMS Development Server console should be displayed with the log window, as you can see in *Figure 13.4*.

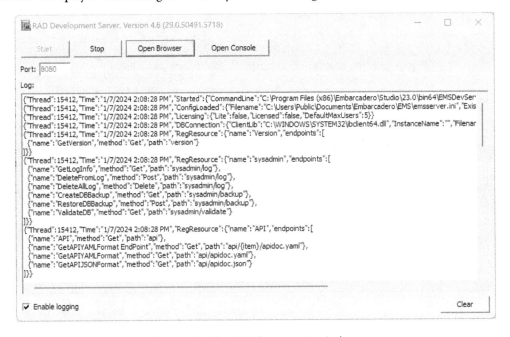

Figure 13.4: The RAD Server main window

In the first three lines of the log, we can see that the `emsserver.ini` configuration file, the location and name of the RAD Server system database (`emsserver.ib`), and the licensing information has been loaded. The following lines provide information about available resources, which can be accessed with corresponding URLs and specific endpoints.

If you now click on the **Open Browser** button, the default web browser will be displayed pointing to the version built-in RAD Server resource, available at the `/version` URL, as you can see in *Figure 13.5*.

Figure 13.5: The built-in version RAD Server resource in a web browser

Notice that the request to version resource has been logged in the console, like any incoming request. You can try accessing other RAD Server built-in resources by replacing `version` with other resource names presented in the log window.

You can also click on the **Open Console** button, which will start the **EMSConsole** executable and automatically open the embedded web server. By default, EMS Server is using HTTP port `8080` and EMS Console port `8081`. Click on the **Open Browser** button, and then in the browser, click on the **Login** button and enter `consoleuser` and `consolepass` as the console username and password, unless you picked different values during the configuration steps discussed earlier.

There are two more fields for entering the tenant name and tenant secret. This is used if RAD Server is running in the multi-tenancy mode, which is all we will be covering in this chapter; we will not be covering advanced configurations. If your configuration added them (depending on the steps you did in the RAD Server Setup Wizard) you'd need to enter the values in this screen for the console to work. The default values are `Initial Tenant` and `Secret`, respectively.

After clicking on the **Login** button, you should see the EMS Console home page (see *Figure 13.6*) with links to different kinds of available information:

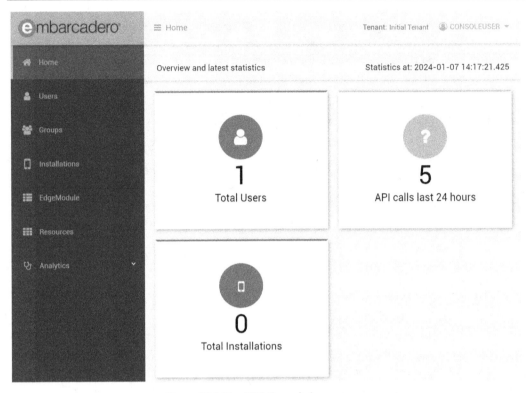

Figure 13.6: The EMS Console home page

The RAD Server has been set up and we can now start publishing our own APIs by creating new packages for the server.

Building RAD Server resources

The RAD Server architecture has been elegantly designed. You can add custom REST API resources through Delphi package library files that are loaded to RAD Server at its startup. The location of packages to be loaded is stored in the `ini` configuration file.

In the last chapter, we used the Web Broker architecture to expose CRUDL operations on the underlying ToDo data stored in the SQLite database as custom REST APIs. Here, we are going to implement a similar solution, but in this case, we are going to expose the same functionality using RAD Server. Initially, we are going to leverage the advanced features of RAD Server including its automatic mapping to database operations. Later on, we'll go back to the architecture we built in previous chapters and expose the `IToDoData` interfaces, following the same process we used in the last chapter with Web Broker.

Open the **New Items** dialog from the Delphi **File** menu. Select the **RAD Server** category and the **RAD Server Package** icon, as you can see in *Figure 13.7*:

Figure 13.7: The RAD Server Package wizard in the New Items dialog

On the first page of the wizard, we have an option to create an empty package or a package with a resource. You'd generally want the second option, although in general, you could use this wizard to create an empty package and then use the RAD Server Resource wizard to add resources to an existing package. In general, in fact, in a single package (a single BPL) there can be multiple resources, associated with different URLs.

On the second page of the wizard, we need to specify the resource name (which will match to a URL) and the base class for resource implementation. If we plan to add any components to a resource, then it is a good idea to choose a data module, otherwise we can go for just a plain unit. For this first demo, enter a name, such as `tododatabase`, and select **Data Module**.

On the third page (see *Figure 13.8*), you can specify which endpoints you want to add to the resource. These endpoints will translate to different HTTP request types and URLs. Instead of going for the manual approach, you can also specify to use a database endpoint. This can be done alternatively to the custom endpoints or in addition to them (in other words, you can use one of the two approaches or combine both techniques at once). For the first demo, I've selected the database endpoints option only, as shown in *Figure 13.8*.

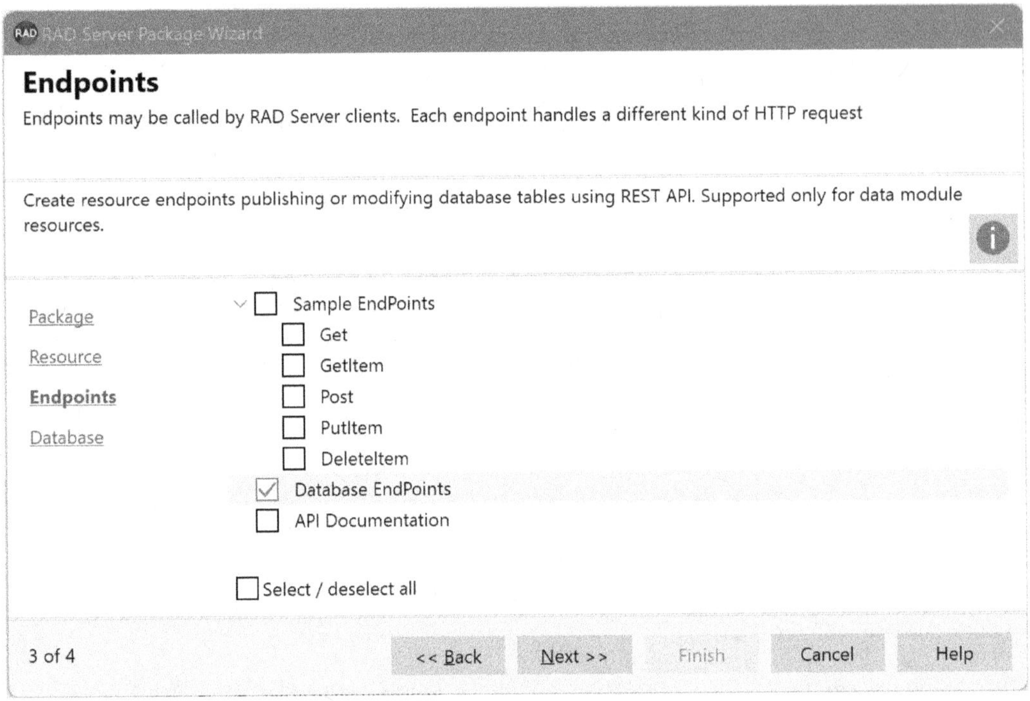

Figure 13.8: The RAD Server Package Wizard Endpoints definition page

On the fourth page, you'll get asked to pick a database connection. Just select the default SQLite connection and pick one of the available database tables. Don't worry about which as we'll replace it with the usual todo list table later on.

At this point, you can complete the wizard and look at the generated data module. This is the only unit of the project, which is a package project. Click the **Save All** button, name the unit RSToDoDatabase_DM and the project RSToDoDatabase, and place them in a specific folder.

Now, make the following changes to the data module components:

1. Open the connection editor for the FDConnection1 component and set the **Database** value to the same one you used in earlier chapters, most likely C:\Users\Public\Documents\ ToDos.db.

2. Rename the TFDQuery component as qryTodo.

3. Change the first line of the SQL property to select * from ToDos, but leave the rest of the generated code as is if you want to keep sorting enabled.

4. Rename the TEMSDataSetResource as dsrTodo and don't make any changes to it.

What's happening here is that this RAD Server module can map HTTP operations to the query via this powerful TEMSDataSetResource component. Its configuration includes a list of enabled operations in the AllowedActions property (they are all enabled by default) and the target database query.

However, the core element of its configuration, as is most often the case for RAD Server, is in the decoration of methods or components in the data module class. If you open the source code of the data module, in fact, you can see the following code:

```
type
  [ResourceName('tododatabase')]
  TTododatabaseResource1 = class(TDataModule)
    FDConnection1: TFDConnection;
    qryTodo: TFDQuery;
    [ResourceSuffix('Categories')]
    dsrTodo: TEMSDataSetResource;
  published
  end;
```

The resource name maps to the initial URL of this module within the RAD Server instance. The resource suffix indicates the subsection of the URL. The [ResourceSuffix('Categories')] text has been generated. You can then replace it with [ResourceSuffix('Todo')].

To better understand the URL mapping, let's see this code in action. Compile and run the application. Now, you cannot really run a package, but the RAD Server Wizard generates a configuration with RAD Server as a host application. So, when you run it, you actually run the host passing the package as a parameter.

You can verify this URL mapping in the RAD Server log that is displayed when the server starts. In the log, you should see a section like this:

```
"RegResource":
  {"name":"tododatabase",
   "endpoints":[
     {"name":"dsrTodo.List",
       "method":"Get",
       "path":"tododatabase/Categories/",
       "produce":"application/json, *;q=0.9"},
     {"name":"dsrTodo.Get",
       "method":"Get",
       "path":"tododatabase/Categories/{id}",
       "produce":"application/json, *;q=0.9"}
     . . .
```

This log indicates that the `tododatabase` resource has been loaded with specific endpoints for the various operations. Now, if you open a browser from the RAD Server UI and replace the predefined URL with the first path listed in the preceding log, `tododatabase/Categories/`, you should see the database table in JSON format, as in *Figure 13.9*.

← → C   ⓘ localhost:8080/tododatabase/Categories/

```
[{"Id":1,"Title":"Update home page","Category":"IT"},{"Id":2,"Title":"Configure database","Category":"IT"},
{"Id":4,"Title":"milk","Category":"food"},{"Id":5,"Title":"Pizza","Category":"Food"}]
```

Figure 13.9: The entire table listed by the RSToDoDatabase RAD Server module

Notice that you can also retrieve a single record (or perform other operations on it, depending on the HTTP verb) by using a URL such as `tododatabase/Categories/4`, where 4 is the ID for one of the records.

This is all we need to do to create a RAD Server module that can expose database data and operations at a web service. If you check the data module source code, there are only some attributes, but zero actual code. All that is left is to write a client for it, in Delphi or a different language. I won't do it here because I'll work on it only after writing a different RAD Server module, which will manually expose the various operations and reuse as much as possible the code of the previous chapters.

The ToDo list in RAD Server

Let's now move to the implementation of a `ToDo` list server based on the architecture of the previous chapters, rather than directly exposing the database. Notice that there is nothing wrong with the approach we used in the previous section, but it's good to get a bit deeper to better understand how RAD Server works:

1. Let's start by creating a proper folder structure for our projects. Create a new folder for RAD Server ToDo resource and client projects. Inside this folder, create three sub-folders: `resource`, `client`, and `shared`.

2. Now, run the RAD Server wizard again. On the second page of the wizard, this time we can just pick a unit and use the resource name `todo`.

3. On the third page, this time we want to pick the endpoints of the wizard (see *Figure 13.8*, again). Select **Sample EndPoints** and all five sub-elements These endpoints will translate to different HTTP request types and URLs. We want all of them because there are five different CRUDL operations to expose on our `ToDo` resource.

4. Click the **Finish** button.

5. The new package project has been generated for us. Click on the **Save All** button. Save the resource unit as `uToDoRes` and the project as `ToDoPckg` in the `resource` subfolder of the project folder.

6. Copy the `uToDoTypes.pas` and `uToDoUtils.pas` units from the last chapter's `ToDoListWebBroker` project to the shared directory and add them to the package project.

7. Copy the `uDMToDo.pas` and `uDMToDo.dfm` files to the `resource` directory.

8. In the project option, add the shared folder in the search path on the Delphi compiler page.

9. Now, open the `uToDoRes` unit generated by the wizard in the code editor. You will find the resource class declaration with five published methods that correspond to all endpoints that we have selected in the wizard. The custom attribute decorating the class contains the actual resource name to be used in the URL pointing to this resource. Depending on the type and parameters of the HTTP request, different methods will be called for processing. This class is similar to the web module class from the `WebBroker` implementation. This is how you can complete the class configuration.

10. Add the `uToDoTypes` unit to the `uses` clause in the `interface` section of this unit.

11. Add the `uToDoUtils` and `uDMToDo` units to the `uses` clause in the `implementation` part.

12. Declare a `FToDoData` private field of type `IToDoData` in the `TToDoResource` class.

13. Also, declare a `GetToDoData` function returning the same interface. Implement the `GetToDoData` method in the exact same way as in the web module of the last chapter.

Let's now start with the actual implementation, beginning with the `Get` endpoint. It will be used to return the list of all ToDo items. The wizard has generated a sample code that we need to modify. RAD Server endpoint implementations are very similar to `OnExecute` events of web action items from the Web Broker framework seen in the previous chapter. In RAD Server, we also have HTTP context and request parameters and we need to put JSON into the response, specifically the `AResponse.Body` value that will be returned from this endpoint:

1. We already have the code for retrieving the generic list of ToDo records from the local database using the data module. We also already have code to convert it to JSON, so our method can generate a temporary string (`RespStr`) and assign it to the response body:

```
procedure TToDoResource.Get(
  const AContext: TEndpointContext;
  const ARequest: TEndpointRequest;
  const AResponse: TEndpointResponse);
begin
  var AToDos := TToDos.Create;
  try
    GetToDoData.ToDoList(AToDos);
    var RespStr := ToDosToStr(AToDos);
    AResponse.Body.JSONWriter.WriteRaw(RespStr);
  finally
    AToDos.Free;
  end;
end;
```

2. Let's check if this works before proceeding. Save all and click on the **Run** button. Again, we are not running our module, we are starting EMSDevServer as shown on the **Debugger** page as a **Host** application, and we pass our module as a parameter to it, as you can see in *Figure 13.10*:

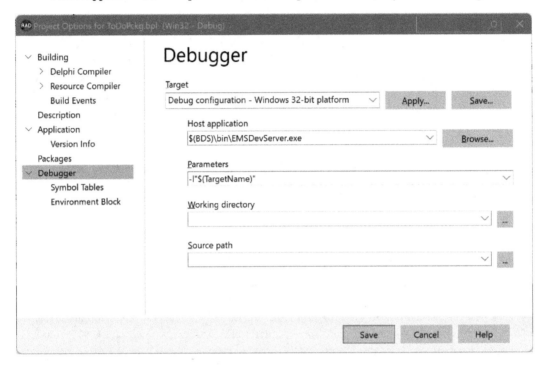

Figure 13.10: The Debugger tab in Project Options in the RAD Server module

3. After you start the RAD Server, open the browser and replace version with todo in the URL. The content that you can see in *Figure 13.11* will be almost identical to *Figure 13.9*, which we saw earlier.

Figure 13.11: The ToDo records listed as JSON in a web browser

4. Now, we can implement the remaining methods. The next one is `GetItem`, which corresponds to the `Read` functionality in our interface. This method is called if the HTTP request type is `GET` and there is a parameter value after the slash, like in `todo/4`. You can see that the code makes access to an individual record and returns it after converting it to a string representation:

```
procedure TToDoResource.GetItem(
  const AContext: TEndpointContext;
  const ARequest: TEndpointRequest;
  const AResponse: TEndpointResponse);
var
  AToDo: TToDo;
  RespStr: string;
begin
  var Id := ARequest.Params.Values['item'].ToInteger;
  if GetToDoData.ToDoRead(Id, AToDo) then
    RespStr := ToDoToStr(AToDo)
  else
    RespStr := 'Failed';
  AResponse.Body.JSONWriter.WriteRaw(RespStr);
end;
```

5. The next method to implement is `Post`, which is invoked if the HTTP request kind is `POST`. This will be used for inserting new ToDo records. In case of a `POST` request, we can pass parameters in its body. That will be just a JSON string with a new ToDo item to be inserted. For this, we'll need one more utility function that takes a JSON string as a parameter and returns a `TToDo` record. This is available in the `uToDoUtils` unit, in the companion code, and I'll omit it from the text.

6. With this function at hand, we can implement the actual `Post` method, which takes the input stream, converts this byte stream into a string using UTF8 encoding, passes it to the `StrToToDo` utility function just described, and finally calls the `ToDoCreate` method of the interface:

```
procedure TToDoResource.Post(
  const AContext: TEndpointContext;
  const ARequest: TEndpointRequest;
  const AResponse: TEndpointResponse);
var
  AStream: TStream;
begin
  if not ARequest.Body.TryGetStream(AStream) then
    AResponse.RaiseBadRequest('no data');
  var Bstr := AStream as TBytesStream;
  var RespStr := TEncoding.UTF8.GetString(Bstr.Bytes);
```

```
    var AToDo := StrToToDo(RespStr);
    GetToDoData.ToDoCreate(AToDo);
  end;
```

Next on the list is the `Put` method, used for updating a `ToDo` record. The implementation is almost identical to the `Post` method. Only the last line of code is different. Instead of calling the `ToDoCreate` method, we are calling `ToDoUpdate`.

The last endpoint to implement is responsible for deleting the `ToDo` item. The identifier of the record to be deleted is passed to this method via the `item` parameter, so that code is actually quite simple:

```
procedure TToDoResource.DeleteItem(
  const AContext: TEndpointContext;
  const ARequest: TEndpointRequest;
  const AResponse: TEndpointResponse);
begin
  var Id := ARequest.Params.Values['item'].ToInteger;
  GetToDoData.ToDoDelete(Id);
end;
```

The RAD Server code is complete. Now, we can move on to implementing the client app. We are going to reuse the main form unit of the previous chapters and will only need to implement a data module that will be calling different `ToDo` endpoints of our RAD Server module.

Creating a client app for RAD Server

Let's now create a client application for the REST API we just built with RAD Server. We'll do this by reusing the UI and some of the code from the previous versions:

1. Create a new, blank multi-device project and save it as `ToDoListEMS` in the `client` folder.

2. Keep the default name of the main form. It does not matter because in a moment we are going to remove it from the project.

3. Add to the project the `uToDoTypes` and `uToDoUtils` units.

4. Add a new data module to the client project. Save it as `uDMToDoEMS` and change its `Name` property to `DMToDoEMS`.

5. Add `uToDoTypes` to its uses clause in the `interface` section and copy the five `IToDoData` interface method declarations from the `uToDoTypes` unit to the public section of the data module. The class should look like this:

```
type
  TDMToDoEMS = class(TDataModule, IToDoData)
  private
```

```
  { Private declarations }
public
  // IToDoData
  function ToDoCreate(AValue: TToDo): Integer;
  function ToDoRead(Id: Integer;
    out AValue: TToDo): Boolean;
  function ToDoUpdate(AValue: TToDo): Boolean;
  function ToDoDelete(Id: Integer): Boolean;
  procedure ToDoList(AList: TToDos);
end;
```

6. Now press *Ctrl + Shift + C* to create empty implementations of all of these methods.

7. Make sure to add the uToDoUtils unit to the uses clause but in the implementation part of the data module.

8. Now, copy the uFormToDoRESTClient unit and form files from the last chapter's Web Broker project to the client folder.

9. Add the form unit to the client project and save it as uFormToDoEMS. Also, change the Name property of the form to FormToDoEMS.

10. Remove the existing main form from the client project and save all.

11. Now, modify the uses clause of the main form unit and change the implementation of GetToDoData to use the DMToDoEMS data module. That's the only modification that needed to be made in the main form unit.

12. The last task is to implement all five methods of the IToDoData interface in the DMToDoEMS module.

13. Drop a TEMSProvider component on the data module. It is responsible for connecting with RAD Server. For testing, enter 127.0.0.1 in its URLHost property and 8080 in the URLPort property.

14. Right-click on the EMS provider component and click on the **Test Connection** item in the context menu. Assuming the server is running, an information message should be displayed with the version of RAD Server. That means the connection is OK.

15. Now, drop five TBackendEndpoint components on the data module. Rename them as BeToDoCreate, BeToDoRead, BeToDoUpdate, BeToDoDelete, and BeToDoList. These will be used to implement the five calls to the matching RAD Server REST APIs.

16. Drop a TRESTResponse component on the data module and rename it as RrespToDo. With the *Shift* key pressed, left-click on each TBackendEndpoint component to select them all at once. Enter ToDo as the value of the Resource property and connect the RrespToDo component to their Response property. In this way, we can change the properties of all five components in just one operation. With this step, we've created a data module like the one in *Figure 13.12*.

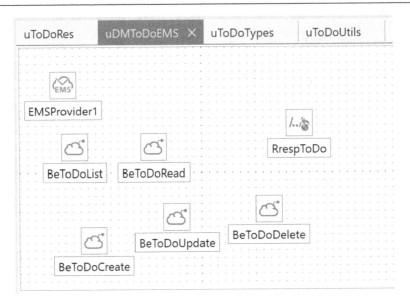

Figure 13.12: The provider, endpoint, and response components on the data module

17. At design time, we can already invoke these backend methods. The first method to try will be GET, which should return all ToDo records. Right-click on the `BeToDoList` component and select **Execute** from its context menu. The message with the response code **200 – OK** should be displayed. Now click on the `RrespToDo` component and in **Object Inspector**, you should see that its `Content` property contains JSON text with the list of all ToDo items. In order to implement all methods of the interface, we need to optionally provide values for expected parameters, call the `Execute` method of a given endpoint, and retrieve the result from the REST response component if a given method returns anything.

18. The implementation of the `ToDoList` method is straightforward. We need to empty the list, execute the backend operation, and fill in the list with the resulting JSON string:

```
procedure TDMToDoEMS.ToDoList(AList: TToDos);
begin
  AList.Clear;
  BeToDoList.Execute;
  StrToToDos(RrespToDo.Content, AList);
end;
```

19. The second variation of the GET endpoint is the `Read` method, which will return just a value of a given ToDo item. To refer to this item by ID, use the `ResourceSuffix` property of the `BeToDoRead` component. In this way, we will be calling the correct GET endpoint, using a specific URL. Now we can implement the `ToDoRead` method:

```
function TDMToDoEMS.ToDoRead(Id: Integer;
  out AValue: TToDo): Boolean;
```

```
begin
  BeToDoRead.ResourceSuffix := Id.ToString;
  BeToDoRead.Execute;
  Result := RrespToDo.Content <> 'Failed';
  if Result then
    AValue := StrToToDo(RrespToDo.Content);
end;
```

20. Let's now move to the `ToDoCreate` method. It will correspond with the POST endpoint, so change the `Method` property of the `BeToDoCreate` component to `rmPOST`. The code in this endpoint at the server is expecting to find a JSON representation of the `ToDo` item to be added to the underlying storage in the request body. Enter the following code in the `ToDoCreate` method, after adding the `REST.Types` units to the `uses` clause of the unit:

```
function TDMToDoEMS.ToDoCreate(AValue: TToDo): Integer;
begin
  Result := 0;
  var StrStr := TStringStream.Create(
    ToDoToStr(AValue), TEncoding.UTF8);
  try
    BeToDoCreate.Params.Clear;
    BeToDoCreate.AddBody(StrStr,
      TRESTContentType.ctAPPLICATION_JSON);
    BeToDoCreate.Execute;
  finally
    StrStr.Free;
  end;
end;
```

21. The next method to implement is `ToDoUpdate`. It will have a very similar implementation to the `ToDoCreate` method above. Just make sure to change the `Method` property of the `BeToDoUpdate` component to `rmPUT`.

22. The last method to implement is `ToDoDelete`. Change the `Method` property of the `BeToDoDelete` component to `rmDELETE`. Now, enter the following code in the body of the delete method:

```
function TDMToDoEMS.ToDoDelete(Id: Integer): Boolean;
begin
  BeToDoDelete.ResourceSuffix := Id.ToString;
  BeToDoDelete.Execute;
  Result := True;
end;
```

That's it. Save all and run the client application. You should just run and display the ToDo data from the underlying SQLite database received from a REST API resource hosted in the RAD Server backend, as you can see in *Figure 13.13*:

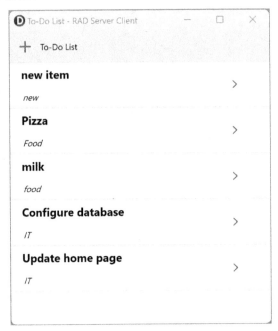

Figure 13.13: The client application using RAD Server, which isn't
any different from other clients in previous chapters

As you can see, RAD Server is a very powerful product. It is the perfect backend for mobile apps written in Delphi. Publishing REST APIs is its core functionality, but it has other features including user and group management, API analytics, and even mobile push notifications.

Summary

In this chapter, we have seen how to use RAD Server to build multi-tier architectures and provide a lot of reusable functionality to build great mobile backends for your cross-platform, mobile Delphi apps.

As Delphi's RAD technology and FireMonkey make you fast at building the UI of an app, compared to other development tools, RAD Server makes you fast at building and publishing web services and the backend of your mobile and desktop applications. This chapter offered only an introduction to RAD Server, as it is a very complex technology with many built-in features.

The next chapter will change focus; we will be getting back to mobile and focusing on the final steps of mobile development: deployment to app stores.

14
App Deployment

Building and deploying your mobile app to your devices is just the beginning. There is a lot more to a successful app. In this chapter, we are going to focus on all of the details of app deployment. We are going to discuss adding artwork, app monetization with ads, and in-app purchases. To be successful in mobile app development, you need to constantly improve your app. For this, you need to automate as many tasks as possible for reduced development and deployment times. That is why, at the end of this chapter, the book offers some suggestions in terms of version control, testing, and continuous integration.

This chapter will cover the following topics:

- Deploying to app stores
- Monetizing with ads and in-app purchases
- Tips to automate the development process

The objective of this chapter is to learn how to successfully deploy and maintain mobile apps for iOS and Android.

Technical requirements

In terms of code, this chapter is a little different. There is no code in the book source code. For this chapter, the MyMoleculeHero app source code is managed separately from the book source and it's available at: `https://github.com/marcocantu/MyMoleculeHero`

Deploying to app stores

You have built your app and tested it on multiple different devices with different versions of supported mobile operating systems, and now you feel that you are ready to make it available in an app store.

Before submitting your app, you need to have artwork in place and a number of screenshots from different devices that you plan to support. You might want to ask a professional graphic artist to provide them with the required app artwork, including app icons and splash screens.

Let's go through the steps of publishing your app to different mobile app stores. As an example, we are going to use an updated version of the **MyMoleculeHero** demo app that Paweł had written and published. The app is a 3D chemical molecule viewer that reads data from a **Protein Data Bank (PDB)** file format and generates models made of spheres and cylinders, which can be watched from different points of view.

The app uses the techniques described in *Chapter 6* of this book, but we are not going to delve into its code. In this chapter, we'll focus exclusively on the steps required to deploy it to app stores. You can see the output of this app in *Figure 14.1*.

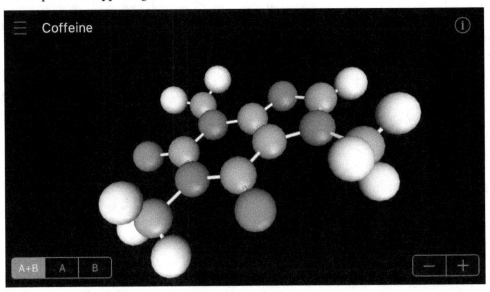

Figure 14.1: The MyMoleculeHero Delphi app running on iOS

The new version of the app is called *MyMoleculeHero*. It is open source with an MIT license and is completely free to use and modify by anybody. You can find it at `https://github.com/marcocantu/MyMoleculeHero` (as mentioned earlier), while the original version is still available at `https://github.com/pglowack/MoleculeHero`.

Apps artwork

Before you can build your app for deployment to an app store, you need to add the required artwork to your project. This is a collection of images in PNG file format that are used as application icons, launch images, and spotlight search icons. When you create a new multi-device app in Delphi, it uses the default FireMonkey icon that can be found in the standard Delphi installation in the bin\ artwork directory. Delphi developers tend to have lots of these icons on their devices; with regard to the demo applications in the book, I have not changed the default icons.

Because we want to deploy the MyMoleculeHero app, we need an icon. I'm going to stick with the image used by Paweł in the first edition of the book. It's going to be used both as the icon and the splash screen at different resolutions. For this to work better, you should start with an SVG file, as a vector image can be scaled much better for different resolutions.

All required graphic files can be configured in the **Application Icons** tab in the **Project Options** dialog. Starting with version 12 of Delphi, the icons and splash screen for different resolutions can be generated automatically using the **Artwork Generator** wizard. To activate the wizard for all platforms, you should select the **All configuration – All platforms** option in the target combo box (see *Figure 14.2*) before starting the wizard.

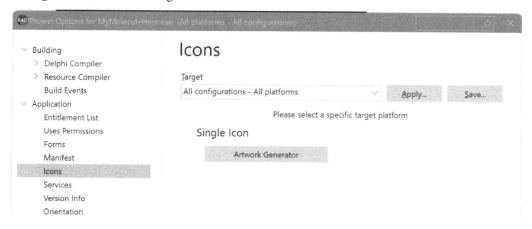

Figure 14.2: Generating the artwork for all platforms

Once you start the **Artwork Generator** wizard, the first key information to provide is the initial image, which, as I mentioned, should be an SVG file if possible, although PNG files are also supported. You can see the initial configuration of the wizard in *Figure 14.3*. I'm not going to cover each individual setting, as most of them are quite intuitive to use.

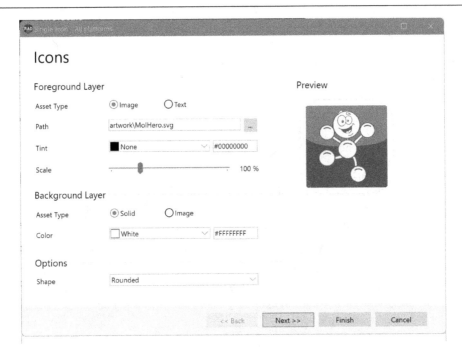

Figure 14.3: The first screen of the Artwork Generator

As you proceed with this wizard, the second page offers further customization for the **Android Adaptive Icon**, a new Android resolution-independent artwork file. You can keep the default settings there.

The next page offers the configuration for **Splash Screens**, where you can customize the size and default scale of the image. Here, you might want to pick a different image, better suited as a splash screen. In my case, I'll just use the same for simplicity, scaling it to a bigger size. Finally, there is a **Splash Screens Dark** page in case you want a different splash screen when the phone is in dark mode.

Once you press the **Finish** button, the wizard will generate a couple of dozen different graphic files and configure them directly in the project settings. This saves a lot of time.

Apps orientation

Another important setting before you deploy an app is its orientation. You can specify it in the **Orientation** tab of **the Project Options** dialog box. By default, it is not enabled, and when you rotate the physical device, the form of your app will also rotate, adapting to the current orientation and firing the `OnFormResize` event. Sometimes, such as in the case of certain games, you may want to disable the rotating of the screen. You can specify that, for example, you only want your app to be displayed in landscape mode.

Publishing on the Apple iOS App Store

The first step toward publishing your app on the iOS App Store is to create a developer account on the `https://developer.apple.com` website. You most likely have one already created to be able to deploy Delphi apps to iOS phones and tablets for testing. As I already mentioned, the Apple developer account requires a payment, which you have to renew every year.

In order to submit an app to the iOS App Store, you need to create an entry for your app on the Apple developer site, creating an application ID configuration or bundle ID.

Next, you need to create and download a **Provisioning Profile** by going to the matching section of the Apple developer website, add a new iOS App Store profile for the Bundle ID you created in the previous step, and pick the **iOS Distribution** category. In this process, you need to provide a request file generated on your Mac using the **KeyChain Access** tool. Once you have generated a signing request, it can be uploaded to the Apple developer site as part of the process to create a certificate.

At the end of the process, you can download the certificate and install it on your Mac. The recommendation is to use **Xcode** to verify that your developer profile and provisioning profile are in place and have been configured correctly.

After doing these steps, you need to prepare your app for deployment. Go to the **Project Options** dialog for your app and , at the top of the dialog, select **All Configurations - iOS Device - 64 bit** as the target.

Select the **Version Info** tab and make sure that the **CFBundleIdentifier** matches the **Bundle ID** that you have created on the Apple developer website. In the case of MyMoleculeHero, that will be `com.marcocantu.MyMoleculeHero`.

The next step is to create an app archive file that you can submit to the App Store. In the **Project Manager**, make sure to select the **Release** build configuration, and under the **Configuration** of the iOS 64-bit target, double-click on the **Application Store** node to make it active, as in *Figure 14.4*.

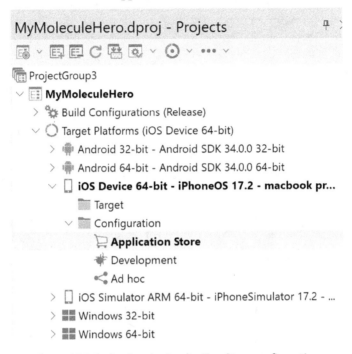

Figure 14.4: Activating the Application Store configuration

Make sure that the Platform Assistant server (**PAServer**) is running on your Mac.

Next, check that you have the proper Provisioning Profile for App Store deployment in place. If you go to the Deployment page of the project options, Delphi will fetch the information from your Mac via **PAServer**, as displayed in *Figure 14.5*:

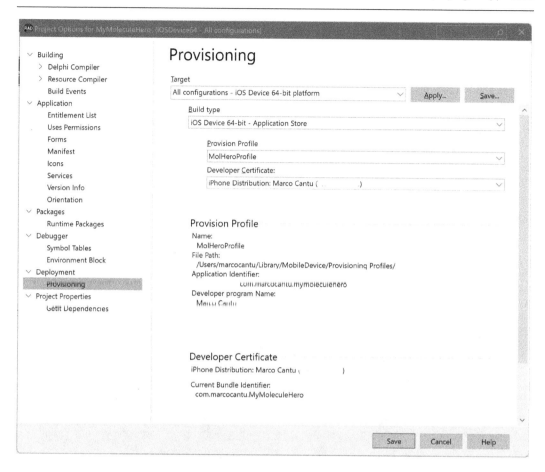

Figure 14.5: App Store Provisioning Profile configuration

Now, right-click on the project node in **Project Manager** and select **Build** from the context menu. Open the **Deployment Manager** window and click on the **Deploy** button. Alternatively, you can use the **Deploy** menu item in the **Project** menu.

If everything has been configured correctly, you should be able to find the ipa file in the `Release` folder of your project. That file is ready to be submitted to the App Store.

To submit your iOS app, given you are not using `Xcode`, you can use the **Transporter** app from Apple, freely available for MacOS. In the Transporter app, select the target store app. Pick the ipa file generated by Delphi and place it directly on your Mac in the **PAServer** scratch directory.

Getting back to the App Store Connect website, you can now create a submission (including a large number of images you can capture from your devices or from the iOS Simulator), configure description, prices, privacy policies, and much more. The website should be able to find your submission and use it for the app. Once you are done, send the app for review. Now your app will go to Apple for testing, and eventually, you will be notified by email if your app has been accepted or rejected by the App Store.

You can see the app description on the Apple App Store in *Figure 14.6*.

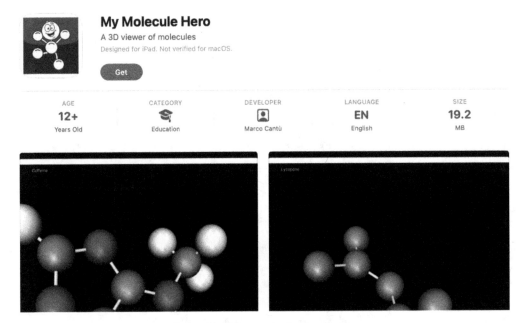

Figure 14.6: The app in the Apple store

Let's now go over the steps to do the same for the Google Android Play Store.

Publishing your Android apps to the Google Play Store

Similarly to the iOS counterpart, the first step to publish your Delphi Android is to create a Google Play developer account on the `https://developer.android.com` website. Like for Apple, this is also a paid account, but you make a one-time payment rather than a yearly one. It is also cheaper. From this site, you'll have to navigate to the Google Play console at `https://play.google.com/console/` to manage your apps.

Before we get into the specifics of the store deployment, we need to make sure the app has the correct permission requests. This, however, is a step you don't need to do for iOS.

In the **Uses Permissions** tab of the **Project Options** dialog box, check if you have selected all required rights that your app will need to have, e.g. access to **Bluetooth** or **Location**. In the case of this app, there is no permission required.

To sign the app for Android, you need to configure a **KeyStore File** in the **Provisioning** tab within the **Project Options** dialog. If you do not have one, you can create it by clicking on the **New Keystore** button and following the steps of the wizard. Once you have the file, you can enter the matching password and see its data in the Delphi IDE, as shown in *Figure 14.7*.

> **Note**
>
> Make sure you keep a copy of the keystore file in a safe place. You will need this specific file in the future to submit a new version of your app.

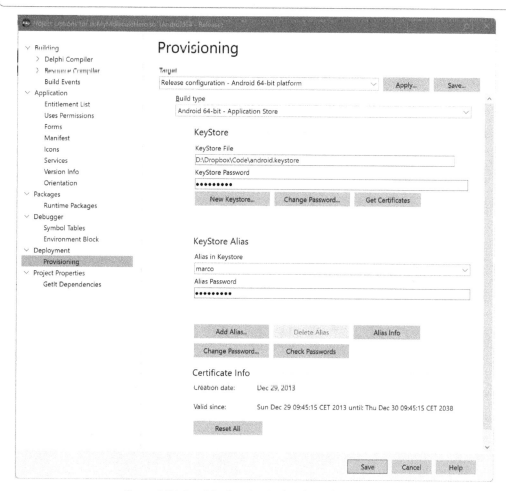

Figure 14.7: Provisioning the Android app for Android

The second specific configuration in the **Project Options** is in one of the **Delphi Compiler** sections and indicates that you want to build a deployment file including both the 64-bit and the 32-bit versions of the app in a single package. This allows your application to be available for a larger number of phones. You can see this configuration in *Figure 14.8*:

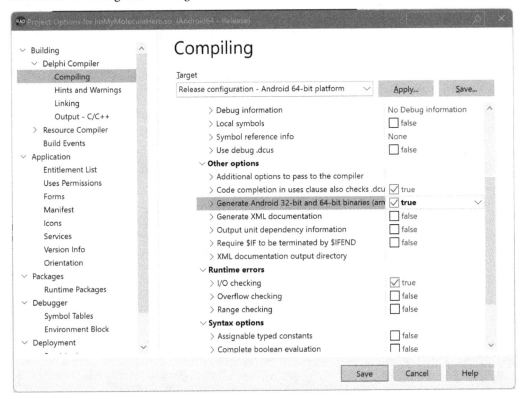

Figure 14.8: Configuring the Delphi compiler to bundle the 64-bit and 32-
bit versions of the app in a single package for the store

Remember to also give a proper internal name to the app. For example, in the **package** field of the **Version Info** page, you can remove the com.embarcadero domain and use either a full name or a name based on your own identity. In my case, I'm using

```
com.marcocantu.$(ModuleName)
```

The next step is to build a signed **Android app bundle** (*.aab* file) that can be uploaded to the store. Go to **Project Manager** and select the **Release** build configuration and the **Application Store** configuration in the Android target node.

> **Note**
>
> Earlier versions of the Android store and Delphi integrated deployment support used the older apk file format rather than the newer aab format. If you go through the online Delphi documentation, you might find references to apk . The role and the steps are the same, only the deployment file is different.

In the **Project** menu, click on **Build** and then on **Deploy** to deploy the menu items. This should create a signed aab file ready for submission to the Google Play Store.

To submit your app, you have to log into the Google Play Developer Console and select **Add new application**. Select the default spoken language of your app and enter the app title, as shown in *Figure 14.9*.

Create app

App details

App name	My Molecule Hero
	This is how your app will appear on Google Play 16 / 30
Default language	English (United States) – en-US ▾
App or game	You can change this later in Store settings
	◉ App
	○ Game

Figure 14.9: Creating a new app in the Google Play Console

There are many configuration pages to fill, including privacy policy information, listing data, and filters. Once you are done with those, you can go to the **Production** tab of the website, move to **Releases**, and select **Create new releases**. Once this is done, you can upload the aab file generated by Delphi's Deploy operation. This can be found by default under the application source code folder, in a sub-folder with a name such as Android64\Release\MyMoleculeHero\bin.

After uploading the file, the information extracted from your aab file (like the package name and its version) will be displayed on the app configuration page. You will have to fill in mandatory information in the remaining tabs that are marked with asterisks and then click **Save**. After all options are displayed with a green check mark, you can send your app for review.

> **Note**
> Unlike the iOS App Store, you should see your Android approved for installation in a matter of hours, not days or weeks.

Your app is now in the App Store and you know that at least your friends are downloading and installing it on their device. However, there are still two important elements to consider for your app. First, you might want to monetize it so that you can cover the development efforts and store costs and work on future extensions if you're not planning to make a real business out of it. Second, you should consider improving the development process to make sure your app remains stable and of good quality over time. Let's focus on app monetization first.

Monetizing with ads and in-app purchases

There are different business models for mobile apps. Rather than expecting users to pay for an app before they can use it, it is fairly common to offer apps for free. In this case, you can monetize your apps by displaying ads or by offering in-app purchases.

Delphi comes with a cross-platform `TInAppPurchase` component that is available on the **Services** tab in the **Tool Palette**. With this component, you can sell virtual content within your app in a single way by using the Google Play in-app billing service on Android and the Apple iOS in-app purchase service on iOS. The details of using in-app purchases are different on both platforms and are very well documented on Embarcadero DocWiki.

Another possible business model is to embed advertisements in your apps. FireMonkey comes with a `TBannerAd` component that you can use to easily display ads in your app. This is a visual component, as you need to indicate which portion of the UI of your application is going to display ads.

The ad is generally configured in code by writing something similar to (the number here is not a valid one; use the one Google assigns you):

```
BannerAd1.AdUnitID := 'ca-app-pub-1234567890';
BannerAd1.LoadAd;
```

FireMonkey offers platform-based ads for iOS (a feature Apple has abandoned) and Android but also Google Firebase Ads for both iOS and Android.

Whether you want to make money with your app or not, that's your decision. In any case, if you want to keep your application available over time by offering updates, it is important to improve and automate the development process as much as possible. Given that updating your app on a regular base is important, you need to make sure you have a smooth release process and a well-organized development process.

Automate the development process

The first release of an app is hardly the last one. This brings us to this question—how can you continue to build and enhance your application? It's important to consider the steps you can and should take to improve the process.

Delphi IDE provides many features that help you with establishing your own custom automated workflows, including version control engine, code editing, refactorings, integrated unit testing, and customizable build events. In the last part of this chapter, I want to introduce some of them.

App versioning

To be able to track errors and understand which version of your app customers are using, it's important for every application to have a good versioning strategy. Every time you release a new build of your app, It should have a new, increased version number.

Most developers use two or three numbers to determine the version of their apps, such as *3.4* or *3.4.2*. The Delphi **Project Options** page lets you set a version number using major, minor, and build numbers, as you can see in *Figure 14.10*.

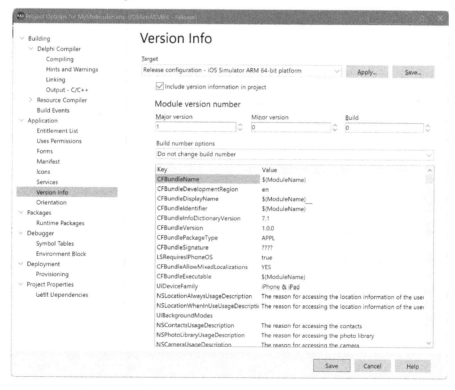

Figure 14.10: The version number in the project configuration

That's perfect for Windows and other operating systems, but a bit tricky on mobile. The issue is that the two mobile platforms, iOS and Android, use different models. The Android Play Store internally uses a single release number, increased every time, for each version, although it can display a version made of multiple numbers to the users. On the other hand, iOS uses major and minor version numbers.

You can, of course, use a different scheme for each platform and track them in your documentation. Throughout the course of my work as an app developer, I adopted an interesting solution. I used an always-increasing build number rather than resetting when increasing the major version and using that as the Android package number. As an example, suppose I'm on build 1.1.8. This will be displayed as version 1.1 and will internally use the number 8. The next version might be 1.2.9, displayed as version 1.2 with the internal Android package number 9. The next big release might be 2.0, but I'll still increase the build number so it's now 2.0.10, displayed as 2.0 to the users and internally as version 10. I found this approach extremely useful, which is why I'm suggesting it here.

Practical version control

Let us imagine this scenario. You have been very intensively working on a new app throughout the whole week. By Friday, your app is already in good shape and its basic functionality works. Over the weekend, you have some clever ideas and make some changes to the source code. Then, it's Monday morning in the office and somehow nothing is working. You wish you could go back in time and put your app in the state when it was last working. This is what version control is all about. Every time you make a change to a source code file or any other asset that belongs to your project, this change is saved and you can easily roll back changes and get back to the last working version of your app.

Delphi IDE comes with an integrated, lightweight version control system. At the bottom of the Code Editor, there is a **History** tab. Every time there are changes in your code and you save your code, a new copy of your file is created in a hidden __history sub-folder where your source file exists. In the **Editor Options**, in the global **Tools Options** dialog, you can control how many recent versions of every file are kept using the **File backup limit** setting. By default, this value is 10, but you can increase it up to 90.

The **History** tab offers the ability to compare files of different versions using the integrated viewer of the embedded Embarcadero edition of Beyond Compare.

On top of built-in version control, it is also possible to configure Delphi to integrate with some popular version control software, including Git and Subversion. These systems have different capabilities and philosophies. The most widely used is probably Git because of its decentralized nature and the popularity of large and partially free hosting services such as GitHub.

Using a version control system should be a mandate for all developers. Even if you are working alone, there is no reason not to use a version control system to keep a backup and a history of your changes over time. Covering Git and Subversion is beyond the scope of this book and there are many sources of information covering them in detail. The only element I want to mention is that the Delphi IDE, and in particular the **History** view, is fully integrated with version control systems. Your app history, in fact, will take into account file versions committed to version control systems and local backup files. An example is shown in *Figure 14.11*.

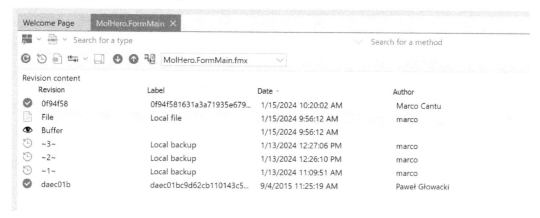

Figure 14.11: The History tab with local backups and version control files

There is much more to version control and hosting your projects on public systems such as GitHub, Bitbucket, Assembla, or similar hosted version control repositories. The goal here was just to remind you that this is a must-have element of your development process. This is the same for the next topic I want to briefly touch on—unit testing.

Sleeping well with unit testing

Writing code is like solving a big puzzle. The more lines of code your app has, the more difficult it is to maintain and evolve. It takes a lot of experience to be able to properly structure your projects. When you add new features, they should not break the functionality of the whole app. Unit testing can help with making sure that every piece of code that you write works as expected. Some developers start writing their code by implementing unit tests that will prove that the code they will write later works.

Delphi IDE comes with two integrated unit test frameworks: DUnit and DUnitX. DUnitX is newer and leverages modern language features such as custom attributes. Delphi integrates a wizard to create DUnitX unit tests for an application (see *Figure 14.12*), offering the ability to populate the test suites with an initial set of test skeletons.

Figure 14.12: The unit test wizard

Once you have prepared the tests, they can and should be run for every single change you apply to the code. Make sure the tests always remain green.

What's the structure of a unit test? In DUnitX, a test fixture class can have methods marked with `Setup` and `Teardown` attributes. The `Setup` method is called before all tests are run and the `Teardown` method is called afterward. These methods can be used to instantiate an object to be tested and free it.

The actual testing happens in methods marked with the `Test` attribute. It should do a number of different operations on the object, testing the results. When designing unit tests, it is important not only to check if a test feature works with standard arguments but also to test corner cases, such as passing illegal parameter values. For example, if we divide by zero, there should be an exception raised.

Summary

Your app is in an app store now and you have become a developer who is capable of writing code once and can natively compile it for all major mobile and desktop platforms from the very same source code files. Nobody can beat your productivity.

In this chapter, we have walked through the steps necessary to prepare and publish your Delphi apps to major app stores. We came to realize that being in an app store doesn't signify the end of your app's life. We also introduced critical techniques you have to master to maintain your app healthy over time.

This is almost the end of the book. There is one more chapter that offers some additional guidelines on what you could focus on next after you finish reading the book.

15

The Road Ahead

You have done it! You have become a developer superhero, and now you have all the necessary skills to rapidly create stunning, native mobile apps from a single code base in record time.

In this final chapter, we are going to review some of the most important mobile development trends and think about the innovative and successful mobile apps you can now build.

This short chapter will cover the following points:

- Review of what we have learned
- Trends in mobile development
- Ideas for new and innovative apps for you to build

The objective of this chapter is to show you the road ahead to be successful in the world of mobile app development.

Review of what we have learned

Throughout this book, we have made the journey through different topics related to Delphi programming from the perspective of building mobile apps. Here, we aim to provide a brief summary while also offering references to more specialized books for further exploration of the topics covered in this book.

The main focus of *Chapter 1* was to install and configure the Delphi **IDE** for cross-platform mobile development. That's the single, biggest feature of Delphi cross-platform development: from one source code base, from one project, just by switching target platforms in Project Manager, you can compile your code to a binary executable for all major mobile and desktop platforms, including Android, iOS, Windows, macOS, and Linux. If you need more information about the IDE configuration, you might want to use the Delphi online documentation, at https://docwiki.embarcadero.com.

Chapter 2 was all about the Object Pascal programming language. From basic concepts and the structure of a Delphi program, we quickly moved to understand more advanced constructs, such as anonymous methods, generics, custom attributes, and using **Runtime Type Information** (**RTTI**). Fluency in Object Pascal coding is very important when it comes to writing your own code or understanding the source of the FireMonkey cross-platform library or other Delphi frameworks. For more information about the language, you might want to get a copy of Marco Cantu's language-focused book, *Object Pascal Handbook* (ISBN *9798554519963*). This is an entire book focused exclusively on the Delphi programming language.

The following chapters of *Part 1* focused on the core building blocks of Delphi's runtime library, including writing multithreaded code with the **Parallel Programming Library** (**PPL**) and processing JSON and XML data. For more information in this area, the best resource is Primož Gabrijelčič's book, *Delphi High Performance* (ISBN *9781805125877*).

Armed with this knowledge, the second part of the book went deeper into the development of the UI of mobile (and desktop) apps using FireMonkey. We touched on UI controls, 3D, the styles of architecture, and much more. There is another book that offers a lot of insight in this area, which is Andrea Magni's book, *Delphi GUI Programming with FireMonkey* (ISBN *9781788624176*).

The last part of the book delved into managing data, from local databases to HTTP-based REST services to cloud access, including the development of backends with WebBroker and RAD Server. The suggestion here, in terms of RAD Server, is to refer to the free online content and the *RAD Server Technical Guide* e-book, made available by Embarcadero. See `https://blogs.embarcadero.com/announcing-the-new-updated-rad-server-technical-guide/` for more information.

Finally, *Chapter 14* covered practical aspects of deploying Delphi mobile apps to app stores and touched on fundamental techniques to use for a well-structured application development process. When your app is finally in the App Store, it's not the end of its life. You also want to have an eye on emerging technologies that you could use in existing and new app projects.

Trends in mobile development

Ideas on how you should structure your software architectures are changing at an even faster pace than ever. Clearly, the technology is becoming more complex, and there are plenty of things to look at.

From the perspective of mobile developers, there are mobile platforms themselves, with new capabilities added with every new operating system version, but there are other areas to keep an eye on, most of which are relevant for each type of application, not just mobile ones.

Think about the exploding world of **artificial intelligence** (**AI**) with new releases and features popping up almost every week, the continuous switch toward cloud-based infrastructures, and the myriad of cloud and REST services (or APIs) you can integrate with to build your applications faster. Even the space of games development, which is a significant part of the mobile app business, is continuously evolving with new libraries and trends.

A single screen is not your limit

Mobile platforms keep evolving. With every new version of Android and iOS mobile operating systems, existing frameworks are being constantly improved, and new ones are added, such as speech recognition or mobile payments. There is a growing number of devices of different types you can deploy your apps to. You can have larger screens, screens with higher pixel density and resolution; you can have phones with dual monitors, and weird shapes due to the camera *notch*. There is no way you can stand still. Also, Google requires you to update your store apps to target newer Android API levels every year, and Apple has similar constraints.

Mobile devices and user experience will continue to evolve, and easier ways of interacting with data and services will keep emerging. **Virtual Reality** (**VR**) is growing, and there are already many mobile apps that provide **Augmented Reality** (**AR**) experiences where the virtual world is projected into the real world. Other mobile devices don't look like phones anymore, but glasses you can wear. These are built to make AR the primary way of interacting with computer systems. Apple, Google, Microsoft, Meta, and other software giants are putting a lot of effort into making these devices as popular as smartphones.

Serverless backends and NoSQL databases

Serverless architectures, *containers*, and *microservices* are some of the hot buzzwords you can hear here and there. With container technology getting more mature, it is becoming practical to start and stop a **virtual machine** (**VM**) just to execute one function. Cloud web services vendors, such as Amazon, provide the underlying infrastructure for building these kinds of architectures, where you can just deploy the source code of a remote function (see `https://aws.amazon.com/lambda/`) that you want to execute, and the whole complex aspect of provisioning VMs, scaling, and load balancing becomes transparent to software architects. With technologies such as API Gateway (`https://aws.amazon.com/api-gateway/`), you can create, version, and manage your own REST APIs at any scale with lots of flexibility and little hassle.

As mentioned, REST APIs are growing, and there are emerging API marketplaces offering a high range of very diverse services. One of them is `https://apilayer.com/`.

Traditional SQL **relational database management systems** (**RDBMS**) are no longer the only choice for storing data. NoSQL and other types of data stores, such as graph databases, are gaining more and more popularity. Some of the most interesting offerings in this space are the MongoDB open source NoSQL database (`https://www.mongodb.com/`) for which Delphi offers direct support via FireDAC, the Amazon DynamoDB NoSQL database (`https://aws.amazon.com/dynamodb/`) where you can configure its desired response time, and the Neo4j graph database (`https://neo4j.com/product`), which offers that whole new way of modeling data where relations between data are as important as data itself. The number of emerging database solutions in the NoSQL space is so large that we certainly cannot adequately cover this space in a short section of this book. This serves as just a starting point to entice your curiosity and encourage you to explore.

The AI revolution

A recent trend, or maybe better call it a *revolution*, is the emergence of AI services and chatbots. There have been services available for some time from many vendors, including the top cloud vendors. However, the new breed of **large language model** (**LLM**)-based systems, the most famous being ChatGPT, has changed the public perception of AI. This revolution is already impacting the IT world and the lives of many people, and it will continue to do so in ways that are difficult to understand and predict.

As a developer, you can use AI as part of your tooling to help you write code faster, write better code, find bugs, and get suggestions and recommendations. GitHub Copilot is the most popular tool in this space today. At the time of writing this book, there are a few third-party Delphi plugins to integrate ChatGPT directly in the IDE. You can find some of them in Delphi's GetIt package manager.

> **Note**
> When using AI services to help you as a developer, it's important to keep in mind two significant risks. The code you are sending to the chatbot might be used for further training, and portions of it might end up being sent as a suggestion to another developer. On the opposite side, the code you are being suggested to use might not be totally free to use and might require you to recognize the owner of the **intellectual property** (**IP**) of the code, even if it's part of an open source library, depending on the license. Different AI tools for developers offer different types of protection for these two risks, so we recommend you read the fine print first.

However, it's equally important to take into consideration the fact that your applications might become more powerful by embedding AI capabilities, and your users would probably love it, as this might significantly increase their productivity. There are open APIs, SDKs, open source frameworks, do-it-yourself AI backends, and so many alternatives that it doesn't even make sense for us to introduce them here. Next month, the entire picture is going to be different again!

Ideas for new and innovative apps for you to build

Your next Delphi mobile app will obviously be very cool and successful. Think big and start small. There are many sources of inspiration and places to learn about Delphi. One source of inspiration for app ideas can be one of the contests for the coolest Delphi app that is regularly organized by Embarcadero. Check out what other Delphi developers are building, and you will be surprised about all kinds of interesting apps built with Delphi.

You can also check out the app stores for successful apps and emerging threads. Mobile apps are different because they can have so much feedback and input from the physical context of execution, using sensors and cameras to understand what the phone and its user are doing. There is no limit to what you can imagine and build.

In case you are not ready to start your own app journey, you can join a Delphi open source project or library and continue learning while you are offering a direct contribution to the community. You can start looking for Delphi open source projects by visiting `https://github.com/topics/delphi`.

Summary

I hope that you have enjoyed reading this book as much as we did writing it. That was a great journey. Delphi is fun. We are sure that the elegance of Object Pascal language and the technical excellence of the Delphi IDE and its libraries will continue to enchant a growing number of software developers now and in many years to come.

Index

Symbols

G

Game of Memory 127
- configuration, storing 139-141
- designing 128
- images 128-130
- main form, building 131-138
- settings form 141-144
- user interface, designing 130

generic type 55-58
gestures 122, 124
Global Positioning System (GPS) 211
glyphs 138
Google Cloud Platform (GCP) 311
Google Play Store
- Android apps, publishing to 374-378

graphical user interfaces (GUIs) 175
Graphics Processing Unit (GPU) 146
grid layout control 245-247
grid panel layout control 248-250

H

HD Form 108
Hello World app 12-23
helpers 53-55
HTTP status codes
- reference link 300

Hypertext Transfer Protocol (HTTP) 300

I

IBLite 270
IBToGo 270
identifiers 49
images
- working with 128-130

inherited views
- working with 194-198

inline variables declaration 51
integrated development environment (IDE) 3
intellectual property (IP) 386
interactive 3D scene
- building 160-166

InterBase 269, 270
- URL 269

iOS
- DelphiHelloWorld project, deploying to 28-31
- vibrations on 231-233

ISAPI dynamic link library (DLL) 325

J

JavaScript Object Notation (JSON) 300
- reading 80-84
- URL 73
- working with 73, 74
- writing 74-79

JSON Data Binding Wizard 84, 85

L

large language model (LLM)-based systems 386
layout controls
- FlowLayout 243-245
- grid layout 245-247
- grid panel layout 248-250
- leveraging 242, 243
- scaled layout 247, 248

Linux
- desktop applications, building 254-256

local file 67

packtpub.com

Subscribe to our online digital library for full access to over 7,000 books and videos, as well as industry leading tools to help you plan your personal development and advance your career. For more information, please visit our website.

Why subscribe?

- Spend less time learning and more time coding with practical eBooks and Videos from over 4,000 industry professionals

- Improve your learning with Skill Plans built especially for you

- Get a free eBook or video every month

- Fully searchable for easy access to vital information

- Copy and paste, print, and bookmark content

Did you know that Packt offers eBook versions of every book published, with PDF and ePub files available? You can upgrade to the eBook version at packtpub.com and as a print book customer, you are entitled to a discount on the eBook copy. Get in touch with us at customercare@packtpub.com for more details.

At www.packtpub.com, you can also read a collection of free technical articles, sign up for a range of free newsletters, and receive exclusive discounts and offers on Packt books and eBooks.

Other Books You May Enjoy

If you enjoyed this book, you may be interested in these other books by Packt:

Delphi High Performance

Primož Gabrijelčič

ISBN: 9781788624060

- Get to grips with algorithmic complexity and learn how to recognize it
- Use tools to determine program runtime behavior
- Speed up programs by doing less instead of more
- Discover the internal workings of Delphi data structures
- Gain an understanding of Delphi's memory manager
- Find out how to write low-level parallel programs with TThread
- Use parallel patterns from the PPL and OTL libraries to write fast code
- Include external code, written in C or C++, in Delphi programs

Expert C++

Marcelo Guerra Hahn, Araks Tigranyan, John Asatryan, Vardan Grigoryan, Shunguang Wu

ISBN: 9781804617830

- Go beyond the basics to explore advanced C++ programming techniques
- Develop proficiency in advanced data structures and algorithm design with C++17 and C++20
- Implement best practices and design patterns to build scalable C++ applications
- Master C++ for machine learning, data science, and data analysis framework design
- Design world-ready applications, incorporating networking and security considerations
- Strengthen your understanding of C++ concurrency, multithreading, and optimizing performance with concurrent data structures

Packt is searching for authors like you

If you're interested in becoming an author for Packt, please visit `authors.packtpub.com` and apply today. We have worked with thousands of developers and tech professionals, just like you, to help them share their insight with the global tech community. You can make a general application, apply for a specific hot topic that we are recruiting an author for, or submit your own idea.

Share Your Thoughts

Now you've finished *Expert Delphi*, we'd love to hear your thoughts! Scan the QR code below to go straight to the Amazon review page for this book and share your feedback or leave a review on the site that you purchased it from.

`https://packt.link/r/1-805-12110-3`

Your review is important to us and the tech community and will help us make sure we're delivering excellent quality content.

Download a free PDF copy of this book

Thanks for purchasing this book!

Do you like to read on the go but are unable to carry your print books everywhere?

Is your eBook purchase not compatible with the device of your choice?

Don't worry, now with every Packt book you get a DRM-free PDF version of that book at no cost.

Read anywhere, any place, on any device. Search, copy, and paste code from your favorite technical books directly into your application.

The perks don't stop there, you can get exclusive access to discounts, newsletters, and great free content in your inbox daily

Follow these simple steps to get the benefits:

1. Scan the QR code or visit the link below

https://packt.link/free-ebook/9781805121107

2. Submit your proof of purchase

3. That's it! We'll send your free PDF and other benefits to your email directly

www.ingramcontent.com/pod-product-compliance
Lightning Source LLC
LaVergne TN
LVHW081511050326
832903LV00025B/1446